Concepts of the Hero

Contributors

Bernard F. Huppé
STATE UNIVERSITY OF NEW YORK AT BINGHAMTON

Morton W. Bloomfield
HARVARD UNIVERSITY

John Leyerle
UNIVERSITY OF TORONTO

G. E. von Grunebaum
LATE OF THE UNIVERSITY OF CALIFORNIA, LOS ANGELES

John Freccero
YALE UNIVERSITY

R. R. Bolgar
KING'S COLLEGE, CAMBRIDGE UNIVERSITY

John M. Steadman
HUNTINGTON LIBRARY AND ART GALLERY

Bruce W. Wardropper
DUKE UNIVERSITY

Eugene M. Waith
YALE UNIVERSITY

Irving L. Zupnick
STATE UNIVERSITY OF NEW YORK AT BINGHAMTON

Vittore Branca
UNIVERSITY OF PADUA

CONCEPTS

of the

HERO

in the

MIDDLE AGES

and the

RENAISSANCE

Papers of the Fourth and Fifth Annual Conferences
of the Center for Medieval and Early Renaissance Studies
State University of New York at Binghamton
2–3 May 1970, 1–2 May 1971

Edited by Norman T. Burns & Christopher J. Reagan

State University of New York Press
Albany, 1975

Concepts of the Hero in the Middle Ages and the Renaissance
First Edition
Published by State University of New York Press
99 Washington Avenue, Albany, New York 12210
© 1975 State University of New York
Printed in the United States of America

Library of Congress Cataloging in Publication Data

Main entry under title:

Concepts of the hero in the Middle Ages and the Renaissance.

1. Heroes in literature—Congresses. I. Burns,
Norman T., ed. II. Reagan, Christopher J., ed.
III. New York (State). State University at Binghamton.
Center for Medieval and Early Renaissance Studies.
PN56.H45C65   809'.933'51   74-34081
ISBN 0-87395-276-6
ISBN 0-87395-277-4 microfiche

Contents

v

Preface

ORAL VERSIONS OF THE ELEVEN ESSAYS collected here were originally presented at two conferences held in 1970 and 1971. The first five papers were given at the conference on the concept of the hero in the Middle Ages, the others in the following year's conference on the concept of the hero in the Renaissance. As a group the essays perhaps belie the theme of the conferences, for they suggest that medieval and Renaissance artists were as unsure of a worthy concept of the hero as we are. If the essayists have not found a hero whom they can confidently propose as a model for their ages, it is surely not because they did not look far enough. The range of inquiry in the essays is notably wide, geographically, chronologically, and generically, and even those essays that focus on a single artist or tradition are not limited in their points of reference.

The essays reveal that the medieval and Renaissance cultures entertained many views of the heroic and that none of them became dominant because no single concept could comprehend the disparate forms of human excellence admired by medieval and Renaissance people. In both cultures the classical and the northern heroic traditions were both vital forces, but the traditional heroic values imperfectly agreed with Christian values and to many Christian artists the heroic *ethos* of their revered past seemed strangely like vainglory. The following essays, therefore, most commonly deal with the attempts of medieval and Renaissance artists to modify or remake the traditional forms to be more suitable vessels for the new wine of a new *ethos*.

Professor Huppé deals with the problem faced by the early medieval authors in reconciling the concept of the hero of classical antiquity—whose inherent virtue lay in prowess in battle —with the Christian ideal of the *imitatio Christi* and the attainment of salvation. The lives of saints, though they portray men who in their life and death may be heroic models of Christian perfection, are not to be considered tales of heroes. The medieval hero must do battle. Heroes of this sort are to be found only in such works as the *Battle of Maldon, Beowulf,* and the *Chanson de Roland.* The basic difficulty in interpreting the early medieval heroic materials lies in understanding the antithetical tension between the heroic and the saintly ideals with which the poets of the early Middle Ages tried to come to terms in formulating the reality of the Christian soldier.

Professor Bloomfield demonstrates that a shift occurred in the attitude of the later medieval writers from the treatment of the hero as a "truly heroic" type towards the creation of a sort of anti-heroic figure, a character whose heroism is somehow compromised. Even personages of low degree may become heroes. Finally, two attempts were made to solve the problem of the hero who was not to be *too* heroic. First, the author himself in certain later works tends to become the center of attraction, both as narrator and chief actor. Second, some authors presented a plurality of heroes in the same work. The first resolution sees its fullest development in the *Divina Commedia* and in the *Canterbury Tales.* The earliest attempts of this sort are to be found in the *Romance of the Rose* and in Alain de Lille's allegorical epics, *De Planctu Naturae* and the *Anticlaudianus.* The ultimate source for the interjection of the author as *persona* may lie in the satires of Horace and Juvenal and in some of the poems of Ovid. Malory's *Morte d' Arthur* and the *Decameron* are the clearest examples of the second resolution. The valiant hero is absent from the later Middle Ages and is exemplified by Tristram, Lancelot, and Troilus. The ambiguity of the unheroic hero is perfectly revealed in *Sir Gawain and the Green Knight.*

Professor Leyerle adopts a theory of literature which sees the heroic narrative organized about the nucleus of game and play. His essay concerns particularly an analysis of *Sir Gawain and the Green Knight,* but he draws corroborative evidence to support his theory from other works as well. The hero is viewed as playing a role in a game which involves eroticism and death within the framework of a definite set of rules which, though they are and must be arbitrary, must also be observed. There are

only two resolutions to the game and play of hero: either the
hero fails in the task set for him and he calls off the contest, or
he sees it through to the end. In the first instance he returns
home to live happily ever after; in the latter the conclusion is
his death.

Professor von Grunebaum discusses the hero in medieval
Arabic prose. The essay exclusively concerns historiography, in
which the biographies and autobiographies of important religious, political, and cultural figures are frequently found. This
concept of the hero is quite different from the views of the
medieval West, a dissimilarity owing as much to the cultural
milieu of the Arabic world as to the genre of literature which
Professor von Grunebaum considers. Concentration on the individual is frowned upon in the Islamic world and therefore
the medieval author of the Arabic world tended to be more
restrained than his European counterpart. There are scarcely
any works in which the life and personality of a hero are systematically treated. (Autobiographies of scholars offer a notable
though not too frequent exception.) The individual is important, but only as a representative type. The only justification for
autobiography lay in the Koranic prescription that one should
not disregard the blessings of the Lord but speak out to everyone about them.

Professor Freccero's paper concerns the figure of Ulysses as
he appears in the *Odyssey* and in the *Inferno*. He points out
that in the *Odyssey* the view of time and human existence is
circular or cyclical. This treatment of time is typical of the epic;
a linear view of time and of the progress of the protagonist is
essential in the novel. The nexus of the new concept with the
old is to be found in the twelfth book of the *City of God*, where
St. Augustine asserts that the coming of Christ cut through the
circle of time and established for universal history as well as
for the individual soul a linear progression in which death
would give new meaning to life. Professor Freccero sees in
Dante's *Divina Commedia* a poetic synthesis of linearity and circularity, and thus the epic and the novel exist side by side in
this one unique work. He compares and contrasts the epic treatment of Ulysses and Dante's view of him in hell. Central to the
investigation is the navigational metaphor which occurs at the

beginning of the poem. For Dante the calamity of Ulysses stands for the disastrous prelude to the preparation of grace. The figure of Aeneas stands in an intermediate position between Ulysses and Dante. Ulysses and Aeneas share a common heroism, but Ulysses lacks Aeneas's *pietas* and providential destiny. Aeneas and Dante share a linear destiny: one is the preordained founder of Rome, while the other is a pilgrim who will return to tell his tale. But the two differ insofar as Aeneas in death can derive no consolation from the eternity of Rome, while for Dante death is a new beginning. It is this new Christian concept of time which is the unifying factor underlying Dante's poem.

In his exploration of European efforts to establish in the *miles Christianus* a heroic type that would be appropriate to a Christian culture, Professor Bolgar introduces the term "anti-hero," a term that frequently is brought to mind, explicitly or implicitly, in the other essays. The heroes of the ancient world and of the Middle Ages, created in heroic poems, romances, or hagiography, were predominantly either warlike, or amorous, or devoted to the love of God (to the detriment of their love of man). Such heroes were undercut by the ethical revaluations of Erasmus and other humanists, who denounced the folly of war and praised the internalized struggle, the integrated personality, the family man zealous in charity toward his fellow man. In comparison with the heroes of the older traditions, the humanist hero was indeed "anti-heroic." It might be added that in literature he proved exceedingly difficult to embody in a form in which he could rival the older heroes in popular appeal.

Professor Steadman examines the problems faced by the Renaissance epic poet in attempting to reconcile the need to present a worthy hero (who, as a kind of *miles Christianus*, was more than a martial or amorous hero) and the need to present an attractive, engaging action—plot being the soul of the poem. Classical epics imitated great actions, but their conventions were suitable only for the depiction of the martial virtues. Allegorical romances like Tasso's and Spenser's left to the allegorical level the presentation of a worthy *psychomachia*, but this was a level which many readers failed to see or understand. Milton, in praising "patience and heroic martyrdom," wrote epic poems that intentionally subverted the ethical values of the classical epic and turned the *heroic* poem into the *divine* poem in which "the heroic example was overshadowed by its divine exemplar."

The humanist revaluation of what makes a heroic character and respect for the decorous behavior of a gentleman had such force that, Professor Wardropper points out, even Spanish writers, who lived in the presence of the great explorers and the heroes of Granada and Lepanto, were disinclined to write about heroic actions on the ancient model. In seventeenth-century Spain, when the adventurous heroes no longer prospered, the satirists mocked the legendary heroes and Calderón created in Segismundo the hero of an Erasmian *psychomachia*, while Gracián established the ethical foundation for this "new hero." When the new hero was conceived as a member of the less important classes, the "surrogate-hero" of modern literature was created, one who excites not our admiration, but our sympathy and love. Thus Don Quixote, like Lázaro before him, cannot hope to be effective in the unheroic circumstances of the post-epic age, but, like Charlie Chaplin, he keeps his integrity and our love.

Professor Waith's essay illuminates Professor Bolgar's point that humanist ethical ideals did not have much effect on the mass audience that was developing during the Renaissance. Despite Erasmus's subversion of the warrior ideal and despite the honor Vivès gives to the state of married womanhood, Heywood's women worthies are not saints of charity or lovers of God, nor are they even prudent wives and mothers. Instead Heywood offered his bourgeois audience viragoes, women who were to be admired for their masculine spirits, who could appeal to the aristocratic yearnings of the largely non-aristocratic audience. Professor Waith suggests that Heywood's notion of the exemplary life favored the eccentric with limited goals, and thus prefigured the popular biography, the "unforgettable character" of our own day.

Sainthood, of course, was one form of the heroic ideal widely accepted through Renaissance society, yet even in this there was room for a multiplicity of concepts of the hero. Professor Zupnick's account of the graphic representations of Saint Sebastian reveals a tradition that usually depicts the human at the apex of commitment to the divine, in the moment of martyrdom, but the treatments show great variety in the artists' view of heroic sanctity. Is the martyr sustained in his torment by God's gift of grace (as he seems to be in the fresco in Sant'Ambrogio, Florence), or by his own ability to concentrate on the celestial realm (as in Titian and El Greco)? Is his aloofness from his executioners rooted in a sense of aristocratic detachment (as in Memling), or is it a hard-won Stoic victory over mundane concerns (as in Mantegna's Louvre painting and in Antonello da Messina's version)? Or is the Saint's humanity so unmodified that the ordeal is scarcely endurable (as in Mantegna's last version)? Professor Zupnick's study leaves no doubt that the legend of Saint Sebastian provided a popular heroic subject throughout the Renaissance, but on the exact nature of heroic sanctity there is little agreement in the tradition.

In their various ways Professors Bolgar, Steadman, and Wardropper all show Renaissance writers to be deeply concerned with portraying a worthy and exemplary hero, but thoroughly uncertain about how to portray such a hero in traditional forms. Even while the ancient heroic poems were held in great esteem, Christian humanist concerns had made the classical epic celebrating the martial virtues an unsuitable vehicle for depicting the more interior and Christianized virtues of an ideal hero of the Renaissance. In Professor Branca's view, it would seem, Boccaccio cut the knot by creating his collection of prose tales of the new heroes of his own culture, heroes not of war but of commerce, merchant adventurers who were fully as audacious as the classical heroes and who had, in addition, qualities (such as wit) essential to their peaceful conquests. Professor Branca also shows that Boccaccio further opened up the idea of heroic virtues by portraying virtuous women (who nevertheless retained their womanliness), heroes of the middle and lower classes, self-abnegating heroes, and, as his capstone, by proposing that poets (notably Dante and Petrarch) should be considered heroes since they are "the maximum expressions of a civilization." Yet, as Professor Branca notes, there is a nostalgic note in Boccaccio's creation of the new heroes because he saw the expansive, communal culture represented by these heroes giving way to a less exuberant and more mechanical commercial economy narrowly motivated by the quest for profits. Thus, in Professor Wardropper's terms, post-Boccaccean heroism "cannot bloom in an unheroic habitat."

The editors of this volume wish to express their gratitude to Professor Aldo S. Bernardo, Co-director of the Center for Medieval and Early Renaissance Studies, for his energetic organization of the Conference, and to our colleagues, Professors Anthony L. Pellegrini, and Khalil I. Semaan, who gave their time and skill unstintingly when asked for advice on matters of translation.

CHRISTOPHER J. REAGAN
NORMAN T. BURNS
STATE UNIVERSITY OF NEW YORK AT BINGHAMTON

The Concept of the Hero in the

Early Middle Ages

Bernard F. Huppé

THE HERO, WE ARE TOLD, has a thousand faces. The
search for him leads into folklore, myth, philosophy,
history, art history, anthropology, and psychology, so
that the literary scholar can be easily tempted into paths where
only a hero should tread. Even at the sacrifice of being considered unheroic, the historical critic of literature should keep
in mind the limits of his discipline, which is the art of literature. His heroes are Homer's Odysseus, Vergil's Aeneas, Beowulf, Roland, Chretien's Erec, the *Pearl* poet's Gawain, for
example. These are the elements of his study. History, art,
folklore may help him to understand better how the poet and
the audience conceive the hero, but his "given" as a literary
scholar is not history, myth, theology, but the hero celebrated
by a literary artist, a poet.

This definition of the concern of the literary scholar pre-
scribes the limits of my concern as an historical critic with the
hero of the early Middle Ages. His faces are blessedly few
in number, granting my restrictions. Indeed he has only three
faces: that of Beowulf, that of Brythnoth in the *Battle of Maldon,* and that of Roland. The Frankish heroic poetry fostered
by Charlemagne has not survived,[1] and the *Waltharius* is an
academic exercise which cannot seriously be considered as a
work of art. The *Ludwigslied,* although a battle poem, is far
from being either "heroic," or a work of art. The Old English
Waldere and the Old High German *Hildebrandslied* are mere
scraps.[2] There are to be sure the lives of the saints; and two
kingly martyrs, Oswald and Edmund, were celebrated by a
literary artist, Ælfric.[3] But the art of the homily and of the

saints' lives is not the art of the epic, of the heroic; Oswald and Edmund are first of all saints and only thus heroes. Saints are heroic, but they are not heroes; they are examples, models of perfect living and perfect dying. The clash of swords, the bang of shields are missing, and the loss is essential. The medieval hero must do battle as did Aeneas, one obvious proto-type for the medieval hero.

Of prime importance in the conception of a hero like Aeneas is that he serve some kind of inner direction. Aeneas is governed by fate, which in the Christian reading becomes divine providence, revealing man's true home as the heavenly Jerusalem. But such a hero is not simply driven; he must himself act, and act heroically. It is only through his actions, and beyond his actions, that we may perceive the playing out of the divine plan of things. The saint, on the other hand, too clearly embodies divine providence as an actual example of its operation. The saint's life is a miracle and is punctuated by miracles which are in fact the invisible hand of God made visible, the embodied evidence of things unseen. The saint is too clearly defined as a manifestation of divine purpose, whereas the heroic is felt in large part as a relationship, frequently strained, between the larger purpose and a human instrument, superhuman though it may be. Except where their conversion may be involved there is a total absence in the lives of the saints of any strain in their relationship to God.

Thus the lives of the saints, who are the obvious theoretical candidates for being the heroes of the Middle Ages, do not provide us with the examples for which we are searching. That is because the saint is simply too exemplary. He exists to give evidence of things unseen. He is a living miracle, not super-human as the hero is, but supra-human. His battlefield is to-tally spiritual, and his actions find their motivation not in human, but in divine purpose. Nothing more clearly illustrates the distinction I am trying to make between saint and hero than Ælfric's homilies on Saint Oswald and Saint Edmund, both warrior kings and martyrs. Oswald's reign is punctuated by two heroic battles, his victory over the heathen Cedwalla and his death and defeat at the hands of the apostate Penda. Such battles cry out for heroic treatment. They are the mighty

substance from which the *Battle of Maldon* and the *Roland*
are made. But Ælfric sees Oswald not as hero, but as saint,
and the battles are deliberately slighted so that the charity
of his reign and the mighty miracles that followed his death
appear as everything. For example, the story of the sick horse
who was cured when it wandered over Oswald's place of death
is more developed than are both battles put together. Here is
how Ælfric describes the first battle (lines 14–24):

> Oswald þa arærde ane rode sona, Gode to wurþmynte, ær
> þan þe he to ðam gewinne come, and clypode to his geferum,
> 'Uton feallen to ðære rode and þone Ælmihtigan biddan þæt
> he us ahredde wið þone modigan feond þe us afyllan wile:
> God sylf wat geare þæt we winnað rihtlice wið þysne reðþan
> cyning to ahreddenne ure leode.' Hi feollon þa ealle mid
> Oswolde on gebedum and syþþan on ærne mergan eodon to
> þam gefeohte and gewunnon þær sige swa swa se Wealdend
> him uðe for Oswoldes geleafan, and aledon heora fynd, þone
> modigan Cedwallan mid his micclan werode, þe wende þæt
> him ne mihte nan werod wiðstandan.

> [Oswald then raised up a cross to the honor of God before he
> came to the battle and called out to his companions, "Let us
> kneel before the rood and pray to the Almighty that he protect
> us against the haughty enemy who wishes to slay us: God him-
> self knows readily that we contend rightfully against this fierce
> king to protect our people." They all then knelt with Oswald
> in prayer and afterwards in the early morning went to battle
> and won the victory as God aided them because of Oswald's
> faith, and they laid low their enemy, the proud Cedwalla with
> his great army, he who thought that no army might withstand
> him.]

In essence the battle consists in the raising and worshipping
of the cross; the victory is that of God's power and Oswald's
faith. Avoided is even a hint of heroic motif—no shields are
raised, no spears brandished. In the second battle "celebrated"
by Ælfric, in which Oswald is defeated by the apostate Penda,
high heroic tragedy is implicit. Yet Ælfric with conscious
artistry erases from the scene all but the motif of Oswald's

saintly martyrdom.[4] Here is Ælfric's account of the second
battle (lines 124–36):

> Hit gewearð swa be þam þæt him wann on Penda, Myrcena
> cyning, þe æt his mæges slege ær, Eadwines cyninges, Cedwallan
> fylste; and se Penda ne cuðe be Criste nan þincg, and eall
> Myrcena folc wæs ungefullod þagit. Hi comon þa to gefeohte
> to Maserfelda begen and fengon togædere oð þæt þær feollon
> þa Cristenan and þa hæðenan genealæhton to þam halgan Os-
> wolde. Þa geseah he genealecan his lifes geendunge and gebæd
> for his folc þe þær feallende sweolt and betæhte heora sawla,
> and hine sylfne, Gode, and þus clypode on his fylle, 'God
> gemiltsa urum sawlum!' Þa het se hæþena cynincg his heafod of
> aslean, and his swiðran earm, and settan hi to myrcelse.

> [It came to pass that Penda waged war on him, Penda the
> king of the Mercians who had aided Cedwalla at the slaying
> sometime before of his kinsman, Edwin the king; and Penda
> understood nothing about Christ, and all the Mercian people
> were still unbaptized. They came then to battle at Maserfield
> and met together until the Christians fell and the heathens ap-
> proached the holy Oswald. Then he saw approach the ending
> of his life and prayed for his people who there fell in death
> and commended their souls and himself to God, and thus called
> out in his dying "God have mercy on our souls!" Then the
> heathen king commanded that his head be cut off, and his right
> arm, and that they be set up as a sign.]

Even the background for the action raises expectations of
the heroic with the evocation of the motif of vengeance for a
kinsman. Ælfric however, merely notes as a matter of fact that
Penda had been allied with Cedwalla when he slew Oswald's
kinsman, Edwin. The lack of development of the heroic motif
of vengeance, in contrast to its prominence in the *Beowulf* and
its important place in the *Roland*, suggests a deliberate negation
of the heroic possibilities in the battle for the purpose of stress-
ing Oswald's saintly character. The organization of Ælfric's
description implies a consciousness of the contrast between
saintly and heroic ideals, and plays one against the other.
Ælfric's narrative of the death of Edmund even more clearly

exemplifies his conscious disavowal of the heroic motif to give emphasis to the saintly. In the scene, the saint and martyr facing a heathen foe, Hingwar, deliberately discards the heroic response, rejecting it to follow Christ's injunction literally:

Hwæt þa Eadmund cynincg, mid þam þe Hingwar com, stod innan his healle, þæs Hælendes gemyndig, and awearp his wæpna: wolde geæfenlæcan Cristes gebysnungum, þe forbead Petre mid wæpnum to winnenne wið þa wælhreowan Iudeiscan. Hwæt þa arleasan þa Eadmund gebundon and gebysmrodon huxlice and beoton mid saglum, and swa syððan læddon þone geleaffullan cyning to anum eorðfæstum treowe and tigdon hine þærte mid heardum bendum, and hine eft swungon langlice mid swipum; and he symble clypode betwux þam swinglum mid soþan geleafan to Hælende Criste; and þa hæþenan þa for his geleafan wurdon wodlice yrre, for þan þe he clypode Crist him to fultume. Hi scuton þa mid gafelucum, swilce him to gamenes, to, oð þæt he eall waes besæt mid heora scotungum, swilce igles byrsta, swa swa Sebastianus wæs. Þa geseah Hingwar, se arlease flotman, þæt se æþela cyning nolde Criste wiðsacan, ac mid anrædum geleafan hine æfre clypode: het hine þa beheafdian, and þa hæðenan swa dydon.

[Lo then when Hingwar came, King Edmund stood within his home mindful of the saviour and cast aside his weapons. He wished to imitate the example of Christ who forbade Peter to contend with weapons against the bloodthirsty Jews. Lo the heathens bound and humiliated Edmund shamefully and beat him with cudgels and then led the confessor-king to an earth-rooted tree and tied him thereto with strong bonds and beat him then for a long time with whips; and he always called out between the blows with true faith to the Savior Christ; and the heathens because of his faith became madly angry because he called upon Christ for aid. They shot at him then with spears as if in a game until he was all covered with their shafts as if with the bristles of a porcupine, just as Sebastian had been. When Hingwar, the heathen pirate, saw that the noble king would not abandon Christ but with steadfast belief ever called upon him: he commanded that he be beheaded and the heathens did so. While still he called upon Christ the heathens drew the

saint to slaughter and with one blow cut off his head, and his
soul voyaged blessed to Christ.]

In this scene Ælfric clearly rejects the heroic. Edmund turns
like his Master meekly to his slayer. His death, even to the
image of the porcupine and the heathen's game-playing, appears humiliating, so that it reflects clearly the triumph in
ignomony of Christ's Passion and that of the martyrdom of
St. Sebastian. Ælfric is aware of the heroic tradition, but in
picturing his kingly martyr-saints he makes use of the heroic
simply as antithetical to the true value of the martyr who rejects the heroic in favor of the saintly.

Ælfric's use of the heroic as rhetorical antithesis is antici-
pated in a very interesting way in the early (perhaps eighth-
century) poem, *The Dream of the Rood:*

iii   Geseah ic þa frean mancynnes
       efstan elne mycle   þæt he me wolde on gestigan;
35   þær ic þa ne dorste   ofer dryhtnes word
       bugan oððe berstan   þa ic bifian geseah
       eorðan sceatas;   ealle ic mihte
       feondas gefyllan   —hwæðre ic fæste stod.
       Ongyrede hine þa geong hæleð   —þæt wæs god ælmihtig—
40 strang ond stiðmod   gestah he on gealgan heanne
       modig on manigra gesyhðe   þa he wolde mancyn lysan.
       Bifode ic þa me se beorn ymbclypte,   ne dorste ic hwæðre
              bugan to eorðan
       feallan to foldan sceatum   —ac ic sceolde fæste standan;
              rod wæs ic aræred,   ahof ic ricne cyning
45   heofona hlaford   —hyldan me ne dorste.
       iv Þurhdrifan hi me mid deorcan næglum,   on me syndon
              þa dolg gesiene
       opene inwidhlemmas   —ne dorste ic hira nænigum sceððan.
       Bysmeredon hie unc butu ætgædere;   Eall ic wæs mid blode
              bestemed
       begoten of þæs guman sidan   siððan he hæfde his gast
              onsended.

[iii   I saw mankind's Protector
       most manfully hasten   to ascend me;

35   through the will of the Lord   I was stayed in my wish
      to crack and bow   when I saw that the boundaries
      of earth were trembling;   truly I had the might
      to fell these foes   —yet I stood fast.
      The young hero prepared himself   —he who was God
      almighty—
40 great and gallant he ascended   the gallows' abject height
      magnanimous in the sight of many   when mankind he
      wished to free.
      I trembled when the Son clasped me,   yet I dared not cling
      to the ground
      or fall to the boundaries of earth   —for I had need to stand
      fast;
      a cross I was erected,   I raised the King
45   of the heavens above   —I dared not bow.
      iv They pierced me with dark nails,   the wounds are visi-
      ble on me
      the gaping blows of hate   —I dared harm none of them.
      Both of us two they besmirched;   I was all besmeared with
      the blood
      which poured from the side of the Man   after he sur-
      rendered his soul.]

The rhetoric of the passage is complex, involving metaphorical extension, metonomy, oxymoron, and antithesis.[5] But for
our present purposes what is important is that the poet used
as an underlying motif the metaphor of battle in the narration
of the crucifixion; Christ is pictured as a warrior preparing
for battle, and the cross as a kind of retainer of the Lord torn
between his desire to attack the enemy and his need to be
obedient to the Lord's command. The effect of his deliberate
use of heroic metaphor is to emphasize the antithesis between
the degradation of the death by crucifixion and the heroic language of battle which describes it. The hypothesis I have employed elsewhere to explain the poet's rhetorical use of the
heroic is predicated on the early date of the poem, and assumes that the choice of metaphor serves the purpose of missionary apology; that is to say, I hypothesize that the poet
had the specific intention of engaging the imagination of an
audience brought up on heroic poetry, or with a fresh memory

of it, so that they could themselves perceive vividly the higher heroism of the penitential life, the way of the cross.[6] The heroic is thus used to celebrate its antithesis, the penitential and humble Christian life. The poet's vision serves as an apologetic for the unpalatable Christian doctrine of humility and penance through suggesting the affinities of such a life with that of the warrior who also suffers privations that he may win triumph and glory. Thus in *The Dream of the Rood* both Christ and Cross appear as soldiers engaged in a conflict which has victory as its goal. Like good soldiers they are absolutely obedient to a command which calls upon them not to strike, but rather to accept in penitential humility. The Cross expresses its feelings about the Crucifixion as if it were a warrior who has strange obligations placed upon him, and in so doing the Cross reveals the tensions inherent in a warrior society whose ultimate values have been put to question. Thus the Cross wishes to engage in active battle against the enemy, but with great fortitude obeys the command to endure; its reward is the palpable reality of a place in the kingdom of Heaven, a reward the Cross promises to all who follow it.

Judging from *The Dream of the Rood*, an early poem, from the *Ludwigslied* (881), and from Ælfric writing much later, the heroic tradition appears to have been very much alive, however negatively, in the consciousness of the early medieval poet and writer.[7] We may also assume that the antithesis between the heroic and the saintly as ideals presented a primary problem to the Christian writer, who first lived with the vivid memory of a pagan heroic ideal and then faced the Viking attacks upon Christendom which called for a warrior-like heroic response. Certainly it appears to be a problem also faced by the poet of *The Battle of Maldon*, who wrote about the same time that Ælfric was writing his *Lives of the Saints*. About a century later the poet of the *Roland* was also dealing with much the same problem of trying to reconcile the heroic and the Christian; that is, to reconcile these antithetical ideals, not simply to use the heroic rhetorically as metaphor for the fortitude of penitential humility, like Ælfric and the writer of *The Dream of the Rood*. It is also, as I will try to show later, a chief problem of the *Beowulf* poet, who wrote at a time roughly contemporaneous with that of the *Rood* poet.

The problem these poets faced cannot be glossed over by hypothesizing the side-by-side existence of two cultures, that of the warrior and that of the clerk, with the heroic poem simply carrying a veneer of Christianity, simply making a bow in the direction of the saintly ideal. There may have been in fact a division in society, but the poetry we have is that of the clerks, of monks.[8] Yet, though the poetry is monastic, the heroic in *Maldon,* in the *Roland,* and in *Beowulf* cannot be explained away simply as rhetorical manipulation by the poets. The heroic in these poems cannot be transformed to become Christian, for example, by any argument or by allegorization. The poets, I believe, were trying to affect a reconciliation, trying to bring together the split halves of their society. These are great poets dealing with what is most profoundly important in their own times, and there could have been nothing more important for them to deal with than the meaning of the Christian soldier, as a reality, not merely as a metaphor for saintliness like St. Edmund. The dilemma they faced is clear: the only valid life was that led in the *imitatio Christi,* yet meek surrender to heathen marauders could not be contemplated in the real world.[9] Men had to do battle for Christendom.[10] One way or another the Christian writers of the heroic poems, *Maldon, Roland, Beowulf,* were dealing with the problem of the relation between the parts of the equation, Christian and heroic.

The Battle of Maldon is a Christian poem of monastic provenance, celebrating a battle in which the Christians led by Brythnoth, a leader of heroic stature, venerated for his piety, were defeated by the heathens. Two matters are of special interest in our attempt to discover how the poet conceived of the heroic in Brythnoth's conduct of the battle. First of all it should be clear that *The Battle of Maldon* is a poem, not an historical account to be judged by the principles of accurate representation. We can probably feel sure that the poet felt free to take what we might call poetic liberties with his accounts of the battle which reached him. At any rate, he handles his poetic account of the battle so that the death of the hero appears not as the climax but as the center of the poem, as in Ælfric's lives of Oswald and Edmund. The first half leads up to the death, and the last part recounts the treachery and the faithfulness of Brythnoth's followers as responses to his death. Thus the poem appears to enclose, to set off Brythnoth's dying speech. (lines 173–80):

Icȝeþancie þe   ðeoda Waldend
ealra þæra wynna   þe ic on worulde gebad;
nu ic ah, milde Metod   mæste þearfe
þæt þu min sawul   to þe siðian mote
on þin geweald   Þeoden engla
mid friþe ferian;   Ic eom frymdi to þe
þæt hi helsceaðan   hynan ne moton.[11]

[I give thee thanks   God of nations
for the well-being   I have had in the world;
now I have the greatest need   Gracious Lord
for you to grant   my spirit grace
so that my soul   may ascend to thee
into your realm   Ruler of angels,
may come in peace;   I call upon thee
that the devils of hell   may not harm it.]

Clearly his speech is presented as that of a martyr, a man who in dying turns toward God in the expectations of eternal life, and of protection from the devils because he is doing battle against the heathens. Yet, the poet has also made clear that Brythnoth's own actions contributed in a decisive way to his defeat and death, and that of his men, for he voluntarily gave up his advantage in holding the ford. He did this recklessly through heroic pride, *for his ofermode,* as the poet tells us quite specifically. In his speech, as Morton Bloomfield has shown,[12] he tempts God (lines 93–95):

'Nu eow is gerymed,   ȝað ricene to us
gunman to ȝuþe;   ðod ana Þat
hwa þære Wælstowe   Wealdan mote.'

[Room has been made,   in rush of battle
come to us now;   God alone knows
who will find himself victor   on the field of battle.]

Brythnoth's action and his speech suggest the heroic; his death is Christian and saintly. The antithesis in Brythnoth pictured

by the poet is the same antithesis as that used for rhetorical
effect in the *Dream of the Rood*, and by Ælfric, except that
here the antithesis is found embodied in a single Christian
hero, Brythnoth. In the poet's handling of the antithesis in
Brythnoth's conduct and in his way of reconciling the heroic
and the saintly may rest the clue to his concept of the Christian
hero.

Brythnoth is "heroic," and this quality as part of his sol-
dierly role appears in the heroic resoluteness (*anræd*) of his
reply to the Viking messenger (lines 45–61):

> 'ȝehyrst þu sælida   hwæt þis folc seȝeð?
> Hi willað eow to ȝafole   ȝaras syllan
> ættrynne ord   and ealde swurd
> þa hereȝeatu þe eow   æt hilde ne deah.
> Brimmanna boda   abeod eft onȝean
> seȝe þinum leodum   miccle laþre spell
> þæt her stynt unforcuð   eorl mid his werode
> þe wile ȝealȝean   eþel þysne
> Æþelredes eard   ealdres mines
> folc and foldan.   Feallan sceolon
> hæþene æt hilde;   to heanlic me þinceð
> þæt ȝe mid urum sceattum   to scype ȝanȝon
> unbefohtene   nu ȝe þus feor hider
> on urne eard   in becomon;
> ne sceole ȝe swa softe   sinc ȝeȝanȝan;
> us sceal ord and ecȝ   ær geseman
> ȝrim ȝuðpleȝa   ær we ȝofol syllon.'

> [Seaman do you hear   what this people say?
> They will give you   a gift of spears
> the poisoned point   and patrimonial sword
> a booty of war   without profit to you in battle.
> Viking messenger   to your men you must bring
> a tale which will be   loathsome in the telling
> that here a leader stands   loyally with his troop
> and will keep safe   this native soil
> the land of my king   of Lord Æthelred
> his folk and his fields.   The heathens shall fall
> here at battle;   it seems to me too base

that you should board   your ships without battle
and with our treasure   now you have traveled
the long way here   into our land.
You shall not gain too softly   a gift of treasure;
the point and the edge   will make our appeasement
rough battle play   before we render you tribute.]

This quality of resoluteness is transformed into vainglory
(*ofermode*) in his "heroic" granting of fighting room to the
heathen enemy. It is because he heeds the demands of his
heroic character that he becomes responsible for disaster. Thus
Brythnoth's heroism has in it something in the nature of a
tragic flaw. Conversely, Brythnoth's Christian piety, his faith,
is made abundantly clear, as in his thanks to God after his first
victorious skirmishes when he had drawn back to give the
Vikings "room" (lines 146–48):

                              Se eorl wæs þe bliþra
hloh þa modi man   sæde Metode þanc
ðæs dæȝweorces þe him Drihten forȝeaf.

                              [The doughty earl
was happy and laughed   gave thanks to heaven
for the day's labor   which the Lord had given him.]

The act of Christian thanksgiving which reveals that Brythnoth's faith is true, and his Christian purpose steadfast, leads
to his dying speech in which as a martyr he expresses his hope
of salvation.

Thus, it is in the act of martyrdom that the poet finds the
resolution of the antithesis between heroic and Christian. He
sees the heroic as human, as part of the human estate which
resulted from the curse of original sin, but he also observes
that the heroic is absolved of the taint of fallen humanity
when it is placed in the service of the faith, and becomes Good
Works. Brythnoth's martyrdom appears as a symbol of the
mystery of the Death of Christ, which through Divine Grace
reconciles erring humanity with God. As in the Christian reading of the *Aeneid*, *The Battle of Maldon* presents its hero as
an agent of Divine Providence. Brythnoth's human heroism
leads to defeat, but his heroic effort serves Christendom, so

that the defeat itself reveals a high, providential purpose by providing a Christian example of holy dying.

Implicit in the poem is the recognition that men who must do battle are likely to be "heroic," that is, self-reliant, proud. That is part of their fallen humanity. The hero, *qua* hero, is without grace; his heroism, however, may be redeemed, given the stature of saintliness, through grace, right faith and holy dying. It is a concept analogous to that of the *felix culpa*. Though heroism is itself sinful, through heroism a higher act of obedience to divine will may be made manifest. In the battle against heathendom, the penitential nature of the act, and of the martyr's death, exculpate the sinfulness of the warrior's heroic conduct. Only the battle for the faith and the martyr's death remain as a model of salvation. In essence, this is what the relation between Brythnoth's folly and his saintly character seems to suggest.

In turning to the *Roland* in search of the concept which the poet has of the hero and the heroic, one is struck by the lack of balance in the poem if its purpose is to celebrate Roland himself as the hero. The poem has three parts which are clearly marked by balanced repetition which places emphasis upon Charlemagne as the chief actor. The poem begins, Laisse I:

> Carles li reis, nostre emperere magnes,
> Set anz tuz pleins ad estét en Espaigne,
> Tresqu'en la mer cunquist la tere altaigne.
> N'i ad castel ki devant lui remaigne,
> Mur ne citét n'i est remés a fraindre,
> Fors Sarraguce, ki est en une muntaigne;
> Li reis Marsilie la tient ki Deu nen aimet. . . .

[Charles the King, our great emperor, has stayed seven whole years in Spain and has conquered the haughty country as far as the sea. Not a single castle resists him any longer; not one wall has yet to be broken nor one city taken, except Saragossa, which is on a mountain and is held by King Marsiliun, who does not love God. . . .] [13]

Laisse LV, which preludes the battle of Roncesvalles begins:

> Carles li magnes ad Espaigne guastede,
> Les castels pris, les citez violees.

> Ço dit li reis que sa guere out finee.
> Vers dulce France chevalchet l'emperere.

[Charles the Great has ravaged Spain, seized its castles, sacked its cities. Now the King declares the war is over. The Emperor rides toward sweet France.]

The third section of the poem, which tells of the actions of the Emperor after Roncesvalles, begins with Laisse CLXXXIX, a prelude to Charlemagne's defeat of his mightiest opponent, Baligant:

> Li emperere par sa grant poëstét
> vii anz tuz plens ad en Espaigne estét,
> Prent i chastels e alquantes citez.
> Li reis Marsilie s'en purcacet assez. . . .

[The Emperor, by the exercise of his great power, has stayed seven whole years in Spain and taken castles and many cities, though Marsiliun has made every effort to resist. . . .]

The effect of this structure of repetition is to emphasize the role of Charlemagne. Further diminishing Roland's part is the fact that his death is told in Laisse CLVI, leaving the entire last half of the poem (Laisse CLVII–Laisse CCXCI) for the account of Charlemagne's accomplishments: (1.) the defeat of Baligant and the total conquest of Spain (CCLXXI), and (2.) the punishment of Ganelon (CCLXXIV).

Roland is the hero of the epic which bears his name, yet not only is his own responsibility for the disaster at Roncesvalles heavily underscored in the poem, but also his death, however glorious, is over-shadowed by the space given to the account of Charlemagne's subsequent activities. Indeed, the structure of the poem diminishes Roland's part so obviously that there have been some who have attempted to redress the balance by canceling the entire Baligant episode as intrusive. However, if the balance given to the events in the poem is deliberate, the fact may suggest a clue to the poet's attitude toward his hero.

The particular force of the repetitive statements introducing the three parts of the poem is to emphasize the fact that Charlemagne's task is unfinished. He has spent seven years at his task, but in the eighth year one city yet remains, Saragossa.

The task of the conquest of Spain for Christendom is not complete, yet the reasons for Charlemagne's not completing his task are curious. In the first part he appears as the victim of the *legerie*, trickery, of the Saracens, but their *legerie* could not have succeeded if it had not been abetted by Charlemagne's Council, over which he seems to lose some measure of control. Certainly the advice of the Council he accepts is suspect, resulting, as it does, from a quarrel between Roland and Ganelon. Roland advises against the Saracen proposal, but unconvincingly because he appears motivated by a desire that previous ambassadors who were killed by Marsiliun be avenged. Ganelon's advice is equally suspect, and Charlemagne's acquiescence in the proposal to leave Spain appears to result from his war-weariness since he has no particular reason to trust Marsiliun, or Ganelon's counsel. Similarly his disastrous decision to send Ganelon as ambassador is first urged by Roland in a spirit of pique. The Council over which Charlemagne presides reflects strife and conflict, and the council surely must reflect Charlemagne himself, for he clearly controls the Council with an iron hand. If the body, as usual, appears to reflect the head, the disorder in the Council would suggest some kind of disorder in Charlemagne himself. At the very least, Charlemagne appears to have been distracted from completing his divinely appointed task of Christianizing all Spain. Something exists within Charlemagne and his followers which is incongruous with his divine mission as the vicar of God, that role which he is given most clearly, Laisse XXVI, when he sends Ganelon off, to become, ironically, a traitor,

> De sa main destre l'ad asols e seignét.
> Puis li livrat le bastun e le bref.

[With his right hand he absolves the count and makes the sign of the cross. And he gives him the staff and the letter.]

For an understanding of Charlemagne's role in the poem, premonitory motifs, for example, dreams and angelic visitations, and their relationship to the three repetitive introductory statements, quoted above, may provide a clue.

In the first introductory passage (Laisse I) emphasis is placed on the completion of the seventh year and on the com-

pletion of Charlemagne's task—except for the taking of Saragossa, which the heathen Marsiliun holds. Ironically what we
learn in the portion of the poem here introduced is that Charlemagne appears ready to take the eighth year not as a time
of final completion, but of rest, for he is shown as eager to
heed the advice which permits him to go home. The beginning
of the poem leads us to an expectation of the fulfillment of
God's work in the eighth year, with the fall of Saragossa. Instead, Charlemagne is tricked into leaving his task unfinished.
He is provided with one highly charged warning of disaster
when Ganelon drops the glove, but Charlemagne chooses to
ignore the omen.

In the second introductory passage (Laisse LV) mention
of the seven years is left out, and the poet has Charlemagne
himself declare, "The war is over." In the action which ensues
Charlemagne is now warned unmistakably by an angelic vision
of impending disaster. The vision darkens his mind, but in
spite of misgivings, he does not act on the clear evidence of
the vision; instead he goes on his way back to France, clinging
to his declaration, "The war is over," and ignoring the evidence of the prophetic vision.

The third introductory passage (Laisse CLXXXIX) which
returns to the emphasis of the first passage, is a prelude to
Charlemagne's conquest of Baligant, his diabolical opponent,
and his punishment of Ganelon. These have been prophesied
in two angelic visions, which come at the end of the second
section. In this third section Charlemagne fulfills his divinely
appointed task; indeed, in his battle with Baligant he goes beyond the mere conquest of Spain to that of the arch-enemy.
In this section increasingly the hand of the angel Gabriel is
made visible, directing Charlemagne in his task, as, for example, in his reviving Charlemagne when he does battle with
Baligant. There is an increasing emphasis on Charlemagne as
the king-hero, the vicar of God, carrying out divine purpose.

In this divine purpose Roland has played his part, as martyr, and as the hero. His heroic folly, his heroic pride in re-
fusing to blow the horn, lead to disaster, but his heroic nature
is transformed into the saintly through the martyrdom of his
death in a battle of ultimate Christian purpose. The battle is

given striking overtones of the penitential by Bishop Turpin when he "blesses them in the name of God, and as a penance he bids them strike hard" (Laisse LXXXIX). The absolution of Roland is completed in his penitential act of martyrdom. His death suggests the Passion; in dying he acknowledges his "guilt," and holds out "his right glove to God." Angels descend out of heaven and come to him. In acting out God's purpose, and through God's grace, Roland achieves saintliness. The hero is transformed, yet his death is part of a large design, the design of God's Providence, and in this design, Charlemagne, the vicar of God, is of basic and critical importance.

It is Charlemagne, the ultimate heroic and Christian king, who is the primary subject of the poem. This intention in the poem is made clear in its curious ending, inexplicable except as part of the design in which Charlemagne is central. The poem ends (L.CCXCVIII) with the baptism of Bramimunde after the execution of Ganelon. We are told the king has gone to bed in his vaulted bedroom. God sends St. Gabriel to him, to say to him:

> Passet li jurz, la nuit est aserie,
> Culcez s'est li reis en sa cambre voltice.
> Seint Gabriël de part Deu li vint dire:
> 'Carles, sumun les oz de tun emperie!
> Par force iras en la tere de Bire,
> Reis Vivïen si succuras en Imphe,
> A la citét que paien unt asise;
> Li chrestien te recleiment e crient!'
> Li emperere n'i volsist aler mie!
> 'Deus,' dist li reis, 'si penuse est ma vie!'
> Pluret des oilz, sa barbe blanche tiret.
> Ci falt la geste que Turoldus declinet.

["Charles, summon all the hosts of your Empire and enter the land of Bire by force of arms, and rescue King Vivien, for the pagans have laid seige to him in the city of Imphe, and the Christians are pleading and crying out for you."

The emperor does not wish to go.

"Oh God," says the king, "My life is a burden"; and the tears run from his eyes and he rends his white beard.]

The end of the poem, with its picture of the weariness of
an old man facing God's implacable challenge to duty, returns us to the beginning where Charlemagne was shown as
equally weary of his seven years of struggle, and apparently
only too willing to relinquish completing the last part of his
task, the destruction of Saragossa. He is the vicar of God; he
is called upon to stern Christian duty; in human weakness he
sometimes falters. At the end of the poem he is weary, but is
clearly prepared to take up his task—difficult as it is.

In this picture of Charlemagne as the vicar of God, Roland
plays his part as the hero who as Charlemagne's "right arm"
is part of the design of Charlemagne's life. Roland's heroism
is itself a weakness; his pride which leads him not to blow
the horn brings upon the Franks the disaster at Roncesvalles.
Indeed his arrogant contention with Ganelon was part of the
original problem in Charlemagne's Council. Roland's heroism
is his tragic flaw, but it is redeemed by the penitential nature
of his battle against the heathen hosts, and by the saintliness
of his death where in an atmosphere which clearly evokes the
imitation of Christ he surrenders his soul to God in the image
of tendering his glove to his creator. His death, at the center
of the poem, mirrors the larger consequences of his emperor's
heroic and saintly life. It is in this way that Roland and Brythnoth are the Christian heroes of the early Middle Ages, heroes
who reconcile the flawed hero and the flawless saint in the
testimony of their martyrdoms, and in exemplifying the providential concept of the *felix culpa*.

Beowulf is central to any attempt to discover the concept
of the hero in the literature of the early Middle Ages. Consideration of the poem cannot be avoided, but, in disregard of
chronology, has been left to last. That is because *Beowulf* presents a formidable problem, one more readily approached when
the developed concept of the hero in the Christian literature
of the early Middle Ages has already been outlined. The literature which has been reviewed celebrates a hero who is un-
qualifiedly Christian, as Beowulf is clearly not. Roland is Christian; his heroic qualities appear as a necessary flaw, and he
is ultimately given heroic stature through the concept of the
felix culpa: he offers his glove to God and flights of angels

sing him to his rest; he becomes one with providential design. But Beowulf, to the contrary, is a pagan and his heroic quality is simply an essential part of his definition as hero.

It is tempting to explain away this difficulty in our hypothesis about the Christian hero by resort to the once popular notion that *Beowulf* in essence conveys a pagan heroic ethic, although with Christian interpolations. This theory, however, provides no solution since the Christianity of the *Beowulf* may be shown to be an essential part of its structure, its form. The milieu of the poem is Christian; its subject is pagan. It is naive to assume that the poet was not aware of the paganism of his hero and of his hero's society. It is equally naive to assume that he would not have deplored such a society, would not have seen it as lacking in the primary theological virtues which alone gave meaning to life.

It is precisely here that we may find the solution to the problem of *Beowulf* with its pagan hero who must somehow fit into a Christian design. The solution rests in the hypothesis that a primary function of the *Beowulf* is to demonstrate the limits of heathen society, the limits of the righteous heathen, the limits of the heroic. Actually once this view is grasped, that the literary world of *Beowulf* is pagan, its point of view Christian, much that is puzzling in its structure can be explained. For example, one of the obvious facts of the poem is its descending line of mood and action, so that in the last half of the poem the omens of disaster of the first half are realized. After Beowulf gives his account of his exploits in Denmark the narrative is concerned with the deadly, internecine Swedish wars, with the tangled net of Higelac's affairs and his death, with the ravaging of the country by the dragon, with Beowulf's death, and with the forebodings of the ultimate disaster to come. Beowulf himself is shown at the end to be more like Hrothgar in contrast to the youthful Wiglaf, who is like the Beowulf of the beginning; the cycle moves from aged Hrothgar to aged Beowulf. More than that, it is a cycle of ineffectuality, that of Hrothgar, as well as that of Beowulf, who hopes that his death has gained the dragon's treasure for his people. To Wiglaf, however, it is perfectly clear that the treasure is more disaster than triumph, so that he hurriedly

buries it, hoping perhaps to lessen the attraction to the Swedes
and other tribes of an attack upon the Geats once they hear
of Beowulf's death. The whole mood of the poem at the end
is a counterpoint of disaster; for example, the speech of the
last survivor on the useless gold is a counterpoint to Beowulf's
dying speech as he gazes at the same useless gold.

   The heroic in Brythnoth and Roland represents a tragic
flaw which precipitates disaster, but which leads through the
mystery of the *felix culpa* to the good of redemption through
martyrdom. The heroic in Beowulf is self-contained; it is the
ethos of the culture, the age imagined by the poet; it must
be self-justified because it cannot, as in the *Roland*, appeal to
a redeeming grace: thus the last words about Beowulf are
about his glory. But the poet's attitude toward this heroic
ethos is Christian and critical; that is why the direction of the
poem is governed by doom, and towards disaster, unrelieved
by any sense of redemption. Beowulf's flaw is tragic precisely
because there are no means available to him by which the flaw
may be redeemed. Beowulf's tragedy rests in his inability to
rise above the ethos of his society, the mores of revenge and
war which govern his actions. In the first half of the poem,
in contrast to Hrothgar, who is aged and ineffectual, and to
Heremod, who is vigorous but evil, Beowulf appears a savior,
a cleanser of evil; in the last half of the poem, particularly at
the end, Beowulf echoes and reflects not beginnings, but end-
ings, and though he remains heroic, his heroism is no more
effective than is Hrothgar's helplessness. Beowulf's death, indeed, reflects one of the dominant motifs of the last section of
the poem, that of the backward-looking last survivor.

   Significant, as we have seen, in the role of the hero is his
being an agent of fate, in Christian terms, of Divine Providence. Beowulf's role as agent of Divine Providence is seen
most clearly at the middle of the poem, not at the beginning
and not at the end. The introduction to the poem, of course,
is not concerned with Beowulf at all but with Scyld Scefing
and his story. The hero Scyld is seen as an agent of some divine power, but the power itself is mysterious; Scyld appears
mysteriously sent by God and disappears into the bosom of
God. It is clear that the agency invoked by the poet is the

Divine Agency. Scyld Scefing, pagan though he is, appears to be directed by God. The point of view, however, which is most vividly expressed appears in counterpoint to this Christian point of view, that is, the viewpoint of Scyld's followers who see in him only mystery, the mystery of the unknown. That is to say, they reveal the limitations of their paganism, the limitations of a viewpoint which is without faith.

The providential aspects of Beowulf's battle against Grendel are given explicit statement. In particular his battle against Grendel's mother is marked by direct divine interposition, when Beowulf is given the sight of the sword through which he is able to conquer her. At the very center of the poem is the story of the hilt of the divinely revealed sword.[14] Beowulf brings back this hilt, which recounts in biblical terms the story of the downfall of the generation of Cain. Here God's hand and Beowulf's place in providential design appear most clearly, and after this the sense of events given in the poem is fatalistic. Much of the action takes place not providentially, but fatalistically: we are given a picture of the inevitable fate of a war-like society governed by the law of revenge; we are shown the uselessness of all things in this world unless they are governed and directed to the end of being useful to salvation.

Thus the movement of the poem is downward toward a tragic end. Beowulf becomes the victim of the dragon, who protects the treasure of the world; the downward path reveals the doom of the one who lacks saving grace. The poem ends, to be sure, with Beowulf's people celebrating him as the mildest of kings and the most worthy of praise. But their praise has the limitations of the merely human; magnificent as is their praise, what they say would have applied equally well to Aeneas, to Hector, or to any good pagan hero or monarch. Specifically, however, the praise lacks any of the Christian overtones which glorify the deaths of Brythnoth and Roland. For in direct contrast to both *The Battle of Maldon* and the *Roland*, Beowulf's death suggests no movement toward redemption. His death is as dissimilar as any can be to the death of Roland, who tenders his glove to God in a scene evoking the hour of the crucifixion; lacking completely in Beowulf's death is Brythnoth's dying plea that his soul may be brought home safely to his God.

Curiously enough the *Beowulf* ends with the death of the hero, which is what we might expect in a heroic poem. As we have seen, the oddity of *The Battle of Maldon* and the *Roland* is that their deaths come at the dead center of the two poems; the death of the hero is not the whole point toward which each poem is moving. In their deaths the fulfillment of Divine Providence is clearly seen, but as part of a larger design. This is particularly clear in the *Roland*, where Divine Providence is revealed in the death of the hero, but much more clearly revealed when Roland's death is seen to be part of the larger design of Charlemagne's mission to defend Christendom, and to enlarge the number of its citizens. When Roland dies, his death serves the purpose of bringing Charlemagne back to complete his task. The real point of the poem, as we have seen, rests here, not in the battlefield death. Conversely the center of the *Beowulf* celebrates and reveals the hand of God, but the death of the hero does not reveal the providential design so much as it reveals the emptiness of Beowulf's heroic life. His death suggests that the heroic ideal is empty, that its best embodiment in a Beowulf or in an Aeneas is as nothing compared with the Christian ideal, the ideal of the service of the Lord. It is here that we feel most clearly the tragic implications of *Beowulf*, can feel most clearly the pathos of his people's celebrating a hero who has left them literally nothing but debts which will be collected.

A fundamental explanation of the marked difference between the purpose of the poet of *Beowulf* and the poet of the *Roland* is to be found in their times of composition. *Roland*, as it were, stands on the threshold of the era of the Crusades. It is not of course a crusading poem, but in the not too distant future looms the time of the first Crusade. In *Roland* is a flowering of a spirit which has seen the triumph of Christendom, its establishment, its sense of permanence, its sense of expansion. *Beowulf*, on the other hand, comes from a much earlier time, a time which is really at the other edge, the edge of the age of the missionary, particularly in England. Specifically it was written at about the same time presumably as the *Dream of the Rood.* We have seen how the *Dream of the Rood* is explicable as a missionary poem using the heroic as a way of catching the imagination of the Christian warrior, so that he could embrace willingly the penitential doctrine. It would appear likely that the *Beowulf* might have served as a Christian apologetic, revealing both the emptiness of the old way, and, by contrast, the fullness of understanding which follows from the Christian faith.[15]

Thus, to conclude, the *Beowulf* and the *Roland*, though different in purpose, are linked in their conception of the hero and the heroic. There can be but one Christian hero, and that is Christ. Whatever is heroic is an imitation of him—the true hero is an imitation of Christ as were the saints. St. Edmund imitated Christ truly, and was a saint. Beowulf is a hero who lacks Christ and reveals that the heroic in itself is empty. Roland is a hero who follows Christ and in so doing redeems that which is merely heroic within him.

Notes

1. See Reto Bezzola, *Les Origines et la Formation de la Litterature Courtoise en Occident*, Pt. I (Paris: 1958), pp. 98–104.

2. See Frederick Norman's edition of *Waldere* (London: Methuen's Old English Library, Series A, 1933), and its bibliography.

3. Both lives are edited by G. I. Needham, *Lives of Three English Saints* (New York, 1966). English translations are my own except where indicated.

4. The *Ludwigslied*, written in late 881 or early 882, shows a similar erasure of the battle between Louis and the Vikings, the "subject" of the poem. Instead the poet concentrates his entire attention on celebrating Louis as the Vicar, even the adopted son of God, executing divine purpose. Louis has no personality in the poem, except for his relationship to God. The emperor, we are told, served God; indeed, when he lost his father, God adopted him as his own son, became his foster father. See lines 3–6 in the *Ludwigslied*, edited by T. Schauffler, in *Althochdeutsche Litteratur*, 2d ed. (Leipzig, 1900), pp. 119–23:

Kind warth her faterlos.   thes warth imo sar buoz:
holoda inan truhtin, magaczogo wart her sin.
Gab her imo dugidi, fronisc githigini,
stual hier in Vrankon.   so bruche her es lange!

For their sins God visits punishment on the Franks by permitting the
Vikings to attack them, and then calls on Louis to defend his people (line
22): " 'Hluduig, kuning min, hilph minan liutin!' " In response Louis
gathers his men to face the Northmen; he takes shield and spear, sings the
praise of God, to which his men reply (line 47) "Kyrieleison!" "The song
being sung, the battle began" (line 48); victory and honor are given to
Louis. Nothing could have higher heroic potential for the poet than such a
battle; in the poem nothing turns out that could be less heroic, or more
obviously, tendentiously, Christian.

5. See. Bernard F. Huppé, *The Web of Words* (Albany: State University of
New York Press, 1970), pp. 85–88.

6. Ibid., pp. 102–4.

7. *Beowulf, Widsith, Deor,* all testify to the lively survival of the "heroic"
literary past. We have also William of Malmesbury's story of how Ald-
helm taught by using old songs (*Gesta Pontificum Anglorum,* vol. 5, edited
by N. Hamilton [London, 1870], p. 336), and Alcuin's famous reference
to mixing Ingeld with Christ (*Monumenta Alcuina,* edited by Watten-
bach and Duemmler [Berlin, 1873], p. 357). For the *Ludwigslied* see
note 4, above. Rhetorical use of the heroic similar to that in *The Dream
of the Rood* is found in *The Wonder of Creation* and *Judith;* see *The
Web of Words,* pp. 37–38, 173–78. It is also found in *Genesis* A, lines
1960–2095; see Bernard F. Huppé, *Doctrine and Poetry* (Albany: State
University of New York Press, 1959), pp. 195–200, 237–38.

8. Bezzola, *Origines,* Pt. 1, p. 19, speaks of the early attempt to train Theodoric's successor, Athalaric, in the arts, and of how his mother was forced by
the unreconstructed nobility to cease, "à marcher dans une direction si op-
posée à l'esprit ostrogoth. Elle se révolta et représenta vivement à la regente
que ce n'etait pas là l'éducation qu'il fallait à un jeune roi de leur race des-
tiné à une carrière querrière et héroique." He argues, pp. 21–22, that it was
monasticism which succeeded as the inheritor of the "*humanitas* de
l'antiquité," but directed toward a new end, the *opus Dei.* The attempt at
Ravenna to make "une synthèse de la *civilitas* romaine avec l'idéal guerrier
des barbares" was thus superseded by the monastic movement. Bezzola also
cites, p. 98, the picture in a poem of Theodulf's of the uneasy confrontation between clerk and warrior at the court of Charlemagne. Theodulf
speaks of his verses, "qui charment les convives a l'exception du seul 'mem-
brosus Wibrodus heros'; se dernier secoue sa grosse tête d'un air menaçant
et farouche, jusqu'a ce qu'il soit corrige par le roi et s'éloigne en boitant,
'Vulcain par la demarche, Jupiter par la voix.' " The use of "heros" as a
designation for Wibrod in this "clerical" poem is especially significant.

9. For one example, see Ælfric's reference to Judith as an "example to you
men that you with weapons should protect your land against the attacking
enemy" (*The Web of Words,* p. 139).

10. In the *Decretum* of Ivo of Chartres, the problem of military homicide is
treated at great length (*PL* 161, 711–30). Although the *Decretum* is of

the eleventh century, it comprises a judicious compilation of received and traditional opinion, largely Augustinian, and is in effect, a precis of views earlier than the eleventh century. The basic problem presented is that of "justifiable" homicide (i.e., judicial and military) in the face of (1.) direct biblical adjurations against homicide, and (2.) the precept of non-violence made explicit in Christ's preaching and example.

The basis for the justification of an act of homicide rests in "circumstance"; it is necessary to consider not simply the act, but the occasions, the motivation. Ivo, chap. 65, col. 711, cites Chrysostom on Matthew, "Non sola igitur respiciamus opera, sed tempus, et causam et voluntatem, et personarum differentiam, et quantacunque alia ipsis operibus acciderint diligentissime requiramus. Non enim possumus ad veritatem aliter pervenire." Specifically, with regard to war, the defense of country against barbarians is ample justification for homicide. Ivo (chap. 97, col. 721) cites Ambrose, "Fortitudo quae vel in bello tuetur a barbaris patriam . . . plena justitiae est." Further Christian teaching does not condemn all war; Ivo cites Augustine (chap. 107, col. 724): "Nam si Christiana disciplina omnia bella culparet, hoc potius militibus consilium salutis petentibus in Evangelio diceretur, ut abjicerent arma, seque militiae omnino subtraherent. Dictum est autem eis: Neminem concusseritis, nulli calumniam feceritis, sufficiat vobis stipendium vestrum [Luc. III]. Quibus propriûm stipendium sufficere debere praecepit, militare utique non prohibuit . . . Non est iniquitatis, sed potius humanitatis societate devictus, qui propterea est criminis persecutor, ut sit hominis liberator." It is necessary that in battle prayer be made to God by whom the event is governed; see Ivo's citation (chap. 109, col. 725) of Augustine: "Gravi de pugna conquereris ut dubites nolo, utile tibi tuisque dabo consilium. Arripe manibus arma, oratio aures pulset auctoris, quia quando pugnatur, Deus apertis coelis spectat, et partem quam inspicit justam sibi dat palmam." To battle for God is righteous (chap. 110, col. 726), according to Augustine, "Bellum autem quod gerendum Deo auctore suscipitur, recte suscipi, dubitare fas non est" and Jerome (chap. 111, col. 726): "Non solum homines ministri sunt et ultores irae Dei, his qui malum operantur, et non sine causa portant gladium, sed et contrariae fortitudines quae appelantur furor et ira Dei". Righteous warfare, however, must never be undertaken with a view to personal gain, again citing Augustine, chap. 125, col. 728: "Militare non est delictum, sed propter praedam militare peccatum est."

11. See the editon of Eric Valentine Gordon (New York: Methuen, 1966).

12. "Beowulf, Brythnoth, and the Judgment of God: Trial by Combat in Anglo-Saxon England," *Speculum* 44 (1969): 547–48.

13. *La Chanson de Roland*, edited by Frederick Whitehead (Oxford: 1946). The translation is by William S. Merwin, *The Song of Roland* (New York: Vintage Press, 1963). Merwin's prose is lean and strong; it catches better than any other I know my sense of the poem. It has the virtue also of being faithful to the text.

14. In an unpublished article Kjell Meling has shown convincingly the importance to the action of the revelation of the cross-shaped hilt.

15. See Larry Dean Benson, "The Pagan Coloring of *Beowulf*," in *Old English Poetry: Fifteen Essays*, edited by Robert P. Creed (Providence, R. I.: Brown University Press, 1967), pp. 193–213.

The Problem of the Hero in the

Later Medieval Period

Morton W. Bloomfield

Yet surely there are men who have made their art
Out of no tragic war, lovers of life,
Impulsive men that look for happiness
And sing when they have found it
                    Yeats, Ego Dominus Tuus

SINCE THE WORD "HERO" HAS MANY MEANINGS, it would be wise to define briefly in what sense I am using the term so that my comments on the late medieval hero may be properly understood. I do not intend to get into an elaborate exercise in exegesis, but if I can at least make clear what I am not talking about when I use that elusive word, I am only doing what any critic or scholar must do—be clear about his subject. An infinite number of negative statements are entailed by any positive statement, but some are more plausible than others. These, then, need to be especially excluded for the sake of clarity.

The primary sense of the word, at least if we go back to Indo-European, is "protector" or "helper," but in Greek, which has given the term to most European languages through borrowing, it came to mean a superhuman or semidivine being whose special powers were put forth to save or help all mankind or a favored part of it. The Greek hero was normally less than a god and yet more than merely human. Our earliest uses of the term in Homer seem to refer to men of great strength, ability or courage especially favored by the gods, but later the word was extended to a special class of beings somewhere between gods and men. Hesiod speaks of an age of

27

heroes. The noun as far as I know was not used as a literary term in antiquity.

Such a being often had a mythic dimension and was usually the subject of tales and stories. There is even ritual associated with some of these names, as with Aesculapius for instance. In the Orient, there were similar characters among whom we may even include the Jewish Messiah. Culture heroes abound in the stories and myths of many peoples—semidivine beings like Prometheus who brought fire to the world, or Jubal, who invented music.

From this rather special sense, the word passed into most European tongues to indicate any outstanding man, perhaps first of all, because of Homer, in martial prowess. Although there is a late fourteenth-century reference, the term did not become widely used in England until the sixteenth century. By about the seventeenth century, "hero," in English, could mean any notable or great human being, while at the same time keeping its more restricted Greek sense. The normal metaphorical process has extended the semantic range of the word so that we can praise any man by calling him heroic. Today any admirable human being can be called a hero—a saint or businessman, baseball player or writer.[1] The term's popularity was much increased by the predilection of the Romantic Age for great men and for individuality. A writer like Carlyle in his *Hero, Hero-Worship and the Heroic in History* did much to extend the meaning of the word and to make it popular. Today it is widely used in psychoanalytic and mythological writings.[2]

The word is also employed in literary criticism and literature, that is, written literature, as a synonym for protagonist or chief character, but it often carries with it a penumbra, if not more, of its earlier meaning of a superior human being. When Thackeray says that *Vanity Fair* is a novel without a hero, he is certainly using it in that sense. It was first used in English in this sense—as the chief male personage in an epic, story, play or poem—by Dryden, I believe. Since then and especially in the nineteenth century, it has been widely used in the discussion of literature. It is strongly connected with the analysis of narrative or drama and hence with action and deeds of some sort.

It is not normally used in discussing the structure of lyric, even one which contains narrative parts. A lyric may of course praise a hero, but usually or normally does not contain one. Primitive praise-songs were perhaps the matrix out of which epic grew, but this does not give the term an ancient literary lineage for lyric poetry. The nature of lyric does not normally demand a literary character. Thus, although literary heroes as such go back to the dawn of literature, oral and written, the particular term "hero" is a relatively modern one in this sense. The fact that a word originally meaning a semi-divine creature has come, in one of its senses, to mean the protagonist in literature, does tell us a good deal about how we conceived the chief personage in literary works from the seventeenth century onwards.

I am here concerned, of course, with the literary uses of the term. "Hero" as used in literature has also numerous particular meanings. There are the epic hero,[3] the romantic hero, the dramatic hero, the tragic hero, the ironic hero, the realistic hero, and even the comic hero and anti-hero. What I am discussing is the hero who is wrestling with fate or fortune in either narrative or drama and who is either epic, dramatic or tragic. He exists in literature, and he is beyond the average of mankind in physical or spiritual power and strength or in both. In other words, I am taking the word in its usual and basic literary sense and not in the various earlier and transferred senses it has had through its long history (or still has), nor in the more specialized literary senses.

Whatever term be used for the major personage or personages of narrative or drama, that these genres have always been presented around such figures cannot be doubted. What I shall attempt here is to argue that there has been a pattern of up and down in the history of the tragic or epic hero, and that the later medieval period is a down period in comparison with the early Middle Ages and the High Renaissance, joining the eighteenth century and twentieth century in its suspicion of the hero.[4] I shall endeavor to show first that this is the case as far as the later Middle Ages is concerned, second, how this period coped with the problem of a hero-less or at least hero-minimizing literature and finally, a possible explanation for this shift. As Marshall Fishwick writes, "Style in heroes, as in everything else, changes." [5]

The tragic hero who carries a magic aura about him is found mainly in the early epic. This genre could be absorbed into a Christian universe, but a desacralized world has made it very difficult to continue the tradition of such a hero in the face of the disenchantment which has been an increasing element in the Western world view since the Renaissance. Military prowess, poetic power, courage, tragic acceptance, demonic power are all the various substitutes offered to effect such heroic charisma when the magic powers of the hero can only be believed in metaphorically. Yet the Renaissance and the nineteenth century made noble tries, with some success, at carrying on in some way the superhuman element in the original hero.

For the original hero in early literature was probably based on the king who died for his people, the warrior who defeated the tribe's enemies, the ruler who invented a new way of life, or the man who discovered a way of making life easier. These men, regarded as supermen in some way, were celebrated in song and story and, through such literary forms, were presented again to the people so that they could participate in their magic. The teller of the tale or the singer of the song had to give the authentic story [6] (at least as it was assumed to be) so that none of the power of the hero would be lost. Even in the oral tales and songs still recited today, we find a remarkable honesty and a slight ambiguity of attitude towards the hero. Only the Romantic period made its heroes all heroic —and even then usually by the less accomplished poets. This ambiguity in early epic existed both for truth and apotropaic purposes. If the truth is told, we can be sure of the reality of the hero. Furthermore, a man must not be praised too much. Otherwise we bring the evil eye on him or tarnish his power. In order to participate in his glory and charisma, we must hear it "like it is."

These myths and legends were both history and religion. They were numinously powerful because they were true, and it was important that the singer stress the truth-value of what he sang. [7] This sense of the true as well as a sense of magic power and a somewhat ambiguous attitude toward the hero

persists in our first written epics—in *Gilgamesh,* the *Iliad* and
the Abraham and Joseph sagas. When these tales were told
in their original settings, the listeners no doubt participated in
a magic experience and hoped that the strength and power of
the hero would come to them. Time would be conquered so
that past could become the present and the future. Mythic
time is not historic time, but another chronological dimension.
Narrative is man's tribute to and acknowledgement of time
and the sequential nature of existence, as well as his protest
against such an arrangement of the human condition. It is a
tribute insofar as a narrative imitates life as closely as language allows it to do; it is a protest insofar as it attempts by
its very existence to get man out of time by bringing the past
or assumed past to life again. Implicit in the very notion of
narrative is an ambiguous attitude toward time, both accepting
and repudiating it simultaneously.[8]

Epic narrative and the heroes have then their ambiguities
from the very beginning. Furthermore the tendency to praise
and exalt heroes is always accompanied by the drive to deni-
grate and abuse them. The epic heroes of *Beowulf,* of *Igor,*
of the *Njalsaga,* of *Roland,* go down to defeat and in some
sense are responsible for their defeat. They are noble and admirable, but we are always left with a niggling and even in
some cases a strong sense that they deserved their doom. However, we know that even in defeat partially of their own doing,
they are heroes nevertheless—men above the common, above
the average, whose drive for glory whether heavenly or earthly,
raises them beyond the ordinary and the average. They are
big persons who are semi-divine, larger than human, who fascinate us by their valor, courage, and even *bravura.* The hero
does not normally fit easily into the moral mould. He is often
both less and greater than ordinary moral categories. Yet he is
also profoundly involved with the moral element in life.

The heroic stream in Western literature has had from the
very beginning then a shadow, an anti-heroic stream both in
the chief protagonist and in his story. Beowulf has his Unferth
just as Othello his Iago. Prince Hal has to exorcize Hotspur
and Falstaff before he can be a hero. This internal split is
present, I believe, in the whole history of the hero in our lit-

erary tradition. What we have, however, is the dominance of either the heroic or anti-heroic pole of this duality at different times. Roughly speaking, in the early Middle Ages the heroic dominates; in the later Middle Ages and early Renaissance the anti-heroic dominates. In the later Renaissance the heroic once again comes to the fore, even though its opposite, as earlier, is by no means dead. The Renaissance split is beautifully illustrated by Cervantes who, even while he was writing the great heroic masterpiece of anti-heroism,[9] was also completing *Persiles,* an heroic novel. But the ideal of heroism dominated in Shakespeare and Corneille, Milton and Latin drama. This period is followed by a dry period of anti-heroism in the eighteenth century, then a new outburst of romantic *Schwärmerei* continuing until the early years of our century. Then the cynical hero and the anti-heroic hero of the post-war period follow. Finally, very recently the tide seems to be turning again, and we find new heroes—in the old sense—gurus and the like.

This rather simplified scheme does, it seems to me, indicate a dialectical movement in the heroic both within and without.[10] What I now want to concentrate on is the later Middle Ages in order to show how the anti-heroic force came to the forefront then and how it manifested itself in opposition to the concept of the epic and even hagiographical hero.

Literature as we know it must have a protagonist or several protagonists even if they are not heroic figures. The force of the narrative must rest on certain characters, even in a book like Dos Passos's *USA,* which tries to present a whole culture. Dos Passos centers on figures, historical and imaginary, as he presents his story. If all men are equal in a democracy, they are certainly not so in narrative and drama. Some human beings must stand out in literature, but they need not stand out so clearly or so heroically in some literature as in other literature. The protagonist or protagonists are always with us, even if the hero and the heroine are not.

This later medieval absence or relative absence of heroes in the sense of men concerned with honor, fame and possessed of charisma has not been unnoticed until now, but normally the emphasis has been elsewhere and the full force of this situation has not, in my opinion, been grasped. For instance in Father

Maurice McNamee's little book entitled *Honor and the Epic Hero*,[11] written some fifteen years ago, we find an important analysis of the heroic and magnanimous from Aristotle to Milton. We have a chapter on Beowulf in the middle of the book after one on Aeneas, and then a chapter on the quality of magnanimity in Augustine and Thomas followed by one on Spenser. In other words there is no epic hero of any sort worthy of note in the English tradition between Beowulf and Spenser. Father McNamee is of course selective in his work and could no doubt easily find a later medieval hero of this stripe, but the fact is that after Roland and some of the heroes of the Norse sagas and of early romances, no hero of any note from the later Middle Ages leaps to the mind calling for treatment in a book of this sort.

The absence of a true charismatic hero who is valiant and noble is a characteristic of most of the literature of the later Middle Ages in Western Europe. Tristram is defeated by fate without transcending it in literature until Wagner; Lancelot represents a new type of man characterized by sensitivity and obedience to love [12]; Troilus is defeated by his decency, and we can only laugh with him at his own life as the poem ends. There is something powerfully wrong with these later medieval heroes which seriously compromises their heroism. This self-destructive heroism, or more precisely this unheroic heroism, dominates all later medieval and early Renaissance literature until Tasso and Shakespeare. The drastic ambiguity of the hero in the later Middle Ages is perfectly revealed in *Gawain and the Green Knight* where the problem of the hero becomes acute. Scholars simply cannot agree on whether Gawain is to be admired or condemned. Is he a noble man flawed or is he a terrible failure? What does the laughter of Arthur's court at the end of the poem signify? Are the courtiers laughing at him for the failure of his test or to cheer him up to put the episode of the temptation in proper perspective? Although I incline to the latter, I must admit that either interpretation is possible.

Furthermore we find romances written about the squire of low degree, and Guy of Warwick is only the son of the steward. The bourgeois is now beginning to be a hero, and charisma can be earned. When the hero becomes a career "ouverte aux talents," we are seeing the erosion of an ideal.

How did the later Middle Ages deal with the problem of the protagonist who was not to be too heroic? I think in various ways, but in particular two: first, by making the author or his persona himself the hero, and second, by creating various heroes in the same work so that no one would stand out by himself.[13] Let us look at each of these solutions in turn. I do want to stress, however, that these solutions are late medieval solutions and not necessarily valid at other times. Certainly a little inspection will show that the author as hero can also be a feature of an heroic age—as for instance in the nineteenth century.

The main protagonist of both the *Divine Comedy* and *The Canterbury Tales* is the poet himself. The concept of persona is not of course the invention of Dante and Chaucer, but these two poets are among the first to increase the role of the author in the narrative work until it overshadows that of all other characters. Both probably learned to focus on the "I" from the *Romance of the Rose* and Alain de Lille's allegorical epics, which are, I believe, the first major literary works of Western civilization which elevated the "I" into a central role in narration.

The "I" of the *Romance of the Rose* is the true hero of the poem, but he does not at least in the first part, fascinate and grip us as the "I" of the *Divine Comedy* and *The Canterbury Tales* does. Yet the three authors use the "I" for straight narration and make the persona the true hero and protagonist. The hero of Dante is more tragic and powerful, the hero of Chaucer is more fascinating and ironic, but these qualities, however modified, are found in the spiritual center, the "I," of the *Romance of the Rose*.

The "I" appears in narrative and other poetry from earliest times, but he occupies a relatively minor position. The epic relates not only an epic but an epic recitation: the poem deals with the poem being told as well as its subject matter. This situation in the poem reflects, I believe, a desire to authenticate the narrative as much as the narrative preamble to old wills, treaties, letters does.[14] With the *Romance of the Rose* however and to some extent with the roughly contemporaneous *Com-*

plaint of Nature by Alain de Lille, we get a strong emphasis on the persona of the author. He becomes the center of the narrative in a way not seen before. Where do Alain and Guillaume learn to develop the "I" as a character? I can do no more than suggest an answer. The "I" occupies a central place in the satires of Horace and Juvenal and in the ironical verse of Ovid; the persona of Horace, Juvenal and Ovid (in some poems) is a fascinating character who dominates the ironic and satirical works of these writers. The attractive poems of Book I of Horace's *Satires* provide a perfect model for centralizing the author of a poem. I am inclined to think that these and comparable Latin poems rather than, say, the personal dialogue of Boethius's *De Consolatione* or St. Augustine's *Confessions,* gave our high medieval poets the proper paradigm. The vacuum created by the lack of faith in the charismatic hero was filled in some measure by the "I," who became more and more central to the poem. Yet this "I" is a representative "I," not a unique "I"—the "I" of various aspects of the human condition.

As we look over Chaucer's poetry, it is surprising how few heroes we find: even the knight is rather disappointing as a hero. Charles Moorman calls him the philosophical knight,[15] but a philosophical knight is the last type of knight we want as a hero. What remains longest in our memories as the hero of all of Chaucer's poetry is not the knight, nor the Wife of Bath, Troilus, Criseyde, the House of Fame eagle, etc., as magnificent as all these are, but Chaucer himself—the modest, ironic, witty and sorrowful man who is always with us and who leads us into strange places. The narrative poetry of Chaucer revolves fundamentally around the character of Chaucer, who is its real hero. He conquers and controls his world. His plenitude recreates God's plenitude. He is a creator who pretends to be at the mercy of his creation.

With the *Divine Comedy,* the effect is similar. The vast panorama of Hell, Purgatory and Heaven with its numerous scenes etched in words of great power comes to us through the person Dante, who found himself at Easter 1300 "nel mezzo del camin di nostra vita" in a darkling wood. The identification of the reader is completely with the visionary Dante even to

the far mystic contemplation of the circles of the Trinity. The
whole universe fixed in location except for Purgatory and the
world both still going through time and both eventually to
disappear, reverberates in our mind because it reverberated in
Dante, the Pilgrim's mind, who at Easter descended as his
master Jesus did to Hell and then, like him, ascended in two
stages to Heaven. The arrangement of the universe, its geo-
politics so to speak, is the anagogical scene both literal and
symbolic at once, on which the divine drama is worked out.
The essence of the *Divine Comedy* to me is the political (as
to location and power) arrangement of the universe as seen
by a man, Dante, both a man and a pilgrim favored by God.
God's politics involves Heaven, Purgatory and Hell as well
as this world, which are all still partly *in potentia*, not fully
actualized or annihilated. The power of the Divine is manifested in a four-fold division which at the end of time will
become two as this world and Purgatory disappear. The other
two will then finally receive their eternal quota and become
perfected. Politics then in the sense of the distribution of power
and sovereignty is in a profound as well as a more superficial
sense at the heart of the *Divine Comedy*.[16] The hero is an "I"
who must learn to relate himself to what is and *is to be* in the
deepest sense, to the divine arrangement of things and of
power. It is the other government Professor von Grünebaum
talks about here; it was there and enabled man to endure this
one. God's government made possible man's government and
set a model for self-governance.

The author's self continues to be a major character and often
the protagonist of later medieval literature. Indeed he takes a
new turn with Petrarch and the modern period and is detached
from an exclusive connection with narrative.

The second way to reduce the heroic in later medieval literature is to split the hero into several heroes. It is characteristic
of this narrative literature to have more than one hero, thereby
reducing the power of each one. In later French romance, this
technique of *entrelacement* [17] reaches complex proportions, but
we see it in Malory's *Morte d'Arthur* as well as in the *Decameron* and *The Canterbury Tales*. It appears as the splitting

of the same episodes as in *Lancelot du Lac* and Malory's *Tristram* part of the *Morte,* as well as having several heroes in the same work whose adventures are not interlaced but actually sequential.

Furthermore, we also find a multiplication of heroic virtues in one hero. Beowulf is praised at the end of his great poem with the words "he was of world-kings the mildest of men and the gentlest, kindest to his people, and most eager for fame" (E. T. Donaldson, trans.). But when Sir Hector laments the death of his brother Lancelot at the end of Malory's *Morte d'Arthur,* this is what he says:

> "A Launcelot . . . thou were hede of all Crysten knyghtes! And now I dare say . . . thou Sir Launcelot, there thou lyest, that thou were never matched of erthely knyghtes hande. And thou were the curtest knyght that ever bare shelde! And thou were the truest frende to thy synful man that ever loved woman, and thou were the kyndest man that ever strake wyth swerde. And thou were the godelyest persone that ever cam emonge prees of knythtes, and thou was the mekest man and the jentyllest that ever ete in halle emonge ladyes, and thou were the sternest knyght to thy mortal foo that ever put spere in reeste."

Besides the difference in the virtues admired—the stress on fame in Beowulf, the importance of *fin amors* in the *Morte,* I merely wish to call attention to the difference in length and variety of qualities shown when one compares one lament with the other. Sir Hector finds it difficult to describe the heroic; the *Beowulf* poet has no such problem.

This multiplication of heroes as well as the attendant multiplication of episodes and heroic virtues has been attributed to the Gothic spirit with its tendency to create clearly differentiated units with a minimum of articulation but unified by an overarching frame. There is probably something of this spirit behind it all, but I think other factors are at work. A strong one, I believe, is the drive to de-heroize literature—to create a group of heroes, possibly suggested by the company of saints or martyrs.

Perhaps the first example in the main line of Western litera-

ture to use this method is Chretien and his continuers in the
story of the Grail, *Perceval,* where Perceval shares the heroic
honors with Gawain. Whether there is a true artistic reason
for this doubling the hero has been matter for dispute. However, there is no doubt that Gawain is not a simple foil for
Perceval, although some have so argued. But it is not really
until the later fourteenth, fifteenth, and early sixteenth centuries that this splintering of heroes reaches its apogee. Some
scholars believe that many of these late romances which di-
vide their protagonists are not at all intended to be unified but
are collections of almost separate works loosely joined. Others
argue for unity of some sort. I do not want to enter this dispute, because for my purpose it does not matter. The fragmen-
tation of the single hero into shining parts can be conceived
either as the combining of separate tales or the assembling of
a group of tales to attain some kind of unity. In both cases, the
charismatic hero is down-graded. A company of heroes without an outstanding one is not equivalent to the "douze pers"
with Roland the glittering figure.

Cedric E. Pickford in his *L'evolution du roman arthurien
en prose vers la fin du moyen age* [18] traces this late fragmenta-
tion to a preference for shorter stories. Furthermore, he argues
that whatever unity these apparently unified late romances
have is due to the copyist: *entrelacement* in his eyes is an attempt by the copyist to give the impression of unity. I am very
dubious of this thesis, not the least reason for which is the
author's attempt to argue, as I have said above, that the taste
for shorter and less elaborate narratives was winning. It is
hard to hold together two opposites. Pickford does argue that
the coypist is also simplifying in his weaving together, but it
is puzzling that he should bother to weave in the first place.
However, the real situation is not my concern. Whatever the
reason I wish to urge that this separation of heroes is due to
a kind of rebellion against the heroic ideal.

I do not wish to imply, of course, that the anti-heroic strain
of the later Middle Ages ever went so far as to create an anti-
hero as hero or to make the really common man a hero. Even
in its rebellion against the heroic, the later Middle Ages did

accept the fact that some men were notable and that high birth
or position did to a great extent create a kind of interest of its
own. Most of the heroes of later romances were of the nobility. However, as we have seen, some bourgeois were beginning
to "make it" in the later Middle Ages. Occasionally, as in the
fabliaux or *Sir Thopas,* the hero was a figure of fun.

Between Chretien's Perceval and the later Middle Ages, the
concept of the hero could be traced in some detail, and I think
a close investigation would indicate a decreasing heroicization.
There have been interesting studies of the hero in various tales,
but much more remains to be done. Recently John Finlayson
has made a study of the hero Arthur in the alliterative *Morte
Arthure,*[19] usually dated around 1360. Finlayson finds something of both the epic and the romance hero in this Arthur,
but something of neither—a kind of blurring brought about
by the attitude of the fourteenth century.

The rising sadness of the later Middle Ages finds its echo
in these later romances: there is a Christian sadness about these
later protagonists which encourages a kind of fatalism. The
heroes or protagonists are victims of fortune, but a fortune
modified by redemptive history. The heroic *virtù* which defeats *fortuna* is not to flower fully until the Renaissance. In
the later Middle Ages, we have only adumbrations of this
coming victory.

These streams of the non-heroic continued into the Renaissance, but the heroic again became more and more important. The individual endowed with power and spiritual force
once again moves into the center of the stage. The Renaissance
was an age of the hero in narrative and drama, to such an extent that a bombastic or near bombastic heroism develops by
the seventeenth century. Honor and all it implies become the
very center of important literature. At the same time the notion is being turned inside out by Ariosto and Cervantes. The
Quixotic hero reveals a completely new type of heroism in
which the heroic can consist of delusion and mad vitality; man
can be heroic through misunderstanding and a kind of inno-
cent honesty. The Ariostian hero is undercut by parody in a
new and sharp way. Ariosto's irony is well characterized near

the beginning of *Orlando Furioso* when he speaks of Angelica's comment that she has still kept her virginity in spite of her long wanderings with Orlando:

> "Forse era ver, ma non pero credibile
> A chi del senso suo fosse signore"
>
> (1. 56)

The heroic Angelica may not really be heroic and virginal.

The notion of the author as hero undergoes some modification and shift in emphasis in the Renaissance.[20] The persona in epic often becomes more of a voice than a person and we feel no closeness to the Spenserian persona. In the Miltonic voice, on the other hand, we do feel a strong if not a dominant person. The new Renaissance hero helped to diminish the reality of the author in his work. These personae are real and sensed in the work, but they do not dominate the scene as Chaucer and Dante do in their poetry. In prose fiction, as in Cervantes, the narrator is on occasion a little more vivid, but even in *Don Quixote* he is not the focus of our concern.[21] If the "I" is the hero, the protagonist of the tale must be somewhat minimized.

An age like the Renaissance with a strong historical ideal admired a different hero from that admired by a non-historical age like the early Middle Ages or own own. Heroes can be representative or individualistic. They may be held up only as a warning, like Macbeth or Othello, or on the other hand as an example to be more less followed, like Henry V or Horatio.[22] It is actually hard in any great literature to find a wholly admirable hero even in terms of the work itself, but maybe Moses and Roland qualify. Sometimes a death enables us to pass over faults. The Renaissance hero with all his faults does have that sense of public virtue, that charisma, which is lacking in his late medieval counterpart, but which unites him with Beowulf, Waltherius and Roland.

The hero is a complex literary phenomenon and demands a detailed analysis. The hero leads into the anti-hero or un-hero, and the rhythm of European history shows such an oscillation. Yet the various extremes are not the same; and the hero and anti-hero manifest different forms owing to various historical factors. Feudal and national aristocracies demand different qualities in their literary heroes and protagonists from those of the bourgeois, managerial, or proletarian classes. In studying the hero and his opposites, whether anti-, un-, or sub-heroes, these class factors must be kept in mind. Furthermore, religious factors operate powerfully. The saint's life in the Middle Ages left its mark on the hero and protagonist just as the enthusiast affected the concept of the Romantic hero. The Calvinist ideal is not the Communist ideal; a justified sinner is not a hero of the Soviet Union.

In literary terms, the hero is the focus of interest in a work of art. Such heroes frequently reflect class, ideological and historical factors which are dominant in the age which produces such works of art. Frequently, however, the most representative heroes are those created by minor works of art. Horatio Alger is more representative of nineteenth-century America than Ahab. The detective is more revealing of our culture than Leopold Bloom. Finally, however, Leopold Bloom says more to us than Philip Marlowe, however revealing the latter may be. The rise and fall of heroes cannot be studied in isolation but need the full sense of a culture both high and low to comprehend their ways.

Returning now to the later Middle Ages, let us ask our basic question: why do we have this retreat from heroism in the later Middle Ages? I may say frankly that I cannot answer it, but I should like to talk briefly about some possible answers as I come to a close. Why this crisis of the hero in later medieval literature?

Perhaps first of all because there is "a tide in the affairs of men" and all beliefs eventually tend to their opposites, not necessarily the exact opposites. There is a kind of Hegelian drive in ideas to become anti-ideas and theses to become antitheses. In other words the excesses of heroism are bound to lead to some kind of suspicion of heroism; just as suspicion of heroism becomes so exaggerated that men clamor once again for the heroic.

Second, the later Middle Ages and early Renaissance was a period of decoration, of elaboration, of complexity in art and literature. To multiply the hero or to decrease the hero by

adding the self may be a literary equivalent to flamboyant
Gothic or to the circumstantial realism of the later Middle
Ages. The desire to control by reason the escaping forms of
life, which helped to give rise to the over-elaborate realism of
detail of the later Middle Ages, is manifested in the tendency
to universalization in the portrayal of the hero. After simplicity we get complexity—and this applies to heroes as well as
to other forms of life.

Third, there is built into the idea of the heroic, the notion
of the value of striving. If we cannot perhaps say that there
is a Pelagian element in heroism, a belief in human freedom
(for men do struggle uselessly against fate and know it), there
is certainly the notion of courage in its manifold forms. Courage implies that there is a race to be won in some way or other
or that even going down to defeat is worthwhile. We cannot
doubt the worth of this world, even if it is only a preparation
for the next. The later Middle Ages developed a strong suspicion of earthly achievement along with a fascination with
it. Troilus when he looks down on this little ball of earth
laughs, for he knows its true vanity. The decline of the hero
in the later Middle Ages must reflect this spirit of denial and
the suspicion of worldly success. It reveals a sense that human
power is finally powerless and human goals finally disappointing. In short, a more pessimistic Christianity than the Christianity of glory which prevailed in the earlier Middle Ages
tended to downgrade earthly fame and its accompanying heroism.

Finally, we find in the Middle Ages a fundamental polarity between fame and conscience. *Conscientia* in Latin has a
broader sense than its modern English reflex has in English;
it is closer to the French *conscience,* which means both conscience and consciousness of self. Augustine is above all the
philosopher of *conscientia.* For him it is the internal religious
organ of man pointing toward God, the center for the recep-
tion of the transcendental; it is the place of self-feeling and
exchange with God, the space where the dialogue of God with
the soul occurs and where God's illumination works.[23] The
awareness of self is at the root of Augustine's argument for
the existence of God. This awareness in its broadest sense is
conscience.

Furthermore there is in Augustine a polarity between conscience and fame.[24] Part of his problem was to show that the
goad of fame, which is the outward parallel to conscience, can
be used by God and transformed to an inner goad. Fame is the
approval of men, whereas conscience is the approval of God.
Fame is the spur to action in this world for this world's sake;
conscience is the spur to action in this world for the next world's
sake. St. Augustine in *The City of God* 5. 13 speaks of God
using the Roman desire for fame and glory to check the wick-
edness of many nations. Then in 5. 18 he goes on to say that
if we do not practice for the glorious city of God the virtues
which, in some sense, are like those which they (the Romans)
practiced for the sake of glory in the city on earth, we ought
to be ashamed; on the other hand, if we do practice them, we
have no reason to be proud. Yet Augustine is not prepared to
eliminate fame altogether. He tells us in *De Bono Viduitatis* 27
that the opinion of men should not be completely despised.
Fame or a good name has importance for others, a good conscience for ourselves.

From a Christian point of view, the idea of the hero in its
literary sense is closely tied up with the idea of fame and its
relation to conscience. Pope Pius II in his *Commentaries* on
the threshold of the Renaissance wrestles with the idea and
puts it very well:

> If the soul dies with the body, as Epicurus wrongly supposed,
> fame can advantage it nothing. If on the other hand the soul
> lives on after it is released from this corporeal frame, as Chris-
> tians and the noblest philosophers tell us, it either suffers a
> wretched lot or joins the company of happy spirits. Now in
> wretchedness is no pleasure even from renown and the perfect
> felicity of the blest is neither increased by the praise of mortals
> nor lessened by their blame. Why then do we so strive for the
> glory of a fair name? [25]

Aeneas Piccolomini is too good a man of the Renaissance to
leave it like that, in spite of his impeccable logic. He finally
goes on to say that the hope of fame does inspire living and
perhaps there is some memory of it in purgatory.

In any case, conscience in the Augustinian sense is in essence
the opposite of fame—the desire for earthly glory and respect

based on a good name. The wicked love "the praise of men more than the praise of God" (John 12:43). The good prefer the praise of God. It is this stress on conscience in the broad sense of the word—self-consciousness and all—which I think weakened the sense of the heroic in the later Middle Ages, concomitant with the revival of Augustinianism in the later Middle Ages. Conscience demands an awareness of self which is manifest in the rise of the author as hero; and it demands a special suspicion of earthly glory which could be somewhat satisfied within the tradition of romance by increasing the number of heroes and their virtues. Pagan love of fame was being brought under control. We must have a protagonist in a romance, but let us weaken him by shifting our focus so that the heroism is split among several men.

The entrance of love into the scene in the later Middle Ages is an extension of the idea of conscience in the broad sense that we have been using it. The "dream of heroism through love" (as Huizinga puts it [26]) as a motive for heroic deeds replaces or supplements the desire for fame. The great lover is motivated by the power of his mistress, who is, in the medieval physiology of love, oneself. We discover ourselves in our mistress and in her eyes in a very physical way. Love actually unites conscience and fame because in "fin amors," the outer becomes the inner and the inner the outer; the proud becomes the humble and the humble the proud. The dialectic of fame and conscience receives in love one of its temporary resolutions. Soon however fame begins to break out of the synthesis. It is no longer enough to be secret about love as in Chaucer and Dante; one must make it known to all:

> So long as men can breathe, or eyes can see
> So long lives this, and this gives life to thee.
>   Shakespeare (Sonnet 18)

Love arises in conscience but ends in fame.[27]

No one of course in the kind of over-view which I am taking can answer the question of why we have this diminution of the heroic in the later Middle Ages, but it is clearly there in all its ambiguity and difficulty. Before there is a leap into a great period of the heroic again, the world pauses and is weary of the nobility of the past and present and attempts in various ways to undermine it. This denigration of the heroic was to make possible its elevation once again. The rhythms of history move in strange fashion.

Notes

1. See, for example, Marshall Fishwick, *The Hero, American Style* (New York: McKay, 1969.) See also Dixon Wecter, *The Hero in America: A Chronicle of Hero-Worship* (New York: C. Scribner's Sons, 1941).

2. See, e.g., Dorothy Norman, *The Hero: Myth/Image/Symbol* (New York and Cleveland: World Publishing Co., 1969) or the books of Joseph Campbell.

3. There are numerous books on this topic. See, for instance, Charles Baudouin, *Le Triomphe du héros, Étude psychanalytique sur le mythe du héros et les grandes épopées* (Paris: Plon, 1952); G. R. Levy, *The Sword from the Rock, an Investigation into the Origins of Epic Literature and the Development of the Hero* (London: Faber, 1953); C. M. Bowra, *Heroic Poetry* (London: Macmillan, 1952); Harry Tegnaeus, *Le héros civilisateur* . . . Thèse . . . à la Faculté des Lettres d'Upsal . . . 25 mai 1950 . . . Studia ethnographica upsaliensia II (Stockholm: Victor Pettersonsbokindustri, A.B., 1950); Arie van Deursen, *Der Heilbringer* . . . Academisch Proefschrift . . . aan de Universiteit van Amsterdam . . . (Groningen and The Hague: J. B. Wolter, 1931); and Joseph Fontenrose, *Python, A Study of Delphic Myth and its Origins* (Berkeley and Los Angeles: University of California Press, 1959).

4. There is some evidence that we are moving back into a period of the hero again in literature, although he may be a guru rather than a warrior. See Frank L. Kersnowski, "Exit the Anti-Hero," *Critique* 10:3 (1968): 60–71 (study of Brian Moore). For a rather good selection of articles on the hero in Western literature, see *The Hero in Literature*, edited by Victor Brombert (New York: Fawcett Premier Books, Paperback, 1969).

5. *Op. cit.*, (note 1 above), p. 5. See also Sean O'Faolain, *The Vanishing Hero, Studies in Novelists of the Twenties* (London: Eyre & Spottiswoode, 1956).

6. See M. W. Bloomfield, "Authenticating Realism and the Realism of Chaucer," *Thought* 39 (1964): 335–58. See also Georges Dumézil, *Servius et la fortune, Essai sur la fonction sociale de louange et de blâme et sur les élements indo-européens du cens romain* (Paris: Gallimard, 1943), p. 241: ". . . pour être socialement et même magiquement efficace, la louange ou la censure doit être juste, doit exprimer une verité."

7. See M. W. Bloomfield, "How to read an Old English Poem," *Annuale mediaevale* 9 (1968): 11 ff.

8. See the very perceptive phenomenological study of time in narration in B. Groethuysen, "De quelques aspects du temps, Notes pour une phénoménologie du récit," *Recherches Philosophiques* 5 (1935–36): 139–95.

9. In another sense, of course, the Don is a hero and what Cervantes is saying is that heroism of another and more profound kind than the traditional is possible. See below, p. 39.

10. This internal ambiguity of the heroic in all ages accounts, I believe, for the contradictory statements about the hero in different periods. For some critics, for instance, the literature of the nineteenth century is not an heroic literature, while for others it is. It all depends how one wishes to emphasize the anti-heroic element in the heroic. I believe that the nineteenth century has, on the whole, an heroic literature, even if the hero is demonic and not an Achilles. The hero of that period has charisma and power.

11. *Honor and the Epic Hero: A Study of the Shifting Concept of Magnanimity in Philosophy and Epic Poetry* (New York: Holt, Rinehart and Winston, 1960). I do not agree with Father McNamee's extremely Christian interpretation of Beowulf, but I do agree with him that the protagonist of the poem is heroic and magnanimous.

12. See Paul Imbs, "De la fin amor," *Cahiers de civilisation medievale* 12 (1969): 265–85. See also J. P. Collas, "The Romantic Hero of the Twelfth Century," *Medieval Miscellany presented to Eugene Vinaver* . . . , edited by Frederick Whitehead, et al. (Manchester and New York: Manchester University Press, 1965), 80–96.

13. Other ways suggest themselves. The rise of the fool as hero, for instance, is one possibility to be explored. The Perceval "dummling" is a good early example. The continual replacement of the medieval hero in certain cycles is another possibility. Arthur became an otiose king after a while; he is succeeded by Lancelot and Gawain, then Perceval and Galahad—so it goes.

14. Babylonian letters for instance always begin "Say to A: thus says B . . ." See also Gene M. Tucker, "The Legal Background of Genesis 23," *Journal of Biblical Literature* 85 (1966): 77 ff., and Samuel Greengus, "The Old Babylonian Marriage Contract," *Journal of the American Oriental Society*, 89 (1969): 505 ff., esp. pp. 516, 517 and 519.

15. *A Knyght There Was, the Evolution of the Knight in Literature* (Lexington, Ky.: University of Kentucky Press, 1967), 76 ff.

16. See Heinz Lowe, "Dante und das Kaisertum," *Historische Zeitschrift* 190 (1960): 517–52.

17. *Entrelacement* is, of course, more a method of interweaving episodes of the narratives of different heroes, than of presenting different heroes themselves.

18. (Paris: A. G. Nizet, 1960). For an early sixteenth-century multiple-heroic romance, see *Amadis de Gaule*. For a recent perceptive study of it

and its impact, see John J. O'Connor, *Amadis de Gaule and Its Influence on Elizabethan Literature* (New Brunswick, N. J.: Rutgers University Press, 1970). In this romance, we have gigantism and complexity gone wild.

19. "The Concept of the Hero in *Morte Arthure*," *Chaucer und seine Zeit, Symposion für Walter F. Schirmer*, edited by Arno Esch, Buchreihe der Anglia (Tübingen: Niemeyer, 1968), 249–74. See also Madeleine Palmer Cosman, *The Education of the Hero in Arthurian Romance* (Chapel Hill: University of North Carolina Press, 1966). Mrs. Cosman is primarily interested in exactly what her title says—the education of the hero as revealed in the "enfances"—and has little to say about the problem of the heroic. Note also William Matthews, *The Tragedy of Arthur* (Berkeley and Los Angeles: University of California Press, 1960) and J. A. Burrow, *Ricardian Poetry: Chaucer, Gower, Langland and the Gawain Poet* (New Haven: Yale University Press, 1971), pp. 93 ff. (on the unheroic heroes of this poetry).

On the dissatisfaction with the notion of the heroic in German literature of the thirteenth century, see Heinz Rupp, " 'Heldendichtung' als Gattung der deutschen Literatur des 13 Jahrhunderts," *Volk Sprache Dichtung, Festgabe für Kurt Wagner*, edited by Karl Bischoff & Lutz Röhrich, Beiträge zur deutschen Philologie, vol. 28 (Giessen: Wilhelm Schmitz Verlag, 1960), 9–25.

20. See, e.g., André Stegmann, *L'Heroisme cornélien*, 2 vols. (Paris: Colin, 1969). Some wise words on the Renaissance hero may be found in Douglas Bush's "The Isolation of the Renaissance Hero" reprinted from *Reason and Imagination*, edited by J. A. Mazzeo (New York: Columbia University Press, 1962), pp. 91–106 (p. 95: "The Renaissance hero was not merely of lofty station; his moral stature, his personality, was commonly enlarged to something like superhuman dimensions"). Although I do not entirely agree with his arguments, see Ronald S. Berman, "Heroic action in the later Renaissance," *Symposium* 18 (1964): 113–27. He has some interesting things to say.

21. On the author in Renaissance epic, see Robert M. Durling, *The Figure of the Poet in Renaissance Epic* (Cambridge, Mass.: Harvard University Press, 1965). See also, from a somewhat different focus, Thomas Greene, *The Descent from Heaven, A Study in Epic Continuity* (New Haven, Conn.: Yale University Press, 1963). On voice in *Paradise Lost*, see Anne Ferry, "The Authority of the Narrative Voice in *Paradise Lost*," in *In Defense of Reading: A Reader's Approach to Literary Criticism*, edited by Reuben A. Brower and Richard Poirier (New York: Dutton, 1962), pp. 76–93.

22. The pure hero as protagonist is not easy to find in Shakespeare any more than in the early Middle Ages, but even the villains are heroic in their evil. See Matthew N. Proser, *The Heroic Image in Five Shakespearean Tragedies* (Princeton, N.J.: Princeton University Press, 1965). The no-

tion of public virtue in the late Renaissance and early medieval hero mentioned below and its absence in the later medieval hero needs investigation.

23. The main source of my discussion of conscience in Augustine is Jo-
hannes Stelzenberger, *Conscientia bei Augustinus, Studie zur Geschichte
der Moraltheologie* (Paderborn: Schöningh, 1959).

24. See, *e.g.*, *De civ. Dei* 22.23, Sermo 355. 1 (*PL* 39. 1569) and *Ep.*
112. 2. 27. For an earlier reference, see Tertullian *Ad. nat.* 1. 7. In *De
civ. Dei* 22, *rumor* (one of the major senses of *fama*) is set against *conscientia*. On this polarity, see Stelzenberger, pp. 43 ff. Boethius also seems
to set conscience and virtue (*conscientiae virtutisque*) against fame in the
Consolatio II, 7 prose 64. For a useful article on fame in the Middle Ages
and Renaissance see Edwin B. Benjamin, "Fame, Poetry and the Order of
History in the Literature of the English Renaissance," *Sewanee Review* 6
(1959): 64–84.

25. Trans. Florence A. Gragg in Smith College Studies in History, vol. 22,
nos. 1–2 (1936–37), p. 9.

26. *The Waning of the Middle Ages* (London: F. Arnold & Co., 1924),
chap. 5. On Spenser's hero and his ambiguities, including the pull between
glory and love, see Michael West, "Spenser and the Renaissance Ideal of
Christian Heroism," *PMLA* 88 (1973): 1013–32.

27. Of course, love as fame is not unknown earlier. The wife of Bercilak in
Gawain speaks of Gawain's fame as a paragon of courtesy. Above we have
also seen Sir Hector's eulogy of Lancelot.

The Game and Play of Hero

John Leyerle

Man only plays when he is in the fullest sense of the word a human being, and he is only fully a human being when he plays.

Friedrich Schiller

T HE WORD *hero* in the title and in the paper is taken as a literary form, specifically as a literary game that can be defined by its rules.[1] Implicit in the inquiry are the interesting possibilities that other literary games exist, each regarded as a paradigmatic structure defined by its own set of rules, and that such literary games taken together may possibly form a specific and detailed grammar of literature. This argument can be developed with reasonable clarity by starting with a specific text.

Some narrative literature in the medieval period can be shown to be organized about a nucleus. The English word is intended; it is first recorded in the O.E.D. in 1704 and is used in its two common senses. The first is kernel, or seed, the latent beginning of growth or development. The second sense is the center around which other parts of a structure are grouped or arranged. Nucleus as a critical term thus means both seed, implying origin and growth, and center, implying surrounding structure of a poem. Use of the word nucleus naturally leads one to think of molecular structure; in this analogy the nucleus is the nodal point about which the manifest structures of a narrative poem are organized. In the view of Northrop Frye [2] the meaning of events in a well-designed literary structure arises from their centripetal force; the nucleus is the focus of this force and the inner core of poetic deep structure. Two examples from Chaucer's poetry will illustrate use of a poetic nucleus.[3] The nucleus of *The Knight's Tale* is bonds, or prison, with the literal force of confinement and the transferred sense of order. *The Miller's Tale,* which follows and parodies *The Knight's Tale,* has as its nucleus holes, with the literal sense of pits or openings and the transferred sense of chaos. When a nucleus exists and is identified, it gives the reader a particularly lucid view of the work by aiding in the "discovery of a work's centre, the source of its life in all its parts, and response to its total movement," which is Helen Gardner's crisp definition of the purpose of critical activity.[4]

A particularly clear poetic nucleus is evident in *Sir Gawain and the Green Knight,* a poem of 2530 lines written in a dialect of the northwest Midlands of England by an unknown contemporary of Chaucer in the late fourteenth century. This nucleus is *gomnez* 'games'. In Middle English the word *gomen* had several related senses, which are arranged in the *Middle English Dictionary* in six categories: (1.) joy, gaiety, mirth; (2 a.) pastime, amusement, festivity; (2 b.) polite accomplishment (uncommon); (2 c.) any of the sports of hunting; (2 d.) amorous play, love-making, especially sexual intercourse; (3.) athletic contest, tournament, battle; (4.) joke, jest, ridiculous circumstances; (5.) action, proceeding, plan, trick, plot; and (6.) game animals, quarry, the catch, any object of pursuit. These six categories present a remarkably complete summary of the poem in all its complex, interlocked structure and also illustrate how *gomnez* are the focus of the centripetal forces arising in the elements of the poem's narrative. These elements are generally known as The Beheading Game, The Temptation, The Hunts, and The Exchange of Winnings. The action takes place at two successive Christmas seasons in two aristocratic courts, Arthur's Camelot and Bertilak's Hautdesert; both are filled with the entertainments and gaiety of the festive season.

Early in the New Year's Eve feast at Camelot during the Christmas season, the splendid and frightening figure of the huge Green Knight enters the hall on horseback and craves of the king a Christmas game:

> "Bot if þou be so bold as alle burnez tellen,
> Þou wyl grant me godly þe gomen þat I ask
> bi ryȝt."[5]   (272–74)

Arthur replies that if his visitor wants *batayl bare* (277) 'actual combat', he will not miss a fight, but the Green Knight corrects Arthur and repeats his request, not for a fight, but for a *Crystemas gomen* (283):

> "Nay, frayst I no fyȝt, in fayth I þe telle,
> Hit arn aboute on þis bench bot berdlez chylder.
> If I were hasped in armes on a heȝe stede,
> Here is no mon me to mach, for myȝtez so wayke.
> Forþy I craue in þis court a Crystemas gomen,
> For hit is Ȝol and Nwe Ȝer, and here ar ȝep mony."
>
> (279–84)

Arthur makes an initial response to this challenge; then Gawain rises, excuses his initiative with some self-deprecating remarks, and asks Arthur that the contest be his. The court agrees to *gif Gawan þe game* (365), which is a battle-like tournament involving a ridiculous contest that has its sequel in the last section of the poem. This two-part tournament involves senses 3, 4, and 5 above and is treated here as one of the three main game-elements of the poem. Another is the two-fold hunt at Hautdesert; the lady hunts Gawain by tempting him to make love to her in the castle while her lord hunts game animals in the fields and woods nearby. These two hunts involve senses 2 and 6 above and are connected by The Exchange of Winnings game; hunting is treated here as the second of the three main game-elements. The poem's Christmas settings involve sense 1 above and are the third main game-element, the festival atmosphere surrounding most of the poem's actions. The reader, like Gawain, only discovers as the narrative concludes that all of the games are interconnected. The three categories of the festival setting, the hunting, and the two-part tournament are treated here one by one for clarity, but the process is somewhat misleading because it unravels the fabric of the poem which is, like the pentangle, an endless knot such that each point is connected to all the others and has positional significance in the whole design.

The first category to be considered is the festival setting, the gaiety and mirth of the Christmas season. E. K. Chambers long ago pointed out that in medieval courtly society "A suc-

cession of gaieties filled the Twelve nights from the Nativity
to the Epiphany".[6] The poem begins, as already noted, in the
Christmas season, *Wyle Nw ʒer watz so ʒep þat hit watz nwe
cummen* (60). Our first view of Camelot is one of the revels
on New Year's Eve:

> Loude crye watz þer kest of clerkez and oþer,
> Nowel nayted onewe, neuened ful ofte;
> And syþen riche forth runnen to reche hondeselle,
> ʒeʒed ʒeres-ʒiftes on hiʒ, ʒelde hem bi hond,
> Debated busyly aboute þo giftes;
> Ladies laʒed ful loude, þoʒ þay lost haden,
> And he þat wan watz not wrothe, þat may ʒe wel trawe.
>
> (64–70)

Amidst the gaiety and mirth of seasonal festivities the men and
women of Camelot play *hondeselle*, an exchange of gifts that
Oliver F. Emerson has identified as kisses [7]; this game in
Camelot anticipates a similar game of exchanged kisses in the
castle of Bertilak a year later. Love as a public game has been
discussed by John Stevens in chapter 9, "The 'Game of Love,' "
of his *Music and Poetry in the Early Tudor Court* [8]; this
valuable discussion shows that such amusement was fairly
common in late medieval and early Tudor writing about aristocratic society. The first game of exchanged kisses in Arthur's
court is part of a courtly custom during festivities, and Gawain
—or the reader for that matter—can hardly be blamed for not
realizing that more is at stake than the temptations of amorous
dalliance in the similar game a year later.

The year runs quickly and Gawain departs from Camelot
after the Feast of All Souls; he arrives at Bertilak's castle on
Christmas Eve. The transition, including the lengthy descriptions of his arming and of the pentangle device on his shield,
takes only about 250 lines and the poet is back to another
season of the gaiety and mirth of Christmas revels, this time
in the ornate castle, described in lines 763–802, located somewhere in or near the Wirral.[9] Gawain is welcomed, given a
change of clothes, and served an elaborate meal. He hears mass
and joins his host, who does not give his name, but calls for
spiced wine and begins to play the hood game (983–85).

> Þus wyth laȝande lotez þe lorde hit tayt makez,
> For to glade Sir Gawayn with gomnez in halle
> þat nyȝt.   (988–90)

On Christmas day the games continue; Gawain is paired off
with his host's wife, and the poet remarks that *hor play watz
passande vche prynce gomen* (1014). For three days these
princely games continue. St. John's Day, December twenty-
seventh, is *þe last of þe layk, leudez þer þoȝten* (1023) and
it concludes with the agreement between Gawain and his host
to exchange winnings on the next day. The poet rather inex-
plicably drops out December twenty-eighth and the action continues on the twenty-ninth as if it were the next day. The
evenings of the twenty-ninth, thirtieth, and thirty-first are
spent, as before, in games, *And euer oure luflych knyȝt þe lady
bisyde* (1657). After the encounter at the old cave on New
Year's Day, the Green Knight reveals that he has been Gawain's host since Christmas Eve and that his name is Bertilak.
He invites Gawain to return to his castle where they can *reuel
þe remnaunt of þis ryche fest* (2401), an invitation that the
vexed Gawain refuses. Bertilak's name is probably a word
play.[10] The second element sounds like the Middle English
noun *layk* (Old Norse *leikr*); the compound name is thus an
onomastic pun on *berȝt layk* 'bright game'. Bertilak is another
Harry Bailey, the host of *The Canterbury Tales* (also a poem
organized about a game), the master of the revels, the *magister ludi* of the Wirral. The last sight we have of Camelot is
at Gawain's return. He is much abashed in telling of his adventure, but *alle þe court als / Laȝen loude þerat* (2513–14).
His green sash is made into a festivity as all the members
of the court decide to wear a similar sash. Gaiety and mirth,
a general sense of *festivitas*, thus provide the entire background
and context of the poem which is, in fact, an interconnected
series of one Christmas game after another. The whole am-
bience is one of laughter, feasting, and games; yet only an in-
sensitive reader can fail to remark an ominous side to these
high-spirited celebrations.

The second category is hunting, the aristocratic accomplishment of taking one's quarry, or game, politely, no matter

whether the sport is afield or abed. This activity in the poem
is largely confined to Bertilak's domain. Late on December
twenty-seventh Bertilak draws Gawain apart, *þe chymné bysyde*
(1030), and suggests a new game. The host proposes these
terms:

> "Quat-so-euer I wynne in þe wod hit worþez to yourez,
> And quat chek so ӡe acheue chaunge me þerforne."
>
> (1106–7)

Gawain agrees at once, the tendency the usual hero has to act
quickly without much thought; a moment's reflection would
have made him wonder what he could possibly win inside the
castle that was not already in Bertilak's possession. A man more
circumspect than Gawain might suspect a snare, yet he can
hardly be blamed for agreeing to one more game after three
agreeable days of doing little else but playing games (1110–
11). As the reader discovers, a *lace,* that is, a snare, is exactly
what he gets.

Next day the lady creeps into Gawain's chamber and woos
him in a very forthputting manner as he lies in his bed while
þe lorde of þe londe is lent on his gamnez (1319) hunting
deer, and, as one afterwards learns, hunting Gawain as well
by using the lady as a lure. The reader only notices in retrospect that the plural expression *his gamnez* is appropriate because Bertilak is playing more than one game and hunting
more than one quarry at a time. The lady praises Gawain's
hendelayk 'courtly play' (1228), and his reputation for polite
behavior in love-making is alluded to several times. Gawain's
resistance is the more remarkable when one sees it in the context of his usual reputation in medieval literature as a lover
of more skill than scruples. B. J. Whiting sums up the matter
neatly: "Gawain as a lover followed a well-defined pattern:
when he met an unattached girl he made love to her; if she
rebuffed him he departed; if, as more often, she welcomed his
attentions, he also departed, but not as soon." [11] Bertilak returns home at evening *And al godly in gomen Gawayn he called*
(1376); he hands over the slaughtered deer and asks, *"How
payez yow þis play?"* (1379). Gawain takes the deer and gives
his host the kiss he had received earlier from the lady. The

host asks where Gawain won the kiss, but Gawain reminds him that such information is not part of the agreement. They both laugh and go to dinner. No further questions.

The pattern is repeated by *þe chymné* (1402) late on the next evening in the poem, December twenty-ninth:

> And efte in her bourdyng þay bayþen in þe morn
> To fylle þe same forwardez þat þay byfore maden.
>
> (1404–5)

The jesting tone again seems to be light-hearted and drink is brought out *in bourde* 'in jest' (1409) to ratify the game for the next day. The reader may feel that Gawain is being very confident of his ability to make a polite refusal or else he is being rather incautious. What, one wonders, would he do if he were to pay over to his host more of the lady's favors than a kiss? Next morning the lady again comes to sit on his bed; Gawain is, obviously, enjoying himself and enters so far into the game that he allows himself to appear to be caught napping. The day before he had been caught in bed; now he allows himself to be found in bed again, not up and dressed as a more prudent guest might have been. The role he is playing dominates his judgment. She says,

> "of alle cheualry to chose, þe chef þyng alosed
> Is þe lel layk of luf." (1512–13)

The statement is ironic, for she is certainly not playing the loyal game of love, but is, on the contrary, trying to trap Gawain; as he afterward learns from Bertilak, in wooing him she is his *enmy kene* (2406). She adds the hope, as she sits beside him, "*To lerne at yow sum game*" (1532). Gawain replies that her coming is a "*gomen to me huge*" (1536). It is, in fact, bigger game than he knows, for he is the quarry; what he risks, without realizing the danger, is his head. Bertilak returns at the end of his second hunt and offers to his guest the head of the boar he has killed that day (1635); it is a visual allusion to the beheading game that encloses the scenes in the castle but is still being covertly played. They again exchange their winnings; Gawain gives his host the two

kisses he received from the lady that day. Then follows dinner
and yet more revelry.

> Quen þay hade played in halle
> As longe as hor wylle hom last,
> To chambre he con hym calle,
> And to þe chemné þay past.   (1664–67)

The third time they agree to exchange winnings in exactly
the same circumstances as before. After an evening of gaiety
and game-playing, they withdraw to the fireplace and the
bargain is made. Everything is done by Bertilak to reduce the
terms to a thoughtless repetition of an established pattern of a
jesting game when his guest is warm with food, drink, and
fire. He keeps the same rules; they have played this game
before. It is all very agreeable and disarming. On the third
day, Gawain receives three kisses and the green sash that will,
so he is told, save his life. He also promises the lady that he
will, for her sake, conceal the gift from her lord. Although
critics call the gift a sash, in the poem it is generally referred
to as a *lace*, which, like its Old French source *laz* or *las*, also
means a 'noose, snare, entrapment.' [12] The word is derived
from Latin *laqueus* 'noose', which is also the source for the
word lasso which originally meant a knotted snare used as an
instrument of death. In Middle English usage the word *lace*
in the sense of a snare is generally applied to the snare of love
or to the snare of death. Consequently, a love gift of a *lace* that
is supposed to protect the wearer from death is almost a linguistic contradiction in terms. Certainly the gift causes Gawain
to break his *trawþ*, because he does not follow the agreement
with his host to exchange all of his winnings. He pays over
the three kisses in exchange for the fox skin, but he keeps the
lace. The fault is small and is no more than a violation of a
game rule made *in bourde*.

The third category is the tournament, the enclosing action
of the poem. The terms of the Beheading Game are explicit
and discussion here can be brief. At the beginning of the poem
is the feast at Camelot on New Year's Eve, which the Green
Knight interrupts by entering and asking for a Christmas game.
Gawain volunteers to accept the challenge of the tournament

and the court agrees to *gif Gawan þe game* (365). A year and a day later Gawain reaches what his host has assured him is the Green Chapel, but it turns out to be neither green, nor a chapel, part, no doubt, of the ridiculous circumstances of the tournament. It is only a cave covered with snow.[13] The only chapel that Gawain visits is the one in Bertilak's castle, where he goes soon after his arrival to hear mass and first encounters the lady and her ancient companion, Morgan le Fay. Only in retrospect does the reader realize that he undergoes *þe chaunce of þe grene chapel* (2399) in Hautdesert against an opponent neither he nor the reader recognizes until later. The castle is where he risks his head without knowing it; the encounter with the Green Knight at the end is a formal ceremony whose outcome has been determined by Gawain's earlier conduct with the lady. The Green Knight starts his swing and Gawain flinches. He is reproached. The Green Knight feints a second blow to test Gawain's steadiness. On the third stroke he merely nicks Gawain's neck. Then he and the reader learn that the games with the lady in the castle have decided the manner of the three blows. Little harm is done him by Bertilak and the nick is for withholding the *lace* in the exchange of winnings, a tiny fault arising from his desire to save his life, not from the provocative blandishments of the lady. The rules of play are revealed as being more complicated than Gawain, or the reader, had been told. The design and decorum of the games are the result of rule-keeping, the holding of *trawþ*, which is a central theme of *Sir Gawain*. The poem is, as already noted, a complex network of overlapping, interlocked games; it is an endless knot, like the pentangle design on Gawain's shield, a design which the poet does, in fact, call a *gomen* (661).

The pentangle has been ably elucidated by John Burrow [14] and little need be added here to his discussion. The first pentad indicates that Gawain is without sin in the five senses, a purity born out by his action in the poem. The second pentad states that Gawain never failed in his *fyue fyngres* (641); this apparently puzzling strength is a reference to the five fingers bent together into a fist, a conventional indication of physical strength. The third pentad refers to his trust in the five wounds of Christ. The fourth refers to his fortitude from the five joys that Mary had from Christ. The fifth pentad is of Gawain's special virtues: *fraunchyse* 'generosity', *felaʒschyp* 'love of fellow men', *clannes* 'purity', *cortaysye* 'good manners of chivalry', and *pité* 'the active manifestation of compassion'. This list supports the earlier remark by the poet that Gawain was *Voyded of vche vylany* 'free from all ill-breeding' (634). Silences in this poet, like those in Chaucer, are to be noted; what is not said is anything about his humility.

The reason is that he shares the *sourquydrye* 'pride' (311) of Arthur's aristocratic court, proud of its lineage and of its accomplishments; *surquidré* (2457) was the precise characteristic that the Green Knight was sent to test. Gawain is too much aware of his excellence; no modest man would employ the pentangle with its symbolism on his shield as his public, heraldic device. Because of his pride he feels disgraced at the end by what is, after all, a trivial fault, a failure to keep all the rules of just one of the many games he plays. His extravagant outburst against himself and against all women when his fault is exposed by Bertilak is the mark of injured pride. What he learns in Bertilak's domain is some humility; he has failed to obey one rule of a polite game by keeping one rule of another polite game. The lady puts a condition of secrecy on her gift of the *lace* that makes him unable to give it to Bertilak and carry out the full terms of the exchange-of-winnings game. She also deceives him by telling him that the lace will protect his life; in fact it does not even protect him from a nick in the neck, and his behavior under the axe indicates that he has no great confidence in its protective power.

No spiritual stigma attaches to such a violation of game rules; consequently, the extended critical discussions about the validity of his confession which he makes during his last full day in Hautdesert (1876–84) or his supposed moral fault in not giving the *lace* to Bertilak attach to Gawain's fault his own exaggerated appraisal of it.[15] His failing is the trivial violation of a game rule and has trivial bearing, if any at all, on his confession. There is no cause to invent a flaw in the absolution he receives from the priest who *asoyled hym surely and sette hym so clene / As domezday schulde haf ben diʒt on þe morn* (1883–84). When the tiny fault of not exchanging the *lace* is revealed, however, he is abashed and feels disgraced; his pride is humiliated, which is precisely what the Green Knight had set out to do. He returns to Camelot, less proud than when he left, wearing his *token of vntrawþe* (2509), the green *lace*; the term *vntrawþ* means here failure to keep plighted word, or, in the context of the poem, breaking a game rule. He exaggerates his fault into *couetyse* 'possessiveness', which had little to do with his reason for keeping the *luf-lace*. The exaggeration indicates that he remains proud and wears the *lace* as a too-prominent token of a trivial fault. He comes home to Camelot carrying his pentangle of *trawþ* and his *lace* of *vntrawþ*, feeling generally undone because the high ideals symbolized by his first device have, he thinks, been compromised when he kept the second. Some symmetry is evidently intended because Gawain returns wearing the green *lace,* which makes a parallel to the green *lace* that is *lapped aboute* (217) on the handle of the Green Knight's axe at the beginning; the poet gives a subtle clue, recognizable only at the end, that the test of the battle axe–the Tournament–is intertwined with the test of the *luf-lace*–the Exchange of Winnings. The green *lace* at the outset is a thread connecting with the green *lace* in Hautdesert, the snare that enmeshes the hero. This symmetry is a further reminder that the poem, like the pentangle which is its device, is something of an endless knot.

Quite systematically the whole society of *Sir Gawain and the Green Knight* is portrayed as constantly engaged in game-playing, especially in amorous dalliance that often is near to actual love-making. All the central figures are hunting. The Green Knight in his *alter ego* as Bertilak pursues as quarry the hart, the boar, the fox, but chiefly Gawain himself. Bertilak's lady is a more adroit hunter than the reader at first suspects; she appears to want his body when her real object is his head. Gawain, in turn, hunts the Green Knight and the Green Chapel to fulfil the conditions of the tournament, whose outcome depends on his behavior under the bed clothes–not under the axe. Gawain, the chief figure, thus is both hunter and hunted. The games account as well for the poem's markedly comic moments; as with most game-playing, the poem has a humorous side. It is entertaining and fun.

As analysis of the text makes clear, the nucleus of *Sir Ga-wain and the Green Knight* is *gomnez*. References in the text are specific and extensive; once attention is drawn to their presence the poem may clearly be seen to be a complex knot of interconnected games, largely summed up in the word *venery* understood in Chaucer's punning use: Venus and venison, so to speak. Don Cameron Allen has traced this metaphoric tradition from classical antiquity into the Renaissance, showing that he "who knew Ovid, knew that love was a hunt." [16]

The game of love and the hunt of game are, then, traditional in their close connection. What is unusual is the emphasis given *gomnez* by the poet who used them to form the nucleus of his complex masterpiece, which is one of the chief ornaments of narrative poetry in English literature. These games have been discussed before, first by Robert G. Cook, whose paper, "The Play-Element in *Sir Gawain and the Green Knight*," is very helpful. [17] The games of the poem present a central problem, however, and it is little acknowledged or discussed. This problem is how a poem that conveys a sense of moral weight and seriousness can be constructed around a nucleus of games. Seriousness and games would appear to be mutually exclusive, even though they manifestly are not in this poem. The seeming paradox of serious play is widely encountered in the literature and culture of the Middle Ages. Examples are fortune's roulette wheel, the dance of death, tournaments, the mortal chess game, and the dance of the seven deadly sins. The seriousness of such playful activities is evident and to resolve the apparent paradox of serious play some consideration of the play-element in culture is necessary.

A basic treatment of the subject is the well-known study by Johan Huizinga, *Homo Ludens;* the main argument of this book is that the "great archetypal activities of human society are all permeated with play." [18] Huizinga points out that play has several general characteristics, which can be outlined briefly here. In the first place, play creates order by establishing rules that are binding. If the rules are broken, the game is ruined; for this reason, society is severe on the spoil-sport, the heretic, and the drop-out, for they destroy the illusion of play. The word illusion is derived from the past participle of the Latin verb *ludere* and is interesting to the student of literary games, as are other related words, such as delusion, collusion, allusion, elusion, and the like.[19] Second, games often involve masks, disguises, and costumes, aspects that shade off into deception, trickery and fraud. Third, play has distinct limits in time and space as part of its rules; the game has a beginning and plays itself to an end. The playground is well marked, whether it be a jousting list, a chess board, a card table, a magic circle, or a stage. These places are often remote, if the rules of the game involve secrecy, as they often do; the games are played in "forbidden spots, isolated, hedged round, hallowed." [20] Fourth, play conduces to repetition; not only can the game be repeated, but also its episodes can be repeated. Fifth, the action of games involves movement, transfer from one place to another. For literature this movement has a special importance because action is a basic element in narrative and transfer is a basic element in all metaphor, which simply means transfer. It applies to diction in which there is displacement of the literal sense. This displacement involves word-play, which means that the language of poetry is inherently playful.

These five characteristics of play, as described in *Homo Ludens*, apply to *Sir Gawain and the Green Knight*. Although Huizinga never refers to this poem and to few other literary texts in his book, *Sir Gawain* presents a literary example of his theory and its characteristics sketched above. One basic difficulty emerges, however; in general Huizinga insists that play is not serious. Occasionally he shifts his ground and suggests that play can be serious, but he gives only the barest hints of how this inconsistency is to be understood or that he is concerned with the seeming paradox of serious play. His book gives any analysis of literary games a beguilingly large framework, but it only deepens the contradiction of how they can be serious. Hardly less troublesome is the fact that Huizinga's analysis is done in broad strokes and is able to provide little help in criticism of a specific literary work centered about games, such as *Sir Gawain*, unless the elements of his argument are developed in ways that allow for focus on specific texts and forms. The theory that play is central to human society proved to be a great stimulus to others and many studies have followed Huizinga's influential work.

An extended account of writing by game theorists is beyond

the scope of this paper and is little needed here for the simple
reason that the seriousness of game-playing is a paradox that
most writers tend to avoid. Their main concern is with the
characteristics of play and its elements. One list will suffice
here. For Roger Caillois,[21] one of the best-known recent authors
on the subject, games have six basic aspects: they must be freely
played; they must be remote from ordinary life; they must be
of uncertain outcome, that is, they must have a determining
element of chance; they must be unproductive economically;
they must be governed by agreed rules; and they must be
"make believe." For a literary scholar, a limitation in the work
of Caillois is that it is written from a sociological point of view
and is relatively little concerned with literature. That presents
less of a problem, however, than the large and increasing volume of work prepared by analysts of political and military
power who have taken to framing theories of national policy
in the vocabulary of game-playing. Use of complex mathematical models and notation make such work inaccessible to
all but experts and of minimal interest to the study of literature, even of texts like *Sir Gawain* that are manifestly games.
Application of game theory to international politics is hazardous because the rules are assumed unilaterally and other countries may be playing quite a different game, or no game at all.
The notorious domino theory of Southeast Asia is a reminder
of what disasters can follow when game theory governs national
policy. Economic and political realities hardly take the shape of
the creative imagination, which is where games are formed,
most obviously, literary games.

One view of why some texts in which games are played are
serious can be found in the work of Sigmund Freud and his
followers. Freud's analysis relied heavily on literary texts for
data and use of his conclusions as non-literary support for
critical theory runs a clear risk of being a circular argument.
Although psychological studies long ago moved away from his
methods and from many of his conclusions, his contribution to
the understanding of the literary imagination was very considerable and his influence on critics continues. One well-known
literary follower of Freud is Norman O. Brown. In his book
Life Against Death,[22] Brown suggests that man is the species

that represses itself: *homo reprimens,* so to speak. The deep urges of the unconscious are expressed in forms that society tends to regard as irrational: madness, dreams and errors. Society is seen as a creation of man to repress the unconscious which is organized about two deep instincts. One is for erotic contact and is a force for life, *eros;* the other is for violent cutting off and is a force for death, *thanatos.* Games are a way of giving these deep wishes experience in play, but because stable society cannot accept the chaotic implications of unrepressed eroticism and violence, it undercuts the deep seriousness of games by dismissing them as "just play." Another follower of Freud is Herbert Marcuse,[23] who also notes that "Free gratification of man's instinctual needs is incompatible with civilized society." As a result these needs are suppressed, or made into a game. The literary form that seems to draw most directly on man's atavistic delight in *eros* and *thanatos* is the treatment of the hero. In Freudian terms the literary game of hero comes from the unconscious drives for erotic satisfaction or violent destruction, for life or death, but it is a formal displacement of these drives by the creation of a fiction where they can be play-acted. Perhaps the formulation should be life *and* death because the two are inextricably combined in literature, as the much-repeated word-play on the verb *to die* somewhat tiresomely attests. The explicit connection of eroticism and violence is the central theme in many of the major texts of western tradition from the *Iliad* and *Odyssey* onwards. Only a few need be mentioned: the Oedipus trilogy, the *Aeneid,* Chaucer's *Knight's Tale,* Malory's account of the court of Arthur, *Hamlet,* and *Othello.*

Sir Gawain and the Green Knight clearly fits the pattern of the game of love and the game of death; as the narrative unfolds one learns that there is but one complex game that involves both. Gawain nearly loses his head, as we say, over a lady. When he finally returns to Camelot, his remorse remains because his pride is humbled a second time at the exposure of his fault to his own society, but the court's *sourquydrye* continues as before; Gawain's personal experience is turned into a public game with the green *lace,* which still is, one must remember, a snare. It is an ominous token for the court because Camelot's fall in Arthur's last battle was a direct consequence of the eroticism of Guinevere and Lancelot. The poet frames his narrative by ending with a terse glance, as at the start, to the flaming walls of Troy, *After þe segge and þe asaute watz sesed at Troye* (2525). That city fell because a visiting warrior without Gawain's caution and chastity first seduced and then abducted the wife of his host. The story of Paris, Helen, and the fall of Troy has obvious parallels with the story of Lancelot, Guinevere and the fall of Camelot. These two traditions were major source versions for the theme of love and death in western literature. The popularity of these traditions is testimony to the enduring fascination that the literary game of eroticism and death has for society.

The literary forms used to express the theme of eroticism and death vary greatly; the discussion here on the literary game of hero is meant to display but one form of that expression, not at all to be a rigid pattern that all texts with the theme must fit. In Chaucer's *Troilus and Criseyde,* for example, play elements are prominent and the main themes are love and death, but the poem differs sufficiently in emphasis and design from *Sir Gawain* to make a separate category valid. *Troilus and Criseyde* is an example of a literary game closely connected to that of hero, but distinct from it, namely the game of courtly love; that, however, is another subject.[24]

One other example of the literary game of hero can be glanced at here to give the argument the benefit of a second leg on which to stand. The story of Arthur had its origins in migration-age history which was elaborated in the centuries that followed into complex, overlapping, and often inconsistent narrative clusters. The closest continental parallel to this tradition is the Nibelungen material, seen, for example, in the *Nibelungenlied.* This strange and moving poem, like *Sir Gawain and the Green Knight,* is about eroticism and violence connected together; it is also an example of the literary game of hero as sketched here, although it is written in a different style and is given a different emphasis. Game-playing is evident in the *Nibelungenlied,* but games do not form a poetic nucleus as in *Sir Gawain.* The action begins with Brünnhilde's wooing game: she competes with her would-be lovers in a three-part game in-

volving spear-throwing, putting the stone, and "jumping after."
The sexual equivalence of this entertainment is clear enough
without comment. Her astonishing vigor is indicated by the size
of the spear, which weighs half a ton, and of the stone, which
takes twelve men to carry. Guthrun is unable to compete, but
is aided by Sifrid in his cloak of invisibility. The ruse works.
Brünnhilde supposes that Guthrun has outplayed her and she
goes back with him to the Burgundian's seat at Worms where
she is royally entertained. There the feasting and fine costumes
so often emphasized in the poem are particularly splendid. She
refuses to accept Guthrun's advances in bed, however.

> She said: "Noble knight, you'd better resign yourself. What
> you're hoping for is out of the question. I intend to remain a
> virgin (and you may as well recognize this) until I find out
> what's at the bottom of the match between Kriemhilde and
> Sifrid." Then Gunther got really annoyed with her. He tried
> to take her by force, and succeeded in getting her clothes off,
> but at that moment the magnificent maiden got hold of her
> girdle, a stout band which she wore round her waist, and pro-
> ceeded to give the King some real trouble.
> To stop him disturbing her sleep any longer, she bound his
> hands and feet together, carried him to a nail, and hung him up
> on the wall. She also forbade any further attempt at love-making
> —but in any case he was lucky to escape with his life, she was
> so strong.[25]

The bed-room scenes of *Sir Gawain and the Green Knight* are
turned up-side-down. Here Brünnhilde's girdle is an article of
defence, not a *lace* of entrapment, although she may be using
it to truss Guthrun up like a game animal. What further attempts at love-making Brünnhilde forbade are hard to imagine
from Guthrun tied up and hanging from the nail.

Guthrun can get nowhere near Brünnhilde until Sifrid comes
again to his friend's help, this time under the cloak of darkness.
During the night he wrestles her to the point of submission;
during this struggle he slips off her ring and the troublesome
girdle. Guthrun replaces Sifrid in the wedding bed, making this
consummation *à trois* one of the bizarre scenes of medieval literature, although not without parallels in Book III of Chaucer's

Troilus. Afterwards Sifrid unwisely gives the ring and the girdle to his wife Kriemhilde. Years later at a tournament the two queens argue as to which of them has the best husband; Kriemhilde chides the proud Brünnhilde by saying that she had been Sifrid's mistress before she became Guthrun's wife. The charge seems unlikely because the text says explicitly that Sifrid had got up in the dark, as if to undress, and "left her lying, still a virgin" [26] for Guthrun.

By twice disguising himself in erotic game-playing, Sifrid helps Guthrun with a deception from which others follow, bringing death to both heroes and grief to their women. To avenge the supposed slight to Brünnhilde, Guthrun and Hagen take Sifrid on a hunt; he slays more game than the others, unaware that he, like Gawain, is the biggest game of all. As he drinks from a cold well, Hagen drives a spear into his back through the one place where the dragon's blood had not touched his skin and given him invulnerability. His costume is important because Hagen had treacherously asked Kriemhilde to sew a cross on his tunic to mark the vulnerable spot so that he could, as he deceitfully claimed, better protect his friend. Kriemhilde uses her second husband, the Hun Etzel, as a means to gain revenge in turn. She persuades him to invite the Burgundians to his court and then stirs up violence, a whetting role often played by Germanic women, notably those in the poems of the *Edda* and in some of the saga literature of Iceland. At the end of the *Nibelungenlied* the courts of the Burgundians and of the Huns are, like Camelot and Troy, destroyed; as often happens in the literary game of hero, unrepressed eroticism destroys the society that tolerates it. The antagonistic aspects of any game involving a contest easily become open hostility and the frequent outcome in literature is the deaths of the principal players.

Destruction on the scale portrayed in the *Nibelungenlied* is not unusual in texts written for the theatre, a form we call play without noticing the implications of the term. Many Renaissance plays are about the combined nexus of eroticism and violence that culminates in the deaths of the chief players involved. *Antony and Cleopatra,* *The Duchess of Malfi* and *Hamlet* are three examples from a long list of such texts. In *Hamlet* the combination of eroticism and violence is explicitly displayed in what Hamlet terms his mousetrap, the interior playlet designed by him to confirm his suspicions about the erotic attachment of his mother and his uncle that led to the murder of his father. The unfolding of the play is too familiar to need comment except to note how the protagonist of this play, like many others in similar texts, has supernatural experience, goes mad or pretends to do so, and makes errors hard to explain on any rational basis. These aspects of his behavior illustrate Norman O. Brown's observation that such irrational conduct expresses, or is used by the artist to express, atavistic desires for eroticism and violence, a combination neatly summed up in the word bloodlust. In such plays supposedly irrational conduct is often dismissed or ignored for a time, but the underlying conflict eventually breaks over the play's society and results in the deaths of many, including that of the hero. Conflict is so central to the chief player that it has entered critical vocabulary of the theatre in the term protagonist; the second element is from Greek *agon* 'contest'. Plays involving conflict that ends in destruction on a large scale are inevitably taken to be serious. Indeed, there is no form of literature judged to be more serious than the Oedipus trilogy, *Hamlet*, *Lear*, *Othello* and other plays with similar forms.

Mention of serious play and its forms takes the discussion back to the problem that arose from the detailed analysis of *Sir Gawain and the Green Knight* at the outset. In *Sir Gawain* a gifted and perceptive poet used games as the nucleus of his work. In doing so he wrote a remarkable poem that provides a valuable insight into the poetics of its own form, an accomplishment so uncommon as to justify application to the poem of that much misused word, unique. Only a daring poet would risk undercutting the seriousness of his work by structuring it about interlocking games and thereby inviting its dismissal by those who suppose poetry to be only fiction and echo the age-old charge that poets tell lies. This structuring gives a clue that the poem itself may be a form of play. Although the author seems to be playing as he writes and certainly portrays Gawain and his society as always playing, all readers recognize that the part he plays is serious for him and serious for his society. The paradox of serious play remains, but progress toward resolving it seems possible using the indications, now becoming apparent, that there is evidence for a literary form, which is here termed the game and play of hero.

This form may be thought of as a paradigm in literature analogous to a grammatical paradigm in language. Such paradigmatic structures in literature would, like those in language, exhibit forms composed of regularly-occurring elements. The structures can be expected to be complex and very numerous because the morphology of literary usage is highly developed and also tends to shift and alter with the passage of time and from one area to another. These alterations gradually change the paradigms, a process parallel to that clear from the historical study of language. For example, the paradigmatic structures of medieval French or Spanish literatures may be expected to differ from each other and from their shared historical origins, just as Old French and Old Spanish differ from each other and from Latin. Monolithic theories of literature have the same drawback as monolithic theories of language: they don't fit the specific facts except in terms too general to be of much practical application. An analysis using paradigmatic structures avoids this weakness because the paradigms arise from usage and are valid only when and where they fit the texts.

Two reasons why the argument has been developed here by beginning with texts should now be apparent: first is the advantage of having theory arise from data (if only because it did in the investigation and thought underlying this paper); second is the value of avoiding circular argument. Two texts were used to establish the possible existence of the paradigm of the game and play of hero, but obviously there is need to examine many more texts than two to establish how widespread the paradigm is in medieval literature or beyond. The start was made where the data are very clear, as they are in *Sir Gawain and the Green Knight*. It is a key text because a poem that has games for its nucleus invites consideration as a form of play itself, that is, of being a game defined by rules. The existence of other literary games may be inferred from the one discussed here.

Such literary games allow great scope for individual expression because they establish patterns that are widely understood and therefore allow great scope for individual variation. In this process of variation the paradigm of the game tends to be changed and developed, especially by an inventive poet. Consequently, the hypothesis presented here is not simplistic or reductionist, because poetic play allows for great freedom with a given form and almost a limitless number of forms. Although any full grammar of literary paradigms is apt to be very complex indeed, the individual paradigms themselves can be identified in texts once the reader is aware of the possibility of their existence. The process of identification involves isolation of the elements, or rules, that define the paradigm. A poet is free to use them or to use only a part of them. No poet need play a given literary game that he does not like, or even to stick to any given set of rules. Yet much literature, especially medieval literature, shows both paradigmatic structure and individual talent within that structure, a combination that indicates that such work is the result of poets at play with words.

The literary paradigm of particular interest here is the game and play of hero. It, like all other literary paradigms, is defined by its rules. The qualifications already made need to be kept in mind as the rules that follow are read. They are merely descriptive, not prescriptive. They apply only to texts that exhibit them and are presented here in tentative terms. A few instances are given that seem to be examples of the game and play of hero beyond the two poems discussed in some detail.

ONE. There is a relatively passive figure of authority, often a king, who tends to be aloof from the action or even ineffective in controlling it.[27] His presence sets an aristocratic and martial tone to the society portrayed in the text. An example is Charlemagne in *La Chanson de Roland*.

TWO. The hero makes a formal commitment to accomplish a notable feat and thereby takes upon himself the playing of a role. This commitment is often the result of a challenge, as in *Sir Gawain*. In early Germanic poetry it is the *beot* 'boast', often rash. A familiar example is Beowulf's boast in Heorot. The feat frequently involves a quest, or hunt, which has, as already noted, a long tradition of erotic associations.

THREE.   The hero has courage, a sense of purpose, and strength beyond that of ordinary men; he often faces opponents with supernatural powers, or even with mythic significance. If the hero's opponents are ordinary men, they tend to attack him in large numbers. Examples may be seen in *La Chanson de Roland* or in *Havelok the Dane*.

FOUR.   The hero has a costume, often armor of magical origin and power. This costume tends to be used for trickery or even deception. Examples are to be found in *King Horn* and in the poetic versions of the Tristan story. These costumes are important because they symbolize the metamorphosis inherent in the hero's assumption of the role he is to play.

FIVE.   Fighting is stylized into single combat. When a hero faces heavy odds, the opponents are encountered one after the other even though we are expected to understand that the hero is facing them in numbers. The stylization frequently takes the form of a tournament; the formal, even regal setting involves a mortal risk, as many episodes in Malory's treatment of the Arthurian material illustrate. The tournament is particularly suitable to the literary game of hero because it allows the ladies, whose sexual favors are usually the underlying issue, to be present and watch as the hero plays his game of combat hoping that it will end in *eros*, not *thanatos*. Sometimes both result, as in *The Knight's Tale* by Chaucer.

SIX.   No one, as the economists say, is gainfully employed. Gold may be won in war and is dispensed by the victor as gifts to his followers for their loyal service. More often, the economic support for the hero and his aristocratic society is simply assumed to be available without effort or concern, like air.

SEVEN.   As in all games, there is an element of chance, the hazard of the play; the outcome depends on the hero's luck, or simply on fate. Since poetry has a limited toleration for abstraction, fate was often presented as a function of the wheel of fortune, an image made popular by Boethius in *De Consolatione Philosophiae* where the goddess Fortuna speaks of the play of her wheel. When the stakes are high, as they usually are, the risk is the life or death of the hero. Often the outcome turns on a mistake which can be no more than a clumsy move or an accident; this is the tragic flaw of tragedy, but clear of the disapprobation of the word *flaw*. The mistake often enough does arise from a flaw, especially the hero's tendency to hubris in defining the role he is to play; the more lofty the hero's conception of this role, the more likely he is to overreach and fall. The events of *Beowulf* illustrate this tendency. Sometimes the hero is borne down with no such mistake evident; it is a risk of the game he plays, a risk inherent in all play. As a consequence, winning or losing may have no specifically moral significance; a tragic outcome is not dependent on a flaw in the hero, nor a happy outcome on the absence of such a flaw.

EIGHT.   The protagonist is a man, never a woman.

The game and play of hero has two basic patterns of resolution. If the hero accepts limitations, even a partial failure in his performance, he calls off the quest or hunt and abandons his role, so ending the text; he goes home, marries, does penance, learns humility—usually all at once. This end-game is the comic resolution and is what we generally call romance. *Sir Gawain* is an example. In this conclusion the hero lives on and tends to regenerate his society. If the hero holds to his commitment and keeps to what he regards as his high destiny— forgetting that he usually has chosen the role himself—he is destroyed, so ending the text. This end-game is the tragic resolution and is what we generally call epic. The *Nibelungenlied* is an example. In this conclusion the death of the hero often involves the destruction of his followers, or even of his society. Examples are *La Chanson de Roland* and *Beowulf*.

No matter which resolution concludes the play, the game demands grace of behavior under pressure. The aesthetics of conduct, how the hero acts, are almost as important as what he does. "There will be valor, art, understanding, and, above all, beauty and great emotion . . . a growing ecstasy of ordered, formal, passionate, increasing disregard for death," which are the words of Ernest Hemingway [28] describing the bullfight, a sport, like many others, which has interesting parallels with the literary game and play of hero.

One valuable result of the analysis presented here is that the actions of a hero can be comprehended fully without need for explaining underlying psychological motivation, a procedure that has serious limitations for medieval literature, in which many figures have little or inadequate motivation for what they do. In *Sir Gawain*, for example, Bertilak's motivation is hardly developed at all and Morgan le Fay's animosity towards Arthur's court is merely stated in a line or two without explanation. The behavior of players in a game needs no further explanation, although it may nevertheless be given; they play by the rules of the game. This gives a pleasing mysteriousness to such texts, especially the French and German poems written about the court of Arthur; figures in these poems are not so much irrational as they are playing by the rules. Their behavior seems less odd, if not less mysterious, when the game-like quality of their actions is understood.

The existence of the game and play of hero as a paradigmatic structure in literature is mainly to be established by examination of the direct evidence of the sort so far presented in this study. Indirect evidence is also available, but can be given only brief attention here. If several paradigmatic structures in literature can be identified, the validity of analysis for any one is thereby reinforced. A brief glance at two others will be adequate to indicate that such indirect evidence is readily available.

One other paradigmatic structure popular in medieval literature is the game and play of pilgrim. It is often cast as a dream in which the central figure's spiritual afflictions are comforted. The process involves gaining a perspective on himself and on his society *sub specie aeternitatis*. These works tend to be didactic and draw heavily on religious writing in Latin, in particular on the Bible. The dreamer is usually the *persona* of the poet and is a real or assumed exile, alienated from himself, his society, or his earthly home. There are various guides, often women, whose wisdom is hard for the pilgrim to grasp quickly because he is shown as being dull, ignorant, or spiritually rebellious. He, like the reader, has to work hard to learn what the events mean; the allusions are difficult to the point of obscurity for the uninstructed. Other figures in such works tend to be allegorical and frequently there is an absence of rounded characterization as a result. The remote goal is often not reached; sometimes the pilgrim actually travels nowhere, discovering that the true pilgrimage is actually within him. The goal is, in fact, much less important than the way to it and the journey tends to lack steady advance. This quality often carries over into poetic structure making the resulting poems notoriously difficult to follow. Langland's *Piers Plowman* and Deguilleville's *Pèlerinage de la Vie Humaine* are examples. Other poets avoid the risk of meandering inherent in the nature of literary dreams by imposing rigid order on their work and the results, like Dante's *Divine Comedy*, are among the supreme achievements of medieval poetry. The *Gawain* poet's exquisitely-wrought *Pearl* has a similar perfection on a miniature scale.

A third paradigmatic structure popular in medieval literature is the game and play of courtly love. Its elements are well recognized because they were quite clearly stated by Andreas Capellanus writing early in the thirteenth century.[29] What he describes has often been understood as social practice of the time, although it seems much more apt to be a literary game. The game begins in a spring season when the man is smitten with love for the lady in the well-known pattern of the physiology of lover's malady; the lady's response follows slowly as she is wooed in the elaborate ritual of courtly love. Some of the action is often set in a walled garden, whether actual or figurative. Both lovers are aristocratic, as is their society, unless elements of parody displace the pattern, as they often do; from the outset of the tradition courtly love seems to have invited parody, which, for example, is present already in the work of Andreas. This tendency is probably inevitable because of the unreal level of ennoblement said to result from such love. The lady is venerated with religious fervor by her abjectly-humble lover who serves her with private devotion and public valor as though he were her worshipper and her feudal vassal. There is usually a go-between who tends to be the master of the game, arranging details with solicitous relish and amusing bawdiness. The affair may involve adultery, but just as often there is no obstacle to marriage. Even so, every effort is made to keep the existence of the love secret. When it becomes known, as invariably happens (else there would be no poetry about it), the game is over. The lovers are separated, often by death of one or both partners. More rarely they marry, but that outcome also ends the game, if not so quickly. Chrètien's *Lancelot,* Juan Ruiz's *Libro de Buen Amor,* and Chaucer's *Troilus and Criseyde* are three well-known examples of this enormously popular medieval literary game. These examples are not typical, however, because its usual expression is in short lyrics, not in narratives.

From the analysis presented thus far there emerge clear indications that a detailed theory of literature can be developed on the model of game-playing. In this theory each literary game would have a paradigm made of the basic rules it follows and would be empirically based because the rules are found in the texts, not imposed on them. Such a theory allows a chance to abandon critical coinage worn thin by time and devalued by careless usage; such undefinable terms as epic, romance, tragedy, comedy, novel, and the like could be replaced with a self-revealing vocabulary that is relatively clear in meaning and easy to remember—no small advantage. On the one hand the theory holds the promise of being precise and specific enough to describe actual texts; on the other hand it also holds the promise of being capable of very complex interconnections and of almost limitless extension. This paper is, in part, presented as an approach to such a literary theory. The approach is hardly past the identification of a tentative paradigmatic structure for the literary game of hero, but it seems to be promising enough to be worth following.

Only a small number of texts have been discussed in developing the structure of the literary game of hero, but it seems to fit a large number of literary works, as the reader will recognize. This fit arises because the game of hero is the literary expression of deep drives in the human psyche and because literature conserves and recycles its own products. Once a pleasing literary game is discovered, it is played over and over, gradually developing new variants and new rules in the process. The central element is the structure of the play, its form, which is created by the rules that govern the game. These rules establish the formal structure, the pattern of play by which a given game is recognized. The rules are rarely codified but arise from usage and are conventional; as a result of this flexibility, changes follow readily. A theory of literature based on game patterns thus allows for a very large number of categories, each of which is open-ended in several directions. The particularities of individual texts can vary endlessly but still provide the data for grouping the texts according to the basic form each displays.

The particularities can be commonplace, or strange, or a combination of both. In *Sir Gawain and the Green Knight* the outlandish shape-shifting and recovery from a beheading are juxtaposed with elegant, but commonplace hunts and an attempted seduction. These events are presented as games in the poem and are entertaining play. What gives the poem its undoubted seriousness is the form involved in the games and the consequent understanding that its life and society have a formal nature. Such an understanding implies the existence of a formal cause and is an argument for the existence of order as a basic characteristic of creation. Without such underlying form, the events in *Sir Gawain* would be little more than a grotesque combination, at once too bizarre and too ordinary for anyone to take seriously. The primacy of rules that establish literary games gives order which is ever-present in their play, and they are serious because of their form, but it is a form which is expressed with great individual freedom. Form thus gives seriousness to literary games and freedom gives delight. The imagination is free, yet structured; perhaps play is the activity where man best realizes fully his rage for order and his innate desire for liberty.

The apparent paradox of ordered liberty is not difficult to resolve and helps to resolve the apparent paradox of serious play. Enough has been said to show that serious play is not a contradiction in terms, but the matter is complex and requires more discussion if the elements of the explanation are to be reasonably clear. In playing a literary game the author freely selects elements from ordinary experience, characterized by

randomness, and imposes patterns on it as he uses the elements
to form the order of his text. This order arises from the rules
that limit and define the game by giving it form, the serious
aspect of play.[30] Form is serious because it imposes order on
undifferentiated, random experience, the process that is generally thought of as creation and characterized by joy in the
performance. A failure of form is a move toward chaos and
disorder, a threat to coherence in life and society. The threat
of disorder is so great that all form-inducing activities are regarded as serious; law and theology are two apparent examples. In ordinary life rules are conflicting, ill-defined, or even
non-existent; there is a constant tug towards chaos. In theological terms this tug is the evil side of life resulting from
man's fall in Eden; chaos is the absence of God, the disordered
randomness of hell, characterized by grief. Consequently, any
activity that imposes form is serious and is characterized by
joy; the combination is what is generally called play in the
doing and game in the formal result. For these reasons music,
the ordering of sound, has long been used as a symbol for
order, whether divine or earthly, and its performance is called
playing. Dancing, a formal movement in time, is closely related to music and has been used in a similar way as a symbol
for harmony and order. Like music, literature is play and a
theory of its structure based on game rules is no more than a
recognition of a basic aspect of the creative act of writing; it is
playful in its inventive freedom and serious in its formal order.
Far from being a paradox, the phrase serious play is a means
to emphasize the importance of formal order in play. The
emphasis is valuable because play is too often dismissed as
no more than trivial invention by those who do not understand
that the rules necessary to all play make it serious by imposing
form on what would otherwise be merely chaotic.

The analysis sketched briefly here has roots in Judaic-
Christian theology, but a connected history of the tradition has
yet to be written. A valuable account of the play-element in
the thought of the church fathers has been given by Hugo
Rahner in his short book *Man at Play*.[31] He discusses the way
that God's acts of creation related in the first chapters of Genesis are often described by the fathers in the specific language

of play. The discussion of the biblical material in these terms presents a very interesting pattern. Creation becomes play, the imposition of form on chaos in an act of inventive freedom. God is the giver of form and establisher of rules which are to be obeyed, although man often fails of this obligation. A consequent central theme of biblical narrative is man's tension between keeping God's rules and attaining the ordered joy of heaven on the one hand and rebelling against God's rules and attaining the chaotic torment of hell on the other hand. The chaotic pull is strong because rules are resisted and man forgets that his freedom exists only in the context of the preexisting form of God's creation. In sum, man himself is seen as a result of God's play because man was given form first at the creation and afterwards freedom; thus freedom exists only within a context of form. Without form there is only anarchy. In medieval terms, the presence of God is heaven and its absence is hell. Rahner's analysis puts the game and play of hero into a religious tradition that starts with Adam and his fall.

A parallel view of the centrality of play in man's condition is evident in the quotation at the head of this paper. Friedrich Schiller wrote about the play element in human society in his letters *On the Aesthetic Education of Man*,[32] a work written when he was deeply immersed in his study of Kant. The tenth letter develops his view that the object of man's play-drive (*Spieltrieb*) is living form (*lebende Gestalt*). Schiller saw in play the human activity that connects man's sensuous impulse and his formal impulse. This important analysis has had very significant influence on subsequent discussions of play where his work was used. Robert E. Neale, for example, gives a valuable account of why play is serious in a discussion that develops and expands Schiller's succinct remarks. Neale sees play as the result of man's need to discharge energy (Schiller's sensuous impulse) and also to design experience (Schiller's formal impulse): "It is the need to discharge psychic energy that relates the individual to the concrete and enables him to become aware of a moment in time and of an object in space. The need to design and organize experience drives the individual toward the formal and enables him to become aware of permanency and universality. The former moves the individual to the specific, and the latter moves him to the abstract. Both discharge of energy and design of experience are necessary for self-awareness." [33]

Neale concludes that play is the principal end-purpose of man, an activity that creates time and space by the use of form. The process is a re-creation because it is capable of re-creating form and order for those involved. As often, the terminology of play sheds light on its inner nature, as in the use of the word recreation as a synonym for play. Neale's point that play leads to self-awareness can be illustrated in the comic resolution of the game and play of hero. The hero experiences the world and may come to know himself in the process. Gawain, for example, learns humility and is aware of his faults at the end in a way that he was not at the outset. When the hero holds to his purpose and is killed, his death is related to instruct those who read or hear his story.

The analysis of play in terms of the form that it creates has special significance for literature; the opening words of the gospel according to John, *in principio erat verbum*, indicate that the primal act of creation was verbal. In this version, creation was the imposition of form, not on matter, but on words, that is, on the expression of inner perception and understanding, which reaches its highest form in poetry. The poets impose form on undifferentiated words to create worlds of fiction both fanciful and formal that never existed but are constantly being revived. The divine afflatus of the poet, often mentioned by Renaissance writers, arises because the poet's creation of verbal order out of his perception of the randomness and mutability of the world repeats the divine act and is serious in its form and playful in the doing. From this basic formal impulse of poetry comes patterns, the rules of the play; these are often complicated, but they can be observed and classified to develop a coherent and specific order of literary forms. Creative criticism itself can also be understood as a form of play from which may come an anatomy of literature that has an attractive theoretical framework as well as specific and unambiguous applicability to texts.

One returns to *Sir Gawain and the Green Knight* with a heightened sense of wonder at the perception of the unknown poet who took *gomen* as the nucleus for his poem and thereby touched an inner source of all poetry. The poem has become for the present writer a nucleating force which has led to a theory, still tentative, that appears to have interesting possibilities for the understanding of literature and the creative process that produces it. The *Gawain* genius, for such he clearly was, touched on a deep aspect of the creative imagination when he presented the society of man as organized about a nucleus of game-playing; a Middle English word for man is *gome*, cognate with Latin *homo*; in the poem *gome* is likely a word play with *gomen* 'game'.[34] *Sir Gawain* shows man as *homo ludens*, or in the language of the poet, *gome gomand*. Other literary works have been constructed with games as a prominent feature, but few signal so clearly as does *Sir Gawain* that play is an underlying basis of poetry and that it is serious because of its formal order, evident in the symmetrical knot of games that constitute the text. The poem also leads to the theory that literature can be analyzed into many paradigmatic structures, or literary games, each defined by the rules it observes. One such form is the game and play of hero; this expression of man's age-old love for *festivitas* is an indication that the concept of the hero is to be understood as both playful and serious, a formal fiction deeply embedded in the creative imagination of man at play.

Notes

1. The first version of this paper, entitled "The Nucleus Image of *Sir Gawain and the Green Knight*," was read in March 1968 at the Fourth Conference of Medieval Studies sponsored by The Medieval Institute of Western Michigan University. Subsequent versions were read at the University of California, Los Angeles, the University of Liverpool, University College, Dublin, and Oxford University. The author received valuable help from discussions following these lectures and from members of a seminar conducted at the Centre for Medieval Studies in the University of Toronto in 1969–1970 on "Fourteenth-Century Narrative Poetry." The epigraph is from Friedrich Schiller, *On the Aesthetic Education of Man*, edited and translated by Elizabeth M. Wilkinson and L. A. Willoughby (Oxford: Oxford University Press, Clarendon Press, 1967), p. 107.

2. *Anatomy of Criticism* (Princeton, N. J.: Princeton University Press, 1957), pp. 73 ff.

3. For a discussion of Chaucer's use of a poetic nucleus, see John Leyerle, "The Heart and the Chain," *Harvard English Studies* 5 (1974): 113–45; this volume, a *festschrift* edited by Larry D. Benson for B. J. Whiting, is entitled *The Learned and the Lewed: Studies in Chaucer and Medieval Literature.*

4. *The Business of Criticism* (Oxford: Oxford University Press, Clarendon Press, 1959), p. 23.

5. All quotations are from *Sir Gawain and the Green Knight*, edited by J. R. R. Tolkien and E. V. Gordon, 2d. ed. revised by Norman Davis (Oxford: Oxford University Press, Clarendon Press, 1967), and are marked with line references to that edition.

6. *The Mediaeval Stage* (London: Oxford University Press, 1903), 1: 391; see also Cesar L. Barber, *Shakespeare's Festive Comedy* (Princeton, N. J.: Princeton University Press, 1959), chaps. 1 and 2. Festivities and relaxation early became so associated with holy days that the compound word *holiday* came to mean a time of diversion and recreation with little or no reference to holiness.

7. "Notes on *Sir Gawain and the Green Knight*," *Journal of English and Germanic Philology* 21 (1922): 365.

8. (London: Methuen & Co., 1961), pp. 154–202. See also Jean Louise Carrière, "*Sir Gawain and the Green Knight* as a Christmas Poem," *Comitatus* 1 (1970): 25–42.

9. For a recent statement on Gawain's journey from North Wales into the Wirral, see John McNeal Dodgson, "Sir Gawain's Arrival in Wirral," in *Early English and Norse Studies Presented to Hugh Smith in Honour of His Sixtieth Birthday*, edited by Arthur Brown and Peter Foote (London: Methuen & Co., 1963), pp. 19–25.

10. The name *Bertilak*, perhaps Celtic in origin, is an appropriate word play on this character's penchant for elaborate game-playing. In Old French what seems to be the same name appears as *Bertolais*; the accusative form is *Bertolai*, earlier *Bertolac*.

11. "Gawain: His Reputation, His Courtesy and His Appearance in Chaucer's *Squire's Tale*," *Mediaeval Studies* 9 (1947): 215.

12. See A. Kent Hieatt, "*Sir Gawain:* Pentangle, *luf-lace*, numerical structure," in *Silent Poetry*, edited by Alastair Fowler (London: Routledge & Kegan Paul, 1970), pp. 118–20. The article shows the opposition between "the rigid, endless, and seamless pentangle of troth and the apparently yielding, incomplete noose of untroth with its ends knotted together" (p. 135).

13. Mabel Day identifies the green chapel as Wetton Mills in Staffordshire in her Introduction to *Sir Gawain and The Green Knight*, edited by Sir

Israel Gollancz, Early English Text Society, Original Series, vol. 210 (London: Oxford University Press, 1940), p. xx. More evidence for this identification is presented by Robert E. Kaske in "Gawain's Green Chapel and the Cave at Wetton Mill," in *Medieval Literature and Folklore Studies: Essays in Honor of Francis Lee Utley*, edited by Jerome Mandel and Bruce A. Rosenberg (New Brunswick, N. J.: Rutgers University Press, 1970), pp. 111–21, 357–58.

14. *A Reading of Sir Gawain and the Green Knight* (London: Routledge & Kegan Paul, 1965), pp. 41 ff.

15. The question was raised by John Burrow, "The Two Confession Scenes in *Sir Gawain and the Green Knight*," *Modern Philology* 57 (1959): 73–79. Disagreement with Burrow's interpretation was given by David Farley Hills, "Gawain's Fault in *Sir Gawain and the Green Knight*," *Review of English Studies* 14 (1963): 124–31. Burrow replied briefly to this criticism in " 'Cupiditas' in *Sir Gawain and the Green Knight*: A Reply to D. F. Hills," *Review of English Studies* 15 (1964): 56, and then modified his views quite markedly in *A Reading of Sir Gawain and the Green Knight*, pp. 129–37. For a recent article taking a view of Gawain's confession similar to the one here, see Michael M. Foley, "Gawain's Two Confessions Reconsidered," *The Chaucer Review* 9 (1974): 73–79.

16. *Image and Meaning*, 2d ed. (Baltimore: The Johns Hopkins Press, 1968), pp. 45–57; the quotation is on p. 46. Also of interest in this connection is the recent book by Marcelle Thiébaux, *The Stag of Love: The Chase in Medieval Literature* (Ithaca, N. Y.: Cornell University Press, 1974).

17. *Tulane Studies in English* 8 (1963): 5–31. John Burrow refers to the games in the poem at various places in *A Reading of Sir Gawain and the Green Knight*; for example see pp. 21–25, 52–53. The subject is also noted by Donald R. Howard, *The Three Temptations: Medieval Man in Search of the World* (Princeton, N. J.: Princeton University Press, 1966), pp. 243–44, 284–85. See also Martin Stevens, "Laughter and Game in *Sir Gawain and the Green Knight*," *Speculum* 47 (1972): 65–78.

18. Johan Huizinga, *Homo Ludens: A Study of the Play-Element in Culture* (Boston, Mass.: Beacon Press, 1955), p. 4.

19. Although not altogether reliable on details, Huizinga's chapter on "The Play Concept as Expressed in Language" (pp. 28–45) is particularly useful to any literary application of his approach.

20. Huizinga, p. 10.

21. *Les Jeux et les hommes* (Paris: Gallimard, 1958).

22. (New York: Random House, Vintage Books, n.d.).

23. *Eros and Civilization* (New York: Random House, Vintage Books, 1962), p. 3.

24. See below, pp. 73–74; the game and play of courtly love is the subject of a separate study now under preparation.

25. Translated by David G. Mowatt (London: J. M. Dent & Sons, 1962), pp. 59–60, slightly repunctuated. Kriemhilde's girdle is used for thwarting Gunther, unlike the girdle of Bertilak's lady, which is used to seduce Gawain from his *trawþ* when all else has failed. In the *Nibelungenlied*, Gunther is hung on the wall just like the axe in *Sir Gawain*. These inversions are no more than coincidence, but illustrate the tendency of similar games to have similar moves and patterns of play.

26. Mowatt, p. 63.

27. When the king has an active role, the result is quite a different literary form, which tends to have political power and succession to the throne as major issues. This form might be called the game and play of king; it was favored by Shakespeare and other playwrights of his time.

28. *Death in the Afternoon* (New York: Halcyon House, 1932), pp. 206–7.

29. *The Art of Courtly Love*, translated by John Jay Parry (New York: Columbia University Press, 1941). A convenient collection of papers on the subject is contained in *The Meaning of Courtly Love*, edited by F. X. Newman (Albany, N.Y.: State University of New York Press, 1968).

30. The best short summary of recent thought on the seriousness of play is given by David L. Miller in "The Kingdom of Play: Some Old Theological Light from Recent Literature," *Union Seminary Quarterly Review* 25 (1970): 343–60. The apparatus of this article provides a useful guide to literature on theories of play. Another useful item is *Yale French Studies* 41 (1968), and issue on "Game, Play, Literature."

31. (London: Burns & Oates, 1965).

32. See note 1.

33. Robert E. Neale, *In Praise of Play* (New York: Harper & Row, 1969), p. 29.

34. Another word in the poem for man is *leude*; a word play on Latin *ludus* would be an attractive parallel, but it appears to be unlikely.

The Hero in Medieval Arabic Prose

G. E. von Grunebaum

TO BE IN A SOMEWHAT MARGINAL POSITION with respect to your field and to your theme is to my mind by no means disadvantageous. It can hardly be considered coincidental that the very first time the topic of the hero in medieval Arabic prose was made the subject of a scholarly meeting it was initiated, not by the American Oriental Society or another body of eastern specialists, but by medievalists who were overwhelmingly oriented toward the western Middle Ages. I mention this because I have my doubts that the typical historian of Arabic literature would have alighted on this subject, and I feel certain in stating that no Arab—medieval or modern—has ever studied the prose of his medieval literature with emphasis on the hero.

This stark contrast of interests and attitudes requires some explanation. The temptation to characterize Arabic literature in a paragraph is not easily resisted but I shall forego generalities that may lead to misunderstandings. The fact must be thought through in all its implications that in the roster of literary genres identified by theorists of Arabic literature, fiction is not included. It is true that in the thirteenth century and later there were authors who attempted to come to grips with what we call fiction. They did so in part under the influence of the Hellenistic tradition, in part on the strength of the examination of their own literature, and in part also on the strength of what they knew of Persian literature. These scholars did analyze imagination. They analyzed poetic creativity both as a concept and as identifiable in a few given cases. Yet it would be difficult in that period to find a rendering of the word "fiction" that would have evoked in their contemporaries the resonance which the term evokes with us.

83

Another fact that must be given its due is the rather strange circumstance that on the strictly literary or standard or educated level, medieval Arabic literature does not possess an epic narrative. There are popular epics and they are in prose, so these would fall under the specifications of this paper. But I am afraid I shall have to take the point of view of the medieval Arab *littérateur*, which is another way of saying that those lengthy and repetitious tales lack the dignity that would qualify them for my notice, the Arabic being overly simple not to say defective, their images vulgar, and their composition disheveled. I must admit, as many a contemporary Arab and every western historian would, that these epic narratives offer many facets to interest scholarship, literary and otherwise. (One should not think of Homer or the *Chanson de Roland* but rather of an almost endless sequence of episodes kept in place by one or two more or less historical figures—avoiding the word hero—and retailed without surcease to edify and to stimulate religious feeling and political antagonisms among the untutored.) But I shall exclude these narratives from this presentation with an all-the-better conscience now that the Accademia dei Lincei has published a comprehensive volume on the heroic epic and its development, in which no fewer than nine excellent chapters have been devoted to the so-called Antar novel and other representative products of this genre (and related developments) which led a lively existence in coffee houses and other public places down to perhaps thirty or forty years ago, yet never qualified as full members of literature in the eyes of their public.

What do these exclusions actually leave me with? There remains historiography, which is very frequently interspersed with biographical and autobiographical episodes, as these may be contained in the sources utilized by the historian, and with characterizations of important religious, political, and sometimes cultural figures. There remains also a large number of so-called *adab* books which may be descriptively defined as compendia of what the educated person was expected to know, compendia that tend to ethicize life and illustrate moral maxims as well as historical experiences and incidents of the social life by novelistic or at least anecdotal inserts. These passages would answer to our qualifications but as a rule they have no heroes in the sense this word is used in our own critical studies, for as I understand it the definition of the hero in the present context is the entity through which the author as spokesman for himself or for the community conveys whatever wisdom, warning, or propaganda he has made it his task to convey. In other words the hero is a means even when we come to as late an author as Balzac, not to speak of the leading figures of socialist realism. He certainly is a means and nothing but a means when it comes to medieval Arab anecdote. This function of his as a tool, not being relieved or enriched as it is in Balzac by deliberate individualization, deprives him of much of the human interest we have come to expect in the protagonists of any narrative whatever.

In struggling with these descriptive definitions and, more generally speaking, with reaching a condensed formula for certain aspects of medieval Arab literature, I am fully aware that I am skirting, perhaps not too successfully, the danger of excessive generalization. For, after all, Arabic literature was produced in the Middle Ages in an area from Marrakesh to Bagdad and beyond. It developed for almost a thousand years and it would by no means be difficult to present alternate definitions. Nevertheless I do believe this summary assessment of the literary material we have to deal with may be defended. So much for what, not without a measure of presumption, may be dubbed the objective part of our considerations.

Even more difficult to circumscribe is its subjective complement, that is to say the outlook on these materials as one might expect to find it in the approach of the medieval Arab himself. In his mind what is the position of the individual and consequently of the individual as the protagonist of narration? And there it must be said that concentration on the individual, or if you prefer, the using of the individual as the unrepeatable person in literary purposes, is considerably less free, less sought after than with us—in fact, even a little frowned upon. It would be foolish in this context to compare the Arab Middle Ages with our *modernissimi*. But even if we limit our contemplation of the western world to the Renaissance or the seventeenth century, we note that by comparison the concern

for the individual by the medieval Arab author is considerably
more restrained than it would be in Europe. By this I do not
mean to say these authors do nothing but repeat patterns and
clichés, but I do mean that as a rule they do not use carefully
worked out personages whose fate it is to serve as model, a
mathal, exemplum, or whose words and actions would symbolize some kind of doctrine or counsel.

To indulge for a moment in the gratifying pedantry of
classification, the hero as protagonist occurs on a number of
different levels without, however, having found his way into
the consolidating systems of the theorists. To descend downward from artistic and rhymed prose, the *maqāmāt* of any
given author (most famous are those of Harīrī, d. 1122) are
told of one and the same person with a second recurring person introduced as observer-narrator. The genre excludes them
from this paper. We further have references to collections of
anecdotes all dealing with the same individual, such as the
anecdotes about the Granada judge Ibn al-Hasan (fourteenth
century) that were collected for the Sultan Abū Fāris 'Abd al-
'Azīz.[1] A notch down toward the popular are the structurally
analogous collections of anecdotes about the celebrated Khwāja
Nāṣir ad-Dīn. Finally we come to the prose *siyar* (pl. of *sīra*)
such as those of Antar or Baibars, already referred to in passing.

To return to our material, there is indeed much clichéism
in it but this clichéism is not so much the work of the authors
as it is that of their society. The society recognizes itself in a
limited number of human images, more limited than has been
the case in the west, at least since the end of the Middle Ages.
The multicoloredness and multifacetedness which certain European literatures have reached since the thirteenth and fourteenth centuries will not be encountered in the corresponding
period in the east.

On the other hand there is one inhibitory factor which I sense
on both sides of the Mediterranean, although perhaps it may
be more operative on its eastern shores. You perceive under
the surface quite frequently a certain rivalry, an uneasy confrontation between the realms of belles lettres and religion,
and this in spite of the fact that religion enters quite freely
into the literary realm. If his treatment in belles lettres tends

to give man prestige when writers use him as an instrument
to convey information and insight, let alone when they offer
striking portrayals of human foibles and accomplishments, religion feels that man, being prone to vanity, self-adulation,
and many another misconception of himself, should restrain
this temptation to pride and arrogance and shy away from
giving space in literature to the unobjective, the transitory—
in short—to the individual. A ninth-century poet said that the
cult of people is worse than idolatry. It is in fact a Persian
whom I am quoting, but the saying might as well have originated with an Arab.[2] This reaction highlights both the temptation and the danger of concentrating on describing and eulo-
gizing persons as well as the lure and the embarrassment which
over-personalization within any literary presentation was apt
to evoke in wide circles of the educated.

All this must be read in a context that sets classical Muslim
civilization apart from other culture areas in that it is one of
the few, and possibly the only, civilization where two types of
education (*Bildung*) and consequently two types of educated
people coexist.[3] No doubt in a considerable number of cases
the two educations blend in personal union, but by and large
and above all in the consciousness of the contemporaries, the
two types are strictly sundered. To keep to the Arab terms, we
have the confrontation and coexistence of the *'ālim* and the
adīb. The *'ālim* is imbued with society's resources in religious
and legal knowledge and with such auxiliary information as
makes the principal areas manageable and applicable to the
needs of the day. He may more briefly be described as a car-
rier and developer of the religious tradition, a tradition that
to the classical Muslim included the political tradition, which
in turn includes the social order and in a sense everything that
goes to make life serious in this world and safe in the other.
The *adīb* is imbued with *adab,* a term not quite easy to trans-
late but which suggests a peculiar type of education extending
to both content and form, a set of manners, a way of bearing
oneself. *Adab* is perhaps not a way of life, but a way of behavior which includes a way of dressing, a way of using the
right perfume in the right situation, a way of using the right
phrases at the appropriate moment, to have the proper quota-

tion and *exemplum* at hand and to achieve usefulness; this implies self-protection and a certain mastery of life by an unerring perceptiveness of the social realities, among them first and foremost the right attitude to power and the powers that be. For among the professions it is the civil service that the *adīb* controls. One may describe *adab* more abstractly as a thoroughgoing stylization of life in all its phases, and whose intellectual substratum is eclecticism: the mind is strained into a cultural anthology which comprises everything essential (from the *'ālim's* point of view, everything seemingly essential) culled from every science there is, with a slight hesitancy of going too deeply into the religious sciences (which carry their own style of life and are the domain of the other, the *'ālim*).

The *adīb* draws heavily on the Iranian tradition. He is by no means antiscientific but in fact the mathematical rigor and the logical severity of the Greek sciences are uncongenial to him, and the predominance of *adab* in the ninth, tenth, and eleventh centuries may be assessed as, among other things, a victory of Iran over Greece and a victory of the essay over the treatise.

Thus there are two tastes, two styles of life, that function in society. I almost said two social orders or, at the very least, two interpretations of existing social order. So if one is to consider the treatment of the individual or of the hero in medieval Arab literature one has to make it very clear whether one attempts to give voice to the ideas of the *'ulamā'* or of the *udabā'*, and this in spite of the fact that not infrequently we meet with personages who unite both these *formations*. Whether or not represented through the same or more normally through different personalities, *adab* and *'ilm* remain structurally and, as I already suggested, genetically quite different: the *adab* and hence the *adīb* represent, knowingly or not, a continuation of the Persian tradition, Islamicized indeed and enriched by a blending with elements of Arab heritage, but nevertheless in form, savoir faire, and also in the political ethos that it conveys deeply beholden to the Persian tradition. The religious education, the life form, and the ideas, and the content of the *Bildung* of the *'ulamā'*, on the other hand, are much more closely tailored to the Arab tradition, needless to say as it was shaped by Islam. There are hardly any books in Arabic prose where the life and the personality of a hero, a ruler, for example, are systematically and also chronologically treated from beginning to end with a view to evoking in the reader a rounded portrait of that personage. This is true when he is sketched for his own sake, or when he represents an ideal type with, by implication, an exhortation to society to allow the next ruler to measure up to some extent at least to the stature of the departed. In fact, one might object to touching upon these books in our context on the formal ground that they tend to be written in rhymed prose, and the objection based on this peculiarity can be sustained by the observation that putting things in *saj'* not only gives greater prestige to the writer and causes us greater difficulty in reading, but unmistakably and intentionally entails a certain stylization. It removes from the pen of the author the ability to deal with the all too menial, the all too technical, the all too petty episodes that might deform the picture of his hero. The form as such carries its own stylization; more precisely, the linguistic form carries a stylization and consequently the life story with the portrait of the hero tends to become a trifle too much of an eclectic work of art to be accepted as a true rendition of what the author knew the person was. With due reservation we may compare these phonetically intoxicating presentations to Baroque paintings of Kings when very rarely, as possibly in the case of Louis XIV, personality and stylization coincide.

I do not think it is generally realized, although it has been noted by some scholars, that the greatest literary achievement of Arab Muslim civilization in the period of classical Islam is neither poetry nor historiography, outstanding achievements though they are, but biography. Our Middle Ages have nothing comparable to offer and it is only with the great polyhistors of the seventeenth century that anything of like scope appears in the west.[4] Strange to say, when it comes to autobiography the distance in level of accomplishment between the medieval Arab and the contemporary European is much less marked. In fact, one may say that what we have of autobiography in Arabic and of autobiography in a variety of languages from the western world from the tenth century onward exhibits more or less the same depth of introspection and also the same linguistic skill to articulate this introspection. It is puzzling for anyone familiar with the biographical literature in Arabic that the auto-biographical does not tower equally over what the Europeans were able to produce at the same time. It seems to me that an explanation may be suggested by what I indicated earlier about the attitude to the individual or the person as such. Although the Muslims of the Middle Ages were certainly extremely keen observers, and witty and precise observers at that, and although they had in the Arabic language a magnificent tool that had been sharpened by literary use in many a genre during a number of centuries, there was lacking a sense of developmental sequence as well as the need to round out characters by showing them in action or rather in a multiplicity of actions, the individual not being considered too important for his own sake. The individual is indeed important, but as a representative of a type. This might be the *'ālim* or the miser, or again, the ideal vizier or the corrupt vizier; it might be the eunuch; it might, in fact, be anyone and everyone, but it must be understood that the individual represents the type not in the sense of our classicism (where the personage is, as it were, a particularized condensation of a given group in its full potential), but rather in the sense in which a model or a mold is representative of all individual shapes and figures that can be cast from it. Consequently—unless this causal connection reflects overmuch the modern approach—dealing too much and too intensely with the psychological experience of one's own self in all its nuances and sentimental finesses was felt to be a kind of almost impious arrogancy, an over-accentuation of something which, in the total economy of the world, did not deserve such emphasis. After all, from the strictly religious point of view man is not even a secondary cause. Hence why deal so elaborately and so lovingly with a being who, in the total machinery of the universe, is of comparatively little influence and conceivably of only moderate transcendental value.

In any case the facts of the matter are that autobiographies are not too frequent and that when they are written they often betray a tendency to type the person. The most obvious exam-

ple is the autobiography of scholars. It does not seem too difficult for a scholar to write an autobiography if you feel you are
entering what is likely to be the last phase of your life, because
you are in ready possession of the relevant data which constitute
a scholar. You know where (but not necessarily when) you
were born; you know that your father and grandfather had
been scholars; you know that they were the most distinguished
ones of their period. You also know that you had the best
teachers and that you are in possession of a number of diplomas
in which those excellent teachers authorized you to transmit
their works. Here is your biographical documentation. Besides,
as everybody knows, scholars have their bibliographies, so as
you can see, there is no real difficulty to put together your
teachers, your learned forebears, the princes who favored or
discriminated against you, the places where you held forth, and
the books you shall be leaving to posterity. Your family life
is irrelevant and hardly ever enters the tale, nor need you say
anything about any switch in your fields of interest, in the institutions or patrons from whom you derive your pay, of the political maneuvers you had to engage in to keep alive, of your
betraying one prince for another, and quite generally of the way
in which your life has been a blend of glory and disgrace. Matters of this kind are not usually included but you do keep
copies of official documents you have written in a particularly
brilliant style and these on reflection you may insert into your
autobiography to serve as model for the scholars that come after
you and to make your writing of greater interest to the European reader of the twentieth century.

In spite of the unquestionable flowering of the genre, autobiography remains a controversial enterprise in need of justification, but, fortunately for us, the urge to immortalize oneself,
or at least to talk about oneself, remained sufficiently strong
to persuade more than a few to choose themselves as their subject. Religion, as I suggested, was somewhat disinclined to
countenance autobiography, but religious motivations may be
turned in various ways. We read in the Koran (93:11) "The
benefactions of your Lord, regard them [or narrate them]"
(*wa-ammā bi-niʾmati rabbika fa-ḥaddith*). This means precisely what it says, to wit, that it would be ungrateful to the

Lord not to speak out on the benefactions with which he show-
ered you, but a further interpretation is not too far-fetched
which reads into the phrase that it would also be ungrateful
to bury in silence the virtues, successes, and glories which He
allowed you to experience. With this interpretation it became
legitimate in the eyes of some to describe their attainments and
accomplishments in the greatest detail possible.

The first document of this order of which I have knowledge
is owed to a theologian Suhrawardī,[5] who in the 1160s insisted
that it was legitimate to boast of oneself provided this be done
with the intention to glorify the Lord, who so signally favored
you, and this rationale tended to be predicated in autobiography
until at least Sha'rānī (d. 1565), another theologian with a
strong mystical bent. The minute detail into which a self-
conscious saint like Sha'rānī goes lifts his mirror image out of
mere typology, but viewed from another angle the endless
enumeration of the "favors" he received makes him even more
true to type in that he wrote as though he had been careful
not to omit a single one of the characteristics which go into the
composite picture of the religious hero. Private incidents, or at
any rate indications such as names of teachers, fellow saints,
officials, suffice to locate the writer in space and time. Dreams
will for moments split the shell of discretion and privacy but
on the whole the generalization stands that the nonprofessional,
nonreligious areas of private existence remain excluded, presumably as irrelevant to the identification which the writer
wishes to establish.

One is reminded of Saint Augustine's *Confessions* with its
very sparing selection of incidents from the private sphere, a
selection that is completely dependent on the function these incidents are allotted in Augustine's spiritual progress. This
parallel is adduced to illustrate, not to compare, for neither
on a literary nor on a personal level do Sha'rānī and Augustine
bear comparison. By and large the diagnosis stands that articu-
lated introspection is restricted, as the case may be, to the author's philosophical, religious, or mystical development. Introspection therefore tends to be presented in a mode of rather
high abstraction; this makes for monotony but pushes analytical
precision. Every now and then the curtain is allowed to slip and

in the characterizations of people with whom you had contact, in some sayings which you quote verbatim, in some lashings applied to your adversaries, you suddenly feel a whiff of the realities of the time. You are abruptly transported into a specific crisis, perhaps a famine or a plague, or again a court intrigue, a fight for appointment to the chair of a madrasa, the death of a king which needs to remain concealed lest the army become mutinous. Thus the tension of life sometimes comes through and one may speculate about the connection between events and the advancement on the mystical path; the horizon breaks open to take in the contemporary scene as a whole, only to disappear and restore us to the conventional habitat of the pious, the court of a mosque, or a nook near the tomb of a saint.

It is not always possible to make one's case without becoming trite. So forgive me for reminding you of what you know. The Middle Ages were indeed a religious period. This platitude serves to emphasize that in terms of our topic most of the heroes of whom we have authentic information or around whom anecdotes, doctrinal debates, and ethical advice were woven were in one way or another professional religionists. They may have been lawyers, that is to say, representatives of the religious law, and hence in some fashion advisors to community and government. They may have been judges and they may have been saints. This designation, which I seem to be using rather lightly, has a very different overtone from that carried by the corresponding Arabic word (*walī*, pl. *awliyā'*). It yet remains the most convenient word to use. The *walī* is someone who has been vouchsafed a more direct knowledge of things divine and of God himself than the rest of us; and this closeness to the Lord is in popular belief independent of his moral qualities. In educated belief it is coordinated with spiritual effort, with consistent endeavor in self-education, with a position implementing the religious law but going beyond it by stripping off anything mechanical or routinized in its observance and making it live by realizing at any moment the Lord's intention to sanctify by his ordinances the "best of communities." As the world and its temptations do not touch him the saint or the truly great scholar without the mystical experience to round out his life of piety becomes an intermediary between the community and its rulers

—more amply put—an intermediary between the community and the vicissitudes of this world. He intercedes to prevent injustice and he carries the desires of the populace to high places, especially when these desires include or imply some action in the religious sphere.

The scholar is almost always city-based. The saint more often than not has his area of influence in the countryside among the peasantry or among the tribes. The tribes, not infrequently the military mainstay of the regime, enjoy a semi-ambivalent position in the community at large. The settled, and especially the urban settled, view the nomad with a mixture of admiration and abhorrence which in Iraq, for example, has survived to our own day.[6] In modern terms the tribes are a great reservoir of national strength; the simplicity of their existence is equated with purity and genuineness. The tribesman symbolizes common sense, brutal honesty, but sometimes brutality and nothing else. He is ennobled by the command of the unpolluted classical tongue that is attributed to him. Tribal usage makes authority but at the same time the scholars who take up residence among the tribes so as to fill their card file with idiomatic expressions are repelled by their ignorance, general backwardness, and dubious assimilation of Islamic precept. The Bedouin is indispensable to keep the cities populated and to protect the burgher from that degeneracy which in the contemporary's view would be tied to a refined standard of living and high sophistication. With all this the Bedouin, as long as they remain within their sturdy social framework, are despised as crude and uneducable, impervious to the deeper demands of religion and, by their unabated quarrelsomeness, barred from integration into an ordered political community. Nevertheless it is Bedouin chieftains and Bedouin tribes that play a most distinguished part in the popular narrative.

Another type of hero which recurs and does so with the same ambiguities (but perhaps with a more didactic tendency) is the ruler. The ruler is discussed in a strangely impersonal way. The ideal ruler is supposed to exhibit a certain number of qualities which I do not propose to enumerate, but samples of which are (1) that he had better be descended of a given family, (2) that he has to be able to interpret the law on his own (in other words, he has to be possessed of a modicum of legal theological training), and (3) that he has to be elected by qualified electors. But these requirements are norms which, without wishing to sound cynical, are rarely more than a pattern that exists not to be followed. The real portraits of the ruler you meet as inserts in annalistic historiography where, when a prince dies, an obituary of varying length tends to be offered and these obituaries are sometimes of a most remarkable honesty and realism. The biographical literature, which in the nature of things is largely interested in the great ones of this world, accumulates an impressive number of portraits of sovereigns, viziers, ministers of lesser rank, and generals; and although the compilers do not as a rule make a special effort to give a sequential description of their lives, let alone trace their internal development, more often than not you do obtain through the simple technique of stringing anecdote to anecdote, and perhaps by means of eulogistic verse (or for that matter lampoons), a strikingly clear picture of what the personage in question must have been like, at least at the particular moment when the authority whom the compiler follows has seen him or expressed his view of the subject.

The most striking exception is Ṣalāḥ ad-Dīn, better known to us as Saladin (r. 1174–93), where the character traits are selected or coordinated by a vision of the prince's moral excellence and religious merit. Saladin has *baraka*. He has a near superhuman power of manipulating the world, including his enemies. It is not that he works miracles but God is sometimes pleased to work miracles at his hand, or rather in his behalf, or at least what to the contemporaries must have appeared as miracles (the question, of course, remains whether this assessment was genuine or a subtle form of courtesy).

An important facet of a ruler's portrait is his relation to the saints of the time, for they are political figures in that it is difficult for the government to touch them, or, at any rate, in that the government risks disturbances which it prefers to avoid in the event that it does lay its hand on them. The religious hero has a freer voice than the ordinary believer. It must be realized that the faithful are in duty bound to stand up for correction of abuses and that they are entitled to speak out and within limits to act, but they do not enjoy protection from reprisal. They follow their religious duty at their own risk. Paradoxically the risk lessened, the higher the religious standing in the eyes of the community, in spite of the fact that in proportion as your standing grows your intercession would become more dangerous to the government. Convention had the religious hero invited to the audience room of prince or vizier who would ask him for advice, whereupon he would regale the powerful with proverbs, pious generalities, and, alas, platitudes (of which that period was as fond as our Middle Ages were and as late antiquity had been). The decisive point, however, is that he had access to the political leaders. He could on occasion redress a wrong. He could hold up, in fact, was expected to hold up, the abstract religious ideal when the ruler was yielding too much to expediency. When the prince rode out with all the symbols of his majesty and surrounded by his guards, he almost expected that at some corner an old man, lean and in rags, would grasp the reins, stop him, and compel him to listen to an address of religious exhortation culminating perhaps in a specific request such as that the taxes be remitted for the current year. How often such scenes really happened we do not know, but as a pattern of allowable action that would be attributed to a hero of popular imagination and somehow also as a technique or method of connecting the politics of the court and the needs of the people, this kind of staging existed and had undoubtedly a considerable psychological and practical importance.

The personalities I have been referring to are, so to speak, relatively harmless, since their prestige stems from the conviction of the people that they possess a supernatural charisma (a prestige which may but need not be bolstered by political initiative), and that by election or psychological labor they have been put into more direct contact with the divinity than the ordinary believer enjoys. But there is more to the relation of saint to community and saint to government than this. A concept is super-added, especially during the later Middle Ages and more particularly in the Islamic west, to wit, that such a saint is not an isolated religious hero but one of a large and in a sense organized group. Its number is not really known although very positive statements about it are met with here and there. Nor is it known who the other saints are, although it is quite often known that such and such an individual is one of them. What is known, however, is that they are ordered in a precisely structured hierarchy which for being invisible is no less effective and is in fact the only real power under God that rules the world. There are certainly a great many saints on the lowest level, with the pyramid narrowing until there are only four *autād* on the last but one and only one, the *ghauth* (lit., 'blessing') or *quṭb* (lit., 'pole') at the apex. When he dies he will be replaced by a choice of the Lord himself from one of the four *autād*, who in turn will be replaced from one of the next lower rank, and somehow, in a not precisely specified fashion, the authority of the minor saints derives from their integration in this hierarchy.[7]

In your everyday experience in facing a religious figure or a beggar or a seemingly feebleminded pious you never know whether you are not confronted with the very highest of saints whose power, thanks to his direct access to the will of God, is truly frightening. Thus in the mind of the community a type of religious hero has developed who is represented at any given time by a whole host, hundreds, and perhaps thousands. There are lists of these classes. Religious writers of the declining Middle Ages seem to enjoy working out the details of the hierarchy and they rarely fail, when dealing with a particular saint, to assign him to a definite position. They are inspired by an acute awareness that they are discussing the members of the real government of this world. It looks like a shadow government but in reality it is the visible government, the potentates surrounded by pomp and circumstance, who are the shadows.

I believe that we have sufficient evidence to state that in the political consciousness of the people and especially of the lower orders during the later Middle Ages, let us say from the thirteenth century onward, this conviction was strong enough to impregnate them with a particular kind of skepticism in regard to the actual representatives and manifestations of power and with something coming close to irony vis-à-vis the frequently rather desperate condition in which the government of the day was compelled to rule them. There was always psychologically this way out, this shunting off of political tribulation, this recourse to the realm of that other government, and it was a relief never to know whether the beggar at this corner or the idiot at the next was not in reality one of the *majādhāb*, one of the enraptured saints who watched over your quarter, every night taking instructions from the *quṭb* in the holy city of Mecca.

There are few systematic exposés of another facet of hierarchic sanctity to which I should like to turn in conclusion. But we do have a number of biographies, whose individual data oscillate between the supremely true and the supremely false, and a large quantity of anecdotes and doctrinal statements which bespeak the strength and reality of the concept in limited circles, at least beginning with the thirteenth and reaching its climax by the end of the fourteenth century. The saints of this category are no longer literary heroes; they have perhaps even outgrown the status of religious hero. They are metaphysical and their highest manifestation is that metaphysical hero who in Arabic bears the name *al-insān al-kāmil*, the Perfect Man, the *aner teleios* of gnosticizing Hellenism. He was created when God wanted to confront his creation, when He wanted to externalize himself by having His creation for Himself to behold, so He created the Perfect Man who is at the same time microcosm and macrocosm. He is the macrocosm because the rest of the created world is created in his image, and he is a microcosm because he is created in the image or the likeness of God.[8] You do not know whether he is not present among us, because in every period he takes on a different form and shape. The Arab writer al-Jīlī (d. 1416–17?), who has given us these ideas in the greatest detail, tells us that one day he realized that his own teacher, a very minor figure from the point of view of literary history and indeed a fairly minor figure in terms of the history of Islam, was the Perfect Man of his age. So perhaps one should say that the hero in Arabic medieval prose, who in a certain sense did not exist, was somehow like those saints, a member of a hierarchy of heroes in which the high point of the hierarchy was the direct likeness of the Lord.

Notes

1. Cf. Wilhelm Hoenerbach, *Islamische Geschichte Spaniens* (Zurich and Stuttgart: Artemis Verlag, 1970), pp. 182 f.

2. Abū Salīk Gurgānī (ca. 900): "but parastīdan bih az mardum-parast." Quoted in Gilbert Lazard, *Les premiers poètes persans*, 2 vols. (Tehran and Paris: Institut Franco-Iranien, 1964), 2: 25. For contrast see Petrarch's *Letter to Posterity* of 1351 in which he is "less concerned for salvation than for the cult of his soul." Quoted by R. Pascal, *Design and Truth in Autobiography* (London: Routledge, 1960), p. 26, from Günter Reichenkron and Erich Haase, eds. *Formen der Selbstdarstellung* (Berlin: Dunkar & Humbolt, 1956).

3. The parallel that may come to mind between the education of the cleric, with its base in Latin and theology, and that of the noble, with its bases in the mother tongue and the largely unwritten Germanic epics and sagas as it exists strikingly in the German-speaking areas during the twelfth and thirteenth centuries, is not in fact of the same order as the division between *adab* and *'ilm*. For one thing both *adīb* and *'ālim* were *litterati*, that is to say, readers, writers, and speakers of the culture language. For another, the alternatives were not rooted in social stratification. And, finally, both *adab* and *'ilm* were complete and self-sustaining bodies of knowledge, a claim that can certainly not be made of the *Adelsbildung*. On the concept of the "lettered" as it developed from antiquity to the Renaissance, see the magnificent study by H. Grundmann, "Litteratus-illiteratus," *Archiv für Kulturgeschichte* 40 (1958): 1–65.

4. In speaking of the Western Middle Ages as parallel to the Islamic it should be borne in mind that at least in the eyes of this writer the parallel ends with the rise of the individualizing scholastics from Duns Scotus's *haecceitas* to Ockham (? 1300–? 1349) and Nicholas d'Autrecourt (? 1300–after 1350), etc. It is here that the decisive divergence starts in metaphysics and aesthetics (and of course in science). For a concise description of this break in scholastic philosophy, see Umberto Eco, "Sviluppo dell' estetica medievale," in *Momenti e Problemi di Storia dell'Estetica*, 4 vols. (Milan: Bompiani, 1968), 1: 115–229, at pp. 187–91.

5. Abū Najīb Suhrawardī (d. 1168)—*Ādāb al-murīdīn*, edited by M. Milson, in press, sec. 205—derives the *rukhṣa* (dispensation) for boasting from Koran 93:11.

6. E. Stetter ("Topoi und Schemata im Ḥadīt," Ph.D. dissertation, University of Tübingen [1965], pp. 28–30) has documented the deprecatory treatment the Bedouin tends to receive in the prophetic tradition. J. Berque (Introduction to "Nomads and Nomadism in the Arid Zone," *UNESCO International Social Science Journal*, vol. 11, no. 4 [1959], 481–98, at

p. 489) sums up the image of the Bedouin as it is consciously sketched and subconsciously reflected in the work of the important contemporary scholar al-'Azzāwī.

7. Similar ideas of hierarchies of saints can be traced in the Kabbala where reference is made to the 36 [Lamed waw] Zaddikim. In early Christianity we find related ideas, e.g., in the so-called *Letter to Diognetus:* "What the soul is in the body the saints [lit., the Christians] are in the world; as the soul sustains the body so it is they who sustain the world." One feels reminded, of course, of the New Testament verse "You are the salt of the earth" (Matt. 5:13). H.-I. Marrou (*Théologie de l'histoire* [Paris: Éditions du Seuil, 1968], pp. 69–70) calls attention to the fact that the word here translated as "sustain," *synechousi,* comes from the Stoic tradition and should be interpreted to mean that those saints are for the world a principle of internal cohesion, of unity, of permanence of life. The quotation is from *Ad Diognetum* (second or third century), edited by H.-I. Marrou, 2d ed. (Paris, 1965), p. 154.

8. The same image could be but was not applied to the community of the faithful as a whole as it had been in a somewhat different context to the Christian Church at least as early as Saint Augustine (cf. his *Ennarationes* in Pss. 118, 16, 6, where we read "tanquam in uno quodam homine diffuso toto orbe terrarum et succrescente per volumina saecuporum" (the unity of the faithful is like unto a single man spread over all the earth who would progress through the "unrolling" of the centuries). For this text see Marrou, p. 45.

Dante's Ulysses

From Epic to Novel

John Freccero

IN ANTIQUITY, history seemed to be made in the image of man. Civilizations, like men, succeeded one another according to the life cycle: a coming-to-be and a passing away to which men and all things of men, as well as the universe itself, seemed forever subject. Time seemed to move in an eternal circle, with repetition as its only rationale. In the face of inexorable destiny, man's only hope for permanence, or at least for its pale reflection, resided in his aspiration to worldly glory and human renown.

For St. Augustine, the advent of Christ changed all of this by introducing into history an absolutely new event. In the twelfth book of the *City of God* he asserts that the "circles have been shattered" for all time. The coming of the Redeemer seemed to cut through the circle of time and to establish a fixed point, making of the circular flux a linear progression toward that new and eternal event. Time seemed at last to have been moving toward its consummation, the fullness of time, which in retrospect gave to all of history a meaning, as a target gives meaning to the flight of the arrow. Christ seemed to have wrought a change not only in universal history, but in the history of the individual soul as well, whose story could no longer be reduced to the curve extending from birth through maturity to death, but was rather a continuous trajectory toward the target: a death that would give meaning to life. It was this new linear conception of time that some have claimed as the ancestor of our own idea of progress.

Whatever the accuracy of such a dichotomy, the circle and the straight line, time as continued repetition and time as a progression toward an apocalyptic goal, these do seem to be logically opposite poles of historiography. They are at the same time logically opposite poles of the narrative art, insofar as that art gives a picture, however idealized, of human existence. Homer's *Odyssey*, for example, seems to reflect in the spatial circularity of the journey's trajectory a temporal circularity as well. The gem-like episodes are strung together as on a necklace, one set of events succeeding another quite independently while the strand measures ten years of the hero's life—Ulysses leaves Ithaca, has his adventures, and to Ithaca he returns. What gives meaning to the adventure is the portrait of the hero in an epic world where there are great dangers and great challenges, but scarcely ever any doubts. The hero may not know what fate has in store for him, but he has no illusions about fate itself or about the limits of his own mortality in dealing with it. Whether the gods are benevolent or malign, their behavior is predictable and the punishment for offending them is equally clear. There can be misfortunes or disasters, monsters and sirens, but from beginning to end the game is fixed and both the reader and the protagonist, confident by tradition about the eventual outcome of the adventure, are more concerned with the "how" of it than with the "why" of the universe in which it is enclosed.

Ulysses' journey was widely read in antiquity as the spatial allegorization of circular human time; Ulysses' *return* to his homeland served as an admirable vehicle for Platonic and gnostic allegories about the soul's triumph over material existence, its gradual refinement back to its pristine spirituality. The return of Ulysses to Ithaca by force of his own wits, the most important element of the story, was taken to represent the most important event of man's spiritual odyssey: the return of the soul to its heavenly *patria* by the exercise of philosophical wisdom. All of human existence seemed to be strung out between the point of departure and the point of return, the homeland of philosophers as well as heroes.

Nothing could be further from the modern form of narrative, the novel, in which linear temporality is of the essence. In any linear narrative, there arises one fundamental doubt that is enough to call the whole world of the novel into question: assuming that there is a goal, will it be reached or not? and the question cannot be answered until the story is fully told. It becomes desperately important to know the outcome because the rules of the game are no longer fixed simply by the character of the protagonist. At any stage along the way, the freedom of the protagonist or the inscrutability of the laws to which he is subject can combine to stop the evolution for reasons which seem not at all to spring from any inner exigency. The reader is often tempted to skip ahead, to ignore the incidental excursions which are the stuff of epic, in order to arrive at the conclusion, awaited with anxiety and suspense. To be sure, a faith in God and the supernatural limited the anxiety that concerned the exterior events, but this had the effect simply of shifting the suspense to a different plane, not of eliminating it: death ceases to be the end of the trajectory and is replaced by the question of the meaning of death—salvation or damnation in medieval language—the definitive ending of any story. Death within a Christian context seems threatening, not because it is the end of life, but because it enters the sphere of human responsibility as the most important moment in life. Like the syntactic silence that ends the sentence and gives meaning retrospectively to all that went before, it is the moment of significance. In the absence of that significance, as in the modern novel, the irreversible linearity of time is perceived, even when its terminal points are shrouded in obscurity, even when the novelist finds himself powerless to improve on the idiot's tale, signifying nothing.

György Lukacs suggested that Dante wrote the last epic and the first novel, so that in the matter of literary genre, as well as in the history of western culture, he bridges the gap between the Middle Ages and the modern world. On one hand, we know from the beginning that Dante's story will have a reassuring ending. In the first sentence, the narrator says "I," an unmistakable sign that he has returned from his adventure in order to tell us his story. At the same time, however, the pilgrim's terror en route, his bewilderment in the world of the beyond, cannot be dismissed simply as dramatic coyness—it is real fear, remaining however in the past. The terror of the pilgrim is gradually refined away until it becomes the confidence of the author who has been with us from the beginning. To understand the *Divine Comedy* simply as a religious epic is to dismiss the transformation of the pilgrim as unimportant. To call it a novel, on the other hand, is to miss the confidence of the poet's voice, perhaps the narrative's most constant theme. Epic and novel exist, side by side, linearity with circularity, in this poetic synthesis which has always been considered a genre unto itself.

As in Homer's epic, so in Dante's story the journey of Ulysses stands as an emblem of human time, but the Homeric story is glossed from a linear, Christian viewpoint, which is to say from the perspective of death. It is for this reason that Dante's Ulysses ends as a shipwreck rather than at home with Penelope. In spite of the fact that, as Benvenuto da Imola tells us, even unlearned people in Dante's day knew that Homer's hero returned safely to Ithaca, Dante has him die within sight of the Mount of Purgatory. This startling transformation of one of the world's most famous stories is the mandatory Christian corrective of the ancient view of human destiny. It is as if the poet had accepted the ancients' allegorical reading of Ulysses' trajectory as a spatialization of human temporality and then had transformed the circularity of the literal journey in order to have it correspond to a linear reading of human time under the aspect of death. The transformation of Ulysses' circular journey into linear disaster is a Christian critique of epic categories, a critique of earthly heroism from beyond the grave.

Death in hell is the determining factor, the moment of significance that defines a human soul, not according to an overall evaluation of life on earth, but rather according to life's last term. For this reason the perspective of Hell very often seems to invert the world's perspective, represented by the perspective of the pilgrim, transforming some of the world's greatest heroes into villains. So it is with Ulysses, whose last voyage is an emblem of his life. In the twenty-sixth canto of the *Inferno*, Virgil does not ask the tongue of flame to recount any of his adventures, the sort of question to which Homer's poem represents the definitive response, but asks instead about the final moment: ". . . ma l'un di voi dica/ Dove per lui perduto a morir gissi." In effect, Virgil asks a novelistic question, left unanswered by Homer.

Such a question can be answered only in the afterlife, from

the vantage point of death. Ulysses can speak with authority about his life only because, like all drowning men, he has seen it panoramically in retrospect, from the ending. This is the privilege, the only privilege, of the souls of the damned. The central fiction of the *Inferno*, the descent into Hell, amounts to Dante's claim to the same vantage point while still in this life. At the simplest level, it is clear that Dante can hear Ulysses because they are in the same place; what separates them is the fact that Dante will return to tell us the story. The descent into Hell, in other words, represents a discontinuity in Dante's life that provides him an Archimedean point from which he can comprehend his own experience as though it were concluded, as though he had in fact survived his own death. Dante's voyage is linear, as are the spiritual odysseys of all men in the Christian view, yet his return as poet enables us to hear of his experience. The paradox of continuity and discontinuity in the midst of life, a spiritual death and resurrection, finds its formal reflection in the poem that is at once novelistic and epic, a linear trajectory that ends with the possibility of a poetic beginning.

Because it provides us with an antitype of Dante's experience, the Ulysses episode is one in which Dante is intimately involved, for all of the pilgrim's silence. Ulysses' itinerary is clearly set forth as an ancient analogue of Dante's adventure: it is for this reason both an episode in the *Inferno* and, unlike any other, a constant thematic motif referred to several times throughout Purgatory and even at the last stage of the journey in Paradise.

It is as a metaphoric shipwreck at the foot of a mountain that Dante begins his poem:

> E come quei che, con lena affannata,
> Uscito fuor del pelago a la riva,
> *(Inf.* I. 22–23)

[like one breathless, coming forth from the open sea to the shore.]

Furthermore, Dante refers to that sea as a

> passo che non lasciò gia mai persona viva,
> *(Inf.* I. 27)

[a pass never left behind by living man]

and when he at last reaches the mountain in sight of which
Ulysses drowned, he refers to the shore as a

> . . . lito deserto,
> Che mai non vide navicar sue acque
> Omo che di tornar sia poscia esperto.
>   (*Pur.* 1. 130–32)

[a desert shore, whose waters were never navigated by a man
capable of returning.]

The waters *are* finally crossed by the angel's bark, bringing the
souls of those who are saved to the mountain of their purga-
tion. The implications of this dramatic theme would seem to be
that one can indeed return home from such an exploration, provided that one can experience a death and resurrection. Exactly
the same point was made by Augustine, in the same terms, in
the *De Beata Vita,* as I have tried to show in a previous essay.[1]
The point I wish to make here is that the tragic death of Ulysses
seems to have as its counterpart the survival of Dante's hero.
The poem is in this sense the view of his own life grasped by a
drowning man who somehow survives to tell his life story. In
other words, the *morphosis* of the soul, the circular return to
the truth read into Ulysses' ancient trajectory, becomes a *metamorphosis*, a death and resurrection, in Dante's poem. What
separates Ulysses' definitive death by water from Dante's baptism unto death and subsequent resurrection is the Christ event
in history, or grace, the Christ event in the individual soul.

In Dante's story, as well as in literary tradition, Virgil's
Aeneas mediates between Homer's Ulysses and Dante's pilgrim. The pilgrim begins his journey with a metaphoric survival of shipwreck within sight of the mountain in the first
canto of the *Inferno,* at a point, that is, where Ulysses met his
death. It happens that Aeneas too begins his journey with a
quite literal near-shipwreck. It must have been clear to Dante
that his readers would assume that only a providential stroke,
"com' Altrui piacque," separated the fate of Dante's Ulysses
from the landing of Aeneas in Book One of the *Aeneid.* Recently Robert Hollander has examined the first scenes of the
Inferno with Book One of the Aeneid in mind and has come up
with some remarkable parallels, although he acknowledges a

great difference in tone between the two episodes.² The providential stroke, of course, was the election of Aeneas and his men
for the foundation of Rome. It is clear to every reader of
the *Aeneid*, however, that Virgilian providence does not extend
to the fate of individuals, who die as everyone must, finding
whatever solace they can in the collective survival of Rome. To
return to the dichotomy with which we began, we may say that
Virgil seems to exempt only Rome from the circular epic destiny. Aeneas's trajectory is linear, but his descent into Hell ends
not in survival, but in Anchises' funereal reminder of the fate
that still awaits individual men:

> manibus date lilia plenis,
> purpureos spargam flores animamque nepotis
> his saltem accumulem donis, et fungar inani
> munere.'
>
> (*Aen.* 6. 883–886)

[Give lilies with full hands; let me scatter bright flowers and
let me at least heap these gifts for my descendant's soul and
perform an empty tribute.']

No reader of Dante need be reminded of the fact that Aeneas's
descent into Hell was the model for Dante's. The difference is
in the kind of Hell presented in each poem. The descent into
the underworld is signaled by the most famous of classical sim-
iles indicating a cyclic view of human destiny. As Aeneas and
his guide prepare to cross the River Styx, the amassing of souls
on the bank recalls to the poet the Homeric comparison of generations of men to falling leaves:

> huc omnis turba ad ripas effusa ruebat,
> matres atque viri defunctaque corpora vita
> magnanimum heroum, pueri innuptaeque puellae,
> impositique rogis iuvenes ante ora parentum:
> quam multa in silvis autumni frigore primo
> lapsa cadunt folia, aut ad terram gurgite ab alto
> quam multae glomerantur aves, ubi frigidus annus
> trans pontum fugat et terris immittit apricis.
>
> (*Aen.* 6. 305–12)

[Hither all crowded and rushed streaming to the bank, matrons and men and high-hearted heroes dead and done with life, boys and unwedded girls, and children laid young on the bier before their parents' eyes, multitudinous as leaves fall dropping in the forests at autumn's earliest frost, or birds swarm landward from the deep gulf, when the chill of the year routs them overseas and drives them to sunny lands.]

The presence of this simile should suggest that, whatever the difference between the linear nature of Aeneas's journey and that of his ancient rival, the two views of individual destiny are the same. For all the eternity of Rome, death remains the common goal for all men, including the poet himself. This elegiac note in Virgil sets the poet off for a brief poignant moment before he too must enter into the cycle which is the extinction of the individual for the sake of the species—a pathos tempered, perhaps, by a collective survival. This ubiquitous tone in the *Aeneid* finds its exact dramatic counterpart in the pathos of the figure of Virgil in the *Divine Comedy,* lighting the way for others, yet unable to help himself. As Rome was the *praeparatio* for Christianity, so Virgil was Dante's poetic *praeparatio,* and his own reward, in the fiction of the poem, is simply the respite from Limbo for the duration of the journey, just as the historic Virgil, presumably, found a respite from the circle of time for the duration of his authorial voice in the poem.

In the poem, Virgil stands between Ulysses and Dante above all as poet and it is as a poet that he addresses Ulysses. It is clear that the two ancient figures speak the same language, right from the beginning of their encounter. Dante wishes to question the flames of Ulysses and Diomed, but his guide says:

> Lascia parlare a me; ch' i' ho concetto
> Ciò che tu vuoi. Chè sarebbero schivi,
> Perchè fuor Greci, forse del tuo detto.'
> *(Inf.* 26. 73–75)

[Let me speak, for I know what you wish. Because they are Greeks, they would perhaps be disdainful of your speech.]

"Speech" in this context is by no means "language"—naive commentators in the past have attempted to gloss this passage

by saying that it means simply that Virgil could understand
Greek, while the poet could not—but Dante's text shows that
such a reading is a misunderstanding, for in the next canto, the
soul of Guido da Montefeltro, who, we presume, has overheard
Virgil dismissing Ulysses, not only has understood their language, but claims to identify a Lombard accent:

> . . . O tu, a cu' io drizzo
> La voce, e che parlavi mo Lombardo,
> Dicendo: "istra ten va, più, non t' adizzo,"
> (*Inf.* 27. 19–21)

[O you, to whom I direct my voice, who spoke lombard just now,
saying, "you can go now, I won't urge you on any more. . . ."]

In other words, the language that Virgil and Ulysses share is a
common style, the high style of ancient epic, whose qualities
are unappreciated in the vulgar company of Hell, where the
language is the *sermo humilis* of Christian *comedia*. Virgil implies as much when he turns to the pilgrim, disdaining to answer Guido, and says

> . . . 'Parla tu, questi è Latino,'
> (*Inf.* 27. 33)
> [You speak, this one is Italian.]

In part, of course, Virgil's disdain for this sinner, who is
guilty of the same sin as that of Ulysses, is a biting commentary
on false counselors in Dante's world, and particularly in the
papal court. The suggestion of the episode is that at least in
antiquity, when men were evil counselors they were still capable of a certain heroic stature and magnanimity, whereas the
meanness and base quality of this thirteenth-century evil coun-
selor puts him beneath Virgil's contempt. At the same time,
there can be little doubt that Dante meant to draw the parallel
between Guido and Ulysses as closely as possible, even to the
navigational figure. As Guido recounts his attempted false conversion to make up for a sinful life, he describes his approaching old age in terms of that figure:

> Quando mi vidi giunto in quella parte
> Di mia etade ove ciascun dovrebbe

> Calar le vele e raccoglier le sarte,
> Cio che pria mi piacea allor m' increbbe,
> E pentuto e confesso mi rendei,
> Ahi miser lasso! e giovato sarebbe.
>
> (*Inf.* 27. 79–84)

[When I reached that stage in life when one ought to lower the sails and coil up the ropes, what had pleased me before I regretted, and I commended my soul to God, contrite and shriven. Alas, it might have worked. . . .]

The major difference between Ulysses and Guido da Montefeltro, therefore, is neither in their material guilt nor in their language, but quite simply in their style.

Virgil's style in his conversation with Ulysses is elevated and rhetorical, beginning with the traditional *Apostrophe*, containing at least one antithesis, and passing quickly to a *captatio benevolentiae* [S' io meritai di voi assai o poco] (*Inf.* 26. 81). Ulysses' tongue of flame flickers with equal oratorical and tragic fervor, and when he addresses his men, he too begins with the traditional *captatio* and manages at least one famous Virgilian figure as well as several lesser oratorical flourishes. Ulysses' speech to his men is of course modelled on Aeneas's speech to his men in the first book of the Aeneid, beginning "O Socii" (*Aen.* 1. 198–207), and it is even conceivable that Dante might have known from a remark in Macrobius that the "O Socii" speech was itself modelled on a Homeric original, as David Thompson has suggested,[3] so that Dante came as close to recapturing Ulysses' original speech as anyone could come who had never seen Homer's text. The speech has been universally admired and widely discussed from the Renaissance to our own day and I have little to add to the sensitive readings it has received, except to insist that, thanks to a series of echoes and parellelisms, there seems to be no difference between the rhetoric used by the character of Virgil and that of Ulysses.

At the same time, there is no doubt that Ulysses is portrayed as an anti-Aeneas, who is mentioned in passing, for he lacks the essential quality of *pietas:*

> Nè dolcezza di figlio, nè la pieta
> Del vecchio padre, nè 'l debito amore,

> Lo qual dovea Penelopè far lieta,
> Vincer poter dentro da me l' ardore
> (Inf. 26. 94–96)

The essential characteristics of Ulysses' rhetoric is that it is completely self-serving, dedicated to a heroic enterprise, without any sense of moral duty. In his speech to his men, the comfort he offers them is their own manhood and stature:

> Considerate la vostra semenza:
> Fatti non foste a viver come bruti,
> Ma per seguir virtute e canoscenza.
> (Inf. 26. 118–20)

[Think of your ancestry. You were not made to live like brutes, but to seek virtue and understanding.]

By contrast, the comfort that Aeneas offers his men is the foundation of Rome, the eternal consolation for individual suffering. Aeneas is portrayed in the *Divine Comedy*, as he is in the *Aeneid*, as the man who is constantly receptive to his providential destiny, who is elected to greatness by God. His descent into Hell was, like Dante's, willed in Heaven, and is by no means simply a consequence of his heroic stature.

The contrast between Aeneas's humility and Ulysses' pride is at least in part the contrast between Greek and Roman ideas of the uses of rhetoric. In a passage in the *De Inventione*, Cicero describes the corrupt orator in terms that serve very well to describe the figure of Ulysses:

> Postquam vero commoditas quaedam, parva
> virtutis imatrix, sine ratione offici,
> dicendi copia consecuta est, tum
> ingenio freta malitia pervertere
> urbes et vitas hominum labefactare
> assuevit. (1. 2.3)

[When a certain agreeableness of manner—a depraved imitation of virtue—acquired the power of eloquence unaccompanied by any consideration of moral duty, then low cunning supported by talent grew accustomed to corrupting cities and undermining the lives of men.]

Dante seems to accept Cicero's judgment about the social function of eloquence when he condemns Ulysses by showing that
his objective was to find virtue and understanding outside of
himself, in a world without people ("il mondo sanza gente").

The providential course of history is represented in the *Divine Comedy*, as it is in the *Aeneid*, by the trajectory of the sun
from East to West. Once it is established that this is the linear
course of history, then it is clear that the proud man who, in
his excess, would outstrip history, or grace, dies a shipwreck
even if enfolded in the arms of Penelope. In other words,
Ulysses' journey in the *Divine Comedy* exists on exactly the
same plane of reality as does Dante's: a journey of the body
which stands for a journey of the soul. If it were otherwise,
then it would be difficult to understand why Dante would use
the figure as a moral *exemplum* as he does in the very beginning of the canto:

> Allor mi dolsi, e ora mi ridoglio,
> Quando drizzo la mente a ciò ch'io vidi;
> E più lo'ngegno affreno ch'i' non soglio,
> Perchè non corra che virtù nol guidi;
> *(Inf.* 26. 19–22)

[I was grieved then and I grieve now, when I fix my mind on
what I saw, and I rein in my genius more than is my wont, lest
it run where virtue does guide it. . . .]

It cannot be coincidental that in the previous canto, Dante's
poetry has reached the heights of virtuosity with the double
metamorphosis of the thieves, a display of his poetic powers
that led him first to challenge Ovid and Lucan and then finally
to repent for letting his pen run away with him. The episode
of Ulysses thus provides a moral *exemplum* metalinguistically
as well, as a poetic representation of such gravity that it both
warns against and atones for a poetic excess beyond the poem's
didactic needs. Dante's warning to himself at the same time
furnishes one more indication of the way in which Ulysses
stands for a kind of writing as well as for a habit of mind.

The navigational image serves admirably as a metaphor both
for the journey of the mind and the progress of the poem. The
metaphoric use of the image is what accounts for the close anal-

ogy that we feel between the figure of Ulysses and Dante himself. We have already seen several examples of its use as a
figure for the pilgrim's journey, but equally obvious is the use
of the figure in the *exordia* of the *Purgatorio* and the *Paradiso*,
Dante's adaptations of an epic *topos* studied in detail by Curtius.[4] The "bark of genius" (navicella del mio ingegno, [*Pur.*
I. 2]) sets sail in Purgatory just as the pilgrim reaches the
shore of the mountain. The use of the word "ingegno" asso-
ciates the journey with the poem—both are in a sense itineraries
of the mind. At a deeper level, the journey is the poem, the
writing of it, for that is the ultimate objective of the pilgrim,
to become the poet that we have been reading from the beginning. In the beginning of the canto of *Ulysses*, it is as an admonition to his *ingegno* that Dante introduces the episode:

"E più lo 'ngegno affreno ch'i non soglio."
(*Inf.* 26. 21)
[I rein in my genius more than is my wont, lest it run where
virtue not guide it.]

For this and other reasons, it seems safe to presume that the
figure of Ulysses, for all of its apparent historicity, is at the
same time a palinodic moment in the *Divine Comedy*, as Bruno
Nardi once suggested, a retrospective view of Dante himself
both as poet and as man, when with confidence and *ingegno* he
embarked upon the writing of the *Convivio*, a work never completed, which began by stating that all men desire to know
and that ultimate happiness resides in the pursuit of knowledge.
Ulysses would then stand for a moment in the pilgrim's life.
In the recapitulation of salvation history, that is, the history of
the Christian soul, Ulysses' would stand for the disastrous prelude to the preparation for grace, a disastrous guide before the
encounter with Virgil. Whatever the validity of the suggestion,
it goes a long way toward explaining at once the greatness of
the figure and the harsh judgement upon him implied by his
position in hell.

The distance that separates Ulysses' point of shipwreck from
the pilgrim's survival, or, for that matter, the *Convivio* from
the *Purgatorio*, is measured by the descent into Hell. This is
literally true, according to the geography of the poem, and

figuratively true as well, as the descent into the self, *intra nos* is the prerequisite for the kind of transcendent knowledge that all men desire. It is a journey that cannot be undertaken without a guide and here too, Virgil spans the gap that separates Dante from the pre-Christian or pre-conversion time represented by Ulysses.

I have said that the contrast between Virgil and Ulysses in the poem is not one of language, but rather of the *uses* to which an almost identical rhetoric is put. In literary terms, Ulysses is the man whose greatness determines epic history, while Aeneas is the man whose greatness is determined by the providential destiny thrust upon him. Both history and the individual follow a circular course in the *Odyssey*, while the pathos of Virgilian epic seems to lie in the discrepancy between the linear destiny of Rome and the cyclical turn of the seasons, to which individual men remain forever subject. Christian time shattered both circles, however, and insisted on the perfect congruence, in the geometric sense, between history and the soul. I should like to turn now to Dante's transformation of that inner circularity, the life of man as seen by the ancients. In dramatic terms, we have seen how the figure of Ulysses is undercut by the *pietas* of Aeneas. We must now examine briefly how *Aeneas* is in turn superseded by the new alter-*Aeneas* in Dante's poem.

Earlier in this paper I described Virgilian pathos with a reference to the simile of falling leaves, borrowed from Homer (*Il.* 6. 146), with which Virgil described the beginning of Aeneas's journey across the River Styx. It happens that Dante imitates that simile as the pilgrim is about to cross the River Acheron, thereby inviting the sophisticated reader to make an important structural comparison of Dante's poem with Virgil's (*Inf.* 3. 112–17):

> Come d'autunno si levan le foglie,
>   l'una appresso dell'altra fin'che il ramo
> Vede alla terra tutte le sue spoglie,
> Similemente il mal seme d'Adamo
>   gittansi di quel lito ad una ad una,
>   per cenni come augel per suo richiamo.

[As leaves fall in autumn, one after the other, until the branch sees its spoils upon the ground, so the evil seed of Adam hurl themselves from that bank, one by one, as a bird to its lure.]

The purpose of the simile in both Homer and Virgil was to render some idea of the vast numbers of men who have fallen before the inexorable law of nature. Generations come and go, multitudinous as leaves which succeed one another. This purpose seems to be directly undercut by Dante's adverbial modifiers "l'una appresso dell' altra," (*Inf.* 3. 113) and "ad una ad una" (*Inf.* 3. 116) in both tercets. If the point of the original simile is in the vast numbers of men who die, then the point is blunted when the poet invites us to follow the fall of each individual leaf from bough to the ground. Dante's simile seems to insist on the fact that this fall is a collective phenomenon which is at the same time very much an individual destiny, leading to a grammatically decisive conclusion: 'fin che 'l ramo Vede a la terra tutte le sue spoglie" (*Inf.* 3. 113–14 [until the bough sees all its spoils on the ground]). The verb personifies the bough in a daring way and substitutes its perspective for that of the detached epic poet. The word *spoglie* 'spoils' moreover, suggests a wanton loss that is far from the inevitability of an autumnal fall. If this branch can look at its own spoils, presumably with sadness, then the implication is that this need not have happened: in short, that God's tree was meant to be evergreen.

The reflexive verbs in Dante's Virgilian imitation, "si levano," "gittansi," seem particularly appropriate, for the point of Dante's verses is that if this fall from God's tree is a destiny, then it is one deliberately chosen. Just as tragedy is out of place in a Christian context, so is Virgil's elegiac tone—these leaves chose to separate themselves from the tree of life. This would seem to be the difference between Virgil's introduction to the world of the dead and Dante's introduction to the world of the damned. Two different deaths are represented by these two similies: Dante would have referred to the Virgilian death as the first death, a death of the body. His own simile, however, refers to "la seconda morte"—a death of the soul (*Inf.* 1. 117).

The death of the *Inferno* is a decision and not a fate. It is also
irreversible. For these leaves, there is not even the biological
comfort of a collective spring to come.

We should note in passing that this distinction between the
two kinds of death is useful for explaining the difference between the Homeric death of Ulysses, largely irrelevant to
Dante, and the death by shipwreck which he in fact portrays.
The first is an organic fact of the body, but the second is a shipwreck of the soul, which can happen at any time and which,
while there is life and grace, can be survived. This probably
explains why Virgil asks Ulysses about his death in a curiously
tortuous sentence:

> . . . ma l' un di voi dica
> Dove per lui perduto a morir gissi.'
> (*Inf.* 26. 83–84)
> [One of you tell / where, lost, death was arrived at by him.]

The strange passive construction was also used by Virgil in the
first canto, when he said that the Emperor of Heaven did not
will that "per me si vegna," that heaven be arrived at *by* me
(*Inf.* 1. 126), the passive construction in both cases indicating
Divine predestination, "com' Altrui piacque" (*Inf.* 26. 141 ['as
pleased another']), in Ulysses' words. Furthermore, *perduto*
'lost' would be a redundancy if this were simply a question of
physical death. As it is, it seems likely that Virgil's question,
'how, when you were lost, did you arrive at death,' refers to
Ulysses' damnation, of which drowning is merely the figure, as
it was for the fathers of the church ever since St. Ambrose.

To return to Dante's transformation of the Virgilian simile,
it would seem to be emblematic of the shift in time, from the
cyclical time of organic nature to the linear time of the soul.
The perspective is shifted as well, from the elegiac to the theo-
centric, from history viewed with the momentary and poignant
detachment of a poetic sensibility to history viewed from the
transcendent aspect of eternity. The basis of the comparison is
changed as well: the point of Virgil's simile is to compare the
almost infinite number of souls to falling leaves: "Quam multa."
Here, however, the comparison is in the manner of the fall—

"Come." By a distortion that would probably be considered a poetic violence in the hands of a lesser poet, a horizontal motion, the crossing of a river, is compared to the downward motion of falling leaves in order to indicate that this crossing is in fact a "fall" in the spiritual sense of the word.

The last part of the simile once more stresses personal choice, in a daring and original way. Turning back to the Virgilian original, the phenomenon of the migration of birds serves to elaborate the theme of the cyclical turn of the seasons: "as birds swarm landward from the deep gulf, when the chill of the year routs them overseas and drives them to sunny lands." Dante accepts the comparison of the flight of birds as an emblem for the flight of the soul—indeed, some of the most exquisite figures of the poem derive from this comparison—but their flight is no longer an instinctive response that changes with the seasons, "Like a bird," writes Dante, "to its lure" (*Inf.* 3. 117). The terms borrowed from medieval falconry seem particularly apt for describing a motion that is at once instinctive and a conditioned response to the falconer's deception, a natural inclination toward a totally alien goal. In terms of this figure, all of the souls in Hell arrived there as did Ulysses, at the end of a "folle volo," a mad flight.

At the very beginning of Virgil's tutelage, the sharp distinctions between the poetry of the *Aeneid* and that of the *Divine Comedy* are perceptible in the most minute details. At the end of Virgil's guidance, the transformation is dramatic and definitive. At the end of the sixth book of the *Aeneid*, the famous *tu Marcellus eris* (*Aen.* 6. 883) passage is perhaps the high point of Virgilian pathos, where human grief for precocious death can derive almost no consolation from the eternity of Rome. Octavia is said to have fainted with grief for her son when the lines were first recited in the presence of Augustus. Virgil's providential history might redeem, or at least pacify the world, but the poet is powerless before death and can do nothing more than offer purple funereal lilies in mourning: "Manibus date lilia plenis" (*Aen.* 6. 883). It happens that this is the only line quoted from the original in Dante's *Divine Comedy*, but it appears, not at the ending of the voyage underworld, as one might expect, but at the ending of the *Purgatorio*, where the angels sing precisely those words to greet Beatrice's return from a precocious death with the white lilies of the Resurrection. It is only after hearing those words that the pilgrim realizes he is for the first time without his guide. The poet pays his model the supreme compliment at the moment when his poem no longer needs him.

At the beginning of this paper, I suggested a distinction between the circular and the linear forms of human time and of narrative structure and said that Dante's poem could be characterized by neither figure because it partook of both. The problematic, tentative view of the pilgrim is a novelistic, almost Dostoevskian striving toward a kind of finality which can be described as a linear goal: the death of the pilgrim and of his story. At the same time, this ending is a new beginning, for it marks the birth of the poet, who has been with us from the start. There is a circularity to the adventure as well: the voice of the poet which ends as it began. This tautology is the tautology of language itself, where the poet's intentionality pre-exists its temporal unfolding in syntax until it arrives at meaning, its point of departure. The point where circle and line, poet and pilgrim meet, is the poem's ending, specifically a vision of the incarnation. The central mystery of Christianity is at the same time the resolution of the epic and novelistic duality. The self that was, the figure of the pilgrim, and the self that is, the voice of the poet, converge in a moment which superimposes the eternity of the Redemption on the hero and now reality of the pilgrim. The detachment of the classic poet, so necessary for finding an historical coherence in the pattern, a logos of intelligibility, joins the flesh and blood experience of the pilgrim, a novelistic linear trajectory. At the final moment, the poet tells us, the circle is squared, in a poetic incarnation which is the unity of the poem and of the belief to which it bears witness.

Notes

1. John Freccero, "Dante's Prologue Scene," *Dante Studies* 84 (1966).

2. Robert Hollander, *Allegory in Dante's Commedia* (Princeton, N.J.: Princeton University Press, 1969), pp. 76 ff.

3. David Thompson, "Dante's Ulysses and the Allegorical Journey," *Dante Studies* 85 (1967):

4. E. R. Curtius, *European Literature and the Latin Middle Ages* (Princeton, N.J.: Princeton University Press, Bollingen Series, 1953), pp. 128–30.

Hero or Anti-Hero?

The Genesis and Development of the
Miles Christianus

R. R. Bolgar

THE TERM "hero" is used to designate the principal character in an action, usually a narrated action,[1] where this character arouses admiration or approval. Heroes have their importance for the history of culture because they serve to show us what traits and types of behavior have enjoyed public favor. Enshrined in the popular fictions, the popularized biographies of an age, they provide a useful index of its values.

Professor Huppé discusses how the warrior hero was depicted in *Beowulf*, the *Battle of Maldon*, and the *Chanson de Roland*.[2] The warrior hero is something of a stock figure. In the traditions of peoples accustomed to hand-to-hand fighting, he has always the same characteristics: skill and strength, courage, self-confidence, even a positive liking for danger. In addition, we often find him endowed with the undesirable concomitants of these qualities: pride, hot temper, a perilous rashness, a habit of taking ruthlessly what he wants. Achilles is the best known representative of the type. And Professor Huppé, if I have understood him correctly, is concerned to demonstrate that this traditional kind of hero—the outstanding warrior, whom other literatures hold up for our admiration—had been represented in the early Middle Ages as a deficient being whose admirable qualities were marred by a disastrous flaw.

The pagan Beowulf tries to cleanse his country of evil in a manner which we are plainly expected to regard as admirable, but he fails in the final accounting "because he lacks the primary theological virtues which alone give meaning to life":

in short, because he is a pagan. His Christian counterparts, Brythnoth and Roland, are also praised for their valor and also fail so long as they put their whole trust in this valor. They attain a truly heroic stature only when they make an explicit surrender to God, so that they take their place within a Christian order. The Christian virtue of submission to the divine power is represented as more important than courage and fighting skill.

The authors of these three works were, we may conjecture, all men educated in monastic schools. Their outlook had been shaped by the clerical culture of the time and reflects its assumptions. Since they lived in an age of violence when the very existence of Christianity was threatened, they were bound to recognize the value of military prowess; but at the same time they were bound by self-interest, and by the system of belief to which they subscribed, to insist on the superiority of religious virtues. It was natural for them to hold valor up to admiration, and natural for them to maintain that valor alone was not enough.

The *Chanson de Roland,* with its repentant hero, was probably composed about 1080. The next age, still struggling with the problem of finding a correct balance between spiritual and military virtues, was to produce a new synthesis. It gives us the concept of the warrior saint, and with this we come to our proper starting point, the beginning of the long road that leads to the *miles christianus.*

Plainly, as its name betrays, this concept of the warrior saint was formed by uniting two elements. One, the warrior, has been mentioned already and is familiar. He is always something of an Achilles. Sanctity, on the other hand, may not, one suspects, prove quite so easy to define since saints present themselves in all shapes and sizes. But, fortunately, when we look at the twelfth century, we find one saint whose contemporary fame outshone all others, who can serve us therefore as an example. It is reasonable to assume that we shall come somewhere near discovering what the men of that age thought sainthood should be if we examine how they depicted Bernard of Clairvaux.

A word of caution is required here. Like Professor Huppé we deal with fiction, not fact. We are considering popular ideals, and so we must take as our guide not Bernard the man, but his legend; not the author of the *De consideratione* and the *Sermones ad cantica canticorum*, but the personality that is presented for our admiration in the *Vita prima*.[3]

Bernard's first biographers painted him as a man whose devotion to the service of God knew no limits. He saw the world simply as a place of trial, and this meant that he had little consideration either for his own or for others' well-being. Here is the account of how he persuaded one of his brothers to embrace the monastic life:

As for Guy, the eldest of the brothers, he was already bound by the bond of marriage. He was a man of high standing, and because of his age he was more securely established in the world than any of the others. Quite naturally he dallied somewhat over his decision, but after thinking things over, he agreed to adopt this new way of life with the others on condition that his wife gave her approval. Yet it seemed impossible that she should agree, for she was a young woman of noble birth with her young daughters to bring up. But Bernard was quite certain that God would show His loving mercy to Guy, and he promised that if she did not give her consent, death would not be long in coming upon her. However, she refused to hear of the idea, and so her husband was inspired by God to formulate a plan worthy of a man of his calibre, and which was an outcome of that unflinching faith which was seen so clearly in his later life. His idea was to give up whatever worldly possessions he had, and to lead the life of a simple peasant by toiling with his own hands, to support the wife whom he might not leave without her consent. After her refusal Bernard, who was going around from one place to another to find more people to join him, arrived at her home, and immediately she was struck down by the serious illness which he had foretold. Knowing that it would be pointless for her to kick against the goad, she sent for Bernard and begged pardon for her hardness, and she herself also asked permission to change her way of life. And so in accordance with the custom of Holy Church, both she and her husband took a vow of chastity, and she went off to join a community of holy women.[4]

This is one of the passages where William of St. Thierry lets us feel his amazement at the extent of Bernard's ruthlessness, but it is an amazement near to admiration. We see little of Bernard the mystic, and not much of Bernard the writer and thinker, in the *Vita*. The ascetic, the fanatic, the spellbinder who can sway a crowd with the fire of his convictions: these are the aspects of Bernard's persona that seem to have caught the imagination of his contemporaries—these and his miracle-working. Bernard had acquired early in his career a reputation for being able to foretell the future and to effect inexplicable cures; and we have only to look at the sixth book added to the *Vita prima* to see how this reputation snowballed into a legend.[5] Bernard's first biographers saw him as a champion of God, resolute, ruthless, gifted with magic powers, a warrior in all but the physical act of wielding the sword.

Once the hagiographers had reached this point, it looks to us as if only one further step remained to be taken: the Bernard figure had to don the accoutrements of a knight, go into battle, kill, or at least unhorse, a paynim opponent. But this step proved impossible to take within a historical framework, however much mythopoiea was prepared to distort historical fact. Admittedly there had been, and still were in the twelfth century, many eminent churchmen who fought energetically on the battlefield; but most of these were ambitious magnates like Odo of Bayeux, who could not by any stretch of the imagination be considered candidates for sanctity.

So in the end we find the ideal of the warrior saint embodied not in a real, but in a purely fictional character. The final stage of the development that began with *Beowulf* and the *Battle of Maldon* was reached when the Arthurian romances were composed. From this reworking of Welsh material by Breton and French writers emerged the conception of the Chevalier Desirré, the unblemished Galahad. It emerged, as Gilson has shown, under Cistercian influence [6]; and the signs of Galahad's sanctity are the ones that the writers of the *Vita prima* had used to set into sharp relief the sanctity of Bernard. One is not surprised to find that, according to a recent theory, William of St. Thierry exercised great influence on the author of the *Queste du Saint Graal*.[7]

The attempt to combine the virtues of the warrior and the saint finds its logical culmination in this work, in which we behold the final fruit of several centuries of myth-making effort. Alas, then, that Galahad should be such a cardboard figure. The compilers of the Arthurian romances were not noted for their skill in drawing character; but even if we allow for a general lack of inspiration in that department of their work, Galahad represents a nadir. We are forced to recognize that to imagine this warrior hero who was at the same time a saint proved beyond the power of the human mind.

His feats of arms are narrated in a mechanical and cursory fashion: "Galahad gave such a display of strength and skill and slew so large a number that he seemed to them no normal man, but a fiend burst in among them to destroy them all. . . .[8]" and again: "Galahad, wielding the sword of the strange belt, smote to right and to left, dealing death at every stroke, and performed such feats that all who saw him thought him no mere mortal but a monster of some sort.[9]" This is not description but labelling, which the author performs with so little attention that he scarcely bothers to vary his labels. Since he was not incapable of depicting a warrior (he does well enough with Lancelot), one can only conclude that he was inhibited by the feeling that a vivid description of the warlike qualities of his hero would detract from the plausibility of the latter's higher, more spiritual side.

Galahad is a being endowed with supernatural powers and wholly surrendered to a supernatural aim. The most spectacular of his achievements owe nothing to a superior skill, strength, or valor: he is able to do what he does because it is his destiny. He is destined to draw the sword out of a stone, destined to sit in the Siege Perilous, destined to win the white shield. The power that enables him to drive out devils, to cure the maimed king, is a magic of divine origin, similar in kind to the power that the popular imagination of the time had attributed to St. Bernard, by means of which he had performed his miraculous cures. And Galahad's other attributes, his austerity, his much-lauded purity, his longing to escape from the world, also call Bernard to mind.

What we have here is not a symbiosis of the warrior hero

with the saint, but a subordination of the former to the latter; and let us note also that it is a subordination for which our minds have been carefully prepared. The Brythnoths and the Rolands of earlier literature had fought for the very existence of Christianity, but the knights errant of Arthurian romance fight to prove their courage or to right private wrongs. At the very best, they are no more than free-lance policemen, and their social usefulness is of a minor sort. Faced with the *Battle of Maldon,* a reader might have been tempted to regard protecting one's country as more important than personal salvation, the warrior as more important than the saint. In the universe inhabited by the paladins of the Round Table, this temptation just does not exist: the supreme value of sanctity remains unchallenged.

The Grail story was to exercise a powerful spell on later ages. Revived by Malory in the fifteenth century, it was to enjoy a further revival in the nineteenth, and since then it has provided material for writers, composers, and artists both good and bad. But when we look at the thirteenth century, the picture we have of its influence is less impressive. We can tell ourselves that perhaps the *Queste* served as an effective counterforce to a fashion that had grown up during the previous hundred years to glorify a merely human courage and success (a fashion that gave us Walter de Châtillon's *Alexandreis* and the several versions of the tale of Troy [10]) or that it served as a counterforce to *Tristan,* which, in spite of the love potion device, may have been regarded as giving sexual passion an undue importance. But even if this was so, the impact which it made does not seem to have lasted very long. The time we are considering came at the end of the period when education had lain entirely in the hands of the clergy; and the figure of Galahad is one of those exaggerated ideals which men construct when they look back on a past that appears to them kinder than the present. It is an ideal which represents a kind of protest.[11] And as decade succeeded decade, in the passage from the Middle Ages to the Renaissance, its grip on people's imagination was to become less and less.

It was not attacked in any specific sense. We must not look in imaginative literature for the thrust and parry of philo-

sophical and political debate. The processes involved in the
development of ideas at this level have a less mechanical, a
more organic character. New conceptions that underline some
weakness in prevailing ideals make their appearance, and they
are repeated with variations. They win popularity until at
last a climate of opinion is built up that is favorable to them;
and then the earlier ideals lose their hold.

The Grail story was a complex imaginative construct related to several fields of human experience. It implied acceptance of a certain view of sanctity, by no means the only view
known to the Christian tradition, but one that found favor
in the twelfth and early thirteenth centuries. It implied also
certain views on the role of the warrior in society and a concept of society that stressed ethical relationships and neglected
politics and economics. But above all it called for a belief in
a world order dominated, in both sum and detail, by unseen
forces, mysterious in their workings.

The Grail story is a romance, so we need not assume that
either its author or its admirers held the views we have listed
in an explicit form. Imaginative literature makes its appeal
outside the sphere of reasoned argument. But what we are
entitled to assume is that in the centuries when the story was
popular, its ideals, values, and presuppositions about the order
of things evoked a measure of sympathy; and what we have
to look for now are indications of the gradual waning of that
sympathy.

I shall arrange my material in this part of the argument
under certain broad headings. That method has, I am well
aware, the serious disadvantage of hiding vital interconnections; but there is no alternative. The cultural history of three-
hundred years cannot be compressed into a short paper.

Perhaps the most important aspect of the Grail story is the
conception of sanctity it embodies. Galahad does no wrong;
he is eager to succor the helpless; he shows traces of natural
affection towards his squire, his father, his friends. But not
even his most ardent champions would claim that he is afire
with Christian charity, any more than is St. Bernard in the
Vita. Now, during the century and a half following the writing
of the *Queste du Saint Graal,* Charity in the human sense of

a love of one's neighbor came to rank as the most important of Christian virtues. Loving one's neighbor is mentioned, as we all know, in the Sermon on the Mount. It formed part— an inalienable part—of the Christian tradition from the very beginning. But its cult was confined to exceptional individuals like Aelred of Rievaulx.[12] The majority of Christian thinkers were, up to the thirteenth century, primarily concerned with that more impressive, that more radiantly spiritual activity, the love of God.

The change which gave love for one's fellow man popular importance in Christian doctrine began even before the *Queste* was written, with the preaching of Francis of Assisi. It touched the imagination of the humble and found indirect expression in the voluntary poverty of the Beghards and the egalitarianism of Jean de Meun's golden age, until after a long preparation the doctrine became finally explicit in the *devotio moderna*.

It is instructive to compare the passage cited above from the *Vita Bernardi* or Galahad's attitude to sinners slain at Carteloise with the account which Thomas à Kempis gives of his master Radewijns.[13] Radewijns held that we should imitate Christ by sympathizing with the poor and afflicted, visiting the sick, comforting widows and orphans, and being ready to perform all menial domestic tasks, that we should never consider our own good but only our neighbor's welfare. Men of his stamp, exponents of the *devotio moderna*, were not likely to look with favor on a type of sanctity that disregarded the world and rested on manifestations of supernatural power; and by the end of the fourteenth century the time was ripe for a reappraisal of the religious element in the Galahad ideal.

This change in men's religious attitudes was matched by a change in their estimation of the soldier's social role. The knight-errantry of the romances was a fictional and exaggerated derivative of a philosophical doctrine that we find in the more serious writing of the time. According to this doctrine, the use of force is justified only when some villainy requires suppression. Sin, crime, heresy, pagan beliefs are its proper targets; and aggressive war initiated for some wanton or selfish cause ranks as a crime. The soldier, in short, is to be a policeman, charged with maintaining the *pax Romana*. What is lacking in this reasonable analysis of the problem of legalized violence is any mention of the state and its interest. It does not provide for situations where the future safety of a community demands a preemptive strike against a turbulent neighbor, where a competitor must be eliminated if some profitable industry is to survive. The ethic of the knights-errant did not in these important respects take account of the real situation in late medieval Europe.

A sense of national identity, of patriotic pride, had existed in France from the twelfth century. We can trace its beginnings in the *Gesta Dei per Francos*,[14] and Villehardouin and Joinville are there to remind us of its subsequent growth. But as in so many other fields, it is with the fourteenth century that we move rather suddenly into a new climate of opinion: it is then that the well-being of the state emerges as all-important. Comparing Dante with Marsiglio, the *De monarchia* with the *Defensor pacis*, we see the shift of values in what may be an unnaturally sharp relief. But the shift was there and had a marked effect of men's estimation of the warrior hero.

The short article devoted to Horatius Cocles in Petrarch's *De viris illustribus* relates the famous story of the bridge and then adds: "His signal courage was not left unrewarded by the state. His statue was put up in the Forum and he was given land at the public expense, as much land as the plough could encompass in a day."[15] The implication is clear. Horatius is to be admired because he served Rome. And in the account that Petrarch gave of another hero, Scipio Africanus— an account he considered so important that he rewrote it twice after the original draft—the point is explicitly stated. Scipio, a general, diplomat and statesman, is seen primarily as a patriot: "He used to declare that he was born to serve his country. Ever eager to praise the Roman people and to turn his own glory to their credit, he would exhort the friends his merits won him to transfer their feelings of friendship to Rome."[16] Petrarch was in advance of his age, but after another 150 years, the outlook he had championed became universal. Heroes were those who served their country.

It is true that chivalric romances continued to be manufactured throughout this period, and that a revival of chivalric ideals was regarded by many as a panacea for contemporary ills. But how significant was this *laudatio temporis acti?* Some of the works that Caxton produced between 1460 and 1489— the anonymous *Boke of noblesse,* Ramon Lull's *Book of the order of chivalry,* Christine de Pisan's *Boke of faytes of armes and of chyvalrye,* Malory's *Morte darthur* [17]—seem at first sight evidence for a continuing interest in the daydreams of the past. But closer investigation proves disillusioning. These three treatises printed by Caxton are not concerned, as were earlier works from *Beowulf* to the *Queste du Saint Graal,* with the problem of the warrior hero and the life of Faith. What interested their authors was the difference between real warfare and the idealizations of knight-errantry. They do not, to take only one example, countenance the use of force by individuals on their own responsibility; it is for the sovereign to decide whether a war is just or not. The welfare of the state has as much importance for them as for Petrarch or Marsiglio. As for the *Morte darthur,* the differences that mark it off from the French Arthurian cycle have been common knowledge since E. K. Chambers's 1922 article [18]; and they are decisive in the present context. What Malory paints for us is not the failure of a man but the collapse of a kingdom. Where his thirteenth-century original focused on Lancelot's inability to achieve his aims since he relied on his own strength alone (making him thereby into a type of the failure-prone warrior hero), Malory centered his tale on the king, Arthur, who had dedicated his life to a noble conception and who saw that conception and his kingdom fall in ruins around him. In spite of the chivalric trappings of his narrative, Malory too belongs to the new age that places the public interest before private salvation.

But perhaps the best example of the reorientation of values that marked the early Renaissance is the biography of the man whom popular history presents as the last of the knights. The *Histoire du gentil seigneur de Bayard* by the Loyal Serviteur is a panegyric of the chivalric ideal written at a time (1527) when the knight with his skill in hand-to-hand combat was becoming an obsolete figure; and it had the effect of linking the real Bayard with the fictional Galahad in the imagination of mankind. The Loyal Serviteur was almost certainly one Jacques de Mailles, an archer in Bayard's company, and since his aim was to make his captain as like a knight of romance as possible, the work mingles biography and fiction in equal proportions. But what concerns us is that despite de Mailles's shameless romanticizing, Bayard, *le chevalier sans peur et sans reproche,* emerges as the polar opposite of Galahad in many important respects. His eyes are not fixed on the next world. A faithful Catholic, he goes to Mass and will breathe a prayer in a tight corner, but this simple piety does not take much of his attention. It is true that he refused to join Alfonso d'Este in a plot to poison Pope Julius II; but he had no qualms about fighting Julius's troops when his king ordered. Not religion, but an unswerving loyalty to his sovereign and to the France that sovereign represented, was the force that governed his conduct.

He was a fighting man, strong, tenacious, fantastically brave, honest, unambitious, and (the quality that endeared him most to his fellows) fantastically generous. But just as he was not, in the full sense of the word, a religious man, so he was not, in any sense, ascetic. Temperate, yes—a fighter was an athlete who had to keep in training. But he had none of Galahad's vaunted purity. De Mailles relates an anecdote which makes this perfectly clear.[19]

One evening, as he was going off to a banquet, Bayard instructed his servant to find him a girl and have her ready for his return. De Mailles recounts this without comment, and there is nothing to suggest that the proceeding was in any way unusual. The servant knew of a poverty-stricken gentlewoman who had a pretty daughter. He went to see her. A bargain was struck, and when Bayard returned, well wined and dined, the girl was waiting in his bedroom. "She was as fair as an angel," de Mailles writes, "but had wept till her eyes were swollen," and when Bayard, who seems to have been surprised at her distress, asked her what the matter was, she flung herself on her knees and begged for mercy. Bayard lifted her up, put a cloak round her, and went immediately to ask the wife of a neighbor to take her in for the night. Nor was this all. The next day he summoned the mother, upbraided her, and then emptied his purse. He gave the girl a hundred crowns for her bridal chest and two hundred as a marriage portion, and he presented another hundred to the mother. Four hundred crowns was a tidy sum—perhaps ten thousand dollars would be a fair equivalent—and Bayard was not a rich man.

The story shows him to have been indeed *sans reproche* and the possessor of a warm heart; but equally it established him as a man who took sexual laxity for granted in a way that would have shocked Galahad.

This difference between the two heroes indicates yet another change in outlook. The heroic poems of the early Middle Ages paid little attention to problems of sex and love. But already William of St. Thierry's life of St. Bernard and the thirteenth-century *Lancelot* present chaste behavior as an essential precondition—if not *the* essential precondition—of sanctity and therefore of perfect knighthood. A knight was expected to serve his lady—indeed to serve any lady who appealed to him for help—but if such service led to illicit passion, as when Arthur lay with his half-sister or Lancelot with Guenevere, the results were painted as inevitably disastrous. Passion, where it appeared, was condemned. Virginity was the ideal. Presumably, in theory, passion could exist in marriage. But the married couples the romances show us are for the most part divided and unhappy. The chivalric tradition was on the whole unsympathetic to sexual as distinct from controlled and idealized love.

But it is unusual for a particular set of values to exercise an exclusive dominion over men's minds; and it is easy to find examples of other approaches to love even in the twelfth and early thirteenth centuries, when the chivalric tradition came into being. We have *Aucassin et Nicolette*, which admittedly may derive from an Eastern source and had little popularity and influence. We have the *Lais* of Marie de France and the uncomplicated seductions described by the *pastourelles*. In Latin we have the letters of Heloise, for it is immaterial in this context whether they are authentic or the creation of some imaginative clerk; and we have the scholars of the time eagerly reading the *Ars amatoria*, a work likely to have some effect on their outlook even though Ovid's tenets for the right man-

agement of courtesans could be and were twisted to serve the
purposes of chivalry. In short, we have an undercurrent to
the mainstream of the chivalric tradition in which some value
is given to naive sexual desire, to love as a sentiment, or to
love as a relationship; and with the second half of the thirteenth century we find this undercurrent running with ever-
increasing force.

The chilling ideal of love as service was now transformed
into the glorification of a love that, while remaining chaste,
genuinely engaged a lover's emotions. We can trace the emer-
gence of this new conception in the rejection of *Aeneid* 4 as
a source for the Dido story. Justin's version, which attributes
the queen's suicide to a determination to remain faithful to
her dead husband, came to be accepted with its emphasis on
chastity as more palatable than the Virgilian tale of seduction,
and because it was more palatable was regarded as more likely
to be true. Eberhard Leube in his recent book *Fortuna in
Karthago*,[20] notes three vernacular accounts based on Justin,
in Spanish, French and Italian, that appeared between 1270
and 1300, and some seventy years later this metamorphosed
Dido was still popular enough to have her story retold by
Petrarch and Boccaccio.

But it is Dante's love for Beatrice that provides our most
perfect example of a chaste passion. Dante moves from the
cult of frustrated love, that Provençal pendant to the chivalric
ideal of service, to a Neoplatonic conception which is then
transcended in its turn. The central eighteenth chapter of the
Vita Nuova shows Dante abandoning the fashionable and
poetically satisfying role of frustrated wooer and dedicating
himself to the worship of that eternal Beauty of which Beatrice
is the exemplar. And then in the *Divine Comedy* there is a
further shift. The Beatrice who meets us in the *Paradiso* seems
something more than the embodiment of an ideal. She is a
person, and what exists between her and the poet is a personal relationship, even though it is conceived as achieving only
a mysterious fruition, *sub specie aeternitatis*.

Dante tried to prove that human love had metaphysical
validity. But at the very time that he was writing the *Divine
Comedy*, another valuation of a less philosophical sort was

becoming current. Passion came to be represented as a sickness, tragic perhaps in its consequences, but glorious all the same; and this glory was its justification. Such was the concept favored by that early feminist Christine de Pisan; and in Armannino, in Boccaccio (remember Fiammetta), in Chaucer, it found skilled exponents. Sexual passion was given the status of a heroic quality, at least in those cases where it appeared in conjunction with some concern for the well-being of the beloved and some desire for a lasting relationship. There was a growing tendency to place love in a human rather than a divine context.

It is interesting to examine one of the later specimens of the chivalric novel with this development in mind. The *Amadís de Gaula* is a late fifteenth-century version by Rodriguez de Montalvo of an original that seems to have existed more than a hundred years earlier. In its revised form it enjoyed a popularity few other books equaled. Edwin B. Place lists twenty Spanish editions before 1600 as well as numerous printings of translations into Dutch, English, French, Italian, and Portuguese.[21] There was even a translation into Hebrew. *Amadís* follows the pattern of the old Arthurian romances: the leader is hurled from one wild duel to another, and the noise is deafening. But behind the conventional clatter of knight-errantry there is a tale of youthful love. The relationship of Amadís and Oriana moves on a different plane from the main adventure story. Their affection dates back to childhood, and it blossoms into a love that is shown to rest on physical attractiveness. Montalvo emphasizes outward appearances and romantic settings in a way that brings to mind the sentimental novelists of a later age; for instance, Oriana and her friend Mabilia are expecting a midnight visit by Amadís:

> They were both at the window, which they opened, having put candles inside that gave a bright light. Amadís saw his mistress in the candlelight, and she appeared to him more beautiful than anyone would believe a woman could be. She wore a garment of Indian silk, embroidered with a multitude of golden flowers in relief; and her hair, which was of a breathtaking beauty, was uncovered except for a rich garland. When Amadís saw

her thus he trembled in every limb with pleasure at the sight, and his heart beat uncontrollably.[22]

The chivalric novel has drifted far from the rigors of the thirteenth century when love was primarily an obstacle to perfection.

We can see how wise Malory was to choose Arthur for his hero. Everything had altered. What men now felt to be important in religious experience, in political life, and in their personal development made the old ideals—which had found a logical, if somewhat exaggerated embodiment in the figure of Galahad—seem insufficient and ridiculous. The age called for a new synthesis.

Since Europe at this time was still a strongly Christian society, there was no question of any but a Christian hero evoking serious admiration and serving as an ideal. Some importance must therefore be granted to the attempts made in the middle of the fifteenth century to establish a reasoned defense of Christian attitudes. These attempts—the work of humanists like Lorenzo Valla [23]—were not, it is true, directly concerned with the creation of a hero figure. Philosophical in character, they belong to the history of ideas rather than the history of ideals. But by formulating the Christian position with respect to the Stoic and Epicurean teachings popular among the humanist avant-garde, they did, one suspects, prepare the way for its formulation at a different, less philosophical level. The synthesis we are discussing here, the development of a Christian hero whom the Renaissance mind could accept, was the work of a later generation and another land. To find it we have to move from Italy to the north, from Valla to Erasmus and his circle.

The personal contribution of Erasmus was twofold. He provided the world with a new picture of the ideal Christian; and he established what was to prove a lasting pillar of a new outlook in a thorough-going condemnation of war and the so-called glories of war.

The *Encheiridion militis christiani* [24]—the Christian knight's handbook or mirror (the Greek word has both meanings)— is a gummy, diffuse piece of writing. We miss the irony, the sharp insights that distinguish the best productions of Erasmus. If the men of the sixteenth century valued the *Encheiridion,* which they seem to have done, it must have been for its general thesis. Its attacks on sensuality, maliciousness, pride, avarice and violence appear no more than the commonplaces of medieval satire until, coming to know the book better, one realizes that they mask a positive ethic. Sensuality apart, which Erasmus seems to have hated unreservedly for its own sake, the vices he singles out for censure are those through which we injure our fellows. He is making a plea for a socially oriented Christianity in which the love of God finds expression through love of one's neighbor. Charity is not shown by attendance at church, by prayers to the saints, by burning a great number of candles. God, he tells us, has no need for trivialities of that sort. Charity is to rejoice in one's neighbor's wealth as in one's own and to make good his losses. It is to teach the ignorant, to lift up the fallen, to comfort the unhappy, and to help him that labors. It is "to bring all your riches and substance, all study, all your care to bear on this, that you in Christ help as many others as you can." [25] And the reference to teaching the ignorant touches on another important issue. Erasmus was convinced that one could not imitate Christ without an understanding of the Scriptures, which in its turn was not possible without some understanding of literature in general and the ancient literatures in particular. Holiness in his opinion presupposed comprehension. Erasmus was not an unconditional advocate of *sancta simplicitas.*

To this view of Christianity, so damaging to the pretensions of authority and power, Erasmus added a radical hatred of war. For the mass of ordinary men the cost of even the greatest victory far outweighed the gain. The only ones to benefit from war were rulers and their favorites, who trapped people into fighting by investing the activity with a false glamor.

In his efforts to deglamorize war, Erasmus received valuable support from his friends, whose suggestions, less extreme than his own, made his pacifism practically acceptable. The views of the group have been ably studied by R. P. Adams,[26] and I shall do no more than summarize his conclusions. In a world of ambitious tyrants, a state had to be prepared to defend itself. But one should regard such defense as a rational police action to be carried through with a minimum of damage to friend or foe. It was more admirable to win by craft without killing anyone than to kill thousands. More makes the point in his *Utopia* that the well-run state would expect every citizen to bear arms, but for these citizen-soldiers fighting would be an unpleasant duty to be carried out without fuss, and then, without fuss, forgotten. The man recommended for our admiration is the unromantic private citizen, sturdy and conscientious, but eager to be quit of his task at the first opportunity: a figure not unlike the artisans, shopkeepers, and small farmers who were to fight for their beliefs in the Protestant armies of the next two centuries.

As for that further aspect of the chivalric hero, his relationship with women, it also received some attention from the fathers of the *miles christianus*—some but not very much. Erasmus was a natural celibate uninterested in sex, while More, who seems to have led an affectionate family life, hesitated perhaps for that very reason to write formally and at length on the subject of love. It was left to Vivès to produce a pendant to the *Encheiridion* in his *De institutione feminae christianae* and his *De officio mariti*.[27] Vivès, on the face of it, is concerned primarily with the duties of marriage, the education and lifestyle appropriate to a Christian woman, and he paints the husband simply as the master of the household. I hope, said Erasmus commenting on the book, that you are kinder to your own wife. The marital relationship pictured by Vivès seems a poor substitute for the loves of Dante and Beatrice or even of Dido and Aeneas. It moves emotionally at a very low level.

Here then we have the new Christian hero, Galahad's unexpected successor: humble, practical, studious, devoted to the Bible, soberly wedded, zealous in the performance of good works; except for his learning—which Erasmus thinks necessary—he is a type of man most readily found in the lower middle class, estimable but not spectacular.

The reformers set themselves deliberately to debunk the exaggerations of the hagiographers. Who could endure, Erasmus writes in his life of Jerome, those who, with ravings worse than those of old women, children, illiterates, or fools, do not exalt the saints, but rather debase them? [28] And here is his disciple Vivès on the fictions of romance:

> What delight can there be in things that are such obvious and foolish lies? One man kills twenty, another thirty, another receives a hundred wounds and left dead rises up again and is hale and hearty the next day, overcomes two giants and goes off laden with more gold, silver and precious stones than a ship could carry away.[29]

Their ideal of sanctity called for understanding and service, not for displays of miraculous powers. And their ideal warrior was as much a rationalist as Shaw's chocolate-cream soldier. Their ideal lover was a sober family man. So they produced what was indeed an anti-hero. But except in puritan circles, these conceptions did not remain unaltered. As they took root in the minds of the general public, they were in their turn subtly transformed.

The population of Europe included in its number nearly as many Don Quixotes as nascent puritans. There were people who lapped up the adventures of Amadís, who crowded to tourneys and royal progresses, and who wanted a Bayard for their hero. The sixteenth century was an age of ostentation as well as an age of middle-class endeavor, and if we look at the generations after Erasmus we find them making determined efforts to add what it is perhaps fair to call some aristocratic color and extravagance to the sober merit of the *miles christianus*.

A detailed account of these efforts, which were not altogether successful, would take us well beyond our appropriate length, and a few brief indications must suffice: the reading public then as now hankered after heroes who were heroic in love; and this was an issue that Erasmus and his friends had left unexplored. The world that we see emerging out of the Middle Ages had not in any case made up its mind about the ethics of sexual love. The medieval ideal of service offered to a woman as if she were a king or a god was one in which, it came to be believed, only a masochist could find satisfaction. The Neoplatonist recommendation that we look for the divine in the human, if stringently followed, would have always resulted in lovers retiring to separate convents, as happens in one of the stories of Marguerite de Navarre.[30] The humanist line, that sexual desire was a natural impulse but that reason should control all passion, led to the advocacy of a cold-hearted indulgence. It cut out precisely those elements in love which the naive thought valuable, while the anti-feminist tradition enshrined in an infinity of tales and *fabliaux* represented woman as an amalgam of whore and scold, alternately deceiving and deceived. None of these divergent viewpoints offered much prospect of happiness; and better men than Panurge found themselves groping helplessly after some satisfactory code of conduct.

When Vivès drew a favorable picture of marriage, he did break new ground. Marriage had admittedly been presented already in the Spanish romances of the fifteenth and sixteenth centuries as the proper finale of a love affair, but it is quite plain that the married relationship of the couple was regarded not as an enrichment of their love but as an inevitable anti-climax. When the secret marriage of Amadís and Oriana is made public and Amadís asks what he can do to repay her for her consenting to this, Oriana replies: "It is no longer appropriate for you, my lord, to offer such courtesies. I have now to follow and observe your will with the obedience which a wife owes to her husband." [31]

But once marriage was established on a pedestal, it offered love an obvious place within the social framework. Marital affection could be pictured as enriching, adultery as debasing, life. Drawing the dividing line between beneficial and destructive love just where the law drew it had practical advantages that do not concern us here. What does concern us is the fact that the ideal relationship between men and women was for the first time presented in a psychologically fruitful form. It may not have been often that romantic love arose in or survived in marriage; but where it did, it could add to the experience of passion a broader concord based on comprehension and mutual kindliness. The ideal marriage did not, like earlier patterns of sexual conduct, lead to the impoverishment of human personality: it could embody the two ideals of Erasmus, understanding and charity.

Vivès did no more than start the ball rolling. A long time
was to pass before the idea came to be at all widely accepted
that lovers could in a meaningful sense live happily ever after.
Perhaps this did not happen till the eighteenth century. But
one can see writers already in the sixteenth century feeling
their way towards the idea that marriage had something important to offer where love was concerned.

In Sidney's *Arcadia*, Pyrocles takes the Neoplatonist line;
he wants love to be a gateway to perfection. Musidorus is a
humanist who holds that passion should be controlled by reason. Physical desire gets the better of both—more obviously
in the first than in the second version of the tale. But they
are redeemed in Sidney's eyes because the goal of their passion
is marriage.

Spenser wrote the *Epithalamion* as well as the *Faerie
Queene;* and even in the latter work, complex and synthetic
as it is, holding divergent traditions in a precarious balance
and paying more than just lip service to the Neoplatonic ideal,
we have Charissa in the House of Holiness, a figure of con-
tented motherhood. The Red Cross Knight may leave Una
to mourn, but the loves of Britomart and Artegall are to end
in happy marriage and produce a progeny who will occupy
England's throne.

Shakespeare a few years later gives us Portia's marriage
speech to Bassanio, the Roman Portia's moving appeal to
Brutus, and Henry and Katharine, to say nothing of Ferdinand
and Miranda and other pairs of fortunate lovers obviously
bound for happy matrimony.

This blend of Vivès's principles with that cult of passion
and romantic love that went back to Boccaccio and Christine de
Pisan was not the only way in which the ideal of the *miles
christianus* was enriched during the sixteenth century. Erasmus's hero (or anti-hero) had been as unglamorous in war as
in love. And here too there came a change.

The pacifist propaganda of the reformers was not without
its effect on the next generation. Humane and enlightened men
became reluctant to condone aggressive war or a delight in violence for its own sake. Their admiration was reserved, as
More's had been, for the patriot who fought in defense of his

country's legitimate interests. But the great national states of
the sixteenth century were not organized like Utopia or early
republican Rome. Their wars—even their defensive wars—
were not waged by citizen levies who dropped their plowshares
to reach briefly for the sword. There was room for trained
courage and military skill. There was room even for *penache.*
Sidney, who had good claim to be regarded as the favored
hero of his generation, was admired for his looks and gallantry,
for being a poet, a scholar, a man of fashion. He went to war
not because he had Bayard's love of fighting, but because he
was a patriot; and the renown he enjoyed for qualities that
have no connection with military glory added to his effectiveness as a leader. He was a *miles christianus* in the aristocratic
mode. Finally, there were problems on the religious side.
Erasmus wanted his ideal Christian to combine the rejection
of all cravings for status, luxury, and power with the great
breadth of learning which he considered necessary for the
understanding of Scripture. But the people who were ready
to accept his social teachings about simplicity, because their
style of life was hardy and simple anyway, were the humbler
middle class of small craftsmen, farmers, shopkeepers; and
they were not as a class interested in the kind of learning he
advocated. Insofar as his ideal found an echo in the popular
mind, it took the form of simplicity of manners, coupled not
with learning but with an uncritical faith in the Bible.

And as the century wore on, this uncritical faith did not escape—in the nature of things could not have escaped—some
questioning. The ways of God to men as narrated in the Scriptures were not always easy to justify. Was Abraham right to
consent to the sacrifice of Isaac? Was Jephtha right to carry
a similar sacrifice into effect? Beza's *Abraham sacrifiant* [32] and
Buchanan's *Jephthes* [33] seem to answer these questions in the
affirmative. All the same, the general effect of the two plays
is to leave the reader uncomfortable. Certainly there is nothing humanly admirable about God's demands, nothing heroic
about Abraham or Jephtha; and the victims, Isaac and Iphis,
seem prompted by filial affection more than by religious faith.
By the end of the sixteenth century we see men working towards a new set of values centered on enduring personal rela-

tionships, family affections, patriotism, and a religion designed
to guarantee the survival of social virtues: a fuzzy amalgam
that in some measure still serves us today.

Now that we have traced in this rough outline the gradual
abandonment of the chivalric concept of the hero and its replacement by the *miles christianus,* a sort of anti-hero whose
dour lineaments were then softened in their turn, we should
take note perhaps of the level on which our enquiry has moved.
It is evident that we have been more concerned with the cre-
ations of mythopoeia than with historical characters or coher-
ently organized ideas. We have never been far from the realm
of fiction, and on several occasions we have crossed its borders.
The Loyal Serviteur's Bayard, the Sidney who meets us in
the poems dedicated to his memory, have a great deal in
common with the fictional heroes of the age; and so has that
child of Erasmus's theorizing, the *miles christianus.* Spenser's
Red Cross Knight is his twin brother. Our field has been one
in which the creative imagination played a most active part.

At the same time, the various concepts of the hero that we
have been examining have not presented themselves as arbitrary in the sense of being chance products of their creators'
fancy. To win and retain popularity a hero had to possess
characteristics of which people approved. Heroes have never
been independent of the social and cultural climate in which
they came to flourish; and the characters and histories of some
fictional heroes were specially devised, as we have seen, to
justify attitudes and activities favored by groups to which
their creators belonged. So social influences must take their
place alongside the mythopoeic, and what future research will
need to examine are the various subtle ways in which these
two sets of factors—social pressures and the creative impulses
of the imagination—combined to mould people's ideas about
the heroic.

The task will not be an easy one. Hitherto the study of
ideology as we find it in the writings of a Weber, a Karl Mann-
heim, a Lukács, has been concerned with relatively coherent
systems of ideas. If we now admit that concepts of a less precise sort, such as we see objectified in fiction or in representative art, have played a formative part in the development of

western culture, we must evolve new categories of description, new techniques of enquiry to handle this new evidence that is more varied and more amorphous than any that students of ideology have handled in the past. We are on the edge of an unexplored field of knowledge, and its difficult exploration may hold much that will be of great interest.

Notes

1. A woman can be a "hero" in the same sense as a man, and in such cases "heroine" merely marks the change of gender. But "heroine" is also used in a slightly different sense to indicate the woman with whom the hero is involved in a love relationship, and who need not be the protagonist of any independently admirable action. We shall not in this paper be concerned with that extension of the word's meaning.

2. See above, pp. 1–26.

3. See William of St. Thierry et al., *Vita prima Bernardi*, translated by Geoffrey Webb and Adrian Walker, in *St. Bernard of Clairvaux* (London: A. R. Mowbray, 1960).

4. Ibid., pp. 26–27.

5. Migne, *Patrologia Latina* 185. 570 ff.

6. Etienne Henry Gilson, *Les idées et les lettres* (Paris: J. Vrin, 1932), pp. 56–91.

7. Myrrha Lot-Borodine, "Les grands secrets du S. Graal dans la 'Queste' du pseudo-Map," in *Lumière du Graal*, edited by René Nelli (Paris: Gallimard, 1951).

8. Albert Pauphilet, ed., *La Queste de Saint Graal*, Classiques français du moyen âge (Paris, 1923), p. 230.

9. Pauphilet, p. 238. For another example where the phrasing is similar to the passages cited, see p. 296.

10. Walter de Châtillon, *Alexandreis*, in Migne, *PL* 209. 460 ff. Note especially, however, the passage in Book 5, where Walter extols the glory of Alexander (col. 518). As for the Trojan story, we have in Latin Simon Capra Aurea, *Poème sur la guerre de Troie*, edited by André Boutemy, in *Scriptorium*, vol. 1 (1946–47), pp. 267–88 ff., written at the beginning of the twelfth century, and Joseph of Exeter's *De bello troiano*, edited by Samuel Dresemius (London, 1825), which dates probably from c. 1175. In French there is the *Roman d'Eneas* in the first, Benoît de Sainte-More's *Roman de Troie* in the second half of the twelfth century.

11. The phenomenon referred to here has many parallels in cultural history. When a particular form of society is distintegrating, we often find ideals formulated by its partisans that would perhaps have been realizable to some extent while that society was flourishing, but whose only function in the existing situation is to serve as a nostalgic manifesto. We have Dante's unrealistic attitude toward Henry VII in the *De monarchia*. We have writers like Joseph de Maistre in early nineteenth-century France glorifying the *ancien régime*. We have writers like Doderer and Roth in republican Austria glorifying the Hapsburg monarchy. And one might add to this list for England the later works of Evelyn Waugh.

12. Aelred of Rievaulx, *Speculum caritatis*, translated by Geoffrey Webb and Adrian Walker (London: A. R. Mowbray, 1962), and *De spirituali amicitia*, translated by Henry Talbot (London, 1942).

13. Cited in Albert Hyma, *The Christian Renaissance*, 2d ed. (Hamden, Conn.: Archon Books, 1965), pp. 50–51.

14. Guibert of Nogent, *Gesta Dei per Francos*, in *Recueil des historiens des croisades*, Historiens occidentaux 4 (1844–95, reprint Farnborough Hants.: Gregg Press, 1967).

15. Francesco Petrarca, *Prose*, edited by Guido Martellotti et al. (Milan: Riccardo Ricciardi, 1955), p. 234 (from *De viris illustribus*).

16. Petrarca, *Prose*, p. 242.

17. On these see Arthur Bowles Ferguson, *The Indian Summer of English Chivalry* (Durham, N.C.: Duke University Press, 1960).

18. Edmund Kerchever Chambers, "Sir Thomas Malory," in Chambers' *Sir Thomas Wyat and some Collected Studies* (London: Sidgwick and Jackson, 1933); the essay was first read to the English Association in 1922.

19. Le Loyal Serviteur, *Histoire du Seigneur de Bayart* (1527, reprint Paris: Editions E. Droz and Cambridge: W. Heffer and Sons, 1927) pp. 218–219 (chap. 55).

20. Eberhard Leube, *Fortuna in Karthago* (Heidelberg: Carl Winter Universitätsverlag, 1960) pp. 31–33, 120 ff., 288 ff.

21. Edwin Bray Place, ed., *Amadís de Gaula* (Madrid: Instituto "Miguel de Cervantes," 1959) 1: xiv–xlvi.

22. 1: 128.

23. This reference to Valla did not appear in the lecture as originally delivered. Attention was drawn to the debt that Erasmus owed to Valla by Professor Maristella Lorch during the subsequent discussion. When one reads the revised text of Valla's dialogue that Professor Lorch's fine edition has made available (Lorenzo Valla, *De vero falsoque bono*, edited by Maristella de Panizza Lorch [Bardi: Adriatica Editrice, 1970]), one sees very clearly that it was from Valla that Erasmus learned to apply philological techniques to the interpretation of religious and philosophical concepts. Valla must also be given credit for showing his contemporaries that

new methods were required to defend Christianity against the new ideas of the Renaissance. But his actual presentation of the Christian case strikes me as highly idiosyncratic. His spokesman, Antonio da Rho, sees his ideal Christian as motivated solely by a desire for pleasure, only it is a future pleasure located in Heaven. I cannot agree therefore that the *De vero falsoque bono* had much influence on the view of religion that we find in the *Encheiridion.*

24. Desiderius Erasmus, *Encheiridion militis christiani* (Antwerp, 1503). None of the English translations is wholly satisfactory since they are all disfigured by omissions and additions. The latest one, by Ford Lewis Battles in *Advocates of Reform*, edited by Matthew Spinka, The Library of Christian Classics, vol. 14 (London: S.C.M. Press, 1953), is accurate but gives only two-thirds of the text.

25. Spinka, p. 345.

26. Robert Pardee Adams, *The Better Part of Valor* (Seattle: University of Washington Press, 1962).

27. Juan Luis Vivès, *De institutione feminae christianae; De officio mariti* (Basle, 1540). The *De institutione* was completed in 1523, the *De officio* in 1529. Cf. Foster Watson, *Vivès and the Renaissance Education of Women* (London: Edwin Arnold, 1912).

28. *Erasmi Opuscula*, edited by Wallace Klippert Ferguson (The Hague: Martinus Nijhoff, 1933), p. 136.

29. Vivès, *De institutione,* cited in Adams, p. 232.

30. Marguerite de Navarre, *L'Heptaméron* (Paris, 1559); the reference is to the tenth story of the first day in this first complete edition.

31. *Amadís de Gaula,* Bk. 4, chap. 39. For a discussion, Mary Frances Patchell, *The Palmerin Romances in Elizabethan Prose Fiction* (New York: Columbia University Press, 1947), pp. 53–71.

32. Théodore de Bèze, *Abraham sacrifiant* (Geneva, 1550).

33. George Buchanan, *Jephthes: tragoedia* (Paris, 1554); the play was acted c. 1542.

Suggested Reading

Adams, Robert Pardee. *The Better Part of Valor*. Seattle: University of Washington Press, 1962.

Caspari, Fritz Wilhelm. *Humanism and the Social Order in Tudor England*. Chicago: University of Chicago Press, 1954.

Ferguson, Arthur Bowles. *The Indian Summer of English Chivalry: Studies in the Decline and Transformation of Chivalric Idealism*. Durham, N.C.: Duke University Press, 1960.

Greaves, Margaret. *The Blazon of Honour: A Study of Renaissance Magnanimity*. London: Methuen, 1964.

Hyma, Albert. *The Christian Renaissance*. 2d ed. Hamden, Connecticut: Archon Books, 1965.

Isler, Alan David. "The Allegory of the Hero and Sidney's Two Arcadias." *Studies in Philology* 65 (1968): 171–91.

Leube, Eberhard. *Fortuna in Karthago: die Aeneas-Dido-Mythe Vergils in den romanischen Literaturen vom 14. bis zum 16. Jahrhundert*. Heidelberg: Carl Winter Universitätsverlag, 1969.

Lewis, Clive Staples. *The Allegory of Love*. Oxford: Oxford University Press, Clarendon Press, 1936.

McNamee, Maurice Basil. *Honor and the Epic Hero*. New York: Holt, Rinehart and Winston, 1960.

Mazzeo, Joseph Anthony, ed. *Reason and the Imagination*. New York: Columbia University Press, 1962.

Painter, Sidney. *French Chivalry: Chivalric Ideas and Practices in Medieval France*. Baltimore, Md.: the Johns Hopkins University Press, 1940.

Patchell, Mary Frances Corinne. *The Palmerin Romances in Elizabethan Prose Fiction*. New York: Columbia University Press, 1947.

Reynier, Gustave. *Le Roman sentimental avant l'Astrée*. Paris: Armand Colin, 1971.

Rose, Mark. *Heroic Love*. Cambridge, Mass.: Harvard University Press, 1968.

Schücking, Levin Ludwig. *Die puritanische Familie*. Bern: Francke, 1964. (English translation by Bernard Battershaw, London: Routledge, 1969.)

Simon, Pierre Henri. *Le Domaine héroique des Lettres françaises.* Paris: Armand Colin, 1963.

Vogt, George MacGill. "Gleanings for the History of a Sentiment: Generositas Virtus, non Sanguis." *Journal of English and Germanic Philology* 24 (1925): 102–123.

Watson, Curtis Brown. *Shakespeare and the Renaissance Concept of Honor.* Princeton, N.J.: Princeton University Press, 1960.

Weise, Georg. *L'ideale eroico del Rinascimento e le sue premesse umanistiche.* Naples: Edizioni Scientifiche Italiane, 1961.

The Arming of an Archetype

Heroic Virtue and the Conventions of Literary Epic

John M. Steadman

T HE ARMING OF THE HERO is a favorite epic motif. Prominent in medieval romance, in the oral tradition of the Slavs, and in the heroic poems of Homer, Virgil, and their imitators, it can be traced back—by those who like to extend the frontiers of literary history into prehistory— to the archaic poetry of the Middle East, to the Babylonian creation epic and to the Canaanite epic of Baal. The metaphorical variants of this motif are almost as familiar—the "moral rearmament" of the virtues and vices in the *Psychomachia* and the spiritual rearming of the warfaring Christian by Erasmus and Spenser and St. Paul. Taking this trope as a point of departure, let us examine a few of the literary and ethical dilemmas that confronted the Renaissance poet in his attempts to invest his pattern hero not only with the martial arms of classical and romantic worthies, but also with the moral and theological virtues of the Christian knight. Like the divine smith who had forged the arms of Achilles and Aeneas, the heroic poet was an armorer. His task was a double one: to endow the conventional military hero with the panoply of the higher virtues, and to equip an ethical abstraction with the material weapons of the warrior prince. Teaching delightfully by force of example, he would on occasion employ the example of force. His labor (and it was a labor of Vulcan if not of Hercules) was to arm an archetype.

i

An Alexandrian poem, *The Argonauts*, has been called "an epic in search of a hero." [1] In Renaissance epic we may observe a comparable quest—the search of the martial hero for the norms of a higher heroism and (conversely) the quest of the heroic ideals for a champion worthy of bearing their image and their name. Inherent in the epic tradition was a series of inner contradictions that seemed almost impossible to resolve: the tension between the customary matter of the virtues and the subject matter of epic poetry; the tension between the ideal form of the epic and the ideal forms of the heroic virtues; the tension between the form and matter of the poem; and, finally, the tension between the aims of pleasure and instruction. Poetry was simultaneously the imitation of an action and the imitation of moral archetypes. While neo-Aristotelian poetics emphasized the plot as the very soul of the poem, the apologists for poetry as a moral discipline stressed its ability to imitate the Ideas of virtue and vice. This dual emphasis on plot-as-pattern and hero-as-pattern sometimes confronted the poet with divergent (though not irreconcilable) imperatives. Even though he might be theoretically committed to entertaining his audience through a narrative fable and to edifying them through moral exemplars, he found it difficult at times to pursue both of these objectives simultaneously.

In the first place, it was hard to excite interest in the fortunes of an abstract idea. To the historian of ideas, the adventures of an archetype may indeed be the fabric of romance, the clash of concepts in a dialectical battle a far more absorbing encounter than the clatter of lance against shield or sword against sword. The duel of intellects in formal disputation and debate, or the struggle of self against self in meditative combat, may appear far more engaging than an ordeal by arms in the lists. To unhorse an idea in learned controversy may seem a greater and far more praiseworthy exploit than to unseat an antagonist at a joust or tournament. But a Renaissance epic poet and his audience might view the matter differently. It is easier to become involved in the fortunes of Orlando and Angelica or Scudamour and Amoret than in the hopes and perils of an abstraction. In a battle scene, one can muster up little sympathy for the wounds (however deadly) of a bloodless and fleshless idea.

Secondly, even though the poet might recognize the close

relationships between logic and poetry, he was usually compelled to acknowledge that their methods were by no means the same. Though Milton's *Fuller Institution of the Art of Logic, Arranged after the Method of Peter Ramus* quoted passages from poets and orators to illustrate the principal *topoi* for argument, he was fully aware that the method of the poet—simple, sensuous, and passionate—differed as significantly from that of the dialectician as the open palm of rhetoric from the logician's clenched fist. As he observed near the end of his treatise, poets and orators may follow the analytic method when they set out to teach an auditor easily and clearly, but "*they do not always move in it and insist on it.*" When the audience is to be "*allured with pleasure or some stronger impulse by an orator or a poet . . . a crypsis of method will usually be employed,*" and the "*order of things will be inverted.*" Their "own doctrine of method," Milton concludes, "is to be turned over to the orators and poets" themselves—"or at least to those who teach oratory and poetics." [2]

Similarly, though Tasso regarded poetry as subordinate to dialectics (insofar as the poet aimed at probability and verisimilitude) or to logic,[3] he was equally conscious of the difference between arguing a proposition and imitating an action. As most Renaissance poets would have acknowledged, the movement of a formal syllogism from premises to conclusion through manipulation of a middle term is a very different sort of progression from the movement of a poetic fable through *its* beginning and middle to its probable or necessary end. The structure of logical thought and the structure of narrative action remain fundamentally distinct even when they are employing the same concepts.

Among the outstanding features of the Renaissance heroic tradition are: first, the proliferation not only of epic poems but (more notably) of epic theories; second, the tension between classical ideals of the heroic poem and the conventions of the flourishing vernacular romance; third, the ambiguous and controversial relationship between the aesthetic aims of heroic poetry and its moral or religious ends; fourth, a predominantly normative and "idealistic" approach to the definition of the epic genre and the character of the "epic person"; and, finally, the

variety of alternative norms or archetypes available both for
the hero and for the heroic poem. The range and diversity of
Renaissance heroic ideals aggravated the problem of accommodating them to an epic action. Not all modes of heroism lent
themselves with equal facility to the requirements of narrative
structure or the traditional techniques of epic presentation. In
varying degrees the conventions of literary epic itself tended
(paradoxically) to "screen out" the values of the "higher
heroism."

By definition, the heroic poem was devoted to the imitation
of heroic action and heroic virtue—and to the praise of "godlike men." Traditionally, these were men of war—military
leaders and princes. Their characteristic virtues were martial
valor joined with tactical cunning or strategic prudence; and the
actions in which they displayed these qualities were military
enterprises. They belonged to a warlike (and frequently a
courtly) culture, and the poetry dedicated to their exploits was
often addressed to a similar society—to an aristocratic audience
upon whose favor the poet himself might be dependent for
patronage.

This conception of the epic as an aristocratic genre portraying the *ethos* of a military elite and directed to a ruling class
of warriors is common to both oral and literary epic—although
this distinction would not have held the same meaning for a
Renaissance critic as for a twentieth-century scholar familiar
with the researches of Milman Parry and Albert B. Lord. In a
society where poet and audience shared the same heroic values
as those of the epic protagonists themselves, there would have
been little real tension between epic and heroic traditions: the
poetic image would have tended to coincide with the cultural
ideal of the hero. The epic poem could serve as mirror, vehicle, and norm for values that were not only traditional in the
society, but were still widely accepted and commonly believed.

Nevertheless, like all other sublunary things, the epic tradition was subject to change—to generation and corruption—and
(inevitably) to revaluation. The Homeric poems themselves
(it has been suggested) reflect a "reconception" [4] of more primitive heroic tales—and, perhaps, an implicit critique of the older
epic heroism. Virgil's epic, in turn, represents a revaluation of

the Homeric *ethos*. At the hands of Milton and Tasso, both Virgilian and Homeric ideals underwent a further revaluation. Once committed safely to paper, the oral epic had become a part of the literary tradition, serving as a potential model for poems composed under radically different circumstances and addressed to audiences reared in very different cultures. Surviving the society that had created it, the Homeric epic had become the cultural heritage of less martial classes in more literate societies; it belonged to an audience of philologists and antiquarians, philosophers and rhetoricians who might treasure it for meanings the poet himself had never intended and for values alien to its original audience.

Even in classical antiquity Homer's poetry had been reinterpreted by Stoics and Neoplatonists repelled by the violence of an earlier heroic age; in their hands it became a vehicle for natural and moral philosophy and for the values of a philosophical heroism. The heroic concept had outgrown the heroic song; the epic itself needed to be transformed from within, reinterpreted and thoroughly moralized in order to accommodate newer and more spiritual ideals.

In many Renaissance epics one encounters significant disparities between the heroic values conventional in the epic tradition and those of the poet's own society—tensions between the traditional *ethos* of the epic hero and the norms of the "higher heroism." [5] Epic and heroic traditions were manifestly at odds, and the task of reconciling them—the problem of harmonizing their conflicting values within a unified poetic structure—was rather like trying to square the circle.

ii

It is one of the ironies of heroic poetry that it should sometimes obscure the very concept that it professes to illustrate. In attempting to subject a heroic action to the requirements of epic form, the poet might feel compelled to modify his own conceptions of heroic virtue; he could distort his idea of the hero in the very process of embodying it in a heroic image. However lofty or however brutal the writer's ideas of heroic virtue might be, he must somehow present them within the framework of an intelligible story, and he must also accommodate them to the tastes of his audience. If his readers expected entertainment, he could not afford to bore them with excessive moralizing. If they expected high seriousness, he could not satiate them with frivolities. If Achilles seemed too savage for their tastes, and Odysseus too crafty, he must temper his images of Homeric types with Renaissance chivalric ideals and the values of a spiritual aristocracy—a *Christiana nobilitas.*

Though the epic hero might sometimes defy human and divine ordinances, he could not consistently violate the principles of epic poetry. His character and actions alike must inevitably be conditioned by the demands of the narrative mode. Let us suppose, however, that the poet (and perhaps his audience as well) actually regards martial fortitude as inferior to Stoic and Christian patience, and that he really prefers the speculative wisdom of the philosopher or the intuitive vision of the saint to the warlord's strategic cunning. Let us assume that he really esteems the intellectual and theological virtues as proper to a higher heroism than physical valor. How is he to portray these loftier virtues in poetic form? As a narrative poet, he is committed to depicting them in and through an epic action. If he celebrates the "better fortitude" of patience and heroic martyrdom—an inner strength manifested in passion rather than action and through suffering rather than doing—he must organize his plot around heroes who do not primarily *act,* but are *acted upon.* If he portrays a contemplative heroism—tested through intellectual exercise rather than in deeds—he must nevertheless construct his narrative fable as an *imitatio actionis,* the imitation of an action. Moreover, unless he deliberately breaks with the established epic tradition and rejects a martial subject, he must depict these higher virtues in a predominantly military context.

At this stage, however, another difficulty arises. Though wars may be the conventional subject matter of heroic poetry, they are not necessarily the most suitable matter for heroic virtue. According to both classical and Christian ethics, the various categories of virtue and vice possessed their own appropriate subject matter, in which they were properly tested, perfected, and exercised. The most suitable matter for illustrating one virtue was not necessarily the matter best fitted for exhibiting a different virtue. One did not normally test temperance on a battlefield, for instance, nor valor at a banquet. Similarly, although martial combat could exercise fortitude and even a certain kind of prudence, it was by no means the most appropriate vehicle for the majority of the higher virtues.

Nevertheless, as long as the poet retained a martial argument, this could profoundly influence his portrait of the higher heroism. Whatever spiritual excellencies he might wish to attribute to his hero, the actual victory must be won on the battlefield through force of arms; it would usually appear to have been achieved less by superior faith or charity or righteousness than by superior tactical skill, agility, and physical strength.

To portray effectively the values of the higher heroism, the poet must somehow introduce the actual *matter* of these virtues into the framework of his epic plot, contriving narrative situations that could adequately and appropriately test these qualities—manipulating incidents and arranging circumstances in order to emphasize loftier motives than wrath, ambition, and lust for glory. In such instances the hero's moral decisions—in some hermit's cell or lady's bower—could conceivably rival or even outweigh his *aristeia* on the battlefield. His inner motivation could become as significant as the external proofs of his valor, and the ends for which he fought more notable than his actual skill in combat. Moral crisis could thus become more decisive than the crisis of battle, and the hero's self-mastery more important than his mastery of arms. For Virgil, Aeneas's piety was more significant than his martial fortitude; and for the modern reader his encounters with Dido and the Cumaean Sibyl overshadow his duel with Turnus. In Renaissance epic, likewise, the divinely-ordained ends for which the hero contended and the ethical motives underlying his commitment to his enterprise could divert emphasis from the physical means whereby he secured his victory—his "gorgeous arms" and his mastery of the techniques of dissection—to his spiritual arms and moral prowess—to the valor and heroism of the mind.

The inherent tensions within the Renaissance heroic tradition —between active and contemplative virtues, acquired and infused virtues, moral and theological virtues; between ideals of the hero as destroyer and benefactor, philosopher and conqueror, inventor and orator, ascetic and lover, martyr and Machiavellian prince—tended to heighten the technical problems that confronted the epic poet in choosing an argument, in adapting it to the formal demands of a narrative plot, and in finding a protagonist strong enough and wise enough to sustain the ethical burden of a pattern-hero. Though Renaissance authors were not equally sensitive to these tensions between conflicting conceptions of the heroic *ethos*, and though some were content to ignore them altogether, Milton and the more "sage and serious" poets among his precursors were acutely aware of these problems and attempted in various ways to resolve them.

iii

Allegorical interpretation had been a convenient and customary refuge for classical moralists dissatisfied with the brutish and sensual *ethos* of the older epic heroes; among Renaissance poets and critics it was still a standard technique for converting the heroic poem into a vehicle for moral philosophy. By this means Sophists and Stoics, Neoplatonists—and even Christian bishops like Eustathius—had rendered Homer's heroic images acceptable to a more fastidious age.[6] Other exegetes had performed a comparable charity for Virgil, moralizing the egregiously moral *Aeneid* and accentuating the piety of its notoriously pious hero. In Renaissance epic and romance, lapses from moral decorum or from probability had been rationalized as allegory and justified on the grounds of their hidden meaning. In editions of Ariosto, Tasso, Graziani, and other Renaissance poets, allegorical commentaries became—not surprisingly—a standard bibliographical feature. Gratifying the contemporary taste for mysteries and enigmas, they could also help to forestall hostile criticism.

For the poet who desired to adapt epic conventions to higher ethical norms the allegorical method offered distinct advantages. Though poetic conceptions of the traditional subject matter of epic narrative and philosophical doctrines concerning the appropriate matter of the virtues remained separate and distinct in theory, they could nevertheless be made to coincide in poetic allegory by superimposing one meaning upon the other.

By exploiting the imagery of the *Psychomachia*, the epic narrator could effectively portray the combat of the virtues and
vices (or the struggle of the soul against world, flesh, and
devil) through the traditional symbol of a military enterprise.
Martial combat could function symbolically as an extended
metaphor for spiritual combat; the crisis on the battlefield
could serve as a concrete image for the crisis in the human
soul. Through the double vision of the allegorist, the values
of the warrior could be transformed into those of the moral
philosopher; and the essential outlines of an ethical system
could be compressed into a poetic fable. Through the process
of poetic hermeneutics both levels of meaning—physical and
spiritual conflict—could be firmly integrated within the framework of a single poem.

Recent criticism has wisely alerted us to the hazards of anticipating a one-to-one correspondence between events on the
literal and the allegorical level. The coincidence of meanings—
like the coincidence of contraries—is (it would appear) occa-
sional rather than systematic. On occasion the narrative fiction
becomes translucent, like the glaze on a Chinese bowl; the ideal
meaning under the surface becomes visible, like the ideogram
incised by the potter or the design in underglaze blue. As an
instrument of moral philosophy (as in theory it claimed to be)
the allegorical method could be eminently successful in com-
municating abstract ideas through concrete forms, in giving
definition and focus to a single isolated concept, in emphasizing
its interrelationships with allied concepts, and in clarifying its
meaning by opposing it to its logical contrary. In scholastic
logic it was axiomatic that the meaning of a given term could be
made more evident by juxtaposing it with its opposite, and both
poet and rhetorician were equally conscious of the persuasive
force of contrary examples. For writers who desired to retain
the conventional epic argument of warfare, the allegorical
method permitted a sharper and more systematic concentration
on the *idea* of heroic virtue and on the dialectical conflict with
its contraries.

Though the allegorical mode might enable the poet to overcome the disparity between martial and ethical content and to
present the trial of virtue in and through the trial at arms, it

did not provide an easy solution to problems of structure. It was difficult to present the scholastic subtleties of formal ethics through heroic poetry, through a medium that was not only simple, sensuous, and passionate, but also demanded a special kind of structure inherited from classical epic, from medieval romance, or from both. Despite the popularity of moral allegory during the Renaissance, it rarely influenced epic structure to the extent that it had affected the structure of medieval poetry. Even though allegorical episodes are fairly common not only in the chivalric epics on Orlando but also in classicizing epics like Trissino's *Italia Liberata,* they remain, as a rule, isolated episodes in an action conceived rather as fictionalized history or fable than as a sustained metaphor. *Parts* of the Renaissance epic are conceived allegorically, but rarely the poem as a whole. Although Tasso and Graziani offered allegorical explanations that comprehended the entire poetic fable—interpreting the principal actions of *Jerusalem Delivered* and *The Conquest of Granada* as symbolic images of the pursuit of felicity—neither allegory is truly organic or intrinsic to the poem itself. To the contrary, both allegories appear to be *ex post facto* rationalizations, like earlier attempts to moralize the *Iliad,* the *Odyssey,* and the *Aeneid.* Formally and structurally, both of these Renaissance poems are essentially classical epics; both have adapted the argument of a Holy War and the magical and erotic paraphernalia of the romance to a formal structure based on Homer and Virgil.

Spenser's epic reflects a rather different treatment of the allegorical mode. Unlike the epics of Tasso and Graziani, the *Faerie Queene* is conceived and executed virtually throughout as allegory; it requires an allegorical interpretation for the full appreciation of the story. Nor are its allegorical patterns merely episodic, like Trissino's allegory of Acratia or Tasso's allegory of Fortuna. In varying degrees and with varying success, Spenser has attempted to organize each book around a particular virtue associated with a particular champion, contriving the various episodes within this book in such a way as to exhibit the attributes of this virtue, its association with related virtues and their goals, and its opposition to its contrary vice or vices. Moreover, the comprehensive nature of Magnanimity—a virtue that, like *Virtus Heroica* and *Caritas,* includes the totality of the virtues—is concretely demonstrated through the role of Prince Arthur (or Magnificence) and his intervention in the actions of the various books devoted to more specialized virtues. In linking together the separate books of his epic through the person of Arthur, through the Order of the Knights of Maidenhead, and through the final—unwritten—scene at Gloriana's court (where all of the principal champions set out on their respective quests), Spenser not only endeavored to combine the variety of the romantic fable with the unified plot structure of classical epic; he also succeeded, in large part, in fusing ethical structure with narrative structure, in accommodating a pattern of ideas to the pattern of incidents and a pattern of incidents to a pattern of ideas.

Nevertheless, there were major limitations to the exploitation of allegory in heroic poetry. Even in the lifetime of Spenser and Tasso, the allegorist was being steadily forced upon the defensive; and this attack was based on moral grounds as well as on grounds of poetic theory. Tasso had argued that the poet ought to delight through his imitation and instruct through his allegorical content; other writers had similarly exhorted the reader to look beneath the veil of the poetic fable to the latent moral sense. Underlying these exhortations was a *topos* that could be traced back to Lucretius and beyond—the conception of the poet as a physician of the soul, and of poetry itself as a honeyed medicine or sugared pill. To these arguments a churlish moralist might reply that the poet was *not* a licensed pharmacist and that his apothecary's shop was crammed with strange and even monstrous remedies—dragon's bones, Chimaera's skins, and even the manifold scalps of the Hydra. Moreover, in compounding his medicines, he usually mixed his ingredients wrongly. Instead of mingling profit and pleasure in equal proportions, he often neglected the *utile* for the *dulce,* the useful for the sweet. The medicinal element was minimal, and the sugar coating infected with vice. Instead of a wholesome pill, he offered his feverish patient an envenomed sweetmeat, a poisoned bonbon.

As the allegorical method had been closely associated with the romance, it inevitably became an issue in the critical controversies of the period. The moral justification of the romance

—and perhaps its chief defense—rested largely on the value
of pleasing fictions as a vehicle for wholesome truths. Beneath
the amours of cavaliers and ladies and the mutual dissections of
fabled knights in battles feigned, the reader was encouraged
to search for a hidden moral; even the improbabilities of the
romantic plot could be rationalized as allegory. On the literal
level, however, the martial and amorous adventures of chivalric epic and romance— their images "of dames, of knights, of
arms, of love's delight,/Of courtesies, of high attempts"—were
vulnerable to the same accusations that Ascham levelled against
Malory's romance, charges of "open mans slaughter and bold
bawdrye." Ariosto might identify Angelica's ring with reason
and suggest that to a judicious reader capable of penetrating
beneath the surface of the fiction to its hidden meaning, much
that seemed "brutto e rio" would appear "bello e buono"—but
this assertion did not protect him against accusations of immo-
rality and improbability. Although Tasso professed to "Anoint
with sweets the vessel's foremost parts" and thus beguile his
audience into swallowing its "potions sharp," he did not manage
to deceive all of his readers, and some of them protested vio-
lently against this mixture of "fictions light . . . with truth
divine." In the eyes of "Stoicke censours," the "Fierce warres
and faithfull loves" of Spenser's epic definitely did *not* "moralize his song." On the contrary, to hostile critics they were
dangerous frivolities—meretricious baits that could seduce his
younger and frailer readers from the arduous trail of virtue into
the smoother ways of dalliance; the opening stanza of Book IV
of *The Faerie Queene* shows Spenser's concern about such critics:

> The rugged forhead that with grave foresight
> Welds kingdomes causes, and affaires of state,
> My looser rimes (I wote) doth sharply wite,
> For praising love, as I have done of late,
> And magnifying lovers deare debate;
> By which fraile youth is oft to follie led,
> Through false allurement of that pleasing baite,
> That better were in vertues discipled,
> Then with vaine poemes weeds to have their fancies fed.

In the long run, however, the censures of literary critics and
the changing tastes of the poet's audience were largely re-

sponsible for undermining the allegory. The romance itself was under attack for disregarding unity of action, for basing its arguments on fables rather than on history, for violating decorum in persons and style, and for failing to observe verisimilitude and probability. Its apologists protested in vain that it was legally exempt from the laws governing the epic; that fiction could be more instructive than history; that variety gave more pleasure than formal unity; and that the romantic poet addressed his fantasies to the imagination, and their allegorical meaning to the reason. One of the crucial points at issue was whether violations of probability and verisimilitude could be justified on the grounds of allegory. In defending Dante's *Commedia,* Jacopo Mazzoni maintained that they could; the "impossible" might nonetheless be perfectly "credible" by virtue of its allegorical content.[7] Tasso's theory permitted ample scope for allegory,[8] but nevertheless demanded verisimilitude and probability in the poet's "imitation."[9] A taste for "Tourneys" and "Trophies" and "enchantments drear,/ Where more is meant than meets the ear" persisted well into the seventeenth century; but the climate in which it struggled to survive became progressively colder and more inclement. Neo-Aristotelian and Horatian criticism left little room for allegory; and it was the rationalistic approach to poetic imitation—the demand for probability and verisimilitude—that eventually triumphed.

The allegorical mode (it would appear) was better suited to the narrative method of the romances than to the plot structure of epics composed on classical models. Its value as a vehicle for ethical concepts depended largely on carefully contrived situations: particular scenes and episodes in which the personified virtue (or its champion) formed alliances with related virtues or decisively defeated a contrary vice. As an imitator of abstract ideas in concrete forms, the allegorist achieved the ethical intent of his art most effectively by sharply differentiating a single concept and subsequently tracing its operation through various situations that could systematically analyze and symbolically clarify its logical relationships to other moral categories. This mode of presentation could be employed to best advantage in a loosely organized plot allowing a variety of individual scenes and episodes, rather than in a tightly structured narrative. It enabled the poet, from time to time, to isolate an idea and bring it temporarily into sharper focus through a visual tableau or verbal emblem. We see it at its best in such episodes as Scuda-mour's vigil in the House of Care and the metamorphosis of Malbecco from jealous husband into Jealousy itself. In the House of Care Spenser combines a wide variety of mythological and musicological themes in a single emblematic tableau of the jealousy of the lover; in the Malbecco episode he begins with a narrative *exemplum* of marital jealousy and ends with a per-sonification. The vice is no longer merely an adjunct of the man, but the man himself.

Though Milton would subsequently introduce allegorical episodes into a neoclassical epic, the fortunes of the allegorical method were too closely interlinked with those of the romance to flourish in the latter's decay. Critical attacks on the multiple actions of the romance, on its interwoven plots, and on its epi-sodic structure thus worked indirectly to the disadvantage of the allegorist. And, indeed, Milton himself would incur the censure of later critics for his allegory of Sin and Death.

iv

The allegorical mode, then, might enable the poet to display the higher virtues within a martial context, but on the literal level it left him vulnerable to hostile criticism; the *overt* moral content of his story and his manner of developing it had been attacked by moralists and literary theorists alike. There re-mained, however, still another alternative. The epic poet might reject a martial argument altogether and select a subject matter more appropriate for exercising the virtues of a perfect hero. To illustrate chastity, for instance, he might recast the stories of Susanna and Joseph in epic form. For the trial of heroic pa-tience he already possessed a divinely-inspired—and divinely-dictated—model in the biblical epic (or tragedy) of Job,[10] as well as a successful neo-Latin epic on the Passion of Christ. Sig-nificantly, one of Milton's juvenilia—an incomplete ode on the Passion—specifically commends Vida's heroic poem on this sub-ject ("Loud o'er the rest *Cremona*'s Trump doth sound"). The young Englishman still regarded himself as a novice; his pow-ers were not yet adequate for Calliope's trumpet, and for the present he must confine himself to lyric modes, the "softer strings of Lute, or Viol." Nevertheless, his "softer airs" are devoted to the same "Most perfect *Hero*" and the same heroic trial in "heaviest plight/ Of labors huge and hard, too hard for human wight." From Milton's point of view—and probably from Vida's—the Passion might seem to be an inevitable subject for sacred epic. It represented in a degree that no other argument could do, the *aristeia* of the "godlike man," for its protagonist was no less than the Logos itself in human form, the divine archetype embodied in a pattern hero. It contained the traditional heroic motifs of deliverance and public safety (*salus*), but transferred from the physical plane to the spiritual, and from the national dimension to the universal. It exhibited the norm of spiritual warfare and victory—combat against demonic principalities and dominions and triumph over Satan's monstrous vicegerents, Sin and Death. It illustrated the conventional heroic pattern of superlative merits acquired through arduous labors and rewarded with apotheosis or glorification. Finally, in the image of the Suffering Servant it exhibited the norm of heroic patience and the fortitude of the martyr. In a culture theoretically dedicated to the *imitatio Christi,* the epic quest for a perfect hero, embodying the heroic archetype in its perfection, would seem to point to the Passion itself as the epic argument *par excellence.* From a somewhat narrower viewpoint, indeed, this might appear to be virtually the only heroic argument. By one definition of the hero—as the son of a deity and a mortal— the epic person of Vida's *Christiad* and Milton's *Paradise Regained* would (in the strictest sense) be the *only* hero.

In this case the problem of finding a subject matter and an epic protagonist capable of sustaining the weight of the heroic virtues would appear to be largely resolved. As an incarnation of the Divine Image the epic person would be more than a symbolic representative of the heroic archetype, more than a personification of an abstract moral ideal, more than an idealized substratum for the virtues—more than an artificial hero created by the poet himself and crushed under the weight of the virtues with which the poet had invested him. In an epic on the Passion the epic hero would actually *be* the heroic archetype. Instead of merely embodying the ideal of *Virtus Heroica* or possessing the heroic virtues as adjuncts, he would *be* heroic virtue; in the language of the Neoplatonists, he would *be* the "exemplary virtues."

By taking the incarnate Logos as his epic person, the *poeta Christianus* was thus able to circumvent one of the major obstacles that confronted his contemporaries in their search for a pattern hero. On the other hand, he faced other difficulties that might prove equally embarrassing. Though these obstacles did not deter Diego de Hojeda, Robert Clarke, and later poets from essaying a *Christiad*, nor discourage Rapin from writing a short heroic poem on *Christus Patiens*, they may perhaps have deterred John Milton from writing an epic on the Passion. It is significant that though he extolled the Passion in both of his epics as the supreme heroic exploit—the *aristeia* of the most perfect hero—and though he once considered it as a subject for tragedy, he did not elect it as an epic argument. In *Paradise Lost* he centered his plot on the contrary pole of the Adam-Christ parallel—the disobedience of the first man and his expulsion from Paradise. In *Paradise Regained* he chose as his argument the temptation of Christ. Though both arguments were proleptic and derived their full significance from their relationship to the Passion, this event actually lay beyond the scope of his epic fable; the Passion was not the actual subject of either epic, nor did it fall within the time-span of the principal action. It could only be indirectly foreshadowed or directly prophesied. In a sense *Paradise Lost* is the *Iliad* of the "celestial cycle" [11]; it points forward to the saga of redemption in roughly the same way that (for a Renaissance audience, reading Homer in the light of Virgil) the action of the *Iliad* points forward to that of the *Aeneid* and to the foundation of new and greater dominions in the West by Brutus, Francus, and other exiled Trojan heroes. (Indeed Milton himself, in his description of Eve, introduced an allusion to the Judgment of Paris.) Just as the destruction of Troy prepares the way for the foundation of Rome and the establishment of Troynovant—British Troy—Adam's exile from Paradise through disobedience sets the stage for Christ's establishment of a new and happier Paradise within and the triumph of the Church, the *regnum Dei* or kingdom of Heaven. *Paradise Regained*, in turn, as an ordeal

of initial choice confronting the youthful hero at the commence-
ment of his heroic career, bears essentially the same relationship to Christ's ministry and Passion that Hercules' Choice and
Scipio's Dream bear to the future exploits of these classical
worthies.

Perhaps the chief disadvantage of the Passion as an epic subject was the fact that the detailed narratives of the Evangelists
afforded the poet comparatively little scope for invention. In
the opinion of many Renaissance critics poetic "imitation" resided in the invention of probable circumstances—fictional incidents and details that would enable the poet to construct a well-
made plot and to develop his narrative with verisimilitude and
probability. Elaborating the suggestions he had found in Aristotle's poetic and logical treatises, Tasso had advised the poet
to select a subject matter capable of receiving the form or idea
of the heroic poem.[12] Ideally, this would be some history remote
and obscure enough to allow the poet ample license to invent or
feign,[13] though Tasso foresaw practical difficulties in a very ancient theme. Though Milton based his epic arguments on Scriptural authority—despite Tasso's admonition against a biblical
theme [14]—in both cases the textual accounts were sufficiently
brief and obscure to allow him full scope for inventing details
and organizing his material according to the formal "rules" of
the epic genre and the example of the ancients.

v

Early readers of *Paradise Lost* were sometimes perplexed as
to its genre—whether it might "be called an heroic poem" or
not—while others were merely irritated by this question. Addison preferred to "waive the discussion of that point," declaring
that nothing was "more irksome" than "general discourses, especially when they turn chiefly upon words." Those who denied
Milton's epic the title of heroic poem might "call it (if they
please) a divine poem." [15] In Jonathan Richardson's opinion,
the question was insignificant (" 'tis of no great importance
whether this be called an heroic or a divine poem, or only, as
the author himself has called it in his title-page, a poem").[16]
All the same, *Paradise Lost was*, in fact, heroic poetry—"properly and strictly heroic, and such Milton intended it, as he has

intimated in his short discourse concerning the kind of verse,
. . . as also in his entrance on the ninth book." Samuel Johnson
similarly dismissed the problem as irrelevant; the questions
"whether the poem can be properly termed *heroick*, and who
is the hero, are raised by such readers as draw their principles
of judgement rather from books than from reason." Like Richardson, he observed that though Milton entitled *Paradise Lost*
"only a *poem*," he "calls it himself *heroic song*." [17]

Nevertheless, from the point of view of the literary historian, the question of genre cannot be dismissed so lightly. In
an age when literary criticism was still a captive of its own inherited categories, still shackled within the theory of literary
kinds and formal rules, this issue was more than a verbal quibble. Unless Milton had altogether outgrown his earlier respect
for generic distinctions and the principles underlying the various literary species, the question of the genre of *Paradise Lost*
would have seemed far from insignificant to him. A full awareness of his innovations in heroic tradition—his variations on the
heroic image and his revaluations of epic heroism—would de-
pend, in large part, on his audience's recognition of the genre of
his epic on the fall. It is simultaneously (and perhaps paradoxically) heroic poetry and divine poetry—heroic inasmuch as its
protagonist is a man initially perfect, though capable of marring
his perfection, and divine, inasmuch as it draws its argument
from Scripture and consistently orders its plot *ad majorem
gloriam Dei*. Insofar as Milton's epic achieves a critique and
partial reorientation of the heroic tradition, it does so within
the framework of heroic poetry and through the conscious juxtaposition of human and divine merits.

Why the title pages of the first and second editions of *Paradise Lost* identified it simply as "A Poem" without further spe-
cifying its genre, and why *Paradise Regained* bore the same
innocuous and non-committal designation, remains uncertain.
Though Milton must have given his consent, the suggestion
could conceivably have come from someone else (possibly the
publisher) aware of what a contemporary audience expected
a heroic poem to be and reluctant to provoke critical attacks if
they could be avoided. To an audience nurtured on cavalier
epics and heroic plays the fall of man might seem, of all arguments, the least promising for heroic poetry; a title like "Para-

dise Lost. An Heroick Poem" might appear self-contradictory. Some of them might admire it as an ingenious paradox or an audacious oxymoron; but others might greet it as churlishly as that earlier generation of browsers who had encountered *Tetrachordon* on the book-stalls:

> Cries the stall-reader, bless us! what a word on
> A title page is this!

Perhaps it was Milton himself, rather than his publisher, who feared that the title "Heroic Poem" might invite ridicule and accordingly selected a more neutral term.

Once safely past the title page, however, the poet could afford to be less evasive. Both in the text of *Paradise Lost* and subsequently in his note on "The Verse" he explicitly identified it (as both Richardson and Johnson observed) as a heroic poem. In the opening lines of Book 9 he deliberately accentuated (and perhaps exaggerated) his break with the epic tradition. Man's disobedience and Heaven's anger constituted a higher argument than the wrath of Turnus and Achilles or Juno and Poseidon. Although warfare had hitherto been the "only Argument/Heroic deem'd," the battle episodes and banquet scenes conventional in heroic poetry had missed the essence of true heroism. They exhibited merely the baser "skill of Artifice or Office mean," not that "which justly gives Heroic name/ To Person or to Poem."

As an experienced polemicist Milton was fully aware of the value of an aggressive defense; in his *Apology for Smectymnuus,* his defenses of the English people, and in his *Pro Se Defensio,* he had conducted a series of raids into enemy territory and had returned with trophies that would have been the envy of any Jivaro tribesman: the scalps of Salmasius and Alexander More, the unkempt tresses of a disgraced serving girl, the crowned head of a British king, and the mitred crania of several English bishops. In defending his epic argument and his unrhymed verse he again undertook the offensive, directing his attack against the weaker spots in the tradition he was attacking. To a modern reader his arguments may appear slightly disingenuous; they are accurate only if one introduces the necessary qualifications that the poet himself cleverly avoided.

In the first place, his charge that warfare was the *only* argument hitherto regarded as heroic is an overstatement. Even though he may have regarded the creation epics of Tasso and DuBartas as divine poems rather than as heroic poetry, he must have known that numerous poets had already extolled the patience of martyrs or had turned (like himself) to the Scriptures for non-martial themes. He could hardly have forgotten his own eulogy of Vida's *Christiad*. If few of these works merited serious consideration, the defect resided in their quality rather than in their quantity. Milton's indictment of the epic tradition is valid only as a general statement covering the majority of heroic poems or (more narrowly) the comparatively small group of epics of truly outstanding quality. Most of the latter *were* martial epics. Horace's dictum concerning the proper subject for heroic verse—"the exploits of kings and captains and the sorrows of war" [18]—had passed virtually unchallenged. In this context Milton's break with the epic tradition in rejecting a military subject was fully as dramatic as he claimed it to be. Moreover, it also represented a reorientation of his own earlier views on the proper subject matter for epic poetry. Though his early plans for tragedies had indicated a pronounced preference for a biblical subject, his early statements concerning his epic ambitions had shown an equally marked preference for a national theme—the exploits of Brutus or Utherpendragon, Arthur or Alfred, or some other king or knight before the Norman Conquest. He had preferred a divine tragedy, but a national epic.[19]

Secondly, the characteristics of the martial epic that he found repugnant to his taste are typical rather of the romance than of the classical epic.[20] Although "Races and Games" are conventional in classical poetry, they usually occupy a minor part in the narrative action; they provide a temporary diversion— and sometimes comic relief—from the tensions of combat or the vicissitudes of a voyage. Other details,

> . . . tilting Furniture, emblazon'd Shields,
> Impreses quaint, Caparisons and Steeds;
> Bases and tinsel Trappings, gorgious Knights
> At Joust and Torneament; then marshal'd Feast
> Serv'd up in Hall with Sewers, and Seneshals . . .

belong primarily to chivalric romance. Fabulous knights and
fictitious battles are also more characteristic of romance than of
classical epic, but even in the romances they are not always fabulous. Behind the romanticized Rolands and Olivers and Charle-
magnes there generally remained a shadow of historical truth.
The charge that the martial epic neglected the "better fortitude" of patience and martyrdom for an inferior mode of heroism is, on the whole, just; and it effectively diagnoses one of
the principal ethical defects of the conventional epic subject.
This accusation, however, serves rather to deflate the traditional
epic argument than to support Milton's own choice of subject.
Despite the emphasis it receives in various episodes of Milton's
poem, the martyr's patience is *not* the central theme of *Paradise
Lost*. The crucial temptation scene, on which the plot turns,
centers upon the trial of obedience (or, more broadly, constancy, loyalty, and love). Though the heroism of the martyr
is depicted in other heroes—in the Son's *kenosis* [21] as Suffering
Servant, in Abdiel's solitary defense of truth against the scorn
of multitudes, and in the constancy of the "one just man"
against the contumely of the world—this is not the principal
virtue subjected to trial in the temptation of Adam and Eve.

As a heroic poem, *Paradise Lost* would inevitably be judged
by the "rules" of its genre, measured against contemporary
ideals of the epic and against classical and modern examples. It
belonged to a well-established (though sometimes ambiguously
defined) tradition and would be read in the light of this tradition. During a century or more of sustained debate over the
norms of heroic poetry and the relative merits of Homer and
Virgil, Ariosto and Tasso, and other ancients and moderns,
critical readers had developed a sharp eye for apparent violations of the "rules" and for variations within the tradition itself. Milton could expect his readers to approach his poem both
as a sacred epic in the tradition of divine poetry and as a heroic
poem in the tradition of Homer and Virgil and Tasso. Insofar
as his poem broke with the epic tradition in choice of subject,
it behooved him to define its relationship to the tradition and
to justify his innovation. This he did, with no little rhetorical
ingenuity, in the passage we have just examined. His *apologia*,
however, did not explore the full extent of his innovations on

the epic tradition. These apparently went far beyond his rejection of a martial argument and his substitution of the wrath of the biblical God for the rage of fabulous divinities and legendary heroes. They involved a reconception of the pattern hero and the role of the epic person. In comparison with Godfrey and Prince Arthur, with Odysseus and Aeneas—and indeed even with Achilles—Adam seems a significantly different kind of epic protagonist.

Theoretically, the Renaissance epic attempted to form an image of heroic virtue, exhibiting this ideal in the person and actions of the epic protagonist. It was within this frame of reference that critics approached the epics of Homer and Virgil and the heroic poetry of their own contemporaries. Poems were judged not only on qualities of style and structure, but also on the comparative merits of their heroes. If Odysseus was a more perfect hero than Achilles, then the *Odyssey* came closer than the *Iliad* to achieving a principal end of heroic poetry—the creation of a heroic exemplar. By the same line of reasoning the *Aeneid* could seem "more heroic" than Homer's epics, and the *Gerusalemme Liberata* superior as heroic poetry to all three.

The moral quality of its protagonist was, of course, merely one of several criteria by which an epic poem might be judged. Renaissance theorists were quite aware that Aristotle had regarded plot as even more important than character, and that pleasure and profit—literary and ethical values—were not precisely the same thing.[22] Nevertheless, they were also conscious of the interrelationships between moral and aesthetic criteria and between character and action. Just as the quality of the epic action partly conditioned the reader's response to the poem, so the quality of the hero's virtue partly determined the quality of his deeds. Heroic action sprang from heroic character; heroic virtue could best be tested and illustrated in and through a heroic enterprise. The epic poem thus provided a dynamic portrait of heroic virtue in action. The heroic image was kinetic energy rather than static power.

The same critic who regarded the plot as the "soul" of the poem (and the chief source of aesthetic pleasure) might simultaneously regard the heroic image as the *raison d'être* of the epic narrative, and the principal source of its ethical value.

Though few theorists would have maintained that the literary merits of a heroic poem depended altogether on the moral qualities of its hero, the majority would have regarded these factors as closely interlinked. Other things being equal (some of them would have argued), the nobler the epic hero, the nobler the epic poem.

Milton himself had formerly sought an epic protagonist in whom he might "lay the pattern of a Christian *Heroe*," [23] and he could expect his readers to look for a pattern hero in *Paradise Lost*. They *did* look—and they disagreed sharply as to what they had found. To some it appeared that Milton had, consciously or unconsciously, taken the devil for his hero. [24] For others the hero was the Son of God. [25] For a third group the hero was Adam. [26] This variety of critical responses is interesting for the light it casts on the actual flexibility of neoclassical criticism in spite of the external rigidity of its methods and the derivative character of its terminology. The point at issue was not as trifling or irrelevant as several of them declared it to be. For many Renaissance theorists it would have seemed a question of primary importance; and for Milton himself (who had formerly written confidently of "that sublime art which . . . teaches what the laws are of a true epic poem," who had once endeavored to find a British king or knight capable of embodying the pattern of a "Christian *Heroe*," who could still condemn the subject matter of martial epic and chivalric romance as wanting "that which justly gives Heroic name/To Person or to Poem," and who would commend "*Sion*'s songs" for praising God and "Godlike men" aright, "The Holiest of Holies and his Saints") it would have been no insignificant quibble. Their disagreement on the hero of *Paradise Lost* may be partly due to the ambiguity of their critical terminology; the word "hero" was itself equivocal, and Milton's critics themselves sometimes employed it in different senses. Moreover, some of them were reluctant to face squarely the tragic implications of Milton's fable and the coincidence of the epic hero with the tragic hero; they were still hampered by the critical commonplace that the action of an epic hero must end fortunately. [27] (Milton's does—ultimately—through the paradox of the fortunate fall; but Adam's restoration lies beyond the scope of the fable itself and it is achieved through the merits of a different hero, "one greater Man"). Primarily, however, their division points to something new and unusual in Milton's poem. He had somehow failed to meet the expectations that his readers customarily brought to the epic, and this failure could not be explained simply by his rejection of the customary martial argument. As the point at issue was the identity of the epic hero, the principal cause of the critic's uncertainty would seem to lie in Milton's variations on the conventional heroic image—in his unusual treatment of the heroic exemplar and the traditional pattern hero.

Part of the difficulty may have resulted from Milton's choice of theme, which permitted him only two human beings; he was compelled, therefore, to amplify his cast of characters with "machining persons"—divine and infernal spirits and personified abstractions. Nevertheless, the principal *locus* of his narrative action remains Paradise itself, the "Silvan Scene" in which the plot unfolds; and, for all the elaborate off-stage machinery, the focal point of the plot is a voluntary human decision, an act of disobedience springing from an act of *proairesis* [28] or moral choice. The central action is man's own action, and the epic person or principal hero is man himself—Adam as progenitor and type of the human race. Satan and the Son, on the other hand, are essentially "machining persons," and in the strictest sense neither of them can be regarded as a hero. Metaphysically they belong to spiritual orders higher than mankind; to mistake them for heroes (or "godlike *men*") is to miss the essential characteristic of the hero—that he is a man raised above the common lot of men by his supernatural parentage, his superlative virtue, or an immortality of glory and fame.

Adam is the epic person and "principal hero" of *Paradise Lost* but is he actually a *pattern* hero? On the one hand, he has been uniquely fashioned by God Himself—created perfect and possessing the divine image in its pristine excellence. He is therefore a unique kind of hero—heroic or "godlike" man in a sense that could not be applied to his posterity, conceived and born in guilt and bearing the hereditary deformity of sin instead of divine resemblance. On the other hand, the action that the poet has chosen to imitate is the hero's transgression. The epic person of *Paradise Lost* is a godlike man who forfeits the divine image, a perfect man who falls from his perfection, a hero stripped of his heroic virtue.

To be sure, Adam repents; and in the last books of the poem we may follow the stages of his inner regeneration. The pattern of the peccant hero who errs and subsequently repents of his error, is not uncommon in heroic poetry; and Milton's readers would have been familiar with this pattern in classical as well as in modern epic. Achilles' abstention from combat both on the island of Scyros and after his quarrel with Agamemnon had been interpreted in this light. Like Ulysses' sojourns with Circe and Calypso and Aeneas's affair with Dido, these episodes represented the obscuration of heroic virtue by unheroic leisure and "ignoble ease." The same pattern could be detected in Rinaldo's infatuation with Armida, Redcrosse's bondage to Duessa, or Samson's seduction by Delilah. Adam's voluntary transgression through his passion for Eve could be read as another variant on the same pattern.

At this point, however, the resemblances cease. In the majority of cases the peccant hero recovers from his temporary lapse, resumes his heroic enterprise, and triumphs decisively over his adversaries. Achilles forsakes Scyros to join the Greek hosts at Troy; on a later occasion he renounces his anger against Agamemnon and returns to the battlefield to wreak havoc on the Trojan forces and to defeat their foremost champion. Odysseus resumes his journey to Ithaca, and Aeneas his voyage to Italy. Rinaldo returns to the crusade and wins the battle for Jerusalem. Lancelot rejoins Arthur to slay the enemy champion and conquer Avaricum.[29] Redcrosse resumes his enterprise, slays the dragon, and delivers a kingdom. Samson regains his heroic virtue and wins his greatest victory over the Philistines. Adam, on the other hand (as Dryden later complained) is driven from his castle "to wander through the world with his lady errant." [30]

It is hardly surprising that Milton's early critics found his variations on the conventional pattern hero disturbing—or that they should have set out, separately, like knights-errant on solitary quests—to locate the missing hero of the poem. Two of the "machining persons," Christ and Satan, had themselves become heroic exemplars, antithetical images of true and false heroism, and their operations had been invested with the imagery and structure of heroic enterprises. On the human level the epic action had been changed into a psychomachia,[31] a moral struggle within the human soul; on the supernatural level the epic machinery had been converted into a daemonomachia or a theomachy, a war of gods and angels. Although other epic poets before him—Homer and Virgil, Tasso and Camoëns—had relied heavily on supernatural forces in organizing and constructing their plots, Milton went far beyond his predecessors in his exploitation of epic machinery. In his hands it became a duel between superhuman combatants, divine and infernal antagonists in a spiritual and cosmic war.

Moreover, unlike the majority of epic poets, Milton had transferred the heroic enterprise from the epic protagonist to the machining persons. Instead of an enterprise planned and executed by the nominal hero of the poem, he gives us an exploit conceived and brought to fruition by his "infernal machine." It is Satan who plans and achieves the conquest that gives unity to the fable, and it is he who, of all the principal characters in the poem, bears the strongest resemblance to the conventional military hero. Though he is inevitably outwitted by Providence (for who can contend against omnipotence joined with omniscience?), Milton's devil is actually the first world-conqueror. One can sympathize (even though one cannot concur) with critics like Dryden who mistook him for the hero of the poem.[32] The Son, on the other hand, is the perfect image of godlikeness, the archetype of that divine virtue of which heroic virtue is only a shadow. Three of the crucial episodes of the poem, the history of the war of the angels, the creation of the world, and the prophecy of the Incarnation and Passion, are devoted to his *aristeiai*. Here again one may readily understand why critics should have mistaken him for the hero of *Paradise Lost*.

As pattern-heroes Milton's Christ and Satan exhibit moral extremes beyond the conventional opposition of virtue and vice or heroic virtue and brutishness. With their extension to the divine and diabolical planes, *virtus heroica* and *feritas* approach absolute zero; they tend to become perfect good and pure evil. On the human level they are more likely to be mixed: "human kind Cannot bear very much reality." [33]

Milton's epic person was nothing less than archetypal Man himself, the original Adam whose likeness all men had inherited by nature and could "put off" only by grace. For the conventional heroic image—an ideal pattern proposed for the reader's emulation—Milton had substituted the image of the "old man" (the "earthy" man) which the regenerate must reject in order to "put on" the image of the "new" and "heavenly" man. In the portrait of Adam before his fall readers would recognize an original perfection no longer accessible to his posterity, an image of what they *might* have been but never could be. In fallen Adam they would perceive an image of themselves—not a pattern of what they *should* be (as with the conventional epic hero), but a pattern of what they *are*. In Adam's gradual regeneration, culminating in recognition of his own frailty and of an ideal of perfection embodied in the Woman's seed, they might behold an external image of the regenerative process operative in themselves and also an example of faith. Taken together, the various facets of Milton's epic hero form a vivid exemplar of man's original dignity and his present misery, of his weakness and his dependency on divine grace, and of his future beatitude.

For the poet and his "fit audience" as for fallen Adam, awareness of the Fall and its spiritual and psychological consequences inevitably narrowed the possibility of heroic virtue and the scope of heroic action. To the natural man there remained little more than the shadow of true heroism. Perfection in action or in character, heroic virtues and meritorious deeds, the excellencies of the divine image—truth, wisdom, sanctity, and filial freedom—these lay inevitably beyond his grasp. His heroic exploits could not be true "acts of benefit," for they lacked solid virtue and essential goodness. His heroic virtues were splendid vices. Heroic activity itself became a pretentious charade: the shadow of heroic virtue pursuing the phantasm of false glory. In the context of the Fall, the heroic image could be little more than an empty mask, a shadow enclosed in armor or a "Headpiece filled with straw." [34]

The heroism of the natural man was specious. The true, substantial heroism was possible only for the regenerate, and in its fundamental principles this differed radically from the conventional epic heroism. Not only did it emphasize different virtues, but it rested on a different conception of man. If classical epic had overstressed the prowess of the martial hero, classical ethics had exaggerated the wisdom of the philosophical hero. "Ignorant of themselves" and of man's fall ("Degraded by himself, on grace depending"), the Greek philosophers had sought virtue in themselves, and "to themselves/All glory arrogate[d]." The ideals of the secular heroic tradition were not only vain and empty shadows; they were also a major obstacle to the realization of the true heroism. Hardening man's pride in his own powers and achievements, they encouraged him to trust in himself rather than in Providence, to rely on his own merits rather than on divine grace, to regard his heroic exploits as his own personal achievements, and to seek his own glory and fame.

For the "new man," on the other hand, heroism was conceivable only as a gift from a higher power; the regenerate man was heroic only by grace. He could become a hero, so to speak, by act of God, as an officer becomes a gentleman by act of Congress. The power and wisdom behind his noblest exploits were those of the Spirit; whatever glory his actions merited belonged properly to the deity who had inspired them. To act heroically he must act as the instrument and agent of the divine, renouncing the merits of his own actions, trusting no longer in his own strength and wisdom, but relying instead on the imputed obedience of "one greater Man." The precondition of the spiritual heroism of the regenerate is a self-emptying, a humiliation comparable to the *kenosis* of the divine exemplar, the filial Logos.

For Milton the true hero was the saint. The truest office of a poet was to praise God "aright" and "Godlike men,/The Holiest of Holies and his Saints." The core of heroic virtue was actually sanctity; and this was contingent theologically upon the process of regeneration (or sanctification).[35] This is the process we see at work in fallen Adam and fallen Samson, manifested through its customary effects—repentance and faith.

If the Fall had narrowed the scope for heroic activity, it had also created the possibility for a special kind of heroism—the patient fortitude of the martyr to truth. Just as Satan's rebellion had provided the occasion for Abdiel's heroic constancy, so Adam's revolt would establish the scene for the martyr's agony and triumph, the stage of a "perverted World." The corruption of man's nature would provide the occasions for martyrdom; the regeneration of man's nature would produce the martyr himself—and the victories of the "one just man."

In the eyes of its author *Paradise Lost* was a heroic poem, but against the background of the epic tradition it presents a singularly altered image of heroic virtue: its epic protagonist is the archetypal sinner. Its infernal machinery carries the burden of the epic enterprise and (like the pillars of some Philistine temple) the weight of the epic plot. Its divine machinery contains the perfect image of virtues "Above Heroic" and the promise of ultimate victories that lie far beyond the scope of the narrative action. Milton's epic (it would seem) not only undercuts the tradition of secular epic, but reduces heroic virtue itself to a contingency. If the hero's highest virtues and noblest actions really belong to the spirit, if he can acquire no valid merits by his own deeds, then the actual praise for his exploits belongs primarily to the divinity who had inspired and directed them. Heroic virtue becomes essentially a manifestation of divine virtue, heroic action the instrument of a divine action.

vi

Rejecting the argument of wars and altering the roles of epic hero and epic machines, Milton recentered the heroic fable on the temptation crisis.[36] Heroic obedience—heroic righteousness and heroic charity—would be tested and illustrated in moral combat. Nevertheless, the poet was still under the obligation of relating an action and constructing a fable in accordance with the principles of legitimate epic imitation. He must still present his temptation crisis within the framework of a narrative plot. The easiest formula was to organize the incidents through the conventional epic machinery[37]: divine or infernal councils, supernatural messengers, or allegorical abstractions. Milton had already exploited this method in expanding the material of the conventional gunpowder-plot epigram into a heroic (or mock-heroic) epyllion[38] and in constructing his masque at Ludlow around a central temptation with demonic machinery. He would utilize the same device in both of his epics, but with greater subtlety and ingenuity.

In a "brief epic" like *Paradise Regained* it was easier to construct a well-made plot around a temptation ordeal than in a "diffuse epic" like *Paradise Lost*. Nevertheless, even the shorter poem confronted Milton with problems of structure. His biblical sources contained three different (and more or less equally stressed) temptations. A lesser poet might have given them equal emphasis, portraying them in three equally balanced episodes and possibly compromising the integrity of the plot. Milton, on the other hand, managed to avoid an episodic organization and to achieve a unified and integrated narrative by subordinating the first and third temptations to the second, by expanding the second temptation to heighten the antithesis between secular and divine kingship,[39] and by linking them together so that each successive incident appeared to develop logically, with verisimilitude and probability, out of the preceding scene. In the first temptation Satan takes his point of departure from the baptism and proclamation scene—the Father's public declaration of his Son and heir—on the banks of the Jordan. The second temptation is linked through the banquet episode with the first and with the final scene of angelic ministrations. The third temptation crisis, motivated by Satan's frustrated rage, follows immediately upon the elemental violence of the storm scene.[40] The first temptation brings the contestants together in an initial encounter, accentuating and counterpointing the disguise-and-detection motif with a subtlety worthy of Homer's Odysseus. The third temptation not only heightens the narrative tensions already developed in the preceding episodes, bringing them to the point of highest suspense (the *summa epitasis*), but also contains a reversal contrary to expectation, and, perhaps, a recognition—a *peripeteia* combined with an *anagnorisis*. Out of the three discrete temptations that his sources afforded him, Milton has molded a "well-made" plot—a unified action progressing, with increasing suspense, from preliminary skirmish through extended moral victory to divine miracle.

Paradise Lost presented more formidable problems in narrative construction. Like other epic writers before him, Milton overcame some of these difficulties through the conventional techniques of epic construction: divine and infernal councils and emissaries, and prophetic or retrospective episodes in direct discourse. His principal solution, however, constituted a marked innovation on epic tradition. This was nothing less than to develop the role of his infernal emissary according to a narrative pattern normally characteristic of human heroes— a pattern common to protagonists as well as to antagonists. In conceiving and executing a martial enterprise—a war of conquest against a walled citadel—Satan has numerous parallels among epic protagonists: the Greeks at Troy, the Crusaders at Jerusalem, the Britons at Avaricum. As a military hero who penetrates an enemy stronghold in disguise and triumphs through ingenious stratagems and plausible deceptions, he recalls Odysseus and Milton's proposed epic on King Alfred. As an epic antagonist who provokes an unjust war against a hero favored by Providence, he resembles Turnus and the Gothic champions at Rome. Even though Milton has renounced a martial subject and centered his epic instead on moral combat and spiritual trial, he nevertheless constructs his narrative action in terms of a martial enterprise, conceived by a council of war and executed by tactical guile. Paradise is lost—and mankind ruined—by divine permission, human weakness, and infernal fortitude and cunning. This is the first —and archetypal—world conquest; whatever its eventual outcome it is initially Satan's victory.

vii

Having briefly considered the role of Milton's infernal machinery, let us turn to his divine machines. The loss of Eden is a temporary defeat for man and a Pyrrhic victory for Satan. Through the merits of "one greater Man" Satan will one day be decisively vanquished and man restored to a fairer Paradise. Satan indeed conquers the world, and will inhabit the air, but he cannot possess the happy garden. From the standpoint of Heaven the loss of Eden is a calculated loss. This temporary surrender of forested and mountainous terrain on the frontier has been foreseen; it is part of the celestial strategy for a total victory in the remote future. Before the Fall, Milton deploys his divine machines to hinder Satan's enterprise. Uriel warns Gabriel, who in turn dispatches his watch to apprehend the intruder; and the Eternal Father Himself drives the devil from Paradise by displaying a "celestial Sign." (Satan is apparently the archetypal astrologer.) Thereupon Raphael is sent to "admonish" Adam "of his obedience" in order "to render Man inexcusable." After the Fall, however, the celestial strategy becomes operative primarily in man's redemption—in the veiled prophecy of ultimate restoration through the Woman's seed, in the regeneration of Adam and Eve (manifested successively in their repentance and faith), and in Michael's survey of world history culminating in the *aristeia* of the future deliverer.

Though Milton has constructed his plot in terms of a holy war, representing his angels as armed warriors and (on occasion) God Himself as a man of war, he nevertheless preserves the essential distinction between military valor and the higher heroism. Satan is a conqueror; the Son and his elect are "more than conquerors." Satan seeks his own honor and glory; like the majority of Homeric heroes, he stands in fear of shame. The Son and his saints, on the other hand, voluntarily shun honor and embrace ignominy, renouncing their own glory for the glory of God. Satanic wrath is counterbalanced not only by divine wrath, but (more significantly) by divine charity. Because Milton's war is essentially a spiritual war, *psychomachia* and *theomachia* rather than a physical conflict, he can present it (paradoxically) as a war between war and peace, as a conflict between the forces of disorder and destruction and the powers of creation and order.

On the human level and on the infernal plane, their conflict appears as warfare. On the celestial level they are reconciled in the unity of the divine intelligence; they are structural elements in a providential design.[41]

Just as Milton's holy war comprehends the struggle between war and peace, his divine machinery comprehends both divine and infernal machines. Through the doctrine of permissive evil, the infernal strategy itself serves divine ends; and Satan's enterprise is an integral part of the providential design, a design reflected in the design and structure of the poem. The Father Himself is firmly in control, governing action and counter-action, supervising divine and infernal agents, inclining their wills to ends that He Himself has pre-ordained, and occasionally intervening directly to alter the course of battle by a divine miracle. In this context the only recourse for any hero who hopes for eventual victory is to ally himself with Providence, trusting unconditionally in divine wisdom and strength. The cardinal heroic virtues, accordingly, would appear to be obedience and faith, constancy and charity.

What happens to the heroic image in this context? In his archangelic rebel Milton constructs an ironically demonic image of the heroic warlord—the traditional conqueror-destroyer intent on glory and glorying in his strength. This pattern is consistently maintained even in the pseudo-hero's bestial disguises, and it is finally completed in his victorious return to Hell. Nevertheless, with equal consistency, Milton undercuts this image at crucial points in the narrative. At the very outset of his enterprise Satan encounters his deformed progeny, Sin and Death. His daughter bears the serpentine image that he must subsequently assume (though he does not yet foresee this future humiliation); and his own doom is inevitably linked with that of his monstrous son. The soliloquy on Mount Niphates, in turn, occurs immediately after Satan has completed a space journey that dwarfs the heroic voyages of classical legend and Renaissance epic—the exploits of Odysseus, Aeneas, and the Argonauts, and the navigations of Columbus and Vasco da Gama. In this scene the classical heroic values—the pursuit of honor and glory and dominion—are exposed as false and hollow; Satan faces—and recognizes—the reality of sin and guilt. His brush with the angelic guard brings further knowledge of the disfiguring effects of sin; he now learns that his glory has been visibly impaired. The sign of the Scales, in turn, reveals the limitations of his strength. After aspiring to equal his Creator, he discovers the finite, and conditional, powers of the creature. Finally, after completing the image of a triumphant world-conqueror, Milton abruptly shatters the heroic portrait (or heroic caricature). On previous occasions a divine miracle had put the devil to flight; on this occasion another miracle transforms the heroic image into an image of brutishness, the contrary of heroic virtue.

Punished in "the shape" in which he had sinned, Satan experiences public shame instead of expected triumph and applause. In this shrewdly timed *peripeteia* Milton has reversed the normal heroic expectations. Instead of the honor his exploits had apparently merited, the pseudo-hero is again brought face to face with the reality of sin; this time the knowledge of sin is brought home by its punishment.

In Adam and Eve the divine image—the essence of heroic virtue—is paradoxically destroyed through acts that themselves possessed heroic associations. Eve's aspirations for divine wisdom and fellowship with the gods resemble the ambitions of the Stoic and Neoplatonic hero and the flight scene in her dream possesses heroic as well as demonic prototypes. Though it recalls the delusions of witchcraft, it is equally reminiscent of the contemplative ascents of the classical sage and the apotheosized hero. Her readiness to test her virtue in moral combat against the Adversary links her, to a degree, with the woman warriors of classical and Renaissance epic.[42] The Vulgate had described her as a *virago* (Genesis 2:23)—a "heroine" or "female warrior"—and her tragedy stemmed in part from her desire to exercise her *virtù donnesca* rather than *virtù feminile*.[43] Adam's decision, in turn, to risk death rather than separation from his lady would be heroic in the context of chivalric romance. In both instances Milton creates a heroic image that results, paradoxically, in the obliteration of the divine image. In both cases the true image of heroic virtue is obscured and defaced by images of a conventional but spurious heroism.

In the final books of the epic the divine image is partly restored in hero and heroine alike, but neither embodies the image in its perfection. The true pattern of heroic (or divine) virtue lies in a pattern hero who rarely intervenes in the action on the human plane. (In the fable he descends once—to judge and to regenerate man—and in the angelic narratives twice—to create and instruct man—and afterwards to redeem him.) Otherwise, the pattern hero remains a "pattern laid up" in Heaven—to be revealed obscurely by types or more clearly through retrospective or prospective episodes. *Paradise Lost,* like *The Argonauts,* is (it would appear) "an epic in search of a hero."

viii

A few years ago a college lecturer, reading his examination papers after a talk on Renaissance epic and patronage, encountered a sentence that baffled him: "Two grandees were paragons of heroic breakdown." Who could these be? Essex and Don Carlos? Torquato Tasso? (but surely the latter's delusions of grandeur had never extended to the peerage). Or perhaps this was an allusion to some poetic hero: King Lear, or Antony, or Timon, or Tamerlane the Great? Or to the madness of Roland or Hercules, or to the debacle of Milton's heroic archangel? Upon checking his lecture notes the lecturer discovered the answer. What he had originally written was less enigmatic but also far less interesting; it was merely "*Few* grandees were paragons of heroic *virtue.*"

This was a happy error perhaps—a *felix culpa*—but I would prefer to regard it as an oracle. The undergraduate had obviously seen farther and more deeply than her instructor. She had recognized the tragic flaw in the Renaissance epic tradition under its deceptively magnificent facade—the breakdown of the epic hero under the strain of his quest for perfection; the dissolution of the heroic image under the stress of conflicting moral and aesthetic imperatives, the narrative requirements of a concrete action and the ethical demands of an abstract ideal. She had perceived the inner collapse of the heroic poem itself, with its inflated enterprises, inflated egos, and inflated styles.

The relationship between heroic idea and heroic image is only one of the problems that confronted the Renaissance poet in attempting to embody an ideal conception of heroic virtue in the protagonist of an epic action. In concentrating on three particular aspects of this problem, we have (I suspect) barely scratched the surface. We have had to neglect the variety of heroic ideals current in the Renaissance, and the range and diversity of Renaissance epic. Our findings have not been altogether encouraging. The purely martial epic could not, on the whole, cope successfully with the higher virtues, since it could not effectively portray the matter in which they could best be illustrated and tried. The allegorical epic possessed a technique for reconciling a martial subject with the actual matter of the virtues, but critical opinion was sometimes hostile both to allegory and to romance—the narrative genre probably best adapted to allegorical techniques. The epic centered primarily on moral combat encountered inevitable difficulties in the construction of the plot.

The difficulties in forming the image of a pattern hero were equally great. The martial hero could rarely provide a perfect exemplar of the higher heroism. The allegorical hero tended at times to become either a frivolous adventurer or a frigid abstraction. The Christian hero could meet the preconditions of the higher heroism only by renouncing his own virtues, his own glory, and his own heroic deeds. To achieve a balance between heroic image and heroic idea lay beyond the capacity of the majority of poets. In the martial hero, the image could all too easily obscure the idea; heroic virtue might be eclipsed rather than illustrated by the epic protagonist. In the allegorical hero there was an equal risk that the idea might overshadow the image. In the Christian hero, finally, the heroic image itself tended to vanish in an ideal of impossible perfection transcending the powers of the hero and the imitative craft of the poet. Fading away like some ancient soldier, the pattern hero became reabsorbed into the archetype. The heroic image became lost in the divine image; the heroic example was overshadowed by its divine exemplar. In Milton's hands (as one of his earliest critics surmised) the heroic poem had vanished imperceptibly into the divine poem.

Notes

1. Charles Rowan Beye, *The "Iliad," the "Odyssey," and the Epic Tradition* (Garden City, N.Y.: Doubleday, 1966), p. 210.

2. *Artis Logicae Plenior Institutio*, edited and translated by Allan H. Gilbert, in *The Works of John Milton*, edited by Frank Allen Patterson (New York: Columbia University Press, 1935), 11: 481–85.

3. Cesare Guasti, ed., *Le prose diverse di Torquato Tasso* (Firenze, 1875), 1:98–99 (*Discorsi del poems eroico*): "Dico adunque che senza dubio la poesia è collocata in ordine sotto la dialettica insieme con la retorica, la qual come dice Aristotele, è l'altro rampollo della dialettica facultà, a cui s'appartiene di considerare non il falso, ma il probabile. . . ." Tasso also suggests that poetry may be "compresa . . . sotto la logica" rather than "sotto la dialettica." All three parts of logic—demonstrative, probable, and "l'apparente probabile, ch' è il sofistica"—can be found in poetry; nevertheless "la perfetissima imitazione, o la propriissima specie della poesia, non si ripone sotto la sofistica, o nuova o antica ch' ella sia, ma sotto la dialettica."

4. Cedric H. Whitman, *Homer and the Heroic Tradition* (New York: Norton, 1965), pp. 154–55, 220.

5. See the *Times* (London) *Literary Supplement*, 8 February 1968, p. 134.

6. For Renaissance allegorical interpretations of Homer and Virgil, see Don Cameron Allen, *Mysteriously Meant: The Rediscovery of Pagan Symbolism and Allegorical Interpretation in the Renaissance* (Baltimore and London: The Johns Hopkins University Press, 1970), pp. 83–105, 135–62.

7. See Robert L. Montgomery, Jr., "Allegory and the Incredible Fable: The Italian View from Dante to Tasso," *PMLA* 81 (1966): 45–55; Allan H. Gilbert, *Literary Criticism: Plato to Dryden*, 2nd ed. (Detroit, Mich.: Wayne State University Press, 1962) pp. 365–88; Murray Krieger, "Jacopo Mazzoni, Repository of Diverse Traditions or Source of a New One?" in *Medieval Epic to the "Epic Theater" of Brecht*, edited by Rosario P. Armato and John M. Spalek (Los Angeles: Hennessey, 1968), pp. 97–107; Irene Samuel, *Dante and Milton: The "Commedia" and "Paradise Lost"* (Ithaca, N.Y.: Cornell University Press, 1966); and my "Allegory and Verisimilitude in *Paradise Lost:* The Problem of the 'Impossible Credible,'" *PMLA* 78 (1963): 36–39. In his *Della difesa della Commedia di Dante*, Mazzoni had elaborated Plato's distinction between icastic and phantastic imitation (in the *Sophist*) and Aristotle's distinction between dramatic and narrative modes of imitation into a complex poetic theory which classified poetry as a "subdivision of . . . sophistic," inasmuch as it paid "more attention to the credible than to the true. . . ." In his *Discorsi del poema eroico*, Tasso challenged this classification, arguing that poetry (or at least the most perfect poetry) belongs not to sophistic, but to dialectic or logic. Cf. Guasti, 1:98–100:

. . . ma 'l sofista, per giudizio d'Aristotle, pur ne' libri della sua Topica, non considera il probabile, ma il probabile apparente: cioè quello che non è veramente probabile, ma par ad alcuni probabile; . . . è dunque il sofista in ciò differente non solamente dal dialettico, ma dal poeta ancora, perciò che quello che per sè è probabile, quello è verisimile." Hence the poet ought to choose subjects that are in themselves probable: ". . . perchè 'l poeta, come ancora il dialettico, è diverso dal sofista più tosto per elezione che per facoltà; quinci avviene che 'l buon poeta si dee affaticare più volentieri di ciascuno altro intorno a' soggetti per sè probabili, come fece Omero, il qual nella persona d'Ettore volle dimostrarci che lodevolissima cosa sia il difender la patria; ed in quella d'Achille, che sia lodevolissima la vendetta, e da magnanimo, e per conseguenza giusta e favoreggiata da gli dei. Le quali opinioni, essendo senza fallo per sè probabili, son verisimili; e per artificio d'Omero divennero probabilissimi o provatissimi e similissimi al vero.

The most perfect poetry is not fantastic imitation, as Mazzoni had asserted, but the imitation of things that are or were or can be, like the Trojan war and Achilles' wrath and Aeneas's piety and the battles between Trojans and Latins:

Molto meno è vero quel che dice il Mazzone [*sic*], che la perfettissima poesia è la fantasica imitazione; perchè si fatta imitazione è delle cose che non sono, e non furono già mai: ma la perfettissima poesia imita le cose che sono, che furono, o che possono essere; come fu la guerra di Troia, e l' ira d'Achille, e la pietà d'Enea, e le battaglie fra Troiani e Latini, e l'altre che furono o possono essere fatti. . . . Ma perchè il poeta, per sentenza d'Aristotele, imita le cose, o come elle sono, o come possibili, o come è fama ch' elle siano, e come son credute, il principale soggetto del poeta è quel ch è, o quel che puo essere, o quel che si crede, o quel che si narra; o tutte queste cose insieme, come piacque ad Aristotele, potendo essere imitate dal poeta, sono il soggetto adeguato della poesia sotto questa consecuzione di verisimile.

8. See Guasti, 1: 301 ("Allegoria della *Gerusalemme Liberata*"):

L'eroica poesia, quasi animale in cui due nature si congiungono, d' imitazione e d' allegoria è composta. Con quella alleta a sè gli animi e gli orecchi degli uomini, e maravigliosamente gli diletta; con questa nella virtù o nella scienza, o nell'una e nell'altra, gli ammaestra. E sì come l'epica imitazione altro già mai non è che somiglianza ed imagine d'azione umana; così suole l'allegoria degli Epici, dell'umana vita esserci figura. Ma l'imitazione riguarda l'azioni dell' uomo, che sono a i sensi esteriori sottoposto; ed intorno ad esse principalmente affaticandosi, cerca di rappresentarle con parole efficaci ed espressive, ed atte a por chiaramente dinanzi a gli occhi corporali le cose rappresentate: né considera i costumi, o gli affetti, o i discorsi dell'animo in quanto essi sono intrinseci; ma solamente in quanto fuori se n'escono, e nel parlare e negli atti e nell'opere manifestandosi accompagnano l'azione. L'allegoria, all'incontra rimira le passioni e le opinioni ed i costumi, non solo in quanto essi appaiono, ma principalmente nel lor essere intrinseco; e più oscuramente le significa con note . . . misteriose, e che solo da i conoscitori della natura delle cose possono essere a pieno comprese. (p. 301.)

9. Guasti, 1: 88, 98 (*Discorsi del poema eroico*): ". . . l'imitazione non è congiunta con la verita per sua natura, ma con la verisimilitudine." ". . . Ma il probabile, in quanto egli è verisimile, appartiene al poeta. . . ."

10. On the book of Job as epic, see Barbara Kiefer Lewalski, *Milton's Brief Epic: The Genre, Meaning, and Art of "Paradise Regained"* (Providence, R.I.: Brown University Press, 1966); Charles W. Jones, "Milton's Brief Epic," *Studies in Philology* 44 (1947): 209–27.

11. See Watson Kirkconnell, *The Celestial Cycle: The Theme of Paradise Lost in World Literature* (Toronto: University of Toronto Press, 1952) for this phrase. On analogies between the epics of Milton and Homer, see Martin E. Mueller, "The Tragic Epic, *Paradise Lost* and the *Iliad*," (diss., Indiana University, 1966).

12. See Guasti, 1: 86–87: "Il fine, dunque, è la forma data da l'artificio del poeta, il quale, aggiungendo e scemando e variando, dispone la materia e dà un'altra imagine e quasi un'altra faccia a l'azione ed a le cose"; pp. 90–91:

> A tre cose dee aver riguardo . . . ciascuno che di scriver poema eroico si prepone: a scegler material tale, che sia atta a ricever in sé quella più eccellente forma che l'artificio del poeta cerca d'introdurci; a darle tal forma; ed a vestirla ultimamente con que' più rari ornamenti ch'a la natura di lei siano convenienti. . . . La materia, la quale da alcuni è detta nuda, perché non ha anco ricevuta qualità alcuna da l'artificio del poeta o dell'oratore, cade sotto l'artificio del poeta in quella guisa che il ferro o legno è considerato dal fabro: perché, come dice Filopono nel principio del suo commento sovra il terzo libro *Priorum Analiticorum,* s'appartiene a colui che sa, non solo considerare le specie delle cose subiette, ma la materia e la disposizione a ricever le forme. . . . Così Aristotele, volendoci insegnare le specie de' sillogismi, prima ci ammaestrò nelle specie delle proposizioni, che sone materie de' sillogismi. Al poeta similmente conviene non solo aver nel formar la materia, ma giudizio ancora nel conoscerla; e dee sceglierla tale, che sia per natura capace d' ogni ornamento e d' ogni perfezione.

> Also, pp. 93–94: ". . . non è dubbio, che l' eccellentissime forme s' introducono meglio nella materia che sia atta a riceverle. . . . Similmente la medesima forma del sigillo molto meglio fa sue operazioni nella cera, ch' in altra materia più liquida e più densa. . . . Queste cose ho dette acciò che si conosca quanto importi nel poema l' eleggere più tosto una che un' altra materia"; p. 113; "ricever la forma del poema eroico. . . ."

13. Guasti, 1: 111–13. After observing that "L' istoria di secolo o di nazione lontanissima pare per alcuna ragione soggetto assai conveniente al poema eroico; però che, essendo quelle cose in guisa sepolte nell' antichita, ch' a pena ne rimane debole ed oscura memoria, può il poeta mutarle e rimutarle, e narrarle come gli piace," Tasso points out the technical difficulties inherent in a subject derived from ancient or modern history. If the poet chooses an argument based on antiquity, he must run the risk of boring his readers by describing the customs and mores of antiquity—its methods of warfare, its banquets and ceremonies, and "altre usanze di quel remotissimo secolo. . . ." If he introduces "l' usanze moderne" into

ancient times, he will resemble an injudicious painter who invests his portrait of Cato or Cincinnatus with the fashions of the Milanese or Neapolitan youth. Modern histories, in turn, "togliono quasi in tutto la licenza di fingere e d' imitare, la quale è necessariissima a' poeti, particolarmente a gli epici." Finally, Tasso appeals to the authority of Aristotle, who had explained in his *Problems* "la ragione . . . perché ci piaccia più la narrazione delle cose non troppo nuove, ne troppo vecchie; la quale è questa, che noi diffidiamo de le cose troppo lontane, ma non possiamo aver diletto di quelle, ne le quali non abbiamo fede; ma l'altre che sono troppo nuove, pare che ancora le sentiamo, però n'abbiamo minor diletto.' Milton's epic argument would not be vulnerable to this objection against "cose troppo lontane," inasmuch as it rested on the authority of Scripture. At the same time the biblical account of the fall was sufficiently brief and obscure to permit the poet to add the probable or necessary circumstances that would give verisimilitude, plausibility, and structural unity to his plot.

14. Guasti I: 110–11: "Nelle istorie della prima qualità a pena ardisca il poeta di stender la mano: ma si possono lasciare nella pura e semplice verità, perchè non si fa fatica alcuna nel trovare, ed a pena par ch' il fingere ivi sia lecito; e chi non fingesse e non imitasse obligandosi a que' particolari medesimi che ivi sono contenuti, poeta non sarebbe, ma più tosto istorico."

15. James Thorpe, ed., *Milton Criticism: Selections from Four Centuries,* 2d ed. (New York: Collier Books, 1969), p. 23.

16. Ibid., pp. 56–57.

17. Ibid., pp. 75–76.

18. Horace, *Ars Poetica,* line 73: "Res gestae regumque ducumque et tristia bella" (Horace, *"Satires," "Epistles," and "Ars Poetica,"* translated by H. Rushton Fairclough (Cambridge, Mass.: Harvard University Press; London: William Heinemann Ltd., 1966), p. 456.

19. See Milton's remarks on his literary ambitions in *Mansus, Epitaphium Damonis,* and *The Reason of Church Government (Works,* 3: 237–41) and the list of dramatic subjects in the Trinity College MS (*Works,* 18: 228–45. In the dramatic notes biblical subjects outnumber the subjects based on British history. All of the more detailed dramatic sketches, including the four outlines for a tragedy on Adam's fall, are based on scriptural narratives.

20. See Wayne Shumaker, *"Paradise Lost* and the Italian Epic Tradition," in *Th' Upright Heart and Pure,* edited by Amadeus P. Fiore, O.F.M. (Pittsburgh: Duquesne Univ. Press, 1967), pp. 87–100.

21. See Michael Lieb, "Milton and the Kenotic Christology: Its Literary Bearing," *ELH* 37 (1970): 342–60.

22. See *Aristotle on the Art of Poetry,* translated by Ingram Bywater (Oxford, 1909), p. 21; "We maintain . . . that the first essential, the life and soul, so to speak, of Tragedy is the Plot; and that the Characters

come second—compare the parallel in painting, where the most beautiful colours laid on without order will not give one the same pleasure as a simple black-and-white sketch of a portrait. We maintain that Tragedy is primarily an imitation of action, and that it is mainly for the sake of the action that it imitates the personal agents."

23. *Works,* 3: 237.

24. See *Essays of John Dryden,* edited by W. P. Ker (Oxford, 1900), 2: 165 ("Dedication of the *Aeneis*"): "And Milton, if the Devil had not been his hero, instead of Adam, if the giant had not foiled the knight, and driven him out of his stronghold, to wander through the world with his lady errant; and if there had not been more machining persons than human in his poem." Cf. *The Critical Works of John Dennis,* edited by Edward Niles Hooker (Baltimore: The Johns Hopkins University Press, 1939 and 1943), 1: 334 ("The Grounds of Criticism in Poetry"): "He was resolved . . . that his Principals should be the Devil on one side and Man on the other: and the Devil is properly his Hero, because he gets the better."

25. For Addison, Adam and Eve were the principal actors in Milton's epic, but neither was the actual hero of the poem. In answering the objection "that the hero in the *Paradise Lost* is unsuccessful, and by no means a match for his enemies," Addison maintained that the poem was an "epic, or a narrative poem, and he that looks for a hero in it, searches for that which Milton never intended; but if he will needs fix the name of an hero upon any person in it, it is certainly the Messiah who is the hero, both in the principal action, and in the chief episodes." (Thorpe, p. 49; cf. p. 31.)

26. Jonathan Richardson insisted that it was not Milton's "fault if there have been those who have not found a hero, or who he is. 'Tis Adam, Adam the first, the representative of human race. He is the hero in this poem, though as in other heroic poems, superior beings are introduced. . . . He is not such a hero as Achilles, Ulysses, Aeneas, Orlando, Godfrey, &c., all romantic worthies and incredible performers of fortunate, savage cruelties; he is one of a nobler kind. . . . He is not such a conqueror as subdued armies or nations, or enemies in single combat, but his conquest was what justly gave heroic name to person and to poem. His hero was more than a conqueror through Him that loved us (as Rom. viii. 37)." Though Samuel Johnson regarded the question of the hero of *Paradise Lost* as pedantic, he censured Dryden for "petulantly and indecently" denying "the heroism of Adam, because he was overcome; but there is no reason why the hero should not be unfortunate, except established practice, since success and virtue do not go necessarily together." Cato, for instance, was Lucan's hero. Nevertheless, "if success be necessary, Adam's deceiver was at last crushed; Adam was restored to his Maker's favour, and therefore may securely resume his human rank." See Thorpe, pp. 57, 76.

27. The basic problem underlying this controversy over the hero of Milton's poem was the difficulty of reconciling Adam's apparent defeat with contemporary beliefs that a heroic poem should end fortunately. Could an epic hero follow the same pattern as a tragic hero, meeting defeat in the crucial encounter and finally disappearing from the stage (like Oedipus the King) as an exile? For Aristotle, epic and tragedy had differed primarily in their length and in their modes of imitation; both imitated the "better" sort of persons (*spoudaioi*)—sometimes even the same heroes and actions—and the same varieties of plot were common to both genres. On the other hand, Tasso had drawn a sharp distinction between the epic and tragic illustrious; in the opinion of many Renaissance critics (but by no means all) the action of an epic hero ought to conclude successfully. Though Johnson challenged this critical dogma, he did not attempt to refute it, and proceeded to argue that Milton's hero had, in fact, been successful in the end, inasmuch as he had been restored to divine favor. Richardson similarly emphasized Adam's regeneration; in the end Milton's hero achieved "a secure recumbency upon and interest in the Supreme Good by the mediation of His Son." (Thorpe, p. 57.) Dryden had based his identification of Milton's hero on Satan's success and Adam's defeat. In countering this argument, Addison could not deny that Adam, the chief actor in the poem, had failed, but he could deny that Adam was the hero of Milton's epic. Rebutting the charge that Milton's hero was "unsuccessful" by identifying the Messiah as hero, he parried the objection that the "event" of Milton's fable was "unhappy" by arguing that it belonged to a "second" kind of implex fable, in which "the chief actor in the poem falls from some eminent pitch of honour and prosperity, into misery and disgrace. Thus we see Adam and Eve sinking from a state of innocence and happiness into the most abject condition of sin and sorrow." (*Thorpe*, p. 48.)

The problem was further complicated by the ambiguity of the word "hero." Since an epic frequently portrayed several persons of heroic character, Renaissance critics sometimes distinguished the protagonist as the "principal hero" or "epic person." Though they might regard his character as imperfect or even vicious, as some regarded Achilles and Odysseus, they nevertheless recognized his position as the principal hero of the poem; he was simply a hero who, insofar as he lacked the essence of true heroic virtue, did not merit his title as such. When Johnson refers to Cato as Lucan's hero, he is alluding not to the principal actor in the poem, but to a model of Stoic virtue; he is using the term primarily in its ethical sense. When Dryden applies this title to Satan, and Addison to the Messiah, both are associating it with victorious action. Addison's distinction between the "hero" of *Paradise Lost* and its "chief actor" would probably have seemed arbitrary to many Renaissance critics, and on one occasion he himself uses these terms virtually synonymously, passing directly from the "principal actors of the *Iliad* and *Aeneid*," whom the authors had "chosen for their heroes," to the "principal actors" (who are *not* the heroes) of *Paradise Lost*. (See Thorpe, p. 47.)

I am grateful to another participant in the Renaissance Conference for pointing out, during the discussion period, that similar critical controversies have centered on the problem of the hero of Lucan's *Pharsalia* and Statius's *Thebaid*—both of them epics of the Silver Age of Latin literature and both of them taking the fratricidal conflicts of civil war as their epic argument.

28. See John F. Huntley, *"Proairesis, Synteresis,* and the Ethical Orientation of Milton's *Of Education," Philological Quarterly* 43 (1964): 40–46.

29. See my "Achilles and Renaissance Epic: Moral Criticism and Literary Tradition," in *Lebende Antike, Symposion für Rudolf Sühnel,* edited by Horst Meller and Hans-Joachim Zimmermann (Berlin: Erich Schmidt Verlag, 1967), pp. 139–54.

30. See note 24 above.

31. See Priscilla P. St. George, "Psychomachia in Books V and VI of *Paradise Lost," Modern Language Quarterly* 27 (1966): 185–96.

32. Ker, 2: 165.

33. T. S. Eliot, "Burnt Norton," *Collected Poems, 1909–1935* (New York: Harcourt, Brace, 1936), p. 214.

34. "The Hollow Men," Ibid., p. 101.

35. Cf. Milton's *Christian Doctrine,* Bk. I, Chap. 18.

36. See James Holly Hanford, "The Temptation Motive in Milton," *Studies in Philology* 15 (1918): 176–94.

37. The conventions of epic machinery would subsequently be satirized, along with other traditional features of this genre, in Pope's "A Receit to make an Epick Poem"; see *The Prose Works of Alexander Pope,* edited by Norman Ault, vol. 1 (Oxford: Basil Blackwell, 1936), pp. 115–20. For the machines, "Scriblerus" advises the poet to *"Take of Deities, Male and Female, as many as you can use,"* separating them in *"two equal parts"* and keeping Jupiter in the middle, to be excited by Juno and mollified by Venus. On all occasions the poet should remember *"to make use of Volatile Mercury."* Since *"no Epick Poem can possibly subsist"* without these machines, the *"wisest thing is to serve them for your greatest Necessities."* For the manners of the hero, "Scriblerus" recommends *"all the best Qualities you can find in all the best celebrated Heroes of Antiquity. . . . But be sure they are Qualities which your* Patron *would be thought to have. . . ."*

38. See Macon Cheek, "Milton's *In Quintum Novembris:* An Epic Foreshadowing," *Studies in Philology* 54 (1957): 172–84.

39. Howard Schultz, *Milton and Forbidden Knowledge* (New York: Modern Language Association, 1955).

40. See Dick Taylor, Jr., "The Storm Scene in *Paradise-Regained;* A Reinterpretation," *University of Toronto Quarterly* 24 (1955): 359–76.

41. See Geoffrey Hartman, "Milton's Counterplot," *ELH* 25 (1958): 1–12; J. R. Watson, "Divine Providence and the Structure of *Paradise Lost*," *Essays in Criticism* 14 (1964): 148–55.

42. On the female worthy and the woman-warrior in Renaissance literature, see Eugene M. Waith's essay "Heywood's Women Worthies" below; Graham Hough, *A Preface to the "Faerie Queene"* (New York: Norton, 1963); R. A. Sayce, *The French Biblical Epic in the Seventeenth Century* (Oxford: Oxford University Press, Clarendon Press, 1955).

43. See Guasti, 2: 203–14, for Tasso's "Discorso della virtù feminile e donnesca," addressed to the duchess of Mantua. After discussing the divergent opinions of Plato and Aristotle on the question of whether "la virtù dell'uomo e della femina" were the same, Tasso argued that the virtues that temper ire are most appropriate for a man, whereas those that temper concupiscence are most fitting for a woman; whereas a man is dishonored by cowardice (*viltà*), a woman is shamed by *impudicizia*. Though a woman may possess fortitude (*fortezza*), this is not absolute courage, but a courage that obeys ("non l'assoluta fortezza; ma la fortezza ch' ubidisce"). The virtue that is most appropriate for a woman (Tasso continued) is temperance; this is a larger and more comprehensive virtue than modesty, inasmuch as *pudicizia* is a part of *temperanza*.

    From this *feminil virtù*, appropriate for a *cittadina* or a *gentildonna privata*, Tasso turns to the *donnesca virtù* befitting a noblewoman "nata di sangue imperiale ed eroico, la qual con le proprie virtù agguaglia le virili virtù di tutti i suoi gloriosi antecessori." For this virtue one no longer uses "il nome di femina, ma quel di donnesco, il qual tanto vale quanto signorile"; and Tasso conceives it consistently in heroic or quasi-heroic terms: ". . . sì come fra gli uomini sono alcuni ch' eccedendo l'umana condizione sono stimati eroi; così fra le donne molte ci nascono d' animo e di virtù eroica, e molte ancora nate di sangue regio, se ben perfettamente non si possono chiamar donne eroiche, molto nondimeno a le donne eroiche s'assomigliano." In heroic ladies this virtù donnesca is "virtù eroica, che con la virtù eroica dell'uomo contende, e delle donne dotate di questa virtu non più la pudicizia che la fortezza o che la prudenze è propria." There is no distinction of works and offices between these heroic women and heroic men, except for purely biological functions. Among recent or contemporary heroines eminent for their *virtù donnesca*, Tasso praises Queen Mary, sister of Charles V; Margherita of Austria, duchess of Parma; Queen Elizabeth of England, in spite of her Protestantism ("se bene la nostra malvagia fortuna vuol ch' ella sia da la Chiesa separata, nondimeno l 'eroiche virtù dell' animo suo e l'altezza dell' ingegno mirabile, le rende affezionatissimo ogni animo gentile e valoroso"); and Caterina de' Medici. The heroines of contemplation (for the contemplative as well as the active virtues are found among "donne eroiche") include Renata di Ferrara, Margherita di Savoia, and Vittoria Colonna. Finally, the Duchess of Mantua herself, along with her sister, possesses all virtues of mind and of heroic intellect (*intelletto eroico*) and embodies *la virtù cristiana* in its perfection.

Suggested Reading

In addition to the studies cited in the footnotes, the reader may consult the following works. For Renaissance ideas of the hero and for the heroic image in Renaissance literature, see Eugene M. Waith, *The Herculean Hero* (New York: Columbia University Press, 1962); Mark Rose, *Heroic Love, Studies in Sidney and Spenser* (Cambridge, Mass.: Harvard University Press, 1968); Maurice B. McNamee, S.J., *Honor and the Epic Hero* (New York: Holt, Rinehart, 1960); Matthew N. Proser, *The Heroic Image in Five Shakespearean Tragedies* (Princeton, N.J.: Princeton University Press, 1965); Victor Brombert, ed., *The Hero in Literature* (Greenwich, Conn.: Fawcett Publications, 1969); Reuben A. Brower, *Shakespeare and the Graeco-Roman Heroic Tradition* (New York: Oxford University Press, 1971); Maurice Evans, *Spenser's Anatomy of Heroism: A Commentary on the Faerie Queene* (Cambridge: Cambridge University Press, 1970).

For the influence of oral composition and transmission on epic style, read Albert B. Lord, *The Singer of Tales* (New York: Athenaeum, 1965); C. M. Bowra, *Heroic Poetry* (London: Macmillan, 1964); Jan de Vries, *Heroic Song and Heroic Legend*, trans. B. J. Timmer (London: Oxford University Press, 1963); and Francis P. Magoun, Jr., "The Oral-Formulaic Character of Anglo-Saxon Narrative Poetry," *Speculum* 18 (1953): 446–67. For the literary epic, one may consult C. M. Bowra, *From Virgil to Milton* (London: Macmillan, 1965); Thomas M. Greene, *The Descent from Heaven* (New Haven, Conn.: Yale University Press, 1963); A. Bartlett Giamatti, *The Earthly Paradise and the Renaissance Epic* (Princeton, N.J.: Princeton University Press, 1969); E. M. W. Tillyard, *The English Epic and Its Background* (New York: Oxford University Press, 1954); Hallett Smith, *Elizabethan Poetry* (Ann Arbor: University of Michigan Press, 1968); Mario A. Di Cesare, *Vida's "Christiad" and Vergilian Epic* (New York: Columbia University Press, 1964); Aldo S. Bernardo, *Petrarch, Scipio and the "Africa": the Birth of Humanism's Dream* (Baltimore, Md.: The Johns Hopkins University Press, 1962).

For Milton's concept of the hero and his epic techniques,

consult Merritt Y. Hughes, *Ten Perspectives on Milton* (New Haven, Conn.: Yale University Press, 1965); idem, "Merit in *Paradise Lost,*" *Huntington Library Quarterly* 21 (1967): 3–20; Burton O. Kurth, *Milton and Christian Heroism: Biblical Epic Themes and Forms in Seventeenth-Century England* (Berkeley and Los Angeles: University of California Press, 1959); E. M. W. Tillyard, *The Miltonic Setting, Past and Present* (Cambridge: Cambridge University Press, 1938); idem, *Studies in Milton* (London: Chatto and Windus, 1951); Frank Kermode, "Milton's Hero," *Review of English Studies* 4 (1953): 317–30; Stella P. Revard, "Milton's Critique of Heroic Warfare in *Paradise Lost* V and VI," *Studies in English Literature* 7 (1967): 119–39; M. M. Mahood, "Milton's Heroes," in *Poetry and Humanism* (New Haven, Conn.: Yale University Press, 1950), pp. 207–51; Arnold Stein, *Heroic Knowledge: An Interpretation of "Paradise Regained" and "Samson Agonistes"* (Minneapolis: University of Minnesota Press, 1957); Stanley Fish, "Standing Only, Christian Heroism in *Paradise Lost,*" *Critical Quarterly* 9 (1967): 162–78; W. W. Robson, "The Better Fortitude," in *The Living Milton,* edited by Frank Kermode (London: Routledge and Kegan Paul, 1962), pp. 124–37; William R. Herman, "Heroism and *Paradise Lost,*" *College English* 21 (1959): 13–17; John Eugene Seaman, "The Chivalric Cast of Milton's Epic Hero," *English Studies* 49 (1968): 97–107; Lawrence A. Sasek, "Milton's Patriotic Epic," *Huntington Library Quarterly* 20 (1956): 1–14; Ida Langdon, *Milton's Theory of Poetry and Fine Art* (New Haven, Conn.: Yale University Press, 1924); F. T. Prince, *The Italian Element in Milton's Verse* (Oxford: Oxford University Press, Clarendon Press, 1954); C. S. Lewis, *A Preface to Paradise Lost* (New York: Oxford University Press, 1961); J. M. Evans, *"Paradise Lost" and the Genesis Tradition* (Oxford: Oxford University Press, Clarendon Press, 1968); John Peter Tchakirides, "Epic Prolepsis and Repetition as Structural Devices in Milton's *Paradise Lost,*" (diss., Yale University, 1968); Martin E. Mueller, "The Tragic Epic, *Paradise Lost* and the *Iliad,*" (diss., Indiana University, 1966); S. H. V. Gurteen, *The Epic of the Fall of Man: A Comparative Study of Caedmon,*

Dante and Milton (New York: Haskell House, 1964); Peter Hägin, *The Epic Hero and the Decline of Heroic Poetry: A Study of the Neoclassical English Epic with Special Reference to Milton's Paradise Lost*" (Bern: Francke Verlag, 1964); Davis P. Harding, *The Club of Hercules: Studies in the Classical Background of "Paradise Lost"* (Urbana: University of Illinois Press, 1962); Roland Hagenbüchle, *Sündenfall und Wahlfreiheit in Milton's Paradise Lost* (Bern: Francke Verlag, 1967); Mason Hammond, "Concilia Deorum from Homer through Milton," *Studies in Philology* 30 (1933): 1–16; Arthur Barker, "Structural Pattern in *Paradise Lost*," *Philological Quarterly* 28 (1949): 16–30; A. S. P. Woodhouse, "Pattern in *Paradise Lost*," *University of Toronto Quarterly* 22 (1953): 109–127; Dennis H. Burden, *The Logical Epic: A Study of the Argument of "Paradise Lost"* (London: Routledge and Kegan Paul, 1967); William H. Marshall, "*Paradise Lost:* Felix Culpa and the Problem of Structure," *Modern Language Notes* 76 (1961): 15–20; C. A. Patrides, ed., *Milton's Epic Poetry: Essays on "Paradise Lost" and "Paradise Regained"* (Harmondsworth, Middlesex: Penguin Books, 1967); John T. Shawcross, "The Balanced Structure of *Paradise Lost*," *Studies in Philology* 62 (1965): 696–718; Ernest Sirluck, *"Paradise Lost": A Deliberate Epic* (Cambridge: W. Heffer and Sons, 1967); T. J. B. Spencer, "*Paradise Lost:* The Anti-Epic," in *Approaches to "Paradise Lost*," edited by C. A. Patrides (London: Edward Arnold, 1968), pp. 81–98; Irene Samuel, "*Paradise Lost* as Mimesis," in *Approaches to "Paradise Lost,"* pp. 15–29; Mario A. Di Cesare, "*Paradise Lost* and Epic Tradition," *Milton Studies* 1 (1969): 31–50; Michael Fixler, "Milton's Passionate Epic," *Milton Studies* 1: 167–92; Dwight C. Marsh, " 'Above Heroic': A Theological Explication of *Paradise Regained* as Anti-Epic" (diss., University of Nebraska, 1969); Hugh MacCallum, " 'Most Perfect Hero': The Role of the Son in Milton's Theodicy," in *"Paradise Lost": A Tercentenary Tribute,* edited by Balachandra Rajan (Toronto: University of Toronto Press, 1969), pp. 79–105; Philip J. Ford, "*Paradise Lost* and the Five-Act Epic," (diss., Columbia University, 1968); Earl Miner, "*Felix Culpa* in the Redemptive Order of *Paradise Lost*," *Philolog-*

ical Quarterly 47 (1968): 43–54; Nan D. Morrison, "Principles of Structure in *Paradise Lost*," (diss., University of South Carolina, 1968); Stewart A. Baker, "Sannazaro and Milton's Brief Epic," *Comparative Literature* 20 (1968): 116–33; Mario A. Di Cesare, "Advent'rous Song: The Texture of Milton's Epic," in *Language and Style in Milton*, edited by Ronald D. Emma and John T. Shawcross (New York: Frederick Ungar, 1967), pp. 1–29; John C. Ulreich, Jr., "Milton on the Fortunate Fall," *Journal of the History of Ideas* 32 (1971): 351–66; K. W. Gransden, "*Paradise Lost* and the *Aeneid*," *Essays in Criticism* 17 (1967): 281–303; Douglas Bush, "The Isolation of the Renaissance Hero," in *Reason and Imagination*, edited by J. A. Mazzeo (New York: Columbia University Press, 1962), pp. 57–69; idem, "*Paradise Lost*" *in Our Time* (Ithaca, New York: Cornell University Press, 1945); Thomas Kranidas, *The Fierce Equation: A Study of Milton's Decorum* (The Hague: Mouton, 1965). For a survey of recent trends in Milton criticism and scholarship, the reader should consult the essay by Douglas Bush in *English Poetry: Select Bibliographical Guides,* edited by A. E. Dyson (London: Oxford University Press, 1971), pp. 76–95, and the essay by Irene Samuel in *Critical Approaches to Six Major English Works,* edited by R. M. Lumiansky and Herschel Baker (Philadelphia: University of Pennsylvania Press, 1968), pp. 209–53.

On Milton's relation to his audience, see Balachandra Rajan, "*Paradise Lost*" *and the Seventeenth Century Reader* (London: Chatto and Windus, 1962); Stanley Fish, *Surprised by Sin: the Reader in "Paradise Lost"* (London: Macmillan, 1967); Anne Davidson Ferry, *Milton's Epic Voice: The Narrator in "Paradise Lost"* (Cambridge, Mass.: Harvard University Press, 1963).

Among recent studies of the problem of Satan's role in *Paradise Lost,* consult Merritt Y. Hughes, "Satan Now Dragon Grown (*PL.* 10. 529)," *Études Anglaises* 20 (1967): 356–69; Amadeus P. Fiore, O.F.M., "Satan Is a Problem: The Problem of Milton's 'Satanic Fallacy' in Contemporary Criticism," *Franciscan Studies* 17 (1957): 173–87; Jackson I. Cope, "Satan's Disguises in *Paradise Lost* and *Paradise Re-*

gained," *Modern Language Notes* 73 (1958): 9–11; Calvin Huckabay, "Satan and the Narrative Structure of *Paradise Lost:* Some Observations," *Studia Neophilologica* 33 (1961): 96–102; idem, "The Satanist Controversy of the Nineteenth Century," in *Studies in English Renaissance Literature,* edited by Waldo F. McNeir (Baton Rouge: Louisiana State University Press, 1962), pp. 197–210.

On the structure of *Paradise Regained,* consult Arthur E. Barker, "Structural and Doctrinal Pattern in Milton's Later Poems," *Essays in English Literature . . . Presented to A. S. P. Woodhouse,* edited by Millar MacLure and F. S. Watt (Toronto: University of Toronto Press, 1964), pp. 169–94; Barbara Kiefer Lewalski, *Milton's Brief Epic: The Genre, Meaning, and Art of "Paradise Regained"* (Providence, Rhode Island: Brown University Press, 1966); A. S. P. Woodhouse, "Theme and Pattern in *Paradise Regained,*" *University of Toronto Quarterly* 25 (1956): 167–82.

For the Renaissance biblical epic and divine poetry, read Lily B. Campbell, *Divine Poetry and Drama in Sixteenth Century England* (Cambridge: Cambridge University Press, 1959); W. F. Schirmer, "Das Problem des religiösen Epos im 17. Jahrhundert in England," *Deutsche Vierteljahrschrift* 14 (1936): 60–74; Hertha Winkler, "Das biblisch-religiöse Epos des 17. Jahrhunderts bis zu Miltons *Paradise Lost*" (diss., University of Vienna, 1949).

For Renaissance epic theory, see Bernard Weinberg, *A History of Literary Criticism in the Italian Renaissance,* 2 vols. (Chicago: University of Chicago Press, 1961); Ralph C. Williams, *The Theory of the Heroic Epic in Italian Criticism of the Sixteenth Century* (Baltimore: The Johns Hopkins University Press, 1917); Marvin T. Herrick, *The Fusion of Horatian and Aristotelian Literary Criticism* (Urbana: University of Illinois Press, 1946); Joel E. Spingarn, *Literary Criticism in the Renaissance* (Reprint New York: Harcourt, Brace, and World, 1963); Torquato Tasso, *Discourse on the Heroic Poem,* edited and translated by Mariella Cavalchini and Irene Samuel (Oxford: Oxford University Press, Clarendon Press, 1973).

Among recent studies of Spenser and Renaissance allegory,

read Rosemond Tuve, *Allegorical Imagery* (Princeton, N.J.: Princeton University Press, 1966); Edwin Honig, *Dark Conceit: The Making of Allegory* (New York: Oxford University Press, 1966); Thomas P. Roche, Jr., *The Kindly Flame* (Princeton, N.J.: Princeton University Press, 1964); Angus Fletcher, *Allegory, The Theory of a Symbolic Mode* (Ithaca, N.Y.: Cornell University Press, 1964); William Nelson, *The Poetry of Edmund Spenser: A Study* (New York: Columbia University Press, 1963); Kathleen Williams, *Spenser's World of Glass* (Berkeley: University of California Press, 1966); Paul J. Alpers, *The Poetry of the Faerie Queene* (Princeton, N.J.: Princeton University Press, 1967); Michael Murrin, *The Veil of Allegory: Some Notes Toward a Theory of Allegorical Rhetoric in the English Renaissance* (Chicago: University of Chicago Press, 1969); Michael West, "Spenser and the Renaissance Ideal of Christian Heroism," *PMLA* 88 (1973): 1013–32.

The Epic Hero Superseded

Bruce W. Wardropper

THE PURPOSE OF THIS PAPER is to investigate the process by which the hero *par excellence*—the noble warrior of the medieval epic [1]—declined in stature until he became little more than the central character in a work of fiction or a great man in what we call "real life." For the most part my illustrations will come from Romania, and particularly from the Iberian peninsula. This circumscription of my inquiry is partly dictated by my relative competence in this area, but also—and mainly—by the fact that in the deflating and replacing of the epic hero Spanish intellectuals and writers played a leading part.[2]

There can be no doubt that today most academics, and not a few lay people, despise heroics. It seemed quite normal to read a few years ago of an airline pilot who, on being ordered to change course to Havana, told the hijacker: "O.K. We're not armed; we're not heroes." No one, as far as I know, has criticized him for acting unheroically. Nor was there anything but sympathy for those Vietnam veterans—some sort of heroes themselves—who threw away their heroically-won medals as a protest against the war. Heroism is not our style. In the twentieth century we must make a tremendous effort any time we want to summon up reserves of heroism for resistance movements or revolutions. Yet for many centuries heroism was, or seemed to be, man's life style or, at least, his ideal. The French or Spanish nobleman considered himself to have been born a hero; the Italian bourgeois aspired to heroism or cultivated it; the lower classes admired it in their superiors as conferring a benefit on them in the spirit of *noblesse oblige.*

The hero by antonomasia was either a great conqueror in history—like Alexander the Great or Scipio—or the subject of epic poems, whether the *Iliad* and the *Aeneid* or the *Roland* and the *Cid*. The qualities which made up his person—*proz, mesura, esfuerzo*, valor, honor, a flowery beard, and the rest— were well known and clearly enough intuited, even if ill-defined. The hero was a leader of willingly led men, who recognized the type just as we recognize it today. But the heroes did not call themselves heroes, and were not so called by their follow- ers. The highest secular human type in the Middle Ages had no vernacular generic name. In most modern languages it was not until the second half of the fifteenth century that the neo- logism "hero" began to appear. And without a name the concept necessarily remained blurred, imprecise, and unstable. But, as I shall argue, when the word achieved currency in the vernacular languages, it did not bring a stricter denotation to the concept; on the contrary, the idea of heroism at once began to evolve in a different direction with no perceptible gain in semantic pre- cision.

The four definitions of a hero given by the Oxford English Dictionary vividly illustrate the course of this change: (1.) A name given (in antiquity) to men of superhuman strength, courage, or ability, favored by the gods; regarded later as demi- gods, and immortal, (2.) one who does brave or noble deeds; an illustrious warrior (1586), (3.) a man who exhibits extraor- dinary bravery, firmness, or greatness of soul, in connection with any pursuit, work, or enterprise; a man admired and ven- erated for his achievements and noble qualities (1661), and (4.) the man who forms the subject of an epic; the chief male personage in a poem, play, or story (1697). The first three of these definitions, dealing with the antique and medieval hero, have much in common: they describe an extraordinary, chosen man of remarkable valor—valor in its dual sense of "courage" and "intrinsic worth." It is the fourth definition that indicates the full extent of the hero's devaluation, and the dividing line between two very different human climates. The epic hero is a hero because of what he is, because he has been selectively fa- vored by divinity; the fictional hero, because of what an author has made him, because he has been arbitrarily favored by an imaginative writer. The hero of fiction, to his enormous detri- ment, has ceased to belong to an established élite.

By the end term of our inquiry, the middle of the seventeenth century, writers were very conscious of the catastrophe
that had befallen the hero. In his preface to his Lucianesque
dialogue *Les Héros du roman*, Nicolas Boileau deplores the
disappearance of grandeur from Mademoiselle de Scudéry's
novels: she presents the heroes of antiquity as nothing more
than precious lovers in a salon, doing, says Boileau, "whatever
seems most contrary to the character and the heroic seriousness
of those early Romans." [3] In their *romans comiques* Furetière
and Scarron wrote not about heroes but about mediocrities,
while an early practitioner of the genre, Charles Sorel, complains that the de-heroizing tendency has gone so far that
"heroes" have become "zeroes." [4] In the novel, the seventeenth
century seems to have lost the capacity for having a genuine
feeling for heroes and heroism. On the stage, of course, Corneille still presented heroes, but they did not belong to that
laconic universe in which, as G. S. Burgess aptly puts it, "heroes
could scarcely handle a subordinate clause." [5] Rodrigue lives
not for *proz, mesura, valor* but for *gloire, vertu, volonté*. In
Serge Doubrovsky's terms, he is not, like the epic hero, "soli-
daire" but "solitaire." [6] He is struggling in vain, in a society of
consciously enfeebled noblemen, to recover his proper status
from a feudal past. [7] In France, as elsewhere in Europe, the epic
hero was finding it extremely hard to survive in the post-medi-
eval world.

Even in the Middle Ages themselves, of course, the epic
hero's character and role were gradually modified. The mature
hero of the twelfth-century *Cantar de Mio Cid* is conspicuous
not only for his energetic courage and his strategic skill, but also
for his prudence and his loyalty to a king whose favor he had
lost. Some three hundred years later, the immature Cid of the
Mocedades de Rodrigo has even more dynamism, but he is rash
and rebellious. [8] This late epic hero truly belongs to the "waning" Middle Ages. But it is in the romances of chivalry that the
greatest changes in the complexion of the hero are discernible.
Translated out of poetic history into realms of pure fiction, the
knight strives to be as noble in love as he is in war. In the *Chanson de Roland*, as Jean Frappier observed, love was present
"accidentally." [9] The Cid of the ancient epic expresses his lov-

ingness only as a husband and a father. The romances aim to give more equal attention to Mars and Venus. The chivalric hero does not dally like Aeneas: unaware of how impossible the task is, he tries to devote all of his time to love and all of his time to battle. The psychological consequences, inevitably, are disastrous. In *Amadís de Gaula* the hero abandons his knight-errantry while doing penance on the Peña Pobre because he has been dismissed by Oriana through a misunderstanding; in the *Orlando furioso* Roland's Italianate successor quite literally loses his wits when he discovers that Angelica has been unfaithful to him. But they were still somehow doughty warriors, superhuman in strength despite the emollience they underwent as a result of their womanizing. Some of the fifteenth-century Spanish romances, however, point to the future destiny of the knightly hero in the novels of Mademoiselle de Scudéry. Diego de San Pedro in the *Cárcel de Amor* no sooner contrives to get his mighty lover onto the field of battle than he invariably interrupts his narrative to say something like: "It would be prolix to tell of the blows exchanged between Leriano and Persio: suffice it to say that Leriano won." Descriptions of single combat were evidently proving tedious to his gentle readers, who were much more attentive to the progress of Leriano's amorous suit of Laureola.

"Arms and the man I sing," began Virgil. But Ariosto adds to this stark evocation of the hero and his accoutrements the soft delights of the fair sex: "The ladies," he begins, "the knights, the arms, the loves, the courtesies, the bold exploits I sing." The literary epics of the sixteenth and seventeenth centuries did continue, however, to recite the prowess of heroes. Some of them—by Camões, by Tasso, by Ercilla—were, and still are, regarded as major literary works. But the great mass of them are forgotten, and even in their own day they were being displaced by the great prose romances. They were almost, in the exaggerated words of Legouis and Cazamian, "the dead part of the literature of that time." [10]

The comparative lack of success of the literary epics is curious, for heroism was thriving in the real life of the Renaissance. The chivalric adventure of crossing the unknown Atlantic had been accomplished; the Conquistadors stoutly faced impossible odds to reconnoiter unknown lands and defeat unknown opponents, and they named some of their discoveries—such as California and Patagonia [11]—after the fantastic place names in the books of chivalry; the battle of Lepanto was seen as a decisive campaign to save Europe from the infidel fought under the heroic generalship of Don John of Austria. Some writers regarded these contemporary exploits—just as, in modern times, did the marching song of the British Grenadiers [12]—as far exceeding the heroic acts so vaunted by antiquity. The unknown author of *El Abencerraje* (in the middle of the sixteenth century) observes that "this Spain of ours holds courage in such low esteem because it is so natural and commonplace that it seems to us that anything that can be done is of little account; we are not like those Greeks and Romans who immortalized and deified a man for having risked death once in his lifetime." [13] And Montalvo, who early in the same century modernized and revised the text of the medieval *Amadís de Gaula*, exclaims in admiration over the hymns of praise that classical historians would have sung had they been alive to witness an event like the capture of Granada.[14] The spirit of heroism and victory reached into every corner of Spanish life. The young girl who would be known as Saint Theresa of Jesus ran away from home with her brother to fight the Moors.[15] Hernando de Acuña, in a famous sonnet, sang of his hope that a theocratic Spanish world empire was imminent: "One Monarch, one Empire, and one Sword." [16]

Singing such pious hopes, however, is a very different thing from singing contemporary feats of arms. Fernando de Herrera did this, but he did so usually in a somewhat elegiac vein.[17] The literary epics themselves seemed so often to misfire. Where were the modern Homers? It was a question asked in the fifteenth century by Pérez de Guzmán and in the sixteenth by Ronsard.[18] In the seventeenth century Quevedo put it well when he said that, although Spaniards deserved historians, they were not historians.[19] Even an early Renaissance poet like Garcilaso de la Vega, who described his life as a grasping for either the pen or the sword,[20] discreetly refrained from writing about war. Even if his lyre had been capable of singing heroes, he modestly explains, he would still write about love.[21] So he poured the sublime style of the *Aeneid* into the mold of the *Bucolics*, thus exalting the traditionally humble style of the pastoral.

This distaste for singing about heroes coincided with the adoption of the word *hero* into the vernacular lexicon. Both phenomena probably reflect the fact that Renaissance men were taking stock of the rapidly evolving—or disappearing—medieval values of chivalry, the empty forms of which in the autumn of the Middle Ages have been well described by Johan Huizinga. Seeing clearly for the first time the connection between the epic heroes of antiquity and those of the Middle Ages, the Renaissance needed to give them a name if those values of which they were paragons were to be preserved in some form or other as an example of praiseworthy conduct in the centuries to come.

The hero, partaking of the divine in antiquity, subsuming his culture's ideals in the Middle Ages, has always offered men a model life to imitate. Writing a scholarly work in 1929, Ramón Menéndez Pidal even proposed the particular virtues of the Cid as worthy of cultivation by anarchical Spaniards in the twentieth century.[22] Renaissance intellectuals, too, recommended the imitation of heroes. But they did so in a very general sense and in conformity with some theory that they were promoting. "Humanity," writes the Neoplatonist Ficino, "honors as divine beings those superior spirits who have deserved well of the human race in this life, and, once separated from their bodies, it venerates those whom the ancients called heroes as gods particularly dear to the supreme God. . . ."[23] The imitation of heroes is recommended on a variety of grounds and in a variety of ways. Machiavelli urges the Prince not to revere them uncritically, but to learn analytically from their successes and failures; the examples set by heroes must be studied as a means of increasing the ruler's efficiency and effectiveness.[24] For his part, Castiglione adduces the heroes of antiquity not so much for their warlike qualities as for their courtesy: Alexander is praised not as a conqueror but for his continence, his respect for letters and philosophy, his love of music, his practice of securing the peace by building great architectural monuments. Conquering heroes, Castiglione thinks, no longer exist.[25] Arms are now merely instruments for developing gentlemanly skills and character. What remains of heroism is seen in what increasingly come to be called "great men." [26] And great men, unlike epic heroes, need not be born to their greatness; they may be self-made, if only they will study past heroes. The old innate quality of heroic *mesura* is redefined in the Renaissance manuals of courtesy as "good breeding." [27]

By the middle of the sixteenth century, heroism has ceased to be, among the intellectual élite of the reborn world, an exemplary conduct worthy of uncritical imitation. It is simply a preterit model of virtue, to be used as a vague source of inspiration or as a way of life from which certain selected qualities may be singled out for emulation.

Some humanists, however, pressed their criticism of the heroic tradition virtually to the point of discarding it. For the more skeptical, heroism was an illusion; all heroes were, in the blinding light of the new-found critical truth, absolute zeroes.

Erasmus, for example, does not shrink from pointing to the painful reality surrounding heroism. Heroism meant winning wars; and fighting wars was an absurdity. Wars meant disaster for most of those who were affected by them. Besides, no issue was ever settled by the winning of a battle. The heroic adage that might makes right had no place in Erasmus's store of traditional wisdom. Who, he asks, reaps the laurels on the field of battle? Heroes, yes, but on closer inspection these heroes turn out to be, in his words, "parasites, scoundrels, thieves, murderers, peasants, imbeciles, beggars—the dregs of the people." [28]

The only acceptable warfare for Erasmus is the psychomachia, the struggle of the *miles christianus* against his passions. To conquer oneself is to conquer indeed. The new spirituality thriving in the sixteenth century under the influence of Erasmus repeatedly reached this same conclusion. The Portuguese friar Heitor Pinto, for example, could conceive of no heroism but a spiritualized one:

> There were and are many captains who have conquered great armies of countless men, of barbarous cruelty, found in an infinite number of places, richly endowed with all kinds of weapons, support, and finance. But when all is said and done, these

are human victories; to be able to conquer oneself, to trample
one's rage under foot, to be long-suffering in adversity, to forgive wrongs, to ally oneself with patience, this is more divine
than human. This is the highest of all victories, for a man to
conquer himself. This is what delivers one's name to perpe-
tuity, a victory worthy of being celebrated in all letters and on
all tongues and of living for as long as mortal memory shall
live.[29]

While *Il Cortegiano* advocated a discreet imitation of ancient
heroes, the anti-courtly literature in the *Beatus ille* tradition
is more akin to the *Enchiridion* in its repudiation of all sem-
blance of heroism. In Antonio de Guevara's *Menosprecio de
corte y alabanza de aldea* traditional heroic values are inverted.
The uncritical society of the courtier has lost the power to
equate the proper words with the human beings they designate:
"At court . . . the coward [is called] prudent [and] the
brave man, rash. . . ."[30] How can heroism survive such a debasement of linguistic currency? In the past, says Guevara, "illustrious men" undertook trials and tasks of heroic dimensions
to further a cause. The courtiers' trials today, however, are
"thankless ones, for we see most of them suffering so much
hardship without gleaning any benefit from it." The times are
not geared to learning and heroism. "How dare we praise in
our century illustrious men of arms and learned men of science,
since now force is used to rob and letters, to deceive?" (p. 158).
This challenging of the hero's authority and of his very existence is not new. In the fifteenth century the biographer Fernando del Pulgar had criticized chivalry as "an over-rigid
formula" and had "made strictures on the moral virtues of famous Roman heroes."[31] But in the sixteenth century the criticism of heroic postures reaches a crescendo.

One might expect such criticism to have found a literary out-
let in satire. There is a sense, no doubt, in which the *Orlando
furioso* may be said to satirize the paladins. But the work was
not read as a satire, and was probably not meant to be read as
one. It was still too early for the hero to be satirized (in the
way Erasmus was satirizing monks), for there was, in spite of
Erasmus's and Guevara's demurrers, too much evidence of her-

oism being practiced in the expeditions of explorers and soldiers. It is not until the seventeenth century that writers began systematically to puncture the bubble of heroism. Satire is the ritual killing of the man being pilloried, arising from bitter feelings on the part of the writer. The poet Góngora, writing in 1581, thus stops short of satire when he suggests that Leander was wrong in risking his life to see Hero because it is so much more comfortable and sensible merely to cross the gulf pouring from one's winepress. He adopts a comic *Beatus ille* attitude; he is not out to destroy the myth.[32] When, however, Quevedo in the seventeenth century pens his *Hero y Leandro en paños menores* ("Hero and Leander in Underclothes"), he calls Leander an "apprentice frog," and continues:

> Ya no hará en sorberse
> el mar mucha hazaña
> un amante huevo
> pasado por agua.[33]

This means that the sea will perform no great feat in swallowing a lover who is a poached egg. But "huevo," as well as meaning "egg," is a nauseating mollusk, and "pasado por agua," the phrase for poaching an egg, refers literally to Leander's swimming through the water. The deliberate ambiguities, the puns, ensure that after forty-six such quatrains there is nothing heroic left in Leander and nothing noble in Hero. He is an idiot and she a whore. This may or may not have been the reality that Quevedo construed as underlying the myth. But he leaves us in no doubt of the savagery with which he regarded heroic legend in general. His baroque satire of Boiardo's *Orlando innamorato* not only utterly degrades the hero, but is gratuitously anti-semitic into the bargain.[34] There are, it is true, other poems by Quevedo in which he shows a respect for heroism.[35] The contradiction is resolved when one realizes that what he cannot stand is the visible debasement in his times of the very spirit of heroism. A century earlier, he says, Spain was still producing heroes; but under the crass rule of Olivares, heroism has been replaced by a mindless dedication to clothing, coaches, and luxury.[36]

Satire is, of course, only one way of debasing heroes. Eras-

mus's criticism finds its way into less vitriolic fiction. Cervantes
has Don Quixote regret that Amadís was such a "llorón," a
crybaby; and elsewhere he comments that Aeneas was not as
pious nor Ulysses as cunning as their authors made them out
to be.[37] Sometimes, too, over-fertile imaginations may embroi-
der a heroic tale to such an extent that the epic hero is de-
meaned. In the *Poem of the Cid,* the epic hero is shown in
all his dignity as he grasps the escaped lion by its mane to
return it to its cage; his cowardly sons-in-law have fled in terror, one to hide beneath the bench on which the Cid has been
napping after lunch, and the other in a dirty winepress.[38] When
the same episode is recounted in the old ballads, the second
son-in-law has fled to a filthy privy.[39] The detail somehow
does not enhance the Cid's bravery; it rather diminishes his
stature. Inevitably the satiric Quevedo eventually seizes on
this cloacal suggestion to turn the hero himself into a gross,
overfed beast, "snoring like a cow." [40] Merely to coarsen the
hero's environment, it seems, is to encourage the sullying of
his impeccability.

A third kind of attack sometimes mounted against the hero
consists of inverting his circumstances without satirizing him
directly. The hero is replaced not by an anti-hero in the literal
sense in which Frank Chandler understood the term,[41] but in
the complementary sense in which modern physicists talk of
anti-matter and literary historians talk of the anti-novel. We
shall see that this treatment of the hero is of fundamental
importance for his future development. The classic example
of this technique is the protopicaresque novel, *Lazarillo de
Tormes,* first published in 1554. The narrator follows the
paradigm—the episodic structure—of the romances of chivalry. The picaroon—an underdog-errant—proceeds from one
adventure, or misadventure, to the next. Though his real name
is Lázaro González Pérez, he prefers to call himself grandly
by a toponymic: if Amadís is "de Gaula," then Lázaro insists
on being called "de Tormes." (The allusion is to the second-
class river running past Salamanca.) Many heroes, from Moses
to Amadís, have been cast on the water shortly after birth.[42]
Lázaro goes them one better by claiming to have been born
"in the river." [43] His mother gave birth to him while they were
living in the water mill in which his father worked. The hero

helped others in temporary distress; Lázaro helps himself in his continual distress. The rarefied society of the books of chivalry, the product of an imagination untrammeled by any sense of reality (as Montalvo himself noted [44]), is replaced by the actual circumstance of the slums or the servants' quarters. The squirearchy, the lowest level of Amadís's acquaintances, is the highest level with which Lázaro has any contact. The picaresque novel begins, then, as a chivalric romance turned inside out. But it is important to realize that, in spite of the inversion of heroic conditions, there is no denigration of the hero in the *Lazarillo*. Instead, the outcast, the beggar, the man who suffers dishonor gladly, becomes a different kind of hero: in Lázaro's life there are courage, constancy, restraint, and daring exploits, just as there were in the Cid's; but they are not directed to an altruistic cause. Heroism has at last been dissociated from nobility.

It is this phoenix-like rebirth of the hero from the ashes of his destruction that seems to me to have been one of the great contributions of the Spanish Renaissance not only to modern literature but even to the modern sensibility. We do not know to whom we owe this innovative re-creation of the hero, for the *Lazarillo de Tormes* is an anonymous work. But as well as to this nameless author, credit for the revitalization of the epic hero must go to two known writers, Cervantes and Calderón.

Cervantes underwent a spiritual crisis in his attitude toward heroism. It becomes necessary, therefore, to consider his life. He was born in 1547. He studied under a pupil of Erasmus. His life was spent soldiering until he was invalided out of the army. After an unsuccessful stint as a bureaucrat working for the Defense Department, he eventually turned to writing as a second—and second-best—career. He was fifty-eight when the first part of *Don Quixote* was published, and sixty-eight when the second part appeared. He was educated, then, in the fullness of the Spanish Renaissance, but he did not start writing until the dogmatism of the Counter-Reformation had been enunciated and imposed by the Council of Trent. The peculiar conditions of his intellectual formation make his attitude toward heroism particularly complex and significant.

Spanish land armies were not defeated until the Battle of

Rocroi in 1643. Then, as R. Trevor Davies puts it, "Spanish chivalry went down at last before the great Condé." [45] The heroic imperial enterprise, which began with the taking of Granada and the drive to America in 1492, continued with unabated impetus through the sixteenth century. Cervantes served in the victorious armies of Philip II until a wound sustained while fighting valiantly at Lepanto in 1571 forced him, as a veteran, to choose a new career. Even after Lepanto, during a long captivity in Algiers, he demonstrated his heroic nature over and over again in his resistance to his cruel captors and in his many attempts to escape. The spirit of heroism died hard within him.

The Erasmian criticism of war seems not to have penetrated very deeply into his intellectual consciousness. But the criticism was proved true by his experience. War was not always heroic; the rabble, ignoble as it was, was often the hero. Cervantes would always cherish the part he played at Lepanto, which he said was "the most memorable and loftiest event that past centuries have ever seen or future ones expect to see." [46] Yet even the glory of Lepanto had its absurd side. When ammunition ran out, a Turkish crew began flinging oranges and lemons at the Christian vessels, a brilliant idea that rapidly spread to "many places" during the battle. This spirit of *nil desperandum* was heroic after a fashion, but an observer noted that the grotesque use of citrous missiles caused everyone who saw it to laugh. [47] The presence of Don Quixote was already felt at Lepanto. For Cervantes it was proving increasingly difficult to sustain the solemnity and the nobility of spirit demanded of the hero. Still and all, Cervantes probably did not lose his faith in heroism at Lepanto, for he always looked back to that engagement as the last and greatest heroic venture in his life.

Not long afterwards (about 1585) he wrote the great tragedy *La Numancia* about the Iberian city that heroically obliterated itself from the face of the earth rather than accept defeat at the hands of Scipio. But even at this early date in his writing the Cervantine conception of heroism is *sui generis*. For him, glimpsing already the signs of Spanish military decline, heroism consists of plucking victory from the jaws of defeat. His formula of "winning while losing" eventually would lead to the reconstitution of the hero in Don Quixote.

But after his return to Spain from captivity, Cervantes's optimistic view of heroism in defeat was to suffer a further blow. Another naval action, intended to be decisive, was fought in the English Channel. With a truly Cervantine irony the Spanish fleet had been officially dubbed the Invincible Armada. Afterwards, the English spread the word that God was obviously on their side since he had sent high winds and waves to destroy the invaders. The Spaniards, incredibly, accepted this explanation of their defeat.[48] Since God always supports heroes, it follows that the sailors and soldiers of Spain could not on this occasion be thought of as heroes. Cervantes, moreover, was dismayed at Philip's indecision and at his refusal, or inability, to follow up the disaster with a second armada.[49] Cervantes was not this time in the forward lines of the battle, but ingloriously pushing a pen on the home front. His accounts were so badly mismanaged that he was jailed for what amounts to embezzlement. No less heroic involvement in an action that just missed being heroic can be imagined. It must have been this experience that caused Cervantes to become so disillusioned about heroism.

That he had lost faith in the myth of a heroic Spain can best be seen in a sonnet he wrote about the Earl of Essex's foray into Cadiz in 1596. The Spanish rescuing army is first seen drilling in Seville under the magnificent, if unhurried, generalship of the Duke of Medina Sidonia. Then, we are told, "the earth thundered and the heavens darkened, threatening total destruction; and, eventually, with considerable self-restraint, the Earl having fearlessly departed, the great Duke of Medina Sidonia entered Cadiz in triumph." [50] Cervantes underlines his point in an equally despondent sonnet on the catafalque of Philip II in Seville, presumably written in 1598. A soldier is in the cathedral admiring the exquisite workmanship of the catafalque: so wonderful is it that the soul of the departed has surely left its heavenly abode to take up residence in it. A listening bullyboy, ferociously handling his sword, challenges all comers to deny the truth of the soldier's statement. He swaggers out, glaring on all sides, and, in the

final words of the poem, "no hubo nada," nothing happened.[51]
These two poems reveal, with infinite sadness and not much
satire, the hollowness that by the end of the century Cervantes
saw in the myth of Spanish heroism. Out of this withering of
a belief nourished by him since childhood Cervantes would
produce the formula for another kind of heroism. First he
had imagined that the heroic bravery of Numantia would rise
again in the invincible spirit of Christian Spain. When that
dream proved unrealizable, he imagined—perhaps—that Spain
herself might somehow rise again in the dogged, never-say-die
spirit of Don Quixote.

But before considering the nature of the heroism in Cervantes's masterpiece, let us take note of how the post-epic
hero—what I shall call the "new hero"—was evolving in a
more standard fashion in post-Tridentine Spain. I shall try
to reveal some of his features as they appear in practice in
Calderón's dramatic art and in theory in a treatise by Gracián,
both of them much younger writers than Cervantes. I choose
them because they give the most brilliant, original expositions
of the orthodoxy of the seventeenth century. In this orthodox
renovation of the epic hero, too, it may be that Spain offered
a solution for the future. Calderón's hero, unlike Corneille's,[52]
still has an acceptable grandeur for us today; and he points
ahead to Carlyle's conception of the hero as any "great man"
capable of providing leadership for the unheroic masses.[53]

In Pedro Calderón de la Barca's *La vida es sueño* (1635)
Segismundo is first seen as a beast-man who, destined to be a
tyrant, is locked up in a tower by his father, the king of Poland,
and condemned to a childhood and adolescence of awful solitude. Drugged, brought to the palace for a day's experiment
to see if he will indeed behave as the stars have predicted,
he shows his violent nature. The king has him drugged again
and returned to his prison. As a result of this experience, Segismundo comes to believe that all life is a dream. But the people, knowing that at last they have a legitimate heir to the
throne, revolt against the king, release Segismundo, and invite
him to lead their revolution. Segismundo, in charge of a popular army, now begins to dream of heroic grandeur: "If today
Rome could see me present at its earliest triumphs," he muses,

"how glad she would be at seeing this remarkable opportunity of having in command of her great armies a beast whose proud spirit would not shrink from conquering the firmament itself!" [54] He has been afflicted with this titanic pride before (lines 329–36), but now, with an army under his command, his ambition has some chance of realization. Rosaura, the Muscovite noblewoman whom he has accidentally seen twice before, in the tower and in the palace, now recognizes in him a "heroic majesty" (line 2691). Accordingly he dreams of two victories—over his royal father and over Rosaura—that will be "heroic strokes of fortune" (line 2973). He feels capable of conquering not only heaven but fortune, his entire adverse destiny. But as a result of his experience in the palace, he has learned the moral lesson that even in dreams, even if life is a dream, the important thing is always to do good, if only for the selfish motive of winning friends and supporters in eternity: the way to do good to oneself is to do good to others. He therefore vanquishes his fortune "with prudence and temperance" (line 3219), and, even more heroically, he vanquishes his own proud passions: he pardons his father and renounces his love for Rosaura so that she may recover her lost honor by marrying the man who has dishonored her. "Since now," he resolves, "my valor expects to conquer in great victories, today the greatest victory of all will be my conquering of myself." [55] Such noble resolutions on the part of a tyrannically disposed and bestial man on a moral—and not on a military or political—plane make him worthy to be a prince, and make his acts worthy of being called by his father "feats" (line 3253), the moral equivalent of a hero's prowess. In Segismundo, Erasmus's *miles christianus* has been raised from the status of a mere infantryman, a foot-slogger, to that of a hero. Segismundo has discovered that the only battlefield proper to a seventeenth-century hero is the human psyche.[56]

Similarly, in Baltasar Gracián's treatise *El héroe* (1637) we learn that heroes are not born but rather that they make themselves by dominating themselves.[57] The eminent man must go out in search of fame, and, if his qualities and actions are not intrinsically deserving of note, he must try hard to make them appear so. With no trace of irony or cynicism,

Gracián explains that for the hero appearances are everything. Excellence, or the appearance of excellence, is what constitutes the hero. In the dedication to his book Gracián explains that the hero was made prudent by Seneca, sagacious by Aesop, bellicose by Homer, philosophical by Aristotle, statesmanlike by Tacitus, and courtly by Castiglione. If any one quality predominates among these, it is statesmanship: "royal—or real —eminence," he asserts, "is found not in fighting but in governing." Gracián thus harks back to the early Renaissance archetypes [58] established by Machiavelli and Castiglione, as well as to the classics, in order to shape a broad definition of the hero as any man of supreme excellence destined to lord it over his fellows.

We have seen how in Calderón's Counter-Reformation reinterpretation of the hero and in Gracián's redefinition of him the conception of the hero has been adapted and refined to make it viable in an age that still felt heroic but could not be heroic. Seventeenth-century Europe was simply not a continent fit for epic heroes to live in. A new kind of heroism had to be called into being. But Calderón's and Gracián's "new heroes" were scarcely radical enough to suit their unheroic world. The movement from their profound modernization of an old ideal type of human being to a totally new surrogate for the epic hero is rather more complex, more difficult to trace. But there need be no doubt that, in creating the modern novel, Cervantes created at the same time a hero-surrogate to dominate it. In this he was greatly indebted to the author of the *Lazarillo*.

The creation of a successor to the epic hero rests on two postulates: (1) What I have called the "new hero"—Calderón's Segismundo—is victorious in defeat; the "surrogate" is merely lovable in defeat. The world has come to love a loser, even if he snatches no substitute victory from his efforts. (2) The "new hero" still belongs to one of the higher strata of society, for it is above all noble birth that enables him to respond heroically to his adverse circumstance; the "surrogate" belongs either to the plebeian, ignoble end of the social scale or to the lowest class of nobility, the despised squirearchy or *hidalguía*. The ironic ideal of the "surrogate" is not a matter of birthright, for anyone can fail in an undertaking. As a result, the ordinary man, if not the common man, comes into his own in literature as well as in early sociological thought. Juan Bautista Avalle-Arce has noted that in the seventeenth century "The Spaniard is no longer master of his circumstance, and he seeks either to obliterate it . . . or to escape it. . . ." [59] I would add that Cervantes comes to terms with this general inability to control circumstance. He shows his hero-substitute to be indomitable in spirit even when the circumstance is crushing him. There is thus a new kind of humanism in *Don Quixote*, one which, while not exalting a hero to the skies, at least raises his successor out of the mire of mediocrity.

The hero-surrogate is not really an ideal type. He is not admirable, but sympathetic: we cannot admire, but we can sympathize with, one who makes the best of a bad job. His dreams of greatness may be futile, but at least he dreams standing up with his feet firmly planted on the ground of everyday reality. He is one of us.

The instigator of the hero-surrogate is undoubtedly Lazarillo. As we have seen, he is a perversion, or an inversion, of the chivalric hero. He looks out for himself, not for damsels in distress. But he looks out for himself only because he must. He has a residual concern for others, as Lázaro illustrates when he shares the food for which he has begged with the impoverished Squire whose servant he is. If Lázaro's good will and charity are largely suppressed, it is because his circumstance has suppressed them, not because he lacks feeling for his fellow man. But for his circumstance he could have been, if not an epic hero, at least a *miles christianus*. His poverty, however, denies him even the possibility of observing normal Christian obligations. The point for us is that his circumstance is so thwarting that it inhibits in him any possible appearance of heroism. But, like Don Quixote's, his human spirit cannot be crushed. While he will never engage in heroics, a latent heroism enables him to face the horrors of everyday poverty, and even to rise in his circumscribed world against all the odds. Far from being Chandler's anti-hero, Lázaro has all the determination and drive, all the courage and daring, all the self-restraint and prudence of the epic hero. It is simply that he directs these heroic qualities against a world unfit for heroes. He even has a cause, the selfish one of survival; but he would surely have adopted a more responsible cause if circumstances had permitted. The author, writing his prologue in the name of his protagonist, leaves no room for doubt on this point. Lázaro's supposed autobiography was written "so that those who have inherited a noble position in society may consider how little credit they deserve, since Fortune was partial to them, and how much more has been accomplished by those who, with Fortune against them, rowed hard and skillfully until they reached a safe haven." [60] Lázaro incarnates the heroism of the little man, remembered in our day in the works of Émile Zola and Charles Chaplin, but never better synthesized than by Victor Hugo when he wrote: "Life, misfortunes, isolation, abandonment, poverty, are battlefields that have their heroes; obscure heroes, sometimes greater than the illustrious ones." [61]

Alonso Quijano, nicknamed "the Good," is not poverty-stricken like Lázaro, but he has come down in the world. He is a country gentleman who dresses poorly and eats badly. He has sold off his few objects of value to acquire a library not of scholarly books from which to learn, but of fictional romances into which to escape. If Lázaro was trying to emerge from his desperately low station in life, Alonso Quijano is eager to flee from his mediocrity. With a heroic gesture he resolves to do so; and with heroic determination he continues —in his new persona as Don Quixote—to do so until, literally, his dying day. That his heroically led life is a mockery of heroism is not his fault. It was the fault of a Spain whose leaders—after Don John of Austria at Lepanto—were something less than heroes, and men unworthy to lead a nation of potential heroes. Heroism has survived, but it cannot bloom in an unheroic habitat.

Henceforth, not only in Spain but everywhere else, heroism would be baffled, foiled, defeated by the unheroic circumstance of the modern world. But the hero-surrogate would live on in literature to remind us that even in what Don Quixote calls "our detestable age of iron" heroism, the noblest ideal of secular man, continues to thrive beneath the surface of all sorts and conditions of men. The Eastern Airlines captain who denied that he was a hero showed heroic courage, moderation, and decision in his acceptance of the unheroic reality that required him to think first of his passengers' safety. Today no one can doubt the truth of Ortega y Gasset's dictum: "I am I and my circumstance." [62] The post-epic hero is a hero in an unheroic circumstance.

Notes

1. Best defined by Ramón Menéndez Pidal, *La España del Cid* (Madrid: Plutarco, 1929), 2: 631–64.

2. Pedro Salinas, "El 'héroe' literario y la novela picaresca española: semántica e historia literaria," in *Ensayos de literatura hispánica* (*Del Cantar de Mio Cid a García Lorca*) (Madrid: Aguilar, 1958), pp. 58–74. This important essay was the point of departure for my thinking about my subject. I should like to express my thanks to the members of my Spanish seminar at Duke—Rafael Aguirre, Juan Alejandro, Alene Delgado, Susan Fischer, Michael Perna, and George Yehling—for the contributions they made to this lecture during many hours of discussion.

3. "Tout ce qui paroît le plus opposé au caractère et à la gravité héroïque de ces premiers Romains." The preface, dated 1710, is entitled "Discours sur le dialogue suivant." See *Œuvres complètes de Boileau*, edited by Antoine Charles Gidel (Paris, 1873), 3: 176.

4. *De la Connaissance des bons livres* (Amsterdam, 1672), cited by Salinas, p. 66.

5. "Some Thoughts on Roland and Rodrigue," *Modern Language Review* 66 (1971): 42.

6. *Corneille et la dialectique du héros* (Paris: Gallimard, 1963), p. 123.

7. ". . . L' 'honnête homme,' pour se sauver de l'impasse où il est engagé, doit devenir ou, plus exactement, redevenir un *héros*. L'aristocrate est forcé, s'il veut survivre dans son dessein originel, de retourner précisément à ses origines, de se retremper aux sources vives de son être." Doubrovsky, p. 82.

8. "Finally, although he is never technically a traitor, his threats to the King and his refusal of obedience give his conduct a treasonable element, and he clearly comes into the general category of rebellious vassals. Such men are the heroes of epic poems from early times on both sides of the Pyrenees, but this happens more often when the epic is in decline, as part of a

general tendency to hold the attention of an audience by startling innovations." A. D. Deyermond, *Epic Poetry and the Clergy: Studies on the "Mocedades de Rodrigo"* (London: Támesis, 1968), p. 21.

9. "Vues sur les conceptions courtoises dans les littératures d'oc et d'oïl au XIIᵉ siècle," *Cahiers de civilisation médiévale* 2 (1959): 139–56.

10. *Histoire de la littérature anglaise* (Paris: Hachette, 1924), p. 531.

11. See María Rosa Lida de Malkiel, *Estudios de literatura española y comparada* (Buenos Aires: Eudeba, 1966), p. 148, where further bibliographical references may be found.

12. "Some talk of Alexander / And some, of Hercules, / Of Hector and Lysander, / And such great men as these; / But for all the world's great heroes / There's none that can compare / —With a tow-row-row-row-row-row— / To the British Grenadiers."

13. ". . . Esta nuestra España tiene en tan poco el esfuerço, por serle tan natural y ordinario, que le paresce que cuanto se puede hazer es poco; no como aquellos romanos y griegos, que al hombre que se aventurava a morir una vez en toda la vida le hazían en sus escriptos immortal y le trasladavan en las estrellas." Antonio de Villegas's *El Abencerraje y la hermosa Jarifa,* edited by Francisco López Estrada (Madrid: Revista de Archivos, Bibliotecas y Museos, 1957), p. 312. Four different versions of this work are known. The attitude expressed in this passage is called "the essence of the Spanish Renaissance" by J. E. Gillet in his edition of *"Propalladia" and Other Works of Bartolomé Torres Naharro,* vol. 4 (Philadelphia: University of Pennsylvania Press, 1961), p. 104.

14. *Amadís de Gaula,* edited by Edwin B. Place (Madrid: Consejo Superior de Investigaciones Científicas, 1959), 1: 7–8.

15. See, for example, Helmut A. Hatzfeld, *Santa Teresa de Ávila* (New York: Twayne, 1969), p. 12.

16. The text may be read, with accompanying translation, in *The Penguin Book of Spanish Verse,* edited by J. M. Cohen (Harmondsworth, Middlesex: Penguin, 1956), pp. 149–50.

17. See his ode "Por la pérdida del Rey don Sebastián," Cohen, pp. 166–70. His sonnet "Por la victoria de Lepanto" (pp. 170–71) is less elegiac.

18. See Aubrey F. G. Bell, *El renacimiento español* (Zaragoza: Ebro, 1944), p. 137.

19. "Quevedo dice que los españoles 'no supieron ser historiadores, supieron merecerlos' (*La hora de todos*)," Bell, pp. 137–38.

20. "Hurté del tiempo aquesta breve suma, / tomando ora la espada, ora la pluma." "Égloga III," lines 39–40, in Garcilaso de la Vega, *Poesías castellanas completas,* edited by Elias L. Rivers (Madrid: Castalia, 1969), p. 194.

21. The allusion is to the opening of his "Canción V" (*Ode ad florem Gnidi*), Garcilaso, pp. 93–94.

22. "Siempre la vida histórica del héroe puede ser ejemplo que nos haga concebir la nuestra como regida por un deber de actividad máxima, de justicia constante, de mesurada energía. . . ." (*La España*, 2: 663–64.)

23. Cited by André Chastel, *Art et humanisme à Florence au temps de Laurent le Magnifique: Etudes sur la Renaissance et l'Humanisme platonicien* (Paris: Presses Universitaires de France, 1961), p. 249.

24. "But as for the exercise of the mind, the prince should read history, and in it study the actions of distinguished men; to see how they comported themselves in war; to examine the causes for their victories and defeats in order to be able to avoid the latter and imitate the former; and above all he should do as some outstanding man before him has done, who decided to imitate someone who has been praised and honored before him and always keep in mind his deeds and actions: just as it is said that Alexander the Great imitated Achilles; Caesar, Alexander; Scipio, Cyrus." *Machiavelli's "The Prince": A Bilingual Edition*, translated and edited by Mark Musa (New York: St. Martin's Press, 1964), p. 125.

25. ". . . Neither are there still men like Caesar, Alexander, Lucullus, and those other Roman commanders." *The Book of the Courtier*, translated by Charles S. Singleton (Garden City, N.Y.: Doubleday, 1959), p. 240.

26. Pierre-Henri Simon, *Le Domaine héroïque des lettres françaises, X^e–XIXe siècles* (Paris: Colin, 1963), p. 14, discusses this change in the concept of the "grand homme."

27. Cf. Margherita Morreale, in the glossary to her edition of Lucas Gracián Dantisco, *Galateo español* (Madrid: Consejo Superior de Investigaciones Científicas, 1968), p. 313: "mesura—'comedimiento,' palabra clave del lenguaje cortés de la Edad Media. . . . En el siglo de oro los lex[icógrafos] la relacionan e identifican con la buena crianza. . . ."

28. Folly asks: "La guerre. . . . n'est-elle pas la source de toutes les actions que les hommes admirent? n'est-ce pas elle qui prépare les champs glorieux où les héros vont moissonner des lauriers?" A page later Folly notes: "C'est à des parasites, à des infâmes, à des voleurs, à des assassins, à des paysans, à des imbéciles, à des gueux, en un mot à tout ce qu'on appelle la lie du peuple, qu'il appartient de cueillir les lauriers de la victoire, lauriers qui ne sont point faits pour les philosophes." I cite from the following translation: Didier Érasme, *Éloge de la Folie* (Paris: Éditions de Cluny, 1937), pp. 33–34.

29. Translated from the Spanish version: Fray Héctor Pinto, *Imagen de la vida cristiana*, edited by Edward Glaser (Barcelona: Juan Flors, 1967), p. 353.

30. Edited by M. Martínez de Burgos (Madrid: Espasa-Calpe, 1942), p. 100.

31. Robert Brian Tate, in the editor's introduction to his edition of Fernando del Pulgar, *Claros varones de Castilla* (Oxford: Oxford University Press, Clarendon Press, 1971), pp. xlii, xliii.

32. The *Letrilla* "Ándeme yo caliente," widely anthologized, may be read in *Poems of Góngora*, edited by R. O. Jones (Cambridge: Cambridge University Press, 1966), pp. 121–22. The stanza alluded to reads: "Pase a media noche el mar, / y arda en amorosa llama / Leandro por ver su Dama; / que yo más quiero pasar / del golfo de mi lagar / la blanca o roja corriente, / *y ríase la gente.*"

33. Francisco de Quevedo, *Obras completas,* vol. 1, *Poesía original,* edited by José Manuel Blecua (Barcelona: Planeta, 1963), pp. 1076–81. The stanza cited is the fourth.

34. "Poema heroico de las necedades y locuras de Orlando el Enamorado," ibid., pp. 1333–84. The anti-semitism occurs in the dedication to Judas.

35. For example, "Túmulo de Aquiles cuando llegó a él Alejandro," ibid., p. 313.

36. See particularly the "Epístola satírica y censoria contra las costumbres presentes de los castellanos . . . ," ibid., pp. 140–47.

37. *Don Quixote de la Mancha,* edited by Rodolfo Schevill and Adolfo Bonilla, vol. 3 (Madrid: Gráficas Reunidas, 1935), p. 57 (Pt. II, chap. 2) and p. 64 (Pt. II, chap. 3): "A fee que no fue tan piadoso Eneas como Virgilio le pinta, ni tan prudente Vlisses como le descriue Homero."

38. *Poema de Mio Cid,* edited by R. Menéndez Pidal, 5th ed. (Madrid: Espasa-Calpe, 1946), pp. 227–28.

39. "Y Don Fernando, el mayor,—por un postigo se ha entrado, / que salía a un corral;—con el temor que ha llevado, / cayó en un lugar, asaz— deshonesto y perfumado." (Guy Le Strange, ed., *Spanish Ballads* [Cambridge: Cambridge Univ. Press, 1920], p. 89.)

40. "Pavura de los condes de Carrión," pp. 1049–53. From Daniel (Daniel 6:16–17) to Amadís (King Perión, chap. 1) and Don Quixote (Pt. 2, chap. 17), heroes have often shown their bravery in encounters with lions. See Félix G. Olmedo, *El "Amadís" y el "Quijote"* (Madrid: Editora Nacional, 1948), pp. 111–12.

41. The term is systematically applied to the picaresque hero by Frank W. Chandler in his *Romances of Roguery* (New York: Columbia University Press, 1899).

42. Otto Rank, *The Myth of the Birth of the Hero* (New York: Brunner, 1959) notes this event as part of the paradigm of the hero.

43. ". . . Con verdad me puedo decir nacido en el río." (*La vida de Lazarillo de Tormes y de sus fortunas y adversidades,* ed. R. O. Jones [Manchester: Manchester University Press, 1963], p. 5.)

44. *Amadís de Gaula,* p. 9: "Otros [escritores] vuo de más baxa suerte que escriuieron, que no solamente edificaron sus obras sobre algún cimiento de verdad, mas ni sobre el rastro della. Éstos son los que compusieron las hystorias fengidas en que se hallan las cosas admirables fuera de la orden

de natura, que más por nombre de patrañas que de crónicas con mucha razón deuen ser tenidas y llamadas."

45. *The Golden Century of Spain, 1501–1621* (London: Macmillan, 1937), p. 23.

46. "Prologo al lector" to the *Novelas exemplares*, edited by R. Schevill and Adolfo Bonilla (Madrid: Gráficas Reunidas, 1922), I: 21.

47. "A tanto furore si giunse e cosi cieco, che in una galea turchesca, mancando ormai ogni munizione di guerra, diedero di piglio perfino a'cedri e agli aranci de' quali avevano gran copia, e cercavano con quelli offendere i nostri . . . . era venuto a tanto in molti luoghi verso il fin del conflitto quella zuffa, che il vederla era anzi cosa da ridere che no." Cited from Stanislav Zimic, "Un eco de Lepanto en la ironía cervantina," *Romance Notes* 12 (1970): 143.

48. Garrett Mattingly, *The Defeat of the Spanish Armada* (London: Pelican, 1959), p. 408, comments: "It is always easier to accept defeat at the hands of God than at the hands of men, and the Judaeo-Christian tradition is rich in resources for explaining apparently irrational behaviour on the part of the Deity. That this time God had let them be defeated did not mean that the Spaniards were not fighting in His cause or that He would not uphold them in the end." This "logic" of the ruling class, however, did not persuade intellectuals like Cervantes and Quevedo.

49. Cervantes expressed his dismay in his "Canción II sobre 'La Armada Invencible.' " See *Poesías sueltas*, edited by R. Schevill and A. Bonilla (Madrid: Gráficas Reunidas, 1922), pp. 56–61.

50. "Soneto a la entrada del Duque de Medina en Cádiz," ibid., pp. 71–72.

51. "Soneto al túmulo de Felipe II en Sevilla," ibid., pp. 73–74. See Elias L. Rivers, " 'Viaje du Parnaso' y poesías sueltas," in *Suma cervantina*, edited by J. B. Avalle-Arce, E. C. Riley (London: Támesis, 1973), pp. 119–46.

52. Corneille's attempt to re-endow the noble with heroism was doomed in an age which has no place for aristocracy: "l'héroïsme aristocratique échoue en tant qu'entreprise singulière d'une époque et d'une classe, parce qu'il est impossible comme manière humaine d'exister." Doubrovsky, p. 29.

53. Carlyle's advocacy of a "hero-archy" is often said to have paved the way for the Nazi state, with its political glorification of the superman. The error of this opinion is clearly demonstrated in Ernst Cassirer, *The Myth of the State* (New Haven, Conn.: Yale University Press, 1946).

54. "Si este día me viera / Roma en los triunfos de su edad primera, / ¡oh, cuánto se alegrara, / viendo lograr una ocasión tan rara / de tener una fiera / que sus grandes ejércitos rigiera, / a cuyo altivo aliento / fuera poca conquista el firmamento!" Edited by Albert E. Sloman (Manchester: Manchester University Press, 1961), lines 2656–63.

55. Lines 3255–58. Segismundo triumphs over his base nature by coming to know who he essentially is, and acting accordingly. The Spanish baroque

expressed this action upon self-knowledge by the formula *Soy quien soy,* "I am who I am." The modernity of this conception of heroism becomes apparent when one examines José Ortega y Gasset's discussion of the hero in his *Meditaciones del "Quijote"* (1914). "Porque ser héroe consiste en ser uno, uno mismo . . . Y este querer él ser él mismo es la heroicidad." *Obras completas* (Madrid: Revista de Occidente, 1953), 1: 389–90.

56. Karl Vossler, *Introducción a la literatura del Siglo de Oro* (Madrid: Cruz y Raya, 1934), p. 71, names as the three major heroes of the Spanish Golden Age the Cid, Don Quixote, and Don Fernando (the protagonist of Calderón's *El príncipe constante*). The heroism of the saint is indeed very apparent from this and other dramas of Calderón. I pass over this aspect of the changing concept of heroism only for lack of space. Strictly speaking, while recognizing the heroic in the lives of saints and martyrs, one should probably regard them as traditionally belonging to another—a different— human ideal. See the table of "personal value types" or "models for emulation," formulated by Max Scheler, and discussed by Ernst Robert Curtius in *European Literature and the Latin Middle Ages* (New York: Pantheon, 1953), pp. 167 ff.

57. Text in *Biblioteca de Autores Españoles* 65: 600–611.

58. For a discussion of the "archetypes" in Gracián and the Renaissance, see E. Tierno Galván, "Introducción" to Baltasar Gracián, *El político*, edited by E. Correa Calderón (Salamanca: Anaya, 1961), pp. 7–9. See also Alfonso Reyes, *Capítulos de literatura española*, 1st series (México: El Colegio de México, 1939), pp. 232 and 267.

59. Introduction to Cervantes, *Three Exemplary Novels* (New York: Dell, 1964), p. 10.

60. ". . . Porque consideren los que heredaron nobles estados cuán poco se les debe, pues Fortuna fue con ellos parcial, y cuánto más hicieron los que, siéndoles contraria, con fuerza y maña remando, salieron a buen puerto" (p. 4).

61. *Les Misérables*, Bk. V, Chap. 1.

62. "Yo soy yo y mi circunstancia, y si no la salvo a ella no me salvo yo." *Meditaciones del "Quijote,"* in *Obras completas*, 1: 322.

Suggested Reading

Baudouin, Charles. *Le Triomphe du héros: étude psychanalytique sur le mythe du héros et les grandes époques.* Paris: Plon, 1952.

Burgess, G. S. "Some Thoughts on Roland and Rodrigue." *Modern Language Review* 66 (1971): 40–52.

Doubrovsky, Serge. *Corneille et la dialectique du héros.* Paris: Gallimard, 1963.

Hook, Sidney. *The Hero in History: A Study in Limitation and Possibility.* New York: John Day Co., 1950.

McNamee, Maurice. *Honor and the Epic Hero: A Study in the Shifting Concept of Magnanimity in Philosophy and Epic Poetry.* New York: Holt, Rinehart and Winston, 1960.

Menéndez Pidal, Ramón. *La España del Cid.* 2 vols. Madrid: Plutarco, 1929.

Nelson, Robert J. *Corneille, His Heroes and Their Worlds.* Philadelphia: University of Pennsylvania Press, 1963.

Rank, Otto. *The Myth of the Birth of the Hero.* New York: Brunner, 1959.

Salinas, Pedro. "El 'héroe' literario y la novela picaresca española: semántica e historia literaria." In *Ensayos de literatura hispánica (Del Cantar de Mio Cid a García Lorca).* Edited by Juan Marichal. Madrid: Aguilar, 1958.

Simon, Pierre-Henri. *Le Domaine héroïque des lettres françaises, Xᵉ–XIXᵉ siècles.* Paris: Colin, 1963.

Heywood's Women Worthies

Eugene M. Waith

A SUBTITLE FOR THIS PAPER MIGHT BE: "From the Exemplary Life to the Pop Biography and the Journalistic Profile," for Thomas Heywood's book not only shows the pressure of several intellectual and social forces on a major component of the heroic tradition—the exemplary life—but also anticipates some of the ways in which this component was later to be transformed and popularized. The work I shall describe is not a neglected literary masterpiece but a valuable piece of evidence in the history of the tradition that this conference and its predecessor were designed to illuminate. While keeping Heywood's nine women worthies in the foreground, I shall make a few excursions into areas to which they seem to point.[1]

The title page of a book that appeared in London in 1640 reads: *The Exemplary Lives and Memorable Acts of Nine the Most Worthy Women of the World: Three Jewes. Three Gentiles. Three Christians. Written by the Author of the History of Women.* These lines fairly burst with clues to the nature of the work described. Ever since Xenophon wrote his fictionalized account of the early life of Cyrus the Great, the *Cyropedia,* the exemplary life had been a recognized and well-loved means of glorifying a historical figure and holding aloft for emulation his noble character and great deeds. In the fifteenth century Christine de Pisan called her life of the French king Charles V *Le livre des fais et bonnes meurs du sage roy Charles V,*[2] leaving no doubt that she was presenting this wise king as a model of virtuous living and memorable deeds. Indeed, her technique seems to be to name the standard virtues and then show that Charles had them all. Since this was the fifteenth century, it is not surprising that she gives prominence to the virtues stressed by chivalry—"noblece de courage"

(1: 10), "bonne renommée," "libéralité et sage largèce" (1: 79 ff.), the attributes of the medieval hero, the perfect "chevalier." In the same century the Italian, Tito Livio, made the point of exemplary biographies embarrassingly clear by addressing his life of Henry V to his unheroic son, Henry VI, with the avowed hope of encouraging him to cope with his enemies as his father had done. Then the anonymous author of the *Life of Henry V*, written in 1513, translated much of Tito Livio, added to it, and offered his work to Henry VIII to stiffen his resolve against Francis I.[3] Of course, the usefulness of these examples was not restricted to reluctant kings, but extended to all readers. As Sidney said of heroic poetry, with which he associated such works as Xenophon's *Cyropedia,* "For as the image of each action styrreth and instructeth the mind, so the loftie image of such Worthies most inflameth the mind with desire to be worthy, and informes with counsel how to be worthy." [4] In other words, heroic literature only does better and more conspicuously what all literature should do —inspire men to be better. Since the didacticism inherent in the conception of the exemplary life was readily adaptable to bourgeois morality, this strain of the heroic tradition was bound to have a strong appeal to the author of *A Woman Killed with Kindness.*

Perhaps it was natural not to summon up remembrance of this play on the title page of a book about exemplary women. Here Heywood billed himself as "the Author of the History of Women." The reference is to *Gunaikeion,* a compendium of 466 folio pages published in 1624, in which Heywood assembled a formidable quantity of information about all sorts of women. With seeming orderliness, which, as Arthur M. Clark says, is quite deceptive,[5] he divided the book into nine sections, each "inscribed" to one of the muses. Goddesses, for instance, are treated under Clio; muses, sybils, vestals, and prophetesses under Euterpe; "Women Incestuous, Adulteresses, and such as haue come by strange deaths" under Melpomene; and "Amazons and other women, famous either for Valour or Beautie" under Terpsichore, because martial discipline consists in "time, number, measure, distance, and order," and "in daunces we keep time to the musicke" (p. 215). There is something for everyone here, as Heywood clearly intended there should be, describing his audience as "an vniuersalitie of Readers, diuersly disposed" (sig. A3ᵛ), but in spite of the inclusion of adulteresses and "women incestuous," the book as a whole is devoted to the greater glory of women. It was, in fact, a major contribution to the long and bitter controversy about women, and one of many answers to Joseph Swetnam's *Arraignment of Lewd, idle, froward and unconstant women* of 1615.

To recall *Gunaikeion* was, therefore, to identify the *Exemplary Lives* as pro-feminist literature. In the epistle "To the Generall Reader" Heywood states flatly that it is a duty to dignify the sex since we all had mothers; that he tried to do so in *Gunaikeion*, but that here, instead of a miscellany of all types, he presents only nine worthy women (sig. **4). One of the forces pressing on the tradition of exemplary biography was this feminist controversy of the early seventeenth century.

In the course of stating his laudable and laudatory purpose, Heywood writes that his choice of nine women alludes to the number of the muses, but this time he is being disingenuous or absent-minded, for the primary allusion is not that at all. The authors of the commendatory verses "To the worthy Reviver of these Nine Women worthies" and "To his worthy Friend Mr. *Thomas Heywood,* on his Nine Female Worthies" show their awareness of what must have been plain to all who read on the title page the division into "Three Jewes, Three Gentiles. Three Christians." Heywood is invoking worthies, not muses.

The medieval tradition of the Nine Worthies was an interesting subdivision of the heroic tradition, consisting in what purported to be a list of the nine greatest men who had ever been. It must be said at the outset that occasionally there were more or less than nine, and that when there were nine, they were not always exactly the same nine. In the fourteenth century, however, appeared a list approaching the status of canonical in the *Voeux du Paon,* an addition by Jacques Longuyon to the *Roman d'Alexandre,* glorifying the heroism of Alexander's enemy, Porus. Not even the greatest men of all time fought more bravely than Porus, according to Longuyon, who then names the three best pagans, Hector, Alexander, and Caesar; the three Jews, Joshua, David, and Judas Maccabeus; and the three Christians, Arthur, Charlemagne, and Godfrey of Bouillon. This passage about what came to be called in French the "Neuf Preux" seems to have been the source of an identical list in *The Parlement of the Thre Ages* of the fourteenth century and perhaps of the reference in the fifteenth-century *Flower and the Leaf,* where they are called the "Nine Worthy." [6] Pageants of the Neuf Preux or Nine Worthies are known to have been presented more than two centuries before Holofernes, Armado, Costard, and the rest made their disastrous attempt, but the tradition was above all visual. Images of these great men appeared in tapestries woven for Charles V, the subject of the biography by Christine de Pisan, and in the tapestries of his son, Charles VI, who also had the Neuf Preuses. Though the tapestries are lost, we know from inventories that the women in this case were not divided like the men into groups of biblical, pagan, and Christian worthies, but were an assemblage of Amazons and of warrior queens such as Tomyris, who is said to have decapitated Cyrus the Great and plunged his head in a bucket of blood. [7] Images of these worthies, to be wondered at and possibly revered on a castle wall, were clearly exemplary like the biographies of which I was speaking. They recalled memorable acts and condensed a story into a single visual impression. As we shall see in a moment, Heywood, too, relied on visual aids.

To whom was he addressing his feminist tract? A question to be asked, but not simple to answer, for there are no less than four prefatory epistles, the first to the wife of a knight, the "Honorable and Eminently Vertuous, the Excellent" Lady Theophila Cooke; the second to the wife of a country squire, the "excellently disposed" Mistress Elizabeth Tanfield; the third "To all Noble and Brave Spirited Gentlemen, with the excellent and vertuously disposed Gentlewomen in generall"; and the fourth "To the Generall Reader." As we descend the social ladder by easy stages, we realize that once again, as in *Gunaikeion,* Heywood is aiming at "an vniuersalitie of Readers." This intention has important consequences for his handling of a once aristocratic tradition.

Of the four prefatory epistles, then, two might be called

dedications. But there is also, in most copies, a frontispiece on
the verso of the first leaf of the first gathering, opposite the
title page, where one might take it for yet another dedication.
In the Elizabethan Club copy at Yale it is not identified, and
it has sometimes been taken to be one of the dedicatees of the
prefatory epistles. In some copies, however, the same engraving appears in a different form (fig. 1), folding out at the
bottom to reveal the inscription: "The most renowned most
mightie & most Excellent HENRETTA MARIA of England,
Scotland, France & Ireland, Queene, etc.," followed by four
lines of verse:

> Copesmate to crowned Charles our Christian king:
> Mother of Princes, blest in Every thing;
> Dame Natures darling, whose vnmatch'd renowne,
> Add's to the glorious luster of the Crowne.

This larger form of the frontispiece had, of course, to be pasted
in, and it was presumably the publisher's intention to cancel
the first leaf of the first gathering in copies with the paste-in,
but the Huntington Library copy, which contains the engraving reproduced here, also has the other form of frontispiece,
while the copy in the Beinecke Library at Yale has neither.
Though, even with the inscription, this engraving, derived
ultimately from a Van Dyck portrait,[8] does not constitute a
dedication in the strict sense, it is proper to put Queen Henrietta Maria at the top of that hierarchy of readers whom
Heywood was addressing. Six years earlier he had written for
her *Love's Mistress, or The Queen's Masque,* part play, part
masque, which had so pleased the court that it had been twice
repeated.

The first woman worthy is Deborah, an engraving of whom
appears opposite the first page of text (fig. 2), as the engravings of her eight successors precede the sections devoted to
them. Heywood tells with considerable verve the Bible story
of Deborah's attempt to persuade Barak to assault the Canaanites under Sisera. Barak is very reluctant to take on the
task imposed by the prophetess, and only agrees to it if she
will go with him. What an admirable beginning for a story
intended to undermine male chauvinism! But much more is

to come, as all readers of the Bible will remember. "That Heroicke and masculine spirited Championesse," as Heywood calls her (p. 15), so inspires Barak that the Canaanites are overcome, and Sisera flees from the battlefield. He takes refuge, as Deborah knew he would, in the tent of an Israelite family living in Canaanite territory. There Jael, the wife, having welcomed him, given him a drink of milk, and put him to sleep, drives a nail through his temples. Heywood paraphrases Deborah's great triumphal song with its praise for Jael, but adds: "Neither did this great honour done unto *Iael,* any way take off or derogate from the merit and magnanimity of *Deborah.* . ." (p. 19). Note "magnanimity," one of the key words for a quality at the heart of the heroic tradition, expressed sometimes in liberality or largesse, sometimes in altruism, sometimes in great deeds or noble aspirations. Deborah had it and Barak did not, until she inspired him.

Next comes Judith, whose well-known head-chopping is vividly memorialized in the accompanying engraving and in paintings throughout the art galleries of the western world. "Match me this woman amongst men," says Heywood in an introductory poem. Like Deborah, she changed the military fortunes of the Jews.

Esther, the wife of the Persian King Ahasuerus, is, as the illustration suggests (fig. 3), a regal worthy of a somewhat milder cast, but also, through persuasion and contrivance rather than bloody deeds, a savior of her people.

In the group of worthies variously called the "gentiles" or the "heathen," first place is given to Bunduca (alias Boadicea or Bondicia), not, surely, to suggest that she chronologically preceded Penthesilea, the Amazon who follows her, but presumably because she was British. Heywood writes:

> How much, *O Brittaine,* are we bound to thee
> Mother, and Nurse of magnanimity?
>
> . . . .
>
> Witnes this *British* Queen, whose masculine spirit
> Shall to all future, glorious fame inherit, . . . (p. 68.)

Boudicca, as she is known to modern historians, was indeed a formidable woman, the queen of the Iceni, who led their re-

volt against Rome in 61 A.D., which, for a while, seriously
threatened Roman control. According to Heywood, she was
not a "martiall *Bosse*, or *Amazonian* Giantesse, but tall of
stature, and moderately fat and corpulent, her face excellently
comely, yet withall incomparably terrible, her complexion very
faire and beautifull, which who will wonder at in a Lady
borne in *Brittaine?*" (p. 72). It may be debatable whether the
engraving does her justice (fig. 4); no doubt it is difficult to
convey the quality of the complexion in this medium. But in
one respect the engraver is at odds with Heywood, who tells
us that she wore her hair to her knees. He finishes his account
of her with the information that Stonehenge was erected as
a monument to her. In this section he is obviously warming
up to his subject.

As a background for Penthesilea (fig. 5) and to advance
the cause of women he explains: "All these Heroyicke Ladies
are generally called *Viragoes*, which is derived of Masculine
Spirits, and to attempt those brave and Martiall Enterprises,
which belong to the honour of men. . ." (p. 96). After dis-
coursing for a time on this subject, he goes on to the story
of her going to Troy to help the Trojans and, as some say,
to be slain in single combat by Achilles.

Artimesia rates on more than one ground. First, her devotion to her husband, Mausolus, was such that after his death
she built the monument to him that became one of the seven
wonders of the world. (At this point Heywood describes the
other six.) She also displayed magnanimity in giving away
her estate. But her other main claim to worthihood was her
fighting with Xerxes against the Greeks in the naval engagement that ended disastrously for him. Finding that Artimesia's
ships had fought on long after the rest had fled, Xerxes said,
"All my men this day have proved themselves women, and
the women onely shewed themselves to be men. . ." (p. 127).
By this time it may strike one that these women are consistently praised for being like the other sex rather than their
own. However laudatory Heywood is, he seems basically to
agree with Henry Higgins in *My Fair Lady* in wondering,
"Why can't a woman be more like a man?"

It is no surprise that the three Christian women worthies

are all British by birth or adoption; but with the exception of Queen Elizabeth, the last of them, the choice of British heroines is unexpected. The first is a lady whom Heywood calls sometimes Elphleda and more often Elpheda, but who appears in our history books as Aethelflaed, the eldest daughter of King Alfred, sister of Edward, who succeeded him, and wife of Aethelred, the ealdorman of Mercia. She materially aided her brother in his wars with the Danes by fortifying several strategic points in Mercia, and after her husband's death ruled that section of Britain for eight years as the "Lady of the Mercians." I need hardly say that Heywood refers to her "Masculine Spirit" (p. 130). He illustrates it with a curious anecdote: "It is further reported of her, that after she had once prooved the paine of travaile in Child birth, shee for ever after abandoned the bed, and embraces of the Duke her Husband: saying, it was neither convenient nor seemely for a Kings Daughter, and Sister to a King, to expose her selfe to any such lustfull action, which might beget those pangs, and throws, which women were inforced to indure in travell, . . ." (p. 144). She then left "all other effeminacies" to devote herself to war. Her husband's reply to her non-negotiable demands is not recorded, but one is left to suppose that he agreed to everything. Continent, beautiful, free, and "masculine Spirited" (p. 143), Elpheda is clearly one of Heywood's favorites.

The eighth worthy is Margaret of Anjou, the wife of Henry VI. To find this tiger's heart, wrapped in a woman's hide, held up as exemplary, rather than cautionary, is initially breathtaking. Heywood admits that through this marriage Henry lost Anjou and Maine, and that many people blamed civil disruptions on the fact that a woman began to take the government of the kingdom into her own hands; but he admires Margaret's "brave and Heroick Spirit" (p. 156), and is soon talking about her magnanimity in the sense of bravery, manifested both in military prowess and in her defiance of King Edward, even when she is in his power (pp. 167, 179). Sheer will and energy command Heywood's respect. He recounts the infamous episode of the taunting and killing of the Duke of York without comment. In this portrait Heywood is perhaps closest to the primitive heroic tradition, which values great-

ness above moral goodness, or assumes that *virtus* is the greatest virtue.

Last, but obviously not least, comes "this rare Heroicke
Elizabeth" (p. 185), to whom Heywood also devoted a two-
part play, a prose tract, and a poem. In this work she is presented quite simply as the sum of the heroic excellences of all
the most virtuous ladies.

From the samples given so far it would be hard to form an
opinion of the style of this book. There are, as one quotation
revealed, sections in verse (they occur at the beginning of each
portrait), but well over ninety percent of the whole is prose.
Though the poems occasionally get up a head of rhetorical
steam, for the most part they jog along with facile rhymes
and no special distinction. The prose is workmanlike, readable,
and well-suited to narrative—far removed from the grandeur
of epic but a natural development of the style of exemplary
biography and popular history. Heywood classifies his work
as a kind of history, which he defines with a parade of learned
terminology. There are four categories of history: nugatory
(comical dramas), adhortatory (Aesop's fables), fictionary
(poetical narrations), and relatory (adhering to truth), this
last being the category to which his tractate belongs. Then,
with a proliferation of schemes worthy of Northrop Frye, he
further divides history into four species, taken from place
(geography), time (chronology), generation (genealogy), and
"gests really done" (annology) (sig. **3). The *Exemplary
Lives* are presumably instances of relatory annology, where
the emphasis falls on truth. Heywood was enough of a scholar
to know that traditional rhetorical decorum prescribed a low
style for such an enterprise.

It is characteristic of Heywood, with his divided allegiance
to court and city, to have chosen a kind of writing that upholds
the values of an aristocratic society while it is addressed to
a far wider audience. One senses the same popularizing of the
heroic tradition in his plays on the Four Ages, in his *The Four
Prentices of London* (those noblemen in disguise who deliver
Jerusalem), and in his enthusiastic comments in the *Apology
for Actors* on the wonderful effect of heroic deeds upon a
theater audience: ". . . what English blood seeing the person

The most renowned most mightie & most Excellent HENRETTA:
MARIA of England, Scotland, France & Ireland. Queene. etc.
Coremate to crowned Charles our Christian king:
Mother of Princes blest in Every thing:
Dame Natures darling. whose vnmatch't renowne.
Adds to the glorious luster of the Crowne.

Fig. 1. Anonymous Engraving of Queen Henrietta Maria.
Reproduced by permission of the Huntington Library, San Marino, Calif.

Fig. 2. Deborah. Engraving by George Glover.

Fig. 3. Esther. Engraving by George Glover.
Reproduced by permission of the Board of Governors
of the Elizabethan Club of Yale University.

Fig. 4. Bunduca. Engraving by George Glover.

Reproduced by permission of the Board of Governors
of the Elizabethan Club of Yale University.

Fig. 5. Penthesilea. Engraving by George Glover.
*Reproduced by permission of the Board of Governors
of the Elizabethan Club of Yale University.*

THE NINE WOEMEN WORTHYS.
Three Iewes Three Heathens Three Christians.
DEBORA
When BARAK fainted, DEBORA cru'de on:
Heartning & Souldiers, when theirr Spiritts weare gone,
Before whome SISERA, whose pride did swell,
With his nine hundred Iron Charriotts fell.

G: Gl: fecit   Are to be sould by Will Peak:

Fig. 6. Deborah. Engraving by George Glover.
Reproduced by permission of the Trustees of the British Museum.

Fig. 7. Alexander (or Hector) in The Nine Heroes Tapestries.
*The Metropolitan Museum of Art, The Cloisters Collection, Gift of
John D. Rockefeller, Jr., 1947. Reproduced by permission
of the Metropolitan Museum.*

DOMINVS PHLIPPVS HISPANVS DESCOLARIS RELATORVICTORIE THEVCROʒ

Fig. 8. Pippo Spano. From Mario Salmi, *Andrea del Castagno*.
Reproduced by permission of the Istituto Geografico de Agostini.

Fig. 9. Esther. From Mario Salmi, *Andrea del Castagno*.
Reproduced by permission of the Istituto Geografico de Agostini.

Fig. 10. Penthesilea. Design by Inigo Jones for *The Masque of Queens*.
Devonshire Collection, Chatsworth. Reproduced by permission
of the Trustees of the Chatsworth Settlement.

of any bold English man presented and doth not hugge his
fame, and hunnye at his valor, pursuing him in his enterprise
with his best wishes. . . ." [9]

Heywood's practice is merely one of many indications of
this widening audience and of the transformations of the heroic
tradition that it effected. The popularity of the Amadis and
Palmerin romances in the late sixteenth century is another such
indication. But the transformation was not always, as in this
last instance, a debasing of coinage; it could also be a simplifi-
cation suited to a program of uplift. Heroic literature, addressed primarily to the noblest and best—that is, to the aristocracy—must always have found readers and listeners among
those with aristocratic sympathies, if not blood, and among the
curious and the dreamers, whose wishes were fulfilled by such
marvelous doings. By the seventeenth century it was technically feasible to reach a rapidly increasing number of readers,
and an author with Heywood's ambition and missionary zeal
could both play upon and encourage their aristocratic yearnings. Though Judith and Margaret of Anjou may not represent what every woman wants to be, they are frankly presented
as examples of what women have achieved and therefore may
achieve. By implication these histories are, after all, adhortatory
as well as relatory.

Before leaving the matter of mixed modes I must also mention the tradition of compendia which asserts its influence on
this work. Heywood seems never happier than when he is
sharing with his reader the hoards of information that he has
busily accumulated here and there, squirrel or magpie of
scholarship that he is. *Gunaikeion* is a catch-all of legends,
history, and anecdotes about all sorts of women. *The Hierarchy of the Blessed Angels*, another monumental work, is not
an orderly disquisition on the functions of each of the angelic
ranks, as one might expect it to be, but a stupefying collection
of information and anecdotes of the most various sorts. In the
Exemplary Lives, where he has supposedly confined himself
to the nine women of his choice, the restriction proves intol-
erable, and by the time he has reached his fifth woman worthy
he can no longer hold himself in. As a background for Penthesilea he runs through the principal facts about eight other

"Heroyicke Ladies" (pp. 96–99). Some of these receive second mention in another list of thirty-five heroic women in all ages, which he rattles off in the Artimesia chapter, and before he embarks on the story of Elpheda he cannot resist digressing on the subject of fourteen women who were the occasion of "much combustion and trouble" and giving yet another catalogue of seven eminent and excellent women (pp. 132–36). In these sections his treatise becomes the *Reader's Digest* of heroic legend.

I have already said that the tradition of the Nine Worthies was primarily visual. In fact, Heywood's book seems to have been inspired by the illustrative engravings, which already existed as a series called THE NINE WOEMEN WORTHYS. *Three Jewes. Three Heathens. Three Christians.*, by George Glover,[10] who also did some of the illustrations for *The Hierarchy of the Blessed Angels.* In this form there appeared in the lower margin of Plate I the title of the series, the name DEBORA, four lines of descriptive verse, the artist's name, and the imprint (fig. 6). Each of the other eight plates had the name of the woman worthy and descriptive verses. Oddly enough, the names of the worthies are not quite identical, for Zenobia appears among the heathen instead of Bunduca, who is placed (under the variant name of "Bonditia") among the Christians. Heywood has moved her into the heathen category, where presumably, she belongs, leaving Zenobia out (though she receives brief mention in two of his lists of heroic ladies) and adding Elpheda among the Christians. The engraving of Zenobia was simply retitled "Elpheda." As a comparison of the two Deborahs shows, Heywood's plates are identical except for the masking of the marginal titles and inscriptions.

A review of the iconic tradition behind this depiction of the nine women worthies is out of the question here, but a very few samples will help to make one or two more points about Heywood's book. Dating from the fourteenth century, approximately contemporaneous with the list of worthies by Jacques de Longuyon, are the Nine Heroes tapestries at The Cloisters, woven for the Duc de Berry. The original three tapestries, depicting three heroes each, were cut up and dispersed, but enough pieces have been found and reassembled to reconstitute the panels showing five of the nine. Reproduced here is one of the heathens, probably Alexander, surrounded by courtiers and warriors (fig. 7). The heroes are identified by their shields, by motifs on their clothing, and by what they hold in their hands. The device on this shield is sometimes given to Hector, but more often to Alexander.

The stiff formality of the figures makes them seem remote, each in his niche, like the figures on the façade of a cathedral. James Rorimer and Margaret Freeman observe that the treatment of the figures is very similar to that in the stained glass windows of the Duc de Berry's Sainte Chapelle in Bourges.[11] The rigidity perhaps confirms one impression made by the arrangement of major and minor figures—a stable order centered on the hero-king (for even Joshua and Caesar are crowned). Each one is a benefactor, surrounded by grateful subjects. But all the figures also have a certain grace and nobility consonant with chivalric romance. The courtly decorum of the entire group suggests a scene in Chrétien de Troyes. These worthies are models and marvels not only of prowess but of magnanimity and courtesy as well.

The early "preuses" who appeared in the lost tapestries of Charles VI or in the surviving frescoes by Iverny in the Castello di Manta in Piedmont were, like most of Heywood's worthies, unusually fierce women, though in the frescoes and in manuscript illuminations they strike graceful attitudes with their spears, battle-axes, and shields. Like their male counterparts, they are set apart, elevated, as it were (and sometimes literally so), the better to be admired.

The medieval images of worthies, male and female, are preserved in an unexpected way on the face cards of the familiar playing deck. The design of American cards derives from British cards, which were based on a sixteenth-century Rouen deck.[12] The French tradition went back to the fourteenth century, to the period of greatest interest in the worthies, several of whose names became associated with cards. The four kings were: Charlemagne (hearts), David (spades), Caesar (diamonds), and Alexander (clubs). The Queen of Hearts was

Judith, the Queen of Diamonds sometimes Penthesilea, but more often Rachel. They have the same stiff formality as the figures in the tapestries.

In the Renaissance, when frescoes succeeded tapestries as the accepted way to decorate a great hall, the depiction of "uomini famosi" continued, but not the same worthies, and not necessarily nine of them. There is an obvious connection between such paintings and all the heroic portraits and statues of the time, but the sets of famous men and women executed as mural programs are related most closely to the worthies tradition. Worthy women were also, most appropriately, often depicted on wedding chests, though some of them, such as Judith, must have seemed like ill omens to young husbands. In the middle of the fifteenth century Andrea del Castagno painted, in the Volta di Legnaia of the Villa Carducci, a splendid set of heroes and heroines, which may be compared with the medieval worthies. Since they were removed from the original walls many years ago, we cannot be sure how they were originally arranged.

Among these worthies is Pippo Spano, whose real name was Filippo Scolari, a Florentine *condottiere* of the late fourteenth and early fifteenth century (fig. 8). He spent most of his life in Hungary and Germany as advisor of the Emperor Sigismund, who made him count (*ispan*) of Temesvar. Though he lived slightly before Castagno's time (he visited Florence for the last time before Castagno's birth), he was a relatively recent hero. Castagno, who may have seen a likeness of him, depicts him as a living man and as an individual. Though his armor and sword are, in a sense, emblematical, the portrait has none of the remoteness or formality of the heroes in the medieval tapestries. One obvious way in which he is made to impinge on our world is Castagno's breaking of the frame he has put around his figure. Pippo, instead of sitting on a throne in a niche, is about to step out. Admirable and outstanding as he is, he is one of us.

The same may be said of Farinata degli Uberti, who is a little more remote in time—a thirteenth-century Ghibelline who appears in the tenth canto of the *Inferno*. Though there may be some effort to give him the costume of his period, his

hat is of a fashion popular in Castagno's time. The immediacy
and credibility of these heroes seem to be Castagno's aim.

For Queen Tomyris Castagno had, naturally, to draw on
his imagination, but he makes her as much a living individual
as Pippo and Farinata. The mere placing of such a worthy
alongside the almost contemporary ones asserts the continuity
of the heroic tradition. Though the decapitator of Cyrus the
Great is shown in an unaggressive pose, the armor beneath her
graceful tunic speaks for what Heywood would call her masculine spirit.

In the half-length figure of Esther, which was designed to
go over a door (fig. 9), Castagno has obviously attempted to
portray the character of a queen who could so influence her
husband that the fate of her people was drastically altered.
No less exemplary than their medieval predecessors, Castagno's
figures are more humanly credible.

After these Renaissance worthies Glover's nine women, with
the exception of Queen Elizabeth, seem strangely decorative
—almost frivolous, with their bits of flying lace—as unreal as
the Medieval worthies, but in a different way. For one thing,
all of them except Elizabeth seem to be either like Deborah
or like Esther. Bunduca and Penthesilea have that same heavi-
ness of feature, that same rather straight hair. Esther, on the
contrary, is closer to being what one might call "cute," with
frizzy hair parted in the middle and brought down on both
sides of her smallish face. Artimesia, Elpheda, and Margaret
of Anjou are remarkably similar. Judith, somewhat puz-
zlingly, has characteristics of both models. Whether or not
these resemblances are fanciful, the impression remains that
these ladies are in fancy dress—that they have put on costumes
to play the roles of worthies.

Such a suggestion leads us inevitably back to Heywood's
association with the court and the world of the masque, where
court ladies, from the queen on down, did indeed play such
roles. Inigo Jones's costume design for Penthesilea in *The
Masque of Queens* shows another elegantly helmeted lady in
a *dress* that *suggests* armor (fig. 10)—not in real armor covered by a tunic, as in Castagno's painting of Tomyris. Glover's
designs are surely more like this than like the depictions of the

worthies in the tapestry or in Castagno's frescoes. Without directly imitating Inigo Jones, Glover seems to show his awareness of the current fashion in designing heroic figures for the court masque.

The masque was a major expression of heroic ideals, closely related to heroic portraiture. As Andrea del Castagno painted Niccolò da Tolentino as an equestrian statue of the Roman imperial sort, while at the same time making both horse and man seem to be full of life, and as Van Dyck painted Charles I, not as he was, but as the perfect warrior and lover, and yet very much a part of the Cavalier world, so the contrivers and designers of masques transformed the noble ladies and gentlemen of the court. In these "spectacles of state" the participants were both themselves and some far nobler extension of themselves. They were given the opportunity to play the heroic roles they read about—to be for a moment what perhaps they truly wanted to be. Charles, for all his ineptitude, may genuinely have wished to be the beneficent lover of his people that Carew made him in the role of Philogenes in *Salmacida Spolia* in the ominous year 1640. And it may be that for many people in the seventeenth century heroism of the sort that is glorified in epic and romance was to some extent a role. The work we are considering, though far removed from the conventions of the masque and not addressed to the court, may share with the masque certain assumptions or hypotheses. Heywood seems to be saying to his female readers, "You, too, Lady Theophila and Mistress Elizabeth, may be a Deborah or an Elpheda." So, at least, the engravings make us think.

In 1637 Heywood wrote a book called *The Phoenix of these late times: Or the life of Mr. Henry Welby, Esq., who lived at his house in Grub-street forty foure yeares, and in that space, was never seene by any, aged 84.* The last number refers to his supposed age at the time of his death. The little book is a eulogy, but also a strange example. Welby lived a fairly active life for forty years, manifesting several of the chivalric virtues, which, by the seventeenth century, had become the marks of a gentleman. "Now courage and courtesie are the two principal decorements that adorne a gentleman," Heywood writes (sig. C 4), going on to speak of Welby's bounty, honor, and humility. Then, in his forty-first year, a traumatic experience changed the course of his life: his younger brother attempted to shoot him. The pistol misfired, however, and the elder Welby disarmed his would-be assassin. After a period of meditation on this event, he decided to retire from the world, and had a house in Grub Street rebuilt in such a way that he need never see anyone, even the servants who took care of him. "What should I say?" Heywood comments (sig. A2), "hee dyed living, that he might live dying: his life was a perpetuall death, that his death might bring him to an eternal life. . . ." Despite the religious tone induced by this sort of rhetoric, the pamphlet is a sort of journalism—a feature story or profile of an odd character who is also exemplary, presented so as to interest the average reader. It is to the heroic tradition what Elbert Hubbard's *Little Journeys to the Homes of Great Philosophers* (1904) is to philosophy.[13]

Yet *The Phoenix of these late times* is not radically different from the *Exemplary Lives*. The heroic tradition blended with other traditions more easily than one might have supposed, so that vestiges of it appear in the most unlikely places. No abrupt shift of sensibility characterizes the development of certain kinds of heroes and heroines into the subject matter of the didactic and sentimental literature of the eighteenth century or of a twentieth-century article on "The Most Fascinating Character I Have Met."

Notes

1. For valuable advice and assistance in the preparation of this paper I am indebted to Professor David Cast of the History of Art Department at Yale University; Miss Helen Chillman, the Art Librarian; Miss Marjorie Wynne, Research Librarian at the Beinecke Rare Book and Manuscript Library; Mr. James Thorpe, Director of the Henry E. Huntington Library and Art Gallery; and Mr. Carey S. Bliss, Curator of Rare Books at that library. For their kindness in allowing me to reproduce illustrative material I am obliged to the institutions cited under the illustrations. In the quotations extended passages in italic have been silently altered to roman type.

2. Edited by S. Solente, 2 vols., (Paris: H. Champion, 1936). On the subject of exemplary biography see O. B. Hardison, *The Enduring Moment* (Chapel Hill, N. C.: University of North Carolina Press, 1962).

                         Eugene M. Waith

3. See *The First English Life of Henry the Fifth,* edited by C. L. Kingsford (Oxford, 1911), pp. 4–7.

4. *Apology for Poetry* in *Elizabethan Critical Essays,* edited by G. Gregory Smith (Oxford, 1904), 1: 179.

5. *Thomas Heywood, Playwright and Miscellanist* (Oxford: Basil Blackwell, 1931), p. 93.

6. For Longuyon see John Barbour, *The Buik of Alexander,* edited by R. L. Graeme Ritchie (Edinburgh, 1821–29), 4: 402–6, where the French is printed opposite the Scottish translation; for *The Parlement* Israel Gollancz's edition (London, 1897), lines 297–583; for *The Flower and the Leaf* W. W. Skeat's edition of Chaucer (Oxford, 1897), 7: 377.

7. See Jules Guiffrey, *Les Tapisseries du XIIe à la fin du XVIe siècle,* in *Histoire générale des arts appliqués à l'industrie du Ve à la fin du XVIIIe siècle,* edited by Emile Molinier, vol. 6 (Paris: E. Lévy et cie., n.d.), pp. 31–32; and Paolo d'Ancona, "Gli affreschi del Castello di Manta nel Saluzzese," *L'Arte* 8 (1905): 94–106, 184–95. For a capricious variation of the tradition see Bruce Dickins, "The Nine Unworthies," in *Medieval Literature and Civilization: Studies in Memory of G. N. Garmonsway,* edited by D. A. Pearsall and R. A. Waldron (London: Athlone Press, 1969), pp. 228–32.

8. See Margery Corbett and Michael Norton, *Engraving in England in the 16th and 17th Centuries* [a continuation of the work of A. Hind], Part III (Cambridge: Cambridge University Press, 1964), under "George Glover," #67.

9. 1612; re-edition New York: Scholars' Facsimiles & Reprints, 1941), sig. B4.

10. Described by Corbett and Norton, *Engraving in England,* under "Glover," #67.

11. "The Nine Heroes Tapestries at the Cloisters," *Metropolitan Museum of Art Bulletin,* n.s., vol. 7 (1948–49), pp. 243–60.

12. See W. Gurney Benham, *Playing Cards* (London, 1931).

13. That Elbert Hubbard also shared Heywood's feminist sympathies is suggested by his *Little Journeys to the Homes of Famous Women* (1897) and his *Little Journeys to the Homes of Good Men and Great* (1895), starting off with George Eliot.

Saint Sebastian

The Vicissitudes of the Hero as Martyr

Irving L. Zupnick

A N ARTIST WHO PORTRAYS a single incident from the life of a saint expresses a particular point of view about what is most significant. In part the selection can be personal, but certainly it also reflects the attitudes of the public for whom the artist creates. Since saints are considered to have been exemplary human beings who are held up as models for mankind, they represent standards for heroism which we expect to be evinced in the significant act that has been portrayed. The fact that the action is usually passive, representing the saint's ordeal as a martyr rather than a scene representing the active confrontation of vice, illustrates the Christian concept of heroism which was popular in the Middle Ages and Renaissance. It is defined in a treatise like Erasmus's *Enchiridion,* in which the virtue Fortitude is equated not with courageous acts, but with the resigned acceptance of God's will.

The subject of Saint Sebastian in art provides an excellent example of this Christian principle. Although frequently his legend was represented in a continuous narrative form, with a picture to depict each highlight in his life, it was more often the case that a single moment was selected to represent the entire legend. The number of alternatives was limited in part by this attitude, and in part by Saint Sebastian's most important function, as intercessor against pestilence. That is, we are usually shown scenes representing his ordeal by arrow and his miraculous recovery afterwards, two subjects that were understood as parallels to illness and the return of health. The frequent repetition of the same subjects over a period of centuries allows us to make comparisons that reveal subtle differences in the way that Saint Sebastian is made to react to his ordeal, and these distinctions, in turn, contribute to our understanding of the way heroism was conceived in different historical periods.

Anyone who has noticed the great number of still-extant paintings and statues devoted to Saint Sebastian soon realizes that beyond question he was one of the most revered heroes of the Middle Ages and Renaissance.[1] He was one of the saints who was heroic in all respects and by any definition, combining the passive qualities of the uncomplaining martyr with those of the uncompromising activist who sacrifices everything, including life, for his strong beliefs. Whatever the reason for his renown, the long duration of his popular appeal makes him an interesting figure for the modern scholar in a number of disciplines. Not only are the art works we have mentioned of great interest to art historians,[2] but he has also inspired dramatists from at least the fifteenth century on,[3] and, as Giovanni Gullace shows, his legend inspired the unusual collaborative effort of d'Annunzio and Debussy in a musical oratorio that had its first performance in 1911.[4] The histories of guilds and confraternities devoted to him are also quite interesting, particularly the association in Rouen,[5] which began as a benevolent society in the twelfth century, performing the useful task of burying victims of pestilence, only to be discussed shortly thereafter by the Rouen Council of 1189 as a nuisance, both political and religious, but one to be excused since there was no one else who wanted to bury the dead. In 1562 this organization was outlawed by the Calvinists only to re-surface in 1774 as Les Chevaliers de la Sport who, I understand, still hold an annual turkey shoot each January twentieth, that is, on Saint Sebastian's Day. Although it would be interesting to consider any one of these historical phenomena, I shall concern myself only with the visual imagery devoted to the saint, considering the changes that took place in the iconography, the characterization, and the compositions of the pictorial depictions of Saint Sebastian's legend which reflect developing views of the heroic nature.

Saint Sebastian's legend hardly suggests the artistic importance he was to have. The original Acts apparently no longer exist, but they seem to have been recounted, together with a pseudo-Ambrosian *Life of Saint Agnes,* in a manuscript in the Laurentian Library.[6] They also appear, among other places, in the vital *Legenda Aurea* of Jacobus de Voragine, one of the seminal works of the thirteenth century.[7]

When we first meet Sebastian (Saint Ambrose tells us that he originated in Narbonne but was a Milanese citizen [8]), he is already a most successful soldier, the commander of the First Cohort of the Praetorian Guard, that is, of the bodyguard of the joint emperors, Maximian and Diocletian, in the third century of our era. Saint Ambrose excuses such establishmentarian signs of success by assuring us that Sebastian soldiered only to be in a position to help his follow Christians through a period of intense persecution. We are told that one of his acts was to inspire the twins, Mark and Marcellinus, to die as martyrs rather than renounce their faith. During his dramatic exhortations to the twins, Sebastian restored the lost speech of a woman named Zoë and converted the entire family of the twins as well as some other bystanders to Christianity, then cured Tranquillinus, the twins' father, of a very severe illness at the very moment that he baptized him. The prefect of Rome, one Chromatius, who was on his deathbed, upon hearing of this medical side effect of Sebastian's religious efforts, sent for the soldier and his helper, a baptizing priest named Polycarp, to see if they could cure him as well. Tiburtius, the prefect's son, a natural-born scoffer, prepared two furnaces to execute the Christians in case they should fail, but they were quite successful. Finding that the symptoms of the disease were caused by a secret chamber for observing pagan mysteries, they destroyed it, thus curing the old man and, as a result of this miracle, converting the entire household to Christianity.

Nearly everyone converted by Sebastian and Polycarp became martyrs, including the prefect, Chromatius, and Tiburtius the scoffer. Before long the new prefect, Fabian, pointed out Sebastian's subversive ways to Diocletian, who showed his anger by ordering the Praetorian Guard to tie their commander to a stake in the Campus Martius and shoot him full of arrows. When they were finished, we are told, he "resembled a hedgehog." They left him for dead, although some sources say that in their love for him (or, one might conjecture, as a measure of their poor marksmanship) they had managed not to hit a vital spot.

Up to this point, the *Legenda Aurea* agrees with the oldest known account in the Laurentian Library, but then, for some reason, it leaves out a crucial detail. It continues by telling us that "not many days after, Saint Sebastian stood on the steps of the palace" and reproached the emperors for their injustices to Christians.[9] Nothing is said to explain what happened in the time intervening between his ordeal and his reappearance. This is a surprising omission because the hiatus does not exist in the oldest sources. Even the pseudo-Ambrosian manuscript in the Laurentian Library tells us that one Saint Irene, the widow of a man named Castulus, came in the night to bury Sebastian, but finding to her surprise that he still lived, she brought him to her home on the palace grounds and nursed him back to health.[10]

In any case, the emperors did not take Sebastian's scolding in the spirit in which it was intended. In fact, they ordered the soldiers to beat him to death with clubs and, as a final indignity, they had his body tossed into a sewer, the Cloaca Maxima, in order to deprive the Christians of relics that might become an incitement to revolt. But again their plan was miraculously foiled. On the following night a woman who was to become known as Saint Lucina saw Sebastian in a dream in which he revealed the exact location of his remains. His body was recovered and buried at the feet of the Apostles, we are told, in a crypt in Sebastiano alla Polveriera, one of the seven great churches of Rome on the Via Appia. This, by the way, is an interesting location because it had formerly been the site of a temple dedicated to Apollo, and Apollo was the pagan deity in charge of plagues.[11]

There were many reasons for artists to depict Saint Sebastian. He was the patron saint of cities such as Rome and Milan, or Soissons, where Bishop Hilduin brought his relics in 826.[12] His relics are preserved at Mantua, Malaga, Seville, Toulouse, Munich, Paris, Tournai, Antwerp, and Brussels.[13] He was also the patron saint of crusaders, lacemakers, crossbowmen and archers, of arquebusiers, iron merchants, and oddly, of hose-makers in France (whose punning slogan was "Ses bas se tiennent" [14]).

His most important function of course, was his role as protector against disease. We have noted that even his legend speaks of cures, and it could be that his own miraculous recovery from arrow wounds was responsible for his association with sickness. *Psalms* 91 links "the arrow that flies by day" and "the pestilence that stalks in darkness," and there are any number of philological connections between weapons and disease. The Greek *toxon*, or bow, has given us the word "toxic." Plague derives from the Latin *plaga*, or blow, and *plangere*, to strike a blow. The French word, *fléau*, or plague, also means "flail." Specifically, we notice that during the great epidemic of 1348, "The Black Death," the figure of speech likening plague to arrows or to darts cast from heaven was much used, appearing in Gabriello de' Mussi's *Ystoria de morbo seu mortalitate qui fuit a 1348*,[15] and in the *Grande Chirurgie* of Guy de Chauliac, the physician of Pope Clement VI.[16]

We are not certain how early it was that Sebastian assumed this protective role. Saint Ambrose's *Enarratio in Psalmum* mentions that the veneration of saints as a means of allaying pestilence was in vogue as early as the end of the fourth century; but probably the best documented and earliest account of Sebastian's supposed intercession for plague sufferers is in Paulus Diaconus's *De Gestis Langobardorum*, which tells us that in the year 680 a severe plague that was particularly virulent in Pavia was brought to an abrupt conclusion when, on the basis of a revelation that came to a Capuchin monk, relics of Saint Sebastian were brought to Pavia and an altar was erected to him in the church of San Pietro-in-Vincoli.[17] This information has caused some confusion because Deacon Paul did not tell us in which city this particular church was to be found. We cannot be certain, that is, whether it was the well-known church in Rome, which in 680 had been under construction for only two years, or if he referred to a no-longer-extant church in Pavia.[18] The answer could help us date a mosaic in San Pietro-in-Vincoli in Rome, a depiction of a bearded, robed figure labeled, "S. Sebastianus," which was given extraordinary im-

portance as the traditional prototype by such an authoritative
Counter-Reformation hagiographer as Francisco Pacheco, who
argued that Sebastian, as a military commander, should be
portrayed as mature and middle-aged rather than as a handsome, alluring youth who distracted worshippers with his
beauty.[19]

What is particularly interesting about this mosaic is that,
except for the inscription, the generalized figure could represent any bearded saint. This lack of specific detail, particularly
of references to the martyrdom, is not unusual in the early
centuries of Christian art, when it seems to reflect a certain
ambivalence in the Church's attitude.[20] That is, although Saint
Ambrose had done much to encourage the cult of saints through
his discovery of relics,[21] and Saint Augustine tells us in *The
City of God* that it was customary to read the miracles of saints
in public in the fourth century,[22] an iconoclastic attitude had
risen to predominance in the succeeding centuries. Thus we
learn from an early-sixth century manuscript, the *Decretum
Gelasianum,* that the legends of the martyrs were not read in
the Roman Church according to ancient custom "because of
their vague origins and doubtful importance." [23] There is also
an interesting exchange of letters in the seventh century between Eulogius, Bishop of Alexandria, and Gregory the Great,
in which Eulogius requests the loan of a *Gesta martyrum* only
to learn from the Pope that none could be found in the official
libraries.[24] The request shows an interest, the reply, official
indifference, towards the legends of the saints. The Second
Council of Nice in 787 was to reinforce the official attitude,
thereby continuing to inhibit the development of an expanded
iconography for some time to come.[25] Thus, although it is conceivable that in Constantine's day cycles of scenes could have
been painted to depict the lives of certain saints,[26] even the
practice of identifying the saints merely by showing the weapons of their martyrdoms seems to have died out from about
440 (when it was still in vogue, according to the dedication
for a no longer extant mosaic that was in Santa Maria Maggiore)[27] until late in the ninth century. Usually, if Sebastian
is represented during this long period of nearly five centuries,
he appears undifferentiated except for his name, as he does in

Sant'Apollinare Nuovo, in Ravenna. In other words, he is given no more importance than he would have had in a liturgical listing of the names of saints.

This indifference begins to disappear around the middle of the ninth century, probably after Gregory IV (827–844) erected a chapel dedicated to Saints George, Sebastian, and Tiburtius in Saint Peter's in Rome, amidst all the pomp of ecclesiastical ceremony.[28] The earliest known series of paintings to depict scenes from the life of Saint Sebastian probably dates from not long after that event. I am thinking of a copy made in 1630 in the *Codex Vaticanus Latinus 9071* at the behest of Cardinal Francesco Barberini, when a series of frescoes was destroyed during his restoration of the Church of San Sebastiano on the Palatine.[29] The five scenes depicted the martyrdom by arrow, the ministrations of Saint Irene, the disposal of Sebastian's body in the Cloaca Maxima, the procession with his body, and his entombment, suggesting that this could have been part of an even more extensive cycle that probably included his miraculous cures. The martyrdom by arrow is particularly interesting since it shows us a symmetrical composition in which the bearded Saint is flanked by two pairs of archers. Ultimately this symmetrical composition descends from the earlier and more common depiction of the Crucifixion of Christ, and it was to become the typical composition used by artists from central Italy for representing the Martyrdom of Saint Sebastian.

In northern Europe the subject of Saint Sebastian's martyrdom begins to appear somewhat later, perhaps not before the twelfth century, and from the first it is treated quite differently, suggesting that the idea for such a depiction was transmitted through verbal accounts rather than through a direct visual example. Not only is Saint Sebastian portrayed as a younger, beardless man, but the composition is usually bilateral, with the saint on one side and the archers on the other. This distinctive compositional format might have been suggested by a new function and location for his martyrdom scene. That is, most often the central Italian pictures were frescoed on walls where they have a completeness and independence that suggests the suitability of a symmetrical com-

position, whereas the northern paintings just as often were part
of triptyches and polyptyches in which the saint, even at the
moment of martyrdom, had to be oriented so that he could
face either the Madonna or, as we shall see, a depiction of the
Resurrection, an interesting juxtaposition that refers to his
supposed curative powers as well as to his own miraculous
survival. The central Italian symmetrical and the north European bilateral compositions were to remain traditional in the
areas in which they originated, with both traditions mixing in
northern Italy.

The *Stuttgart Passional,* a mid-twelfth century manuscript,[30]
contains an extreme example of the bilateral composition,
showing the emperor and his archers at the base of the
left-hand page and the martyr at the top of the right-hand
one. Such a splitting of the composition can be noted in several
eleventh-century manuscripts in which the subject was not
Sebastian but the *Adoration of the Kings,* and in which the
royal figures were similarly separated from the spiritual, theological ones.[31] It would be hazardous to come to any conclusion based upon a few, scattered examples, but it is possible
that the separation of kings and madonnas is a sign of deference
to a higher power and a suggestion of royal humility, just as
the multiplication of images of kings ordering the deaths of
martyrs might, in certain historical periods, have specifically
political undertones.

Nearly contemporaneous with the *Stuttgart Passional* is an
example that is somewhat unusual because it appears on a
column capital in the Church of Saint-Nectaire in Auvergne.[32]
On the northern face of this capital a bearded, robed figure
stands in a mandorla with his arms raised while a single archer
faces him from the eastern side. On the southern face there
appears to be an eroded remnant of a scene that shows the
saint's death by beating.

After four centuries of relative quiescence, Europe began
to suffer frequent pandemics from about 1094 on, with the
most severe and memorable one, the so-called "Black Death,"
falling between 1347 and 1350, when millions died.[33] So
traumatic was this experience that even now historians find it
a handy reference point, often blaming it for accelerating the

end of the medieval era. Supposedly it accomplished this by creating a shortage of serfs and a scarcity of laborers and artisans, thus bringing serfdom to an end, increasing the relative powers of the burghers and their guilds, and concomitantly weakening the authority and influence of the church. It is possible that because of Saint Sebastian's antibiotic repute, these epidemics spurred interest in him as an artistic subject.[34] As Gasquet tells us, the churches of the fourteenth century after the period of the Black Death were "literally encumbered" with donations of altarpieces, statues, and glass windows depicting Saint Sebastian—as well as Saints Anthony, Roch, Barbara, Denis, and the Madonna—as intercessors against disease.[35]

This renewed interest in Saint Sebastian was accompanied by changes in his imagery. Even when he is shown alone, as a simple icon, he often wears a soldier's uniform instead of the generalized cloak that he sported in earlier times, and as early as the middle of the fourteenth century it was not uncommon to show him almost completely nude, as he might have appeared at the moment of his martyrdom. This last change reflects the growing popularity of the martyrdom scene that, starting with a minimum cast of the saint and the requisite archers, began to acquire onlookers and other details added to contribute to the verisimilitude as well as to the aesthetic interest of the compositions. The frontispiece of the *Statute Book of the Venetian Glassmakers' Guild of 1346* provides an interesting early example,[36] but even more representative are the panel attributed to Giovanni del Biondo in the Duomo of Florence [37] and the partly-damaged fresco in Sant'Ambrogio, Florence,[38] both of which have obviously been inspired by contemporary representations in which the crucifixion of Christ is observed by throngs of onlookers. The *bearded* saint—who is usually attended by angels who reward him with the martyr's crown or the palm—passively, as if anesthetized, accepts the ordeal of the arrows, these creating a loosely symmetrical pattern of wounds over most of his body. The saint's pose in the fresco in Sant'Ambrogio is particularly interesting since it was used in a lost fresco in Sant'Andrea da Katabarbara [39] and possibly goes back to a third-century statue from Pergamon representing Marsyas waiting to be flayed with his wrists tied together above his head.[40]

If we can judge from the frequency of his depiction in art, the high point of interest in Saint Sebastian seems to have been reached after about 1450, receding only by the middle of the sixteenth century. As a reflection of the increasing secularization of religious art in general, the ordeal of Saint Sebastian was subjected to a variety of interpretations which reveal the personal ideological positions of the artist and his patrons.

Some artists succeeded in depicting characterization and emotional expression with increasing subtlety, while others emphasized the aesthetic and abstract features inherent in the subject in the belief that there is a greater truth than that of surface appearances. Those seeking a classical interpretation depicted the saint as a clean-shaven young man, an "athlete of Christ," in Italy as well as in the north. In the work of other artists a new historicism placed the time of his story more accurately in the Roman past and this encouraged a didactic impulse that pointed out that pagan glories had succumbed to the spiritual invulnerability of the meek inheritors of the earth. Some artists, that is, showed his martyrdom taking place among the ruins of ancient Rome to illustrate the point that was made by Poggio Bracciolini in 1448 (in his book *De fortunae varietate* [41]) that the glories of the ancient pagan world were either picturesque ruins or the current sites of Christian churches.

The fact that even personal interpretations are subject to change shows up excellently in the work of Andrea Mantegna, who applied the Paduan precision of his style to three versions of the *Martyrdom of Saint Sebastian* painted during three different periods in his career. The earliest example, the version in Vienna (fig. 1), dates from about 1460.[42] Here Mantegna is preoccupied with the physical anguish of the martyr, depicting him as youthful and vulnerable in order to add a pathetic element to the subject matter. For perhaps the first time we can see the reflection of Bracciolini's ideas in the ruins of the ancient world. The horseman who appears disguised as a cloud, Paul Kristeller suggests, may represent Theodoric of Verona, who was lured to the gates of hell by a stag that he hunted, a subject that Mantegna could have seen on a *bas* relief on the facade of San Zeno in Verona and which he might have understood as an allegorical reference to those who will be punished for persecuting the godly.[43] Sebastian's suffering, graphically expressed in the sinuous writhing of his body and the tortured look in his eyes, is reinforced with almost sadistic insistence by the location of arrows between his eyes and in his throat and others which enter and then re-emerge from his legs.

Shortly before 1480, Mantegna repeated the subject for a member of the Gonzaga family in a painting now in the Louvre (fig. 2).[44] Compared to the earlier version, this one is suffused with classical calm; possibly the influence of Venetian art and his contact with his in-laws, the Bellini, are responsible for the change. Although the arrows are still quite apparent, the upper part of Sebastian's body is relatively free of them. Not only is he more mature and robust, but apparently he is capable of stoical control over his pain. His body maintains a balanced *contrapposto* pose, and only a facial grimace reminds us of his suffering. The architecture is also less of a distraction, although it still reminds us of the destruction of paganism. The clouds on the right seem to show the threatening head of an angry god, and below it the head of the Christ Child. The vines at Sebastian's feet more than likely symbolize eternal life through Christ, and thus emphasize the contrast with paganism that is in ruins all about. Mantegna, through this means, makes us realize that Sebastian's martyrdom occurred early in history, when the might of Roman emperors was directed against Christianity. The saint's heroic martyrdom, with its paradoxical note of triumph then, is shown as a positive contribution to the eventual victory of Christian ideals.

Mantegna's last version of the subject was painted for Cardinal Gonzaga, the Bishop of Mantua, in 1505 or 1506 (fig. 3).[45] Unlike the two earlier interpretations of the subject, this has neither landscape nor competing figures to distract us from contemplating the ordeal of the saint. The artist has concentrated entirely upon the martyr's violent physical suffering, in what amounts almost to an apotheosis of pain. The figure treatment gains new monumentality from a confining pilaster enframement and the sheer power of its massive anatomical structure, but most striking of all, I think, is the awesome facial expression, which seems to suggest what it might be like to look into the eyes of Death. Interestingly, Mantegna has

not forgotten the didactic message of his earlier works: an
expiring candle at the foot of the painting is wrapped in a
ribbon that bears the inscription "Nil nisi divinum stabile est,
caetera fumus," pointing to the fugitive quality of human existence (pagan or otherwise) in contrast to the everlasting permanence of divine power.

Evidence that Mantegna's sadistic approach reflects a personal preoccupation is forthcoming when we consider the relatively calm interpretations created by his contemporaries in
Venice. Among them is the influential Antonello da Messina,
a Sicilian who was trained in Naples (where Flemish influence
was then very strong) and came to Venice in 1475–76, staying
just long enough to have a powerful impact upon Mantegna's
brother-in-law, Giovanni Bellini, the most important local artist of the period. Antonello's *Martyrdom of Saint Sebastian* of
1476 (fig. 4)[46] is a remarkable contrast to Mantegna's interpretations. The picture shows the saint tied to a tree in the
middle of what seems to be a Venetian piazza; only three
arrows, foreshortened to minimize distraction, have struck the
saint, who calmly and stoically faces his ordeal. The casual
gestures of the chatting soldiers, the mother who holds a child
in her arms as she stares at the execution, the curious girls who
watch from their balcony, and the sleeping soldier (whose
foreshortened figure recalls Uccello's experiments with perspective), all tend to give a somewhat surrealistic quality to
this matter-of-fact statement of the manner in which a saint
is subjected to martyrdom by his fellow man in the broad
daylight of an everyday world.

Giovanni Bellini, who also depicted the saint several times
in his career, seems to demonstrate that Antonello da Messina's
concept of martyrdom as a stoical acceptance of one's lot was
closer to the Venetian ideal than Mantegna's pain-filled one.
In Giovanni's earliest known version, the 1462 triptych painted
for the Carità,[47] this was already apparent, and in the polyptych
painted perhaps in 1464 (in honor of Saint Vincent Ferrer for
the Church of San Giovanni e Paolo in Venice[48]) he continues
in much the same vein. It is true that the muscularity of his
youthful Saint Sebastian may owe something to Mantegna,
and that the wounds are relatively bloody; however, the saint's

reaction to pain is quite restrained, and the artist devoted enough attention to the landscape to show that Sebastian's ordeal is not his only concern. In fact, in passing we should note that Giovanni was not above a cold-blooded use of the arrows as abstract elements in his design, in this case giving them a staccato rhythm that contrasts with the symmetrical regularity of his earlier painting. Finally, in his famous *San Giobbe Altar* of the late 1480s (fig. 5),[49] in which the nude Sebastian balances out the nude figure of Job, Giovanni portrays our hero as if he were experiencing the same calm rapture that he shows in his earlier versions of the subject.

The incongruity of the two nude saints in the midst of an otherwise formal, courtly gathering of martyrs and saints makes it quite clear that this type of composition, sometimes called a *conversazione sacre*,[50] owes its characteristics to the fact that it is a later, better-unified invention which functions in recognition of the traditional concept that prayers to higher authorities might be carried by one's patron saint, who in earlier polyptyches appeared on a separate panel. It is only because the nude representation of Saint Sebastian's ordeal by arrow had succeeded by this time in replacing almost any other way that he might be recognized by the public, that it was possible to suspend the sense of the incongruity of his nudeness in the context of the *San Giobbe Altar*.

There is an antithesis between the realism of the Venetians and the highly abstract stylizations of the Florentines that finds parallels in the contrast between the art theory expressed in the Florentine Marsilio Ficino's Neoplatonic *Commentary on Plato's Symposium* of 1469[51] and the strictly materialistic point of view expressed by the Venetian, Agostino Nifo (whose attack on Ficino, *De pulcher*, appeared in 1531[52]). Thus, the emphasis in the *Saint Sebastian* in the Louvre, painted by the Umbrian Perugino,[53] is not upon the realities of the ordeal or the characterization of the saint, but rather upon the graceful disposition of the saint's massive anatomical structure. Even more to the point is Botticelli's famous painting in Berlin, created in 1473 or 1474 for Santa Maggiore in Florence.[54] Here, as always, we find that very personal sense of interior melancholia which seems to pervade all of this master's work,

and as usual that firm but sensitive Florentine line that pre-
sages sixteenth-century Mannerism. It is the same subtle line,
the underlying drawing, that, as far back as 1455, the sculptor
Lorenzo Ghiberti had elevated to the level of artistic theory
in his *Commentarii*.[55] In Botticelli's case, more than in most,
his graceful line seems to be the direct expression of his personal feeling for his subject matter.

Perhaps the epitome of Florentine abstraction appears in
Antonio Pollaiuolo's famous *Martyrdom of Saint Sebastian*
(fig. 6), painted in 1475 for the Pucci Chapel of Santa Maria
dei Servi and now in the National Gallery in London.[56] The
symmetrical arrangement of four archers across the foreground,
front and rear views of two men loading and two shooting their
bows, starts a rhythmic process that carries throughout the
main figure composition. For good measure, archers demon-
strating two more variants of the bowman's manual of arms
appear in the middle ground. The saint is raised up upon the
truncated branches of a tree that is located at a distance from
the foreground to help create a rational sense of space; however, because of his elevated position he becomes the apex of
a two-dimensional isosceles triangle and the climax of the carefully contrived grouping of figures whose garments and curv-
ing limbs echo the abstract curves of the weapons of martyrdom. The sinuous pose of Sebastian and the taut muscular
tension of his executioners almost draw attention away from
the saint's highly expressive face, which conveys an unmistakable impression of his suffering. It is only after we overcome
the spell of the major figure composition that we realize that
Pollaiulo's heavily detailed landscape background, with its
predictable commentary on the transience of the pagan world,
has an independence and neutrality with regard to the major
theme that makes it seem to be not much more than a contrasting backdrop.

Luca Signorelli, who probably borrowed Pollaiuolo's composition for his own painting (fig. 7), made for the Church
of San Domenico at Città da Castello in 1496,[57] placed his
own wine in the bottle, breaking up the rhythmic regularity
of the archers' composition in order to heighten the sense of
reality, and depicting the saint's face as if it were contorted to

voice a scream of agony. This new note of intense suffering and the realism of the painting's cityscape suggest that the artist was in touch with contemporary north-European developments. The saint's odd pose, with one arm raised, probably owes its inspiration to some work by an earlier artist, perhaps to something as easily portable and mobile as an engraving. One example that comes to mind is an engraving that apparently copies a drawing of Mantegna [58]; and the unknown Rhenish "Master E. S.," who created four engravings devoted to Saint Sebastian between 1450 and 1470, also used this pose.[59] Whoever invented it, this pose, and other similar variants that seem equally inefficent solutions for binding the saint to his execution post, were to become very popular throughout Europe.

In northern Europe, German depictions of the martyrdom tended to emphasize Saint Sebastian's agonies [60] whereas Flemish artists showed considerable restraint. As an example of the latter approach, there is the *grisaille* imitating a statue of Saint Sebastian on Rogier van der Weyden's *Last Judgment Altarpiece*, a commission ordered by Nicolas Rolin, chancellor of Phillippe le Beau, for the Hôtel-Dieu of Beaune, and finished probably in 1448.[61] Here we find not too much emphasis on suffering, but a rather melancholy, yet stoical, acceptance of the ordeal.

Similar restraint is to be found in two important versions of St. Sebastian's martyrdom by Hans Memling, who, although he might have been a German by birth, is an exemplary representative of Flemish artistic traditions. His interpretations of Saint Sebastian seem to epitomize what the courtly society of Bruges might expect of its heroes, since in each case the saint exhibits a certain cool detachment, almost a disdain for the poor "form" of the Emperors. In the first of these (fig. 8), a panel in the Musée Royale in Brussels that dates from about 1470,[62] the bilateral composition of the painting suggests that it could have been on the left side of a triptych. The saint's graceful pose, *à la ballet*, seems to be an absurdly incompetent way to tie someone to a tree, but we have already noticed it in engravings by the "Master E. S." and by an artist in the circle of Mantegna. More than likely it is based upon one of the variants used in classical statues of Apollo. What is un-usual is that it appears this early in the north, where classical influences were less in evidence at the time, but it does make one think of a possible source somewhere between Praxiteles' graceful *Hermes* and a sleeping figure of the type represented by the *Barberini Faun*. What is more important to us in the present context, however, is the imperturbability of Saint Se-bastian in Memling's painting in Brussels. By the time that the artist returned to the subject some twenty years later, in about 1490, when he depicted the martyrdom on the narrow left wing of his *Resurrection Altarpiece* in the Louvre,[63] Mem-ling's portrayal of the self-controlled and aloof hero has become exaggerated to the point that Sebastian seems to look upon his ordeal as if it were a crashing bore!

German art, as we have implied, was much more emotional and naturalistic. In the engraved *Saint Sebastian* by Martin Schongauer (fig. 9),[64] for example, the saint's reaction to his ordeal is observed with almost clinical rectitude. He seems to be faint from shock and sags against his bonds with his lips drawn back in a painful grimace. The saint's pose, like that used to represent *Marsyas*, had been popular earlier in Floren-tine art, but could have been suggested to the artist through some other indirect source.[65] Albrecht Dürer is equally insis-tent upon the human frailty of the saint. In his engraving of circa 1498 (fig. 10),[66] Sebastian's head is pinned to the column with a sadistically placed arrow, recalling that some four years earlier Dürer had copied some engravings by the equally rig-orous Mantegna. In another engraving, possibly based upon a drawing by Dürer of circa 1505 (fig. 11),[67] the *Marsyas* pose is combined with an expression of the human debility of the saint, as if in recollection of Schongauer's interpretation. It is not easy to decide if these examples represent an increase of Italian influence on northern art or a closer rapprochement be-tween north and south. The *Augsburg Triptych*, now in the Alte Pinakothek in Munich, which was painted by Hans Hol-bein the Elder between 1515 and 1517 for the Convent of Saint Catherine in Augsburg,[68] suggests that the latter is prob-ably closer to the truth. Here the saint's pose with one arm raised recalls Memling's; the expression of pain is Teutonic;

and the symmetrical composition, although it is a natural outcome of the design of the particular triptych, is Italian.

Meanwhile the center of the stage in sixteenth-century Italian art was occupied by Michelangelo, who was to make his
own intuitive discovery of the possibilities of the raised arm
pose. It is hard to say whether he drew his inspiration from
the Hellenistic statue that haunted this era, the *Laocöon*, which
was recovered in 1506,[69] or from some other source, but it
was such writhing, tormented figures as these that influenced
the depictions of Saint Sebastian for some time to come. The
pose of the martyr with bound wrists that appears on the left
side of Michelangelo's Sistine *Last Judgment*, for example,
was outrageously paraphrased by the Dutch "Romanist" Jan
van Scorel in his *Saint Sebastian* in the Boymans Museum in
Rotterdam.[70] A more original artist, someone of Titian's cali-
ber, could approach Michelangelo's concept of using bodily
poses to express emotion on a more equal footing, absorbing
the general idea without copying any specific example. Thus,
in 1520, when Titian depicted Saint Sebastian on the right-
hand panel of his *Resurrection Altarpiece* (fig. 12),[71] he abandoned the Giorgionesque type that he had portrayed ten years
before at Santo Spirito in Isolo [72] to pay homage (but not sub-
servience) to Michelangelo's *Rebellious Slave*.[73]

The same spell seems to have overcome another important
Venetian artist, Tintoretto, who in the 1570s used an odd pose
—but one that is characteristic for him—in depicting Saint
Sebastian in a fresco in the Scuola de San Rocco (fig. 13).[74]
The pose is so remarkable—the leg as well as the arm being
raised so that the figure seems off-balance—that one immediately begins to look for prototypes. The type of the *Sleeping
Faun* (as represented in a bronze from Herculaneum, for example)[75] seems possible because of the common association
between sleeping and death. There is also a stereotypic "victory
pose" that has been associated with Mithras, a god who created
life from the death of the mythic bull,[76] a pose commonly associated with all sorts of victories, as for example in the *Amazon Sarcophagus* in the British Museum (fig. 14).[77] However,
if we are looking for a more direct prototype we need go no
further than Michelangelo, who used a similar pose both for

his statue of *Victory* and for the martyr, who holds up a cross on the upper right side of his *Last Judgment* (fig. 15), a major work that sixteenth-century artists studied by the hour.

El Greco, in painting his *Saint Sebastian* for the Cathedral of Palencia toward the end of the 1580s (fig. 16), combines the classically-inspired pose developed by Michelangelo and Tintoretto with the sculpturesque style that he learned in Venice and Rome [78]; in the long run, however, it was the less violent, more spiritual quality of Titian's *Saint Sebastian* in the Hermitage (fig. 17)[79] that seems to have inspired El Greco's later versions of the subject. We can see this influence very palpably in the two half-length, close-up interpretations that El Greco created later, one dating from about 1600,[80] and another (fig. 18) probably painted after 1605 and showing some signs of workshop assistance.[81]

These latest examples, which show the saint in isolation at the moment of his martyrdom, and which eliminate the archers, emperors, prefects, onlooking crowds, birds, animals, and so forth, reflect the attitude inspired by the Council of Trent in its efforts to limit artistic license in religious art. The Inquisition that tried Veronese in 1573, accusing him of representing "dwarfs, Germans, and dogs," which were not in the Scriptures,[82] made the point that embellishment of subject matter with picturesque details not part of the textual tradition was no longer an acceptable practice. A number of authoritative theologians published new hagiographies at this time (among them, Lippomanus, Surius, Molanus, and Baronius), further limiting experimentation.[83]

Among these hagiographers was Francisco Pacheco, who added information for artists to his *Arte della pintura*, which he published in 1616.[84] Pacheco was the censor of painting for the Spanish Inquisition and an artist in his own right, although some might claim that his greatest distinction in that direction was that his daughter married Velasquez. His *Saint Sebastian Nursed to Health by Saint Irene* (fig. 19), painted for the Hospital of San Sebastian in Alcalá in 1616, is a somewhat unusual version of a subject that gained extraordinary importance in the seventeenth century.[85] Pacheco portrays Sebastian with a beard because, as he notes in his *Addiciones*, that is the way he is shown to be in the oldest known example, the mosaic in San Pietro-in-Vincoli in Rome.[86] No one else follows his example of showing the saint in a hospital bed, being cured by eating a bowl of hot soup.

Nevertheless, it was probably the growth in the number of hospitals, many of them serviced by religious orders, that gave such a strong impetus to the Saint Irene theme. Rensselaer Lee has shown that another factor behind the interest in the Saint Irene theme is to be found in the romantic attitudes of the seventeenth century which inspired a number of subjects of similar feeling, among them that of Rinaldo being helped by Armida, a tender moment from Tasso's *Jerusalem Delivered*.[87]

Generally in depictions of the Saint Irene theme, the wounded Saint Sebastian is unconscious,[88] shifting the major emphasis from the violence and painfulness of his ordeal to the tender and sympathetic ministrations of Saint Irene. Sometimes, as in the painting by Antonio Balestra in the Hermitage,[89] there is something romantic, if not erotic, about the situation, which may explain why the subject was also interesting for nineteeth-century artists like Delacroix.[90]

Among the more intriguing artists to make a specialty of the Saint Irene theme in the seventeenth century is Georges de la Tour, who painted the subject for Louis XIII and the duke of Lorraine during the great plague that afflicted Lorraine in the 1630s. One of these paintings could be the version in the Detroit Institute of Arts (fig. 20).[91] Occasionally, as in the picture by Tanzio da Varallo [92] in imitation of the Donatello-Mantegna-Bellini composition of the *Dead Christ Supported by Angels*,[93] rather handsome women, wearing wings, treat his wounds. There is something noticeably miraculous about all of these nursing scenes when one thinks about the nature of arrow wounds, by the way. In no case does the treatment follow the required surgical procedures, either of pushing the arrow through so that the barbed head can be removed, or of enlarging the wound to free the barbs. Instead the women and the angels merely pluck out the arrows as if they were so many feathers.

Representations of the martyrdom showing the saint as an isolated figure gained stronger dramatic intensity in the seventeenth century, particularly because of the influence of Caravaggio and his followers. The *Saint Sebastian* by an unknown artist in the Fogg Museum at Harvard,[94] or Gerard Honthorst's painting of the subject in the National Gallery in London (fig. 21),[95] are typical, using stark, dramatic spotlighting and striking poses that create strong diagonal accents in the compositions. We are brought rather close to the saint as he undergoes his ordeal, and the artists show with unflinching realism that he is not a superman at all, but rather a simple human being who has lost consciousness in the midst of his suffering.

And finally, but not for the last time, since the subject still continues to have relevance, there is the tiny etching by Jacques Callot (fig. 22), made in 1621 when he returned from his travels in Italy,[96] a representation that seems to me to show that the Renaissance is over. Here, in the eyes of an artist who was later to depict the disasters of war in a series of brutal and frank etchings, the martyrdom seems to be a comment upon the historical dehumanization of man, of events without heroes. For the first time Saint Sebastian has been deprived of iconographic importance, and he is removed a great distance from us to where he becomes little more than a target for the bowmen, a pretext for a spectacle.

Thus we have seen how a saint, whom scientistic hagiographers (the Bollandists, for instance; protect us from our friends!) would do away with, has continued to exercise the imagination and devotion of mankind through centuries. A brief survey of the history of his pictorial imagery has revealed to us the fact that heroism is not necessarily an unchanging ideal, but rather that it is shaped and reshaped by society in accordance with other principles and purposes.

Notes

1. The present study is intended to bring up to date the dissertation, "Saint Sebastian in Art," which I completed at Columbia University in 1958. I began to work on it some seven years earlier with the encouragement and guidance of Rennselaer Lee, and then, after his departure for Princeton, I continued with Julius Held, Millard Meiss, and H. McPharlin Davis.

Needless to say, my indebtedness to such distinguished mentors can never be repaid.

2. Among the studies devoted specifically to the subject are Detlev von Hadeln, *Die wichtigsten Darstellungsformen des H. Sebastian in der italienischen Malerei bis zum Ausgang des Quattrocento* (Strassburg, 1906), and Victor Kraehling, *Saint Sébastien dans l'art* (Paris, 1938).

3. For example, see Gustav Quedenfeldt, *Die mysterien des Heiligen Sebastian, ihre Quelle und ihr Abhangigkeitverhältnis* (Marburg, 1895), which compares fifteenth-and sixteenth-century mystery plays. More recently, Leonard R. Mills published "Une Vie inédite de Saint Sébastien," *Bibliothèque d'Humanisme et Renaissance* 28 (1966): 410–18, a fourteenth-century poem that was found in a manuscript (MS fr. 1555, fols. 201–5) in the Bibliothèque Nationale in Paris. In addition, see Raymond Lebegue, *La Tragédie religieuse en France (1514–1573)* (Paris, 1929), p. 35, and the text published by François Rabut, "Le Mystère de Saint Sébastien," *Mémoires de la Societé Savoisienne d'Histoire et d'Archéologie* 13 (1872): 259–73. For seventeenth-century examples, see Kosta Loukovitch, *L'Evolution de la Tragédie religieuse classique en France* (Paris, 1933), p. 123, and Henri Busson, *La Pensée religieuse française de Charron à Pascal* (Paris, 1933), p. 527.

4. "The French Writings of Gabrielle d'Annunzio," *Comparative Literature* 12 (1960): 207–28.

5. See Charles Ouin-Lacroix, *Histoire des Anciennes Corporations d'Arts et Métiers et des Confrèries religieuses de la Capitale de Normandie* (Rouen, 1850), especially pp. 415, 420–21, and 479.

6. *Vita B. Agnetis et Acta Sancti Sebastiani*, Codice Laurenziano, LXXXIX, supp. 74, 52–53. Other important sources are M. Lenain de Tillemont, *Mémoires pour servir à l'Histoire Ecclésiastique*, 2d ed. (Paris, 1701), 4: 515–36; the *Acta Sanctorum* (Paris, 1863), 11 January, 621–60; and P. Migne, *Patrologia Cursus Completus, Series Latina* 17.657 ff. (hereafter cited as *PL*).

7. Granger Ryan and Helmut Ripperberger, *The Golden Legend of Jacobus de Voragine* (New York: Longmans, Green, 1941), 1: 104–10.

8. See Saint Ambrose's *Enarratio in Psalmum*, CXVIII in *PL* 65.1497.

9. Ryan and Ripperberger, 1: 109.

10. See n. 6 above (Cod.Laur. LXXXIX).

11. Could Michelangelo have been thinking of this when he depicted a nude Saint Sebastian who brandishes arrows in his famous *Last Judgement* in the Sistine Chapel? See Henry E. Sigerist, "The Historical Aspects of Art and Medicine," *Bulletin of the Institute of the History of Medicine* 4 (1936): 271–72, and "Sebastian-Apollo," *Archiv für Geschicte der Medizin* 19 (1927): 301–17.

12. As pointed out by Hippolyte Delehaye s.v. "Saint Sebastian," *Encyclopaedia Britannica*, 11th ed., this transference helped spread Saint Sebastian's cult north of the Alps. The information comes from Eginhardus, *Annales*, DCCCXXVI (*PL* 104.503), which points out that Pope Eugene II sent the relics that were requested by Louis le Debonnaire. The migration of the relics into Burgundy is described in *Mémoires de l'Académie de Dijon* (1923): 29–61. See also, Mills, p. 410, n. 3.

13. Sabine Baring-Gould, *Lives of the Saints* (Edinburgh, 1914), 1: 300–1.

14. Edmond Haraucourt, *Medieval Manners Illustrated in the Cluny Museum* (Paris, n.d.), p. 72.

15. Published in *Giornale Ligustico* 10(1883): 139 ff.

16. Guy de Chauliac, *Grande Chirurgie*, edited by E. Nicaise (Paris, 1890).

17. Paulus Diaconis, *Historica de gestis Langobardorum*, in *Monumentis Germaniae recusa* (Hannover, 1878), 6:5 (*PL* 95.628).

18. Josef Wilpert, *Die römischen Mosaiken und Malereien* (Freiburg im Breisgau, 1917), 2: 1001, maintains the existence of a church called San Pietro-in-Vincoli in Pavia. As he points out, *Le liber pontificalis* (edited by Duchesne [Paris, 1886], 1: 350) does not mention the erection of such an altar in Rome in 680, which it certainly would have if an event of such importance had transpired. In addition, we should note that Girolamo Bossi's manuscript, *Storia Pavese*, V (according to Constance J. Ffoulkes and Rodolfo Maiocchi, *Vincenzo Foppa* [London, 1908], p. 143, n. 3) describes a similar ceremony that took place at a church called San Pietro-in-Vincoli in 1479. To show how confusing the whole story was even in the fifteenth century, a painting that has been erroneously attributed to Antonio Pollaiuolo was installed in the Roman Church in commemoration of Saint Sebastian's intercession (see G. Clausse, "Deux représentations de la peste de Rome en 680," *Gazette des Beaux-Arts* 2 (1904): 225 ff.). Voraginus does not help either, mentioning an altar in Pavia and another at San Pietro-in-Vincoli in Rome (see Ryan and Ripperberger, p. 110).

19. Francisco Pacheco, *Arte della Pittura*, edited by G. C. Vilaamil (Madrid, 1866), 3: 289–91.

20. Among the earlier examples of pictorial representations of Saint Sebastian, none of which single him out with specific references to characterization or the details of his martyrdom, are: a fifth-century fresco in the Catacomb of Saint Calixtus (Josef Wilpert, *Die Papstgräber und die Cäciliengruft in der Katakombe des Hl. Kallistus* [Freiberg im Breisgau, 1909], fig. IV); another from about the same period in the so-called "Platonia" of San Sebastiano on the Appian Way (Anton de Waal, "Die Apostelgruft ad Catacumbus an der Via Appia," *Römische Quartalschrift*, suppl. 3 [1894], fig. 1); and the mid-sixth century mosaic of Sant' Apollinaire Nuovo (Corrado Ricci, *Tavole storiche dei mosaici di Ravenna* [Rome, 1934], 12: 4, fig. 27).

21. Frederick H. Dudden, *The Life and Times of Saint Ambrose* (Oxford, 1935), chap. 12.

22. *City of God*, 12.8. In addition, Henry O. Taylor, *The Medieval Mind* (Cambridge, Mass.: Harvard University Press, 1949), 1: 54, n.2, reports on evidence that cults of Mary and certain saints had developed as early as the third century.

23. Emil von Dobschütz, *Das Decretum Gelasianum de Libris recipiendis et non recipiendis*, in *Texte und Untersuchungen zur Geschichte der altchristlichen Literatur*, 2d series, vol. 8, no. 3 (1912), p. 9; and Eduard Schwartz, "Zum Decretum Gelasianum," *Zeitschrift für Neutestamentliche Wissenschaft* 29 (1930): 161–68.

24. Vincent L. Kennedy, *The Saint in the Canon of the Mass* (Vatican, 1938), p. 87.

25. René Gilles, *Le Symbolisme dans l'Art religieux* (Paris: Mercure de France, 1943), p. 165, shows that the Council placed invention and composition strictly under control of the church fathers, anticipating the decisions of the Council of Trent by nearly eight centuries.

26. Wilpert, *Römischen Mosaiken*, 2: 951 ff.; Joseph A. Martigny, *Dictionnaire des Antiquités Chrétiennes* (Paris, 1865), vol. 2; and Johaness Reil, *Die altchristlichen Bildzyklen des Lebens Jesu* (Leipzig, 1910), p. 1.

27. Giovanni Battista de Rossi, *Inscriptiones christianae Urbis Romae septimo saeculo antiquiores* (Rome, 1935), 2: 71, 98, 139.

28. *Liber pontificalis*, 2: 74 and 83, n.4.

29. Wilpert *Römischen Mosaiken*, vol. 2, figs. 494–98.

30. Albert Boeckler, *Das Stuttgarter Passionale* (Augsburg, 1923), p. 20.

31. For example, in the Pericope of Heinrich II (1002–14), reproduced in Hans Jantzen, *Ottonische Kunst* (Munich: Bruckmann, 1947), figs. 46, 47.

32. Louis Bréhier, "Une Représentation du Martyre de Saint Sébastien a Saint-Nectaire," *Révue d'Auvergne*, October 1921, pp. 1–2.

33. Among sources of information about pestilence that are particularly interesting I would mention Cornelius Walford, *A Statistical Chronology of Plagues and Pestilences as Affecting Human Life* (London, 1884); Raymond Crawfurd, *Plagues and Pestilences in Literature and Art* (Oxford, 1914); Anna M. Campbell, *The Black Death and Men of Learning* (New York, 1931); Justus F. C. Hecker, *Die grossen Volkskrankheiten des Mittelalters* (Berlin, 1865); Heinrich Haeser, *Lehrbuch der Medizin und der epidemischen Krankheiten*, 3d ed. (Jena, 1882), vol. 3; R. Honiger, *Der schwarze Tod in Deutschland* (Berlin, 1882); and, of course, Francis A. Gasquet, *The Great Pestilence* (London, 1893.)

34. Millard Meiss in *Painting in Florence and Siena after the Black Death* (Princeton, N.J.: Princeton University Press, 1951) brilliantly considers the connection between the epidemic and changes in style and iconography in Trecento art in Italy.

35. Gasquet, p. xviii.

36. Reproduced in Prince d'Essling, "Le Premier Livre xylographique italien, Imprimé à Venise vers 1450," *Gazette des Beaux-Arts* 2 (1903): 255.

37. The cult of Saint Sebastian in Tuscany seems to have been greatly stimulated after his relics were brought to the Duomo in 1348. See Richard Offner, *A Critical and Historical Corpus of Florentine Painting* (New York: New York University Press; Berlin: A. Frisch, 1947), iii–5, 162, n.1; and Meiss, p. 77, n. 19.

38. Meiss, p. 78, n. 21; Bernard Berenson, *Pittura Italiana* (Milan, 1936), p. 183; Offner, iii–5, 162, n. 1.

39. Hadeln, Plate I, fig 1.

40. The best example, that from Pergamon, is in the Louvre. Other examples are in Rome and Istanbul. See Arnold Schober, *Die Kunst von Pergamon* (Vienna: Österreichischen Arcäologischen Institut, 1951), pp. 72–73 and figs. 24 and 25.

41. *Poggii Florentini de Fortunae Varietate Urbis Romae, & de ruina eiusdem descriptio*, in Poggius Bracciolinus, *Opera Omnia*, edited by R. Fubini, Monumenta Politica et Philosophica Rariora, Ser. 2, no 4 (Turin: Bottega Erasmo, 1964), I: 131–37; also, Poggius Bracciolinus, *De varietate fortunae*, edited by Georgius (Paris, 1723), pp. 5–25.

42. Giuseppe Fiocco, *Mantegna* (Milan, 1937), pp. 43 ff.; Paul Kristeller, *Andreas Mantegna* (Berlin, 1902), pp. 168, 175, and 438 ff.; and Erica Tietze-Conrat, *Mantegna* (New York: Phaidon Press, 1955), p. 200.

43. Kristeller, p. 439.

44. Kristeller, p. 438 ff., and Fiocco, pp. 43 and 202.

45. The painting is now in the Ca'd'Oro in Venice; Giovanni Paccagnini, *Mostra di Andrea Mantegna* (Venice: N. Pozza, 1961), p. 64.

46. The painting is now in Dresden; Steffano Bottari, *Antonello da Messina* (Messina, 1939), pp. 22–23 and fig. LV; and Raimond van Marle, *The Development of the Italian Schools of Painting* (The Hague, 1935) 15: 524–25.

47. Giles Robertson, *Giovanni Bellini* (Oxford: Oxford University Press, 1968), pp. 39–40 and Plate xxa; George Gronau, *Giovanni Bellini* (Stuttgart, 1930), pp. 8–9.

48. Robertson, pp. 43–46, and Plates xxv and xxvic; Van Marle, 27: 236–37. A drawing by Bellini (Van Marle, 27, fig. 210) in the British Museum, perhaps a study for the painting, shows the influence of Mantegna even more clearly.

49. Robertson, pp. 83–87 and plate lxvi; Van Marle, xvii, 283–85.

50. This type of composition seems to have appeared as early as Fra Angelico and Domenico Veneziano, and reflects either a desire for a more unified

Fig. 1.   St. Sebastian. By Andrea Mantegna.
Kunsthistorisches Museum, Vienna (Alinari photo).

Fig. 2. St Sebastian. By Andrea Mantegna.

Louvre, Paris (Alinari photo).

Fig. 3. St. Sebastian. By Andrea Mantegna.
Ca'd'Oro, Venice (Alinari photo).

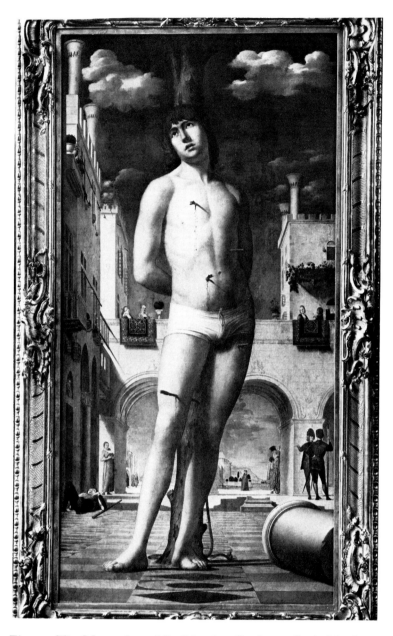

Fig. 4. The Martyrdom of St. Sebastian. By Antonello da Messina.
Pinakothek, Dresden (Alinari photo).

Fig. 5. San Giobbe Altarpiece. By Giovanni Bellini.

Accademia, Venice (Alinari photo).

Fig. 6. The Martyrdom of St. Sebastian. By Antonio Pollaiuolo.
Photo courtesy of the National Gallery, London.

Fig. 7. The Martyrdom of St. Sebastian. By Luca Singorelli.
Pinacoteca Comunale, Città di Castello (Alinari photo).

Fig. 8. The Martyrdom of St. Sebastian. By Hans Memling.
Photo courtesy of the Musées Royaux des Beaux-Arts, Brussels.

Fig. 9. St. Sebastian. By Martin Schongauer.

*Photo courtesy of the Rosenwald Collection,
the National Gallery of Art, Washington, D. C.*

Fig. 10. St. Sebastian. By Albrecht Dürer.
Photo courtesy of the British Museum, London.

Fig. 11. St. Sebastian. By Albrecht Dürer.
Photo courtesy of the British Museum, London.

Fig. 12. The Resurrection Altarpiece. By Titian.

The Church of Saints Nazaro and Celso, Brescia (Alinari photo).

Fig. 13. St. Sebastian. By Tintoretto.
Scuolo di San Rocco, Venice (Alinari photo).

Fig. 14. *Detail of* the Amazon Sarcophagus.
Photo courtesy of the British Museum, London.

Fig. 15. *Detail of* The Last Judgement. By Michelangelo.
The Sistine Chapel, Rome (Alinari photo).

Fig. 16. St. Sebastian. By El Greco.
The Cathedral, Valencia (author's photo).

Fig. 17. St. Sebastian. By Titian.
Photo courtesy of The Hermitage, Leningrad.

Fig. 18. St. Sebastian. By El Greco.
The Prado, Madrid (author's photo).

Fig. 19. St. Sebastian Nursed to Health by St. Irene.
By Francisco Pacheco.
Hospital San Sebastian, Alcalá (author's photo).

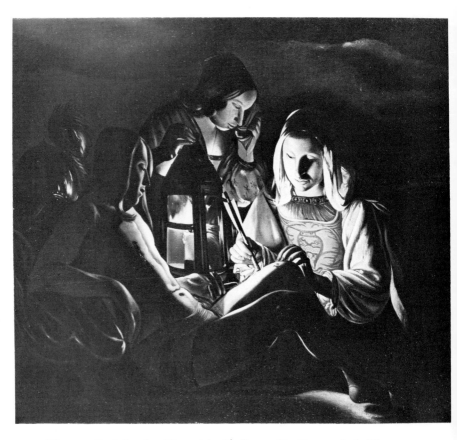

Fig. 20. St. Sebastian Nursed by St. Irene. By George de la Tour.

Photo courtesy of the Detroit Institute of Arts.

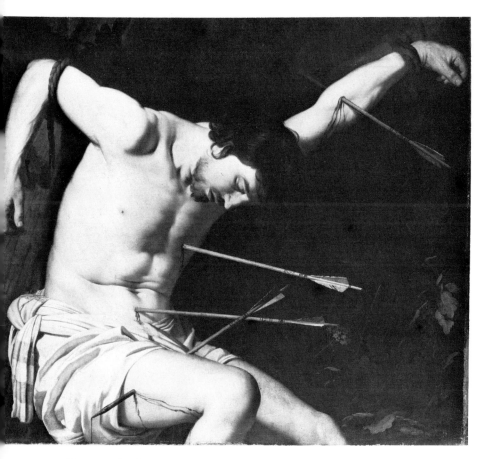

Fig. 21. St. Sebastian. By Gerard Honthorst.
Photo courtesy of the National Gallery, London.

Fig. 22. The Martyrdom of St. Sebastian. By Jacques Callot.
*Photo courtesy of the Rhode Island School of
Design Museum of Art, Providence.*

composition, an effort to economize on the costliness of the polyptych format, or, most likely, a change in the functional use from an altar that was capable of changing with the religious occasion to a painting that became an unchanging monument to the Madonna and Saints.

51. See *Marsilio Ficino's Commentary on Plato's Symposium*, text and translation by S. J. Jayne, in *University of Missouri Studies*, vol. 9, no. 1 (1944): 1–247.

52. *Augustini Niphi Medicis ad Illustriss. Ioannam Aragoniam Tagliacocii Principem de Pulchro Liber* (Vatican, 1531).

53. Walter Bombe, *Perugino des Meisters Gemälde* (Stuttgart and Berlin, 1914), p. 236.

54. Gabriele Mandel, *The Complete Paintings of Botticelli* (New York: H. N. Abrams, 1967), p. 89. Mandel and Giulio Carlo Argan, *Botticelli* (New York and Paris: Skira, 1957), pp. 51–52, suggest that this panel was painted in 1473 for Santa Maria Maggiore (which may or may not be the case). It has been suggested that Botticelli's painting could have been influenced by the example of Pollaiuolo's lost painting for the Church of San Jacopo above the Arno. See Guiseppe Richa, *Notizie istoriche delle Chiese Fiorentini divise ne' suoi Quartieri* (Florence, 1762), 10: 355. See also Van Marle, 12: 60–61; Jacques Mesnil, *Botticelli* (Paris, 1938), pp. 33–34; Wilhelm Bode, *Sandro Botticelli* (London, 1925), pp. 44–45; Adolfo Venturi, *Botticelli* (London, 1927), pp. 27–28; and Yukio Yashiro, *Sandro Botticelli* (London, 1929), pp. 21–22.

55. See, for example, Richard Krautheimer and Trude Krautheimer-Hess, *Lorenzo Gbiberti* (Princeton, N.J.: Princeton University Press, 1956), 14, in which the world *liniamente* is used in this fashion.

56. Alberto Busignani, *Pollaiuolo* (Florence: Edizioni d'Arte Il Fiorino, 1970), p. 91 and plate cxxxvi, informs us that the painting was made for the Pucci Chapel of the Oratorio of St. Sebastian at the Annunciata in 1475. Considerable debate has ensued over what part Antonio's brother, Piero, had in painting the picture, but probably this problem is not to be solved.

57. Now in the Pinacoteca communale. See Giovanni Colacicchi, *Antonio del Pollaiuolo* (Florence: Chessa Editore, 1943), figs. 34–37; Van Marle, 11: 386; M. Cruttwell, *Pollaiuolo* (London, 1907), pp. 159–60; and, more recently, Mario Salmi, *Luca Signorelli* (Novara: Instituto Geografico de Agostini, 1953), p. 53.

58. Passavant 108.34. See Arthur M. Hind, *Early Italian Engraving* (Washington, D.C. and London: B. Quaritch, n.d.), vol. 5, Pt. 2, p. 29 (#23), reproduced in vol. 6, plate 521. The pose, of course, echoes a familiar classical variant in statues of Apollo.

59. All four engravings are reproduced in Max Lehrs, *Geschichte und kritischer Katalog des deutschen, niederländischen, und französischen Kupferstichs in XV Jahrhunderts* (Vienna, 1910), vol. 2, figs. 59, 42, 29,

and 167; the engraving in question is figure 59. See also, Max Geisberg, *Der Meister E. S.* (Leipzig, 1924); and Henry S. Francis, "Saint Sebastian by the Master E. S.," *Bulletin of the Cleveland Museum of Art*, vol. 38, no. 9 (1951), pp. 207–8.

60. For example, see the impressive collection of popular prints in Paul Heitz and W. L. Schreiber, *Pestblätter des XV Jahrhunderts, Einblattdrucke des XV Jahrhunderts* (Munich, 1901), vol. 2; or Elizabeth Mongan and Carl O. Schneiwind, *The First Century of Print-making* (Chicago: Art Institute, R.R. Donnelly & Sons, 1941), p. 21 and fig. 9.

61. Max Friedländer, *Rogier van der Weyden and the Master of Flémalle*, Early Netherlandish Painting, vol. 2 (Leyden: A. W. Sÿthoff, 1967), pp. 62–63, and Herman T. Beenken, *Rogier van der Weyden* (Munich: F. Bruckmann, 1951), pp. 62–65 and plate 60.

62. Max Friedländer, *Hans Memlinc and Gerard David*, Early Netherlandish Painting, vol. 6 (Leyden: A. W. Sÿthoff, 1971), p. 52. Ludwig von Baldass, *Hans Memling* (Vienna: Anton Schroll, 1942), p. 43. Also, see Alphonse J. Wauters, *Sept Études pour servir à l'Histoire de Hans Memling* (Brussels, 1893), pp. 79–80, 85.

63. Friedländer, *Memlinc*, p. 46 and plate 24. Also see Karl Voll, *Memling, des Meisters Gemälde* (Stuttgart, 1909), fig. 113, and Baldass, p. 48.

64. Alan Shestack, *The Complete Engravings of Martin Schongauer* 1969), fig. 64; and Jacob Rosenberg, *Martin Schongauer Handzeichnungen* (Munich: R. Piper, 1923), p. 123 and fig. 10.

65. See n. 40, above, and also André de Hevesy, *Jacopo de Barbari* (Paris, 1925), pp. 20, 23, and plate 10, for a version by the important transmitter of Italianism, Jacopo.

66. Erwin Panofsky, *Albrecht Dürer* (Princeton, N.J.: Princeton University Press, 1943), 2: 47.

67. H. Tietze, *Albrecht Dürer* (Augsburg, 1928), 1: A24, attributed the engraving to Dürer himself; however, at present most art historians follow the opinion of Panofsky, *Dürer*, 2: 47.

68. Norbert Lieb and Alfred Stange, *Hans Holbein der Ältere* (Augsburg: Deutscher Kunstverlag, 1960), pp. 71–72 and fig. 112. Also Curt Glaser, *Holbein* (Leipzig, 1908), p. 228, and Alfred Woltmann, *Holbein und seine Zeit* (Leipzig, 1874), figs. 225, 228–29, and 232–33. Uffizi Inv. 2282 is a copy of the original painting.

69. See, for example, Charles Avery, *Florentine Renaissance Sculpture* (London: John Murray, 1970), p. 181.

70. The date of 1542 places it one year later than the completion of Michelangelo's fresco. See *A Review of the Annual Art and Antique Dealer's Fair in the Years 1949–1953* (Delft: Prinsenhof Museum, 1954), fig. xiv.

71. Painted for the Church of Saints Nazaro and Celso in Brescia. See Hans Tietze, *Titian, Paintings and Drawings* (New York: Phaidon Press, 1950),

p. 367 and figs. 51, 53, and 54. Also see Harold E. Wethey, *The Paintings of Titian* (London and New York: Phaidon Press, 1969), vol. 1, *The Religious Paintings*, pp. 126–28. As Wethey points out (*Titian*, 1: 143), the *Saint Sebastian* panel of the altarpiece was already complete in 1520, and at least ten copies are known to have existed. In another altarpiece, painted perhaps a few years later for San Niccolo dei Frari of Venice (now in the Pinacoteca Vaticana; see Wethey, *Titian*, 1: 107–8, or Tietze, *Titian*, p. 392 and fig. 137), Titian changed back to the Giorgionesque type, portraying Sebastian as if he were almost adolescent.

72. Currently this painting, a *Saint Mark Enthroned*, is in Santa Maria della Salute, Venice. See Wethey, *Titian*, 1: 143, or Tietze, *Titian*, p. 398 and fig. 14.

73. As noted by Wethey, *Titian*, 1: 143, who points to the influence of the Louvre *Slave*, if not the *Laocöon*, on the drawings in Berlin and Frankfort made by Titian in preparation for the painting. See also, Erwin Panofsky, *Problems in Titian, Mostly Iconographic* (New York: New York University Press, 1969), p. 20. For a reproduction of the *Rebellious Slave* in the Louvre, see Frederick Hartt, *History of Italian Renaissance Art* (New York: Prentice-Hall and Harry N. Abrams, n.d.), fig. 542.

74. Erich von der Bercken and August L. Mayer, *Tintoretto* (Munich, 1923), vol. 2, fig. 132; and Hans Tietze, *Tintoretto, the Paintings and Drawings* (New York and Oxford: Oxford University Press, 1948), fig. 210.

75. As an example of this type of figure, see Joseph Jay Deiss, *Herculaneum, Italy's Buried Treasure* (New York: Crowell, 1966, p. 50.

76. For example, see Fritz Saxl, *A Heritage of Images* (Harmondsworth, Middlesex: Penguin, 1970), pp. 19–21 and figs. 21 and 22.

77. Saxl, p. 18 and fig. 18.

78. Harold E. Wethey, *El Greco and His School* (Princeton, N.J.: Princeton University Press, 1962), 2: 147–48. Maurice Legendre and K. Hartmann, *Domenico Theotocopouli, dit El Greco* (Paris, 1937), fig. 470.

79. Wethey, *Titian*, 1: 155–57 and Tietze, *Titian*, figs. 265–66. This unfinished painting, among his last works, was found in the artist's studio at his death.

80. Wethey, *El Greco*, 2: 147–48; Legendre and Hartmann, fig. 469; and Ludwig Goldscheider, *El Greco* (New York, 1938), figs. 147–48.

81. Legendre and Hartmann, fig. 469.

82. Elizabeth G. Holt, ed., *Literary Sources of Art History* (Princeton, N.J.: Princeton University Press, 1947), 245–48.

83. See, for example, Charles de Job, *De l'Influence du Concile de Trente sur la Littérature et les Beaux-Arts chez les Peuples Catholiques* (Paris, 1884), pp. 4, 242–43. Luigi Lippomano's six-volume folio edition of 1560 was expanded by Laurentius Surius's *Historiae seu Vitae Sanctorum* a few years later. In 1570 Molanus, or Jean ver Meulen, published his influen-

tial *De Picturis et Imaginibus Sacris* in Louvain, an errudite defense of
the cult of saints. Caesar Baronius, *Martyrologium Romanum*, published in
Antwerp in 1613, was also most important. In 1564 Andrea Gilio da Fab-
riano's famous attack on Michelangelo's lack of decorum, the *Dialogo degli
Errori dei Pittori*, attempted to set standards other than iconographic.

84. Pacheco, 3: 289–91.

85. Kraehling, plate xxvii.

86. Pacheco, 3: 289–91.

87. *Poetry into Paintings; Tasso and Art* (Middlebury, Vt.: Middlebury
College, 1970).

88. For example, in the composition attributed to Caravaggio that was copied
in paintings in the Palazzo Campori of Modena, the Villa Albani in Rome,
and the Museums of Vicenza and Tours. Cf. Paul Vitry, *Le Musée de
Tours* (Paris, 1911), plate 12; E. Valeri, "Caravaggio," *Chronache d'Arte*
1 (1924): 245, 247, and 249; E. Ricci, *Mille Santi nell'Arte* (Rome,
1931), p. 366; and see Charles N. Cochin, *Voyages en Italie* (Paris,
1769), 1: 77–78.

89. E. Bruiningk and A. Somoff, *Katalog Kartinnoi Galerei* (Leningrad,
1899), p. 19; also in 1912 Hermitage catalog, vol. 1, #309.

90. Delacroix, a keen student of Baroque painting, depicted the subject more
than once. One version painted for the 1836 Salon, and now in San
Michele, Nantua, as well as in a second copy in the Schmitz Collection in
Dresden (See Louis Hourticq, *Delacroix, L'Oeuvre du Mâitre* [Paris, 1930],
p. 61), closely follows Rubens's *Pietà* in the Lichtenstein Gallery. Again,
in the 1850s, Delacroix painted several variations on the theme, exhibiting the 1858 version in his final Salon the next year. This painting
was last in the A. Kahn Collection in Paris (see Alfred Robaut and Ernest
Chesneau, *L'Oeuvre Complet de Eugène Delacroix* [Paris, 1885], figs.
1190, 1353, 1381, 1382, 1780, and 1781; also Hourticq, p. 174).

91. See Georges Pariset, *Georges de la Tour* (Paris: H. Laurens, 1948), pp.
200, 340, notes 3, 4, and 393–94; Paul Jamot, *Georges de la Tour*
(Paris: Floury, 1948), p. 44; and Edgar P. Richardson, "Georges de
la Tour's 'Saint Sebastian Nursed by Saint Irene,'" *Art Quarterly* 12
(1949): 81–88. Georges de la Tour painted several copies with the same
composition to be found in Detroit; the example in Rouen might have
been the original version, and others are also to be found in the Fiorillo
Collection in Paris, and at the Church of Notre Dame de Grâce in Hon-
fleur. A somewhat different composition was used in the better known
version in the Kaiser Friedrich Museum in Berlin, and in a copy at Bois-
Anzeray (see Pariset, plates 26 and 27.1.), in which the wounds are not
being treated, and one gets the impression that the saint has died from
his wounds and is being mourned by the Holy Women.

92. *The National Gallery of Art Book of Illustrations*, 2d ed. (Washington,
D.C.: National Gallery of Art, 1942), p. 192 and fig. 302.

93. For an exacting study of the half-length and other close-up forms of representation, see Sixten Ringbom, *Icon to Narrative*, Acta Academiae Aboensis, Series A, vol. 31, no. 2 (Åbo: Akademi Åbo, 1965).

94. Attributions concerning the artist differ; Roberto Longhi in *Vita Artistica* (Rome, 1927), pp. 9–10, saw the painting as Caracciolo's while in *The Arts* 3 (1929): 122, it was attributed to Caravaggio. The latest opinion seems to agree with Arthur McComb, *Baroque Painters in Italy* (London, 1934), p. 123, who cautiously describes it as a work of "the school of Caravaggio."

95. *National Gallery Illustrations; Continental Schools* (London, 1937), p. 168.

96. Pierre-Paul Plan, *Jacques Callot, Maître Graveur* (Brussels, 1914), p. 35, and Karl Pollhammer, *Jacques Callot als Illustrator* (Vienna, 1925), plate 7. A drawing in the Victoria and Albert Museum seems to have been made by Callot in preparation for the etching (see James Laver, "Callot's Martyrdom of St. Sebastian," *The Burlington Magazine* 51 [1927]: 80–85), and there are at least nine pirated engravings and at least two oil sketches that are known (see Edouard Meaume, *Recherches sur la vie et les ouvrages de Jacques Callot* [Paris, 1860], 1: 107–10; and J. Guiffrey and P. Marcel, *Inventaire Général des Dessins du Musée du Louvre et de Versailles* [Paris, 1907–13], no. 1761, Inv. 9570). More recently N. S. Trivas, "Callot's 'Martyrdom of St. Sebastian'," *Art Quarterly* 4 (1941): 205–9, made a similar claim for a drawing in the E. B. Crocker Art Gallery in Sacramento, California, arguing that certain discrepancies suggest that "while repeating his drawings on the copper plate, the artist *quite naturally* made a number of changes," and that "the spontaneity of these changes is the best proof of the authenticity of the Sacramento drawing." Since then, in the *catalogue raisoneé, Jacques Callot, 1592–1635*, by the Department of Art, Brown University (Providence, R.I., 1970), pp. 75–76, the suggestion has been made that the Sacramento drawing was the first of several studies for the engraving, the Victoria and Albert version being the last, since it is closest to the final version. Jules Lieure, *Jacques Callot* (1927; rpt. New York: Collectors Editions, 1969), 7: 30–31 (# 670) identifies a number of Roman landmarks in the background and lists nine copies of the original etching and a painting that reproduces the composition with some variations.

The Myth of the Hero in Boccaccio

Vittore Branca

THE CONCEPT AND MYTH OF THE HERO were evolved decisively during the autumn of the Middle Ages principally through the work of Boccaccio. They were developed by him vigorously in a way that was not so much Renaissance as fundamentally modern because he introduced successively the commercial middle class, the world of women, and the poet conceived as bard, in a bold spirit of innovation and an all-embracing human sensibility.

As the classic studies by Joseph Campbell and Sidney Hook demonstrate, strength, in an anthropological and historical sense, is at the center of this myth. And in a very striking essay Simone Weil has revealed in the *Iliad* its unsurpassable expression because the poem deeply approves of the destruction of strength itself and therefore sympathizes with those who are overcome by it.[1] Strength is the soul and sign of the hero—the hero in war, in love, in sustaining peoples, or in redeeming them by overcoming death. Even the most emblematic hero-saint—that is to say the martyr or the ascetic—overcomes physically by his own strength the strength of his persecutors or of the demons: he is in fact "the athlete saint" *par excellence.*

Apart from the epic of power of Charlemagne and Roland, feudal civilization tried, with Tristan and Launcelot, to graft the element of love onto the one of physical strength, but love remained above all an ideal goal, a point of arrival beyond actions and representations that were still mostly concerned with violent adventures and war.

All Boccaccio's first works reflect this uncertainty, this vacillation between strength and love in the literature of chivalry, when he portrayed his heroes. After all, these were works written in the atmosphere of the French culture characteristic of Angevin Naples where, as we know, he lived during his apprentice literary period from 1327 to 1340.

With Troilus, the chief character in his first poem *Filostrato* (1335?), Boccaccio takes us back to the Homeric setting of Troy besieged by the Greeks precisely because of his warlike adventures and his unhappy love. He is the strongest of all the Trojans after Hector and is the terror of the Greeks. But this Troy of his is a "great and delightful city" that "during times of truce" enjoys a peaceful, busy life like any great medieval commune. Those warriors—they may be called Troilus or Diomedes, Pandarus or Ulysses, Hector or Achilles—are not mythical heroes but knights of the court, people belonging not to epic but to romance. In spite of the superabundance of heroes presented, the story in fact aims (recalling Benoît de St. Maure) not at creating human models but at focussing through examples upon a love story, leaving it suspended between lyrical poetry and narrative. Boccaccio works effectively within that process which was to establish, through Chaucer, the contrasting portraits of Troilus and Cressida (the first of the bewitching portraits of women that Boccaccio created) as a supreme, completely amorous emblematization—of passion and coquetry as well—in the play by Shakespeare.

From the chivalrous poem to the romance, that is to say from *Filostrato* to *Filocolo* (1336–38?), the game is inverted but the results are similar. The setting is once more fictitiously classical, in the late Roman period, but is in reality communal and courtly. Florio, son of the king of Marmorina, which is Verona, goes on an entirely amorous quest to find his Biancofiore, who has been carried off, but he does so according to the most usual and characteristic models and *topoi* of the traditional hero. He overcomes his enemies in battle and in tournament by his vigor, and even conquers monstrous powers; he regains his beloved by storming a heavily defended castle, founds several cities, and subdues nations; he becomes a defender of the Faith and converts entire populations. Because of all this the figure of Florio is left uncertain between abandoned and sentimental sighings of love and expressions of power typical of armored champions with swords. For this reason *Filocolo* remains a composite work.

Neither does Boccaccio succeed in the *Teseida* (1339–41?)
in overcoming these ambiguities, nor in offering a clearly defined figure of the hero, in spite of the abundance of his mythical Hellenic settings. Yet it is a decisively epical poem and,
furthermore, a reply to a complaint expressed by Dante in his
De vulgari eloquentia (2. 2. 10). Boccaccio replied (12. 84)
ideally by asserting that he was the "primo a cantare di Marte
Nel volgar lazio" (the first to sing of Mars in the vulgar
tongue of Latium). But Theseus remains an abstract figure, a
conventional silhouette of a warrior and defender of peoples.
Instead the chief characters are Arcite and Palemone, the two
Theban youths, rivals for the Pisanelloesque Amazon Emilia,
and in battling, jousting and duelling they are typical Arthurian
knights scaled down, very obviously, to suit middle-class taste.
The doleful grief at the death of Arcite is not of sublime
Homeric origin, but is, instead, as has recently been demonstrated,[2] closely modeled on the Tristan pattern.

In short, in the whole period of his literary apprenticeship
at Naples, Boccaccio did not succeed in going beyond the
schemes of the literature of romantic chivalry. He did not
succeed in offering a new, or even a clear, model of a hero.
The protagonists themselves in these works are the ambiguous
and composite results of hints drawn from earlier contrasting
literary traditions.

His removal, between 1340 and 1341, to the communal and
mercantile city of Florence, to a cultural atmosphere that was
for the most part didactically allegorical and moralistic, caused
a decisive modification in his view of the world and of life, and
also in his artistic choices.

A great and splendid theme that asserts itself ever more
decisively, from the *Comedia delle Ninfe* to *The Decameron*
and then on to the moral-historic erudite works of his maturity,
takes the place of the tales that vacillate among themes of
love, adventure, and arms; it is the representation—continually varied but always more clear and systematic—of the
measure that man gives of his capacities for good or ill in the
face of the great forces that, as instruments of Providence,
dominate the world: Power, Wealth, Fortune, Love, and Wit.
This is the great "human comedy" that has to complete the

"divine comedy" admired so enthusiastically by Boccaccio. It is the theme that emerges from the various and hard experiences he gained in the refined and cosmopolitan Angevin court; in the adventurous and carefree communal environment of his own family; in the gay and gilded life of the Neapolitan youth; in the literary and erudite broodings of his hard and long hours of study; in the stormy vicissitudes of the Florentine commune caught between the economic power of its great bankers, who dominated Europe, and the greedy aspirations of Angevin and papal politics. From his father's accounts, from his own direct experience as a young clerk to one of the most powerful companies (that of the Bardi family), most of all from the experience of having personally lived through the struggle, Boccaccio day by day came to understand the gradual yielding of political, military power to economic power. The solemn King Roberto of Naples, the pretentious Pontiffs at Avignon, the haughty Bohemian and Germanic emperors, even those sovereigns on either side of the English Channel, all revealed themselves to be like "tinkling cymbals" before the resolute and unscrupulous Italian bankers. The so-called "Powers" were in reality at the mercy of the *mercatanti,* who not only exacted from them titles, solemn acknowledgments, and heavy tributes, but also dictated fundamental lines of policy, alliances and agreements, and decisions regarding war and peace. In many royal palaces in Europe Tuscan businessmen could, with good reason, anticipate by way of variation the daring statement to be made many centuries later: "L'État, c'est nous." The kings of France and England were obliged to lay down their arms when the Peruzzis and the Frescobaldis, their bankers, ordered them to do so, because war was ruining trading relationships in which the bankers were particularly interested. The Emperors, from Ludwig of Bavaria to Charles of Bohemia, were docile instruments in the hands of the merchants, who presented their demands together with elegant purses bulging with thousands of gold florins. The Angevins had had to cease their action against the rebellious Sicilians when the Bardis and the Canigianis (who were their purse-holders) had stopped financing them because trade with Sicily and Catalonia was advantageous to them. Precisely in those years Niccolò Acciaiuoli, bosom friend of the youthful Boccaccio, had become through the power of his bank "facitore e disfacitore di re" (maker and destroyer of kings), as one chronicler wrote of him, and arbiter of the Mediterranean kingdoms and empires. The power of armies was replaced by the power of the banks and the trading companies; the sword and the spear by the florin, the true dollar of the Middle Ages; military and political strategy by the new economic techniques that had been discovered by the Tuscan companies—the bill of exchange, the double entry, and the economic and productive systems. The strength of intelligence and human foresight rose up, youthful and full of confidence, in the path of physical and material strength. It seemed to bring true in history the eternal myth of Jack and the Beanstalk, the exemplary biblical story of the giant Goliath overcome by clever little David.

In this profound restructuring of the hierarchy of the powers, in this reversal of the relationship between strength of arm and strength of brain, a way could be opened also to a fresh social appraisal of the works of the spirit. They might easily be felt to be decisive and necessary elements in that restructured society, not just precious ornaments of aristocratic life or elegant courtly or ecclesiastical exercises. Just as the new capitalist leadership sought its justification in Franciscan and Thomist thought, so did the new ruling class make the most modern art and literature its own. It was not by chance that the first quotations from Dante appeared, as I demonstrated some years ago,[3] in the diary of Domenico Lenzi, a corn merchant, and that the first readers and transcribers of the *Divine Comedy* should have come from the society of notaries and bankers. It was not by chance that the most diligent and well-informed chroniclers (the Villanis and Stefani) and the most honored poets in those years (the Frescobaldis, the Rinuccinis, and the Puccis) belonged to the merchant families or to the legal classes who were closely linked with commercial life (Lapo Gianni, Cino da Pistoia). It was not by chance that the newest and most inspired artists, from Giotto to the Gaddis and Orcagna, worked for the chapels of the new middle class and for the Guilds, that is to say, for the productive organizations of a Florence that was the financial center of civilized Europe, the Wall Street in Medieval economy.

It was precisely in this social framework and through the direct personal experiences of the writer himself in the life of this new ruling class that the completely reformed portrait and myth of the exemplary man—the hero—became distinguishable. Already in Boccaccio's second Florentine work, the *Amorosa Visione* (1342), the scale of values and the presentation of the exemplary hero based on it, reveal a radical reform. As we know the poem introduces into literature the theme, or rather the genre, of the "trionfi," a genre that was immediately taken up and established authoritatively by Petrarch and later on developed enthusiastically all over Europe, at least until the sunset of the Renaissance and into the Baroque period itself. Boccaccio presents the great figures of antiquity and the Middle and Modern Ages, right down as far as his own contemporaries, arranged around the symbols of forces (Wisdom, Power, Wealth, Love, and Fortune who overthrows and levels them all) of which they were, pre-eminently, the exemplary representatives, that is, heroes. They are not just enumerations as in the epic tradition, or a row of marvellous names to increase authority, as in the *Caroccio* by Rambaldo, or in the *Roman de la Rose,* or in the *Tesoretto* by Brunetto (to cite only three masterpieces in the three Romance literatures). They are tributes to the heroes of the greatest powers that function in humanity—minutely gauged and studied tributes— in the exemplary and heroic sense, precisely as I have shown in my works.[4] But side by side with the traditional categories of the heroes of strength and love (in which the customary figures reappear—from Hercules and Samson to Roland and the Saladin, from Jove in love to Paris, Tristan, and Launcelot), a place has been made, with explicitly declared intentions, to introduce novelty, for those of Wisdom and Wealth. In these two triumphs figures contemporary or almost contemporary with Boccaccio himself also appear in heroic attitudes: Dante and Giotto, for the first time placed on Olympus with the great figures, and also the merchants of the time, even led by an agent of the Bardi family, that is, by Boccaccio's own father.

It is, from a literary and social point of view, a bold and

surprising innovation on the plane of concept and custom, both
for the two new values that decisively take their place among
the traditional ones, and for the audacity of presenting modern,
indeed contemporary, persons as heroes, thereby showing an
exceptional insight into the continuity of certain values through
the biblical, classical, and modern worlds. It is an innovation established in an abstract way, very stiffly and uncer-
tainly, in the *Amorosa Visione*. Only some years later, after ten
years of varied experiences of life and culture, did Boccaccio
embody it humanly and artistically in *The Decameron*, the
masterpiece and *summa* of narrative in Medieval Europe.

Already in the unified structure of the work (which I have
been able to identify and describe [5]), the profound originality
of the situations is reflected. In fact *The Decameron* develops
exactly like a highly calculated representation of what man
can accomplish, both for good and for ill, in the face of the
great forces of Fortune, Love, and Wit. Boccaccio describes
the ascending (in a certain sense Gothic) itinerary of *jeder-
mann* from vice, which is represented on the first day, to glorified virtue on the last, through the various trials offered to the
paragon, with Fortune (on Days II and III), with Love (Days
IV and V), and with Wit (Days VI, VII, and VIII). From
the champion of vice, Ciappelletto, the protagonist of the first
novella who is portrayed, through a characteristic language,
as a modern Judas, we come, in the last *novella*, to the heroine
of virtue, Griselda, stylized by richly purposive allusions to
the Virgin Mary. Just as the harsh and bitter censure of vice
does on the first day, so does the exaltation of virtue on the
last embrace the three orders of the ruling class in communal
Italy in the sunset of the Middle Ages: the powerful in material strength, economic domination, and intellectual preparation. But in this splendid comedy of man, Boccaccio wanted
most of all to make the new hero—the merchant—stand out;
through his manifold initiative, he had so captured Boccaccio's
attention in those years that the artist created an almost Pro-
methean figure when he described (in his *De Canaria et in-
sulis noviter repertis*) his hero's invincible audacity in discovering new lands and new worlds.

In *The Decameron*, for the first time in European literature, the work and world of the mercantile companies received, in this way, high literary tribute. Between the thirteenth and the fourteenth centuries the mercantile movement was decisive for the history of Europe and the Mediterranean. It created a socio-economic unity from Cadiz to Damascus, from Tunisia to Scotland, on the wreckage of the by then disintegrated Franco-German Empire and on the ruins of the Byzantine one, by then overwhelmed by the great Islamic wave. It was a unity fostered by the real heroes of enterprise and human tenacity, by a handful of exceptional men who launched into the conquest of Europe and Asia and into the discovery of new lands in the West and East. Still isolated in Dante's world in a circle of aristocratic contempt "per la gente nova e i subiti guadagni" (for upstart people and quick profits), ignored as inferior or alien by a man of Petrarch's refined sensibilities, this class, in the hands of Boccaccio, burst into the human comedy of *The Decameron,* and dominated it with exuberant vitality. We are not only referring to the crowd of themes, settings, characters, customs, or to the various references that endow more than half the *novelle*—60 out of the 100—with bright and optimistic colors suitable to this world. Being the author's central concern in the work's ideal design, in the work's artistic and exemplary human impact, the portrayal of this class is the distinguishing and indispensible element in Boccaccio's imagination. The legend of man placed between Vice and Virtue could not have found examples of more potent and overwhelming visual eloquence in that age. After the iron-clad champions of strength and the gilded knights of the sword and of love, it was only a world of merchants that, during the thirteenth and fourteenth centuries, could afford more lively and exemplary champions in the human struggle. It is in that world, to quote Stendhal, that "the plant man" grew more vigorously and gave us people who were able to assert themselves as heroes to be admired and imitated as incarnations and symbols of values and forces that by this time gave a new feeling to life. They were men who—as Boccaccio shows in *The Decameron*—spread themselves all over the world and were always on the alert for the traps and pitfalls of Fortune, always ready to try their graceful agile humanity in the most

varied love affairs, always eager to overcome, with their wits,
the plans and intrigues thought up by the wits of others. Kings
and princes, paladins and knights, ecclesiastics and scholars,
had traditionally always supplied the characters in literature
for the adventures of Fortune, Love, and Wit. Now they
were being ousted by the achievement and energy of these new
heroes of communal life and the last stages of medieval civilization: heroes with open minds, ready wit, solidly based culture, and aspirations that even soared to princely ambition and
royal pride. They were tenacious and audacious. They left
everywhere the imprint of such a powerful personal image that
it roused princes to timid flattery and populations to admiration mixed with rancor as towards someone who held their
destinies in the palms of their hands. They came from far-off
lands loaded with experience and wealth to use the one and
the other in high politics and in sublime works of art, embodying them in splendid public and private palaces, churches, convents, and hospitals, as well as in the universities that have
perpetuated the civilization of that century. The very evocation of the brilliant life of those merchants, as expressed in an
entire literature from Gilles li Muisis to Villani, is invested
with the colors of a golden and heroic legend. Their example,
to quote Renan, is "la plus grande leçon d'energie et de volonté
de l'histoire" (the greatest lesson of energy and will in history).

Boccaccio therefore chose his characters from among them
to represent, in an exemplary way, the history of mankind. Or
rather he chose those champions who are models for the behavior of every man—authentic heroes.

The most subtle and elegantly victorious prudence is portrayed in exemplary style in Melchisedech (1.3), and steadfast religious faith, unassailable by any contingency whatsoever,
in Giannotto and Abramo (1.2). Scrupulous and invincible
loyalty to promises has its apologetical champion in Alessandro
Agolanti, rewarded as he is at the end of the *novella,* fabu-
lously, with the crown of Scotland (2.3). Conjugal chastity
and faithfulness have their high apodictic expression in Ber-
nabò and Ginevra (2.9), to be emblematized by Shakespeare,
who took them from this very *novella,* in his *Cymbeline.* Love,

that love which is both total and chaste, most abandoned and yet exemplary, is stylized in Lorenzo and Lisabetta, in Pasquino and Simona, in Girolamo and Salvestra (4.5, 4.7, and 4.8). The most audacious and enterprising spirit of adventure, almost at the risk of life itself, is embodied in its human values in unsurpassable models such as Martuccio and Gianni da Procida (5.2 and 6). The most discreet and lofty human kindness has its exemplary knights, spotless and peerless, in Federigo and Torello (5.9 and 10.9). Generosity carried even to the spontaneous offer of his own life shines paradigmatically in the fabulous figure of Natan (10.3).

All these—and many others like them—are figures belonging to the world of commerce, and they are all presented and portrayed as the great heroes of the new humanity. And with the process that was usual in epics and representations of heroic societies, to the Achilles and Rolands of trade are opposed the Thersites and Ganelons—ser Ciappelletto, a sink of iniquity (1.1); Ambrogiuolo, all lying cowardice (2.9); the Milanese merchant woman, the incarnation of base greed (8.1)—as if to give greater definition, by the sharpness of the contrast, to the light and exemplariness of those champions of diverse and lofty virtues.

Thus we have, through these figures, the new image of the hero. He too is beautiful in his person and a good talker, like the heroes in the old myths; a ruler not by the strength of his arm but by his intelligence and prudence; an inspired assessor of world situations and crises, ready to take advantage of occasions (even the most complex and remote like the ones offered by the Crusades and the Mongol transmigrations); openhearted and generous, loyal and faithful, sensitive to all human interests.

The champions of this irrepressible enterprise, of this insatiable curiosity about men and countries, are made of this stuff; in history they have had such names as Marco Polo, Guido and Ugolino Vivaldi, Niccolò Acciaiuoli; and, in Boccaccio's legend, Alessandro Agolanti, Landolfo Rufolo, Antigono di Famagosta, Natan, and Mitridanes. These new heroes emerge in *The Decameron* in a twilight, as do all the authentic heroes in the epics, like those Homeric ones in the sunset of

Achaean civilization before the impact of the Doric hurricane.
The difficulties and crises of the forties of the century, caused
by the new European political adjustment of the great kingdoms, had been precipitated by the terrible scourge of the
Black Death in the year 1348, which had destroyed nine-tenths
of the population of Florence. A more cautious and systematic
organization that aimed exclusively at the greatest profits had
followed the expansive and explosive force of the generation
spanning the thirteenth and fourteenth centuries. Then began
the reflective moment in Tuscan capitalistic economy that was
dominated by the law of the "ragion di mercatura" (reason of
commerce). It was a law inflexible and ruthless (just as two
centuries later "ragion di stato" [reason of state] was to be);
hard and inhuman as censured in the introduction to *The
Decameron;* as devilishly portrayed in the first *novella;* as
continually condemned by Boccaccio because, as he writes (6.9,
4), "tutte ha discacciate. . . le belle e laudevoli usanze" (they
have chased away all the fine and praiseworthy customs).

At the very sunset of this society that, in the autumn of the
Middle Ages, had created the premises of the new civil and
social life, Boccaccio wrote his multiform and intensely human
comedy with a lively and sensitive awareness of the values and
limitations of the earlier dynamic stage of that great movement,
but his reservations in no way diminished his admiration and
nostalgic longing for the vital energy of those exceptional
men. And of those real and new heroes of a humanity that
put its trust, above all, in the strength of its intelligence and
initiative, always looking towards new horizons, unyielding
before the blows of misfortune and youthfully trustful in its
own power and destiny, Boccaccio constitutes himself the im-
passioned singer, the inspired *trouvère.*

At the center of the *epos* of the autumn of the Middle Ages
in Italy as *The Decameron* is, the splendid *quête* of the boldest
forerunners of modern society had, perforce, to take place;
there had to loom large in the foreground the *chanson de geste*
of the new heroes, the paladins of commerce.

The creation of the myth of the new hero was possible in
The Decameron because Boccaccio had understood with acute
penetration the exceptional humanity and abundant spiritual

force of the great merchants. Looking beyond all prejudice or material appearances, he had identified this as the essential motive force of their actions and of the splendid civil movement that had set in motion modern capitalistic society. He had seen—as he repeatedly does in his most inspired portraits in *The Decameron*—that the best models of that new middle class had really brought civilization to Western Europe and to the whole of the Mediterranean, that they had opened up the way to progress, yet without arms, without violence, and without great display of brutal force. He had identified the spirit of their dynamic task and their triumphant success in the intensely human and lofty precept that headed one of their statutes: "Niuna impresa per minima che sia può avere cominciamento o fine senza queste tre cose: cioè senza potere, senza sapere, senza con amore volere" (No undertaking, however small it may be, can have a beginning or an end without these things: that is, without power, without knowledge, without desiring with love).

These qualities—power, knowledge, desire—were all interior qualities that, quickened by love, characterize the new hero beyond all the conceptions of strength of the ancient and medieval myths. This break with the old patterns, this transformation of values, had opened new heroic perspectives to Boccaccio even beyond the world of commerce. Most of all it had widened the traditionally limited horizon of men. It had also introduced decisively women as heroines of the flesh as well as of the spirit, bold both in license and in virtue, but always full of humanity and at times genuine examples of those capacities for good and ill that characterize mankind. They were not, like those of Ovid or of Boccaccio's own youthful works, heroines only because they were *grandes amoureuses* (according to Hauvette's definition [6]) and they did not belong only to the upper classes, to the class of the princesses and great ladies of Arthurian or any other romance literature. Gilletta, Ginevra, Andreuola, Simona, Giovanna, Lisa, Griselda, of middle-class families or even just humble working-class women, are all presented in an atmosphere of refinement and strength, with such admirable and pronounced characteristics as to be in no way inferior to the new heroes of *The Decameron*.

This is an extension that, already achieved in Boccaccio's masterpiece, was to have a more systematic confirmation ten years later in *De mulieribus claris*. By upsetting the canonical classical and medieval tradition of the treatises on heroes and illustrious men (reconfirmed just then by an authority like Petrarch with his *De viris*) Boccaccio for the first time was to portray 106 women, from Eve to Queen Joan of his own times, as protagonists in human history. Furthermore, side by side with these illustrious characters, he was to find a place also for women raised to the rank of heroines because they were exquisite artists (Sappho, Leunzio, and Cornificia in, respectively, 47, 60, 86), or because their exemplary behavior was worthy to be held up as a model. Thus he presents the poor little woman of Apulia who so courageously succoured the Roman fugitives of Canne, polemically declaring that she was superior to Alexander himself (69); or the barbarian Galata who, like a new Judith, cut off the head of the Roman centurion who had raped her (83); or the generous and brave middle-class women of the Italian communes, Gualdrada and Camiola (103, 105); or even, with some moral license, intrepid and generous prostitutes like Leena and Epicari (50, 93) because, he argues, "est [virtus] ubique preciosa, nec aliter fedatur, scelerum contagione, quam solaris radius ceno inficiatur immixtus" (virtue cannot be soiled by contact with crimes, just as the ray of sunshine is not soiled by the mud that it strikes). The clear allusion to the famous *canzone* by Guinizzelli is striking here, having exceptional significance for its exemplary value.

The Decameron and *De mulieribus* were both to be, in 1370, on Boccaccio's desk to be revised and recopied in two autograph copies that Pier Giorgio Ricci and I have had the good fortune to find recently in Florence and in Berlin. So the extraordinary extension of subject matter, the result of twenty years of working with the classical and medieval myth of the hero, deeply affected Boccaccio in his maturity and even now in the enthusiastic classicist commitment of his last decades.

But that view of the hero, seen above all as an exceptional model of willpower and natural gifts, while opening the way to characters who, being both female and socially inferior, were until then excluded, also decisively expands the heroic prospect in a spiritual sense. The Count of Anguersa, shut up in the dignified silence of an unjustly condemned man; a vagabond beggar like the Dantesque figure of Romeo di Villanova (2.8); Girolamo, who suffers in silence even till death in order not to compromise his beloved, who has been given in marriage to another (4.8); Master Ansaldo, who overcomes his sensual passion through chivalrous compassion for Dianora (10.5); all are genuine heroes whom Boccaccio portrays and presents with controlled emotion and offers as models. The intellectual and moral victories count no less than the material and warlike ones; on the contrary, they characterize the hero much better. Federigo degli Alberighi, exemplary in this sense, is superior to all the others (5.9). His renunciation, quiet and free from all spectacular gestures; his silent and dignified poverty; his readiness, completely uncalculated, to sacrifice to his beloved (even if she is always unresponsive) this last relic of his aristocratic life—his beloved falcon; all these establish his figure in a heroic light that is rich in new human feelings. Being pure and unadorned, these feelings are perhaps deeper and certainly more intimate than those represented in the great frescoes of the generosity of princes and knights. The humble actions of Federigo thus take on exemplary solemnity no less important than the heroic combat of a paladin for his lady. And the knight of the arduous interior renunciations, of the silent struggles, the knight of a humanity that is spiritually fine and generous, can stand side by side with the knight of the sword and the warlike strength, and can have a more intimate and persuasive dignity. In this way too, as in *The Decameron* generally, Boccaccio thus shows himself to be exceptionally sensitive to the continuity that, despite appearances, links all the various forms of human expression. Just as he felt the uninterrupted message of poetry through different civilizations and languages—from Homer to Dante and his own contemporaries, from the most aristocratic to the most popular forms—so did he perceive and represent the meeting between two societies that had different myths and models: the feudal one bristling with iron and gold, solemn in its nobly statuesque attitudes, and the other of the more splendid communal age, displaying all wisdom and human courtesy in the measured grace of its gestures and words. Federigo degli Alberighi and Lisabetta da Messina have a human nobility not inferior to King Charles of Anjou or to Ghismonda, the Norman princess (5.9; 4.5; 10.6; 4.1); Gentile de'Carisendi is no less chivalrous than King Pietro d'Aragona (10.4; 10.7); Andreuola has an aristocratic resolve not inferior to that of the Marchioness di Monferrato (4.6; 1.5). These middle- and lower-class characters are not crowned or covered with precious stones like those of the preceding generation, but they are rich in a deeper humanity that is nearer to our sensibility, with a simpler but more intimate capacity for sacrifice that is yet heroic in an exemplary way.

Boccaccio seemed to return to just this contraposition of models more explicitly when, years later, writing to Jacopo di Pizzinga (*Ep.* 18), he says: "in spem venio atque creduli-tatem, Deum ytalico nomini misertum, dum video eum e gremio sue largitatis in ytalorum pectora effundere animas ab antiquis non differentes, avidas scilicet non rapine vel sanguine, non fraude vel violentia, non ambitione vel decipulis sibi hon-ores exquirere, sed laudabili exercitio, duce poesi, nomen pre-tendere in evum longinquum, conarique ut possint viventes ad-huc volitare per ora virorum" (at last I can feel hope since I see God, taking pity on the Italians, is infusing them with souls no longer avid for the acquisition of glory with war and with blood, with violence and with deceits, but most of all desirous to acquire fame and to be in the mouths of all men through the exercise of the virtues and under the guidance of poetry). It was exactly for this reason that he proclaimed Jacopo to be a hero and a model.

Along with the representation of character through exam-ples of wit and virtue there now decisively enters Boccaccio's more conscious concern with the sacred power of poetry. In the years after the composition of *The Decameron* Boccaccio had assiduously meditated upon the very essence, as well as upon the ideal and social motives, of poetry. In 1350 he had begun the *Genealogia deorum gentilium,* which concludes with the great synthesis of the eternal reasons of poetry. In 1351 he had written the first draft of the *Vita di Dante,* in which these reasons are referred to as related to a great concrete experience such as Dante's. In the same year he had discussed his convictions with Petrarch at Padua, reading with him several essential texts (the *Pro Archia,* Petrarch's pages in a letter to his brother Gherardo [*Fam.* 10.4], and a verse letter to Zoilo [*Metr.* 2.11]).

In Boccaccio's thought during the fifties and sixties of that century, the hero of meditation and of poetry is placed side by side with the hero of action, whether he is an expression of material power or of moral-social enterprise. He is a hero who —in keeping with the convictions of the new middle-class society—was already present in the stylizations of the *Amorosa Visione* and, in a certain sense, already present before that in the rhetorical portraits in those still earlier epistles that are so full of glosses. The figures of Dante, Cavalcante, and Giotto could then, with good reason, take their place in the Olympus of the heroes of *The Decameron,* being in any case presented and exalted in such an exemplary way, almost as if they were emblems of the supreme dignity of art.

But during Boccaccio's last twenty years the myth of the hero shifted decisively—consistent with his first approach and in accordance with his further cultural development—onto a plane of thought and poetry. The temptation to see in this shift a pre-humanistic development would be quite natural if the example of Petrarch and his school did not belie it so strongly. In fact, in the continual series of heroic models that Petrarch offers us— in the *Africa, Rerum memorandarum, De remediis,* and *De viris* (and again later on in his suggestions for the frescoes in the Da Carrara hall with the thirty-six figures of famous men) —the man of action predominates, and dominates still in the same kind of writings by his most authoritative disciples, from Lombardo della Seta to Coluccio Salutati. After all, this is the concentrated and massive classical tradition from Xenophon to Plutarch and Suetonius, Cornelius Nepos, and Valerius Maximus, a tradition to which the revived classicism of Petrarch remained scrupulously faithful. The biographical genre itself, which by its very nature tends to turn its chief figure into a

hero, was severely limited to the great men of action, of war
and politics, or even, in hagiography, to those of still more
radical action—to the saints. Apart from some philosophers
who were considered masters (like Socrates and Epictetus), in
the case of men of letters or artists biographical news for the
purpose of useful information was sometimes furnished (Quin-
tillian, Suetonius, St. Jerome, and Priscian all gave a little) to
illustrate the whole work or separate texts. They were certainly
not exemplary or heroic biographies; on the contrary, from the
Alexandrine age and from the Middle Comedy on a frequently
anti-heroic trend in the biographies of writers was established.

Boccaccio intervened vigorously in this tradition too. On the
one hand he completely renewed the genre and on the other he
created and offered a new heroic myth, that of the man of letters as teacher of consciences and corrector of private and social
customs. Thus the poet-bard is placed at the apex of the scale of
heroes. In fact, as he explains in the *Genealogia* (14.7), the
poet is characterized and almost consecrated by a fervor that—
like the Holy Ghost, "ex sinu Dei procedens" (proceeds from
the bosom of God)—is given to very few and makes them superior to all other men, their guide and their model.

Boccaccio goes on to say, in fact, that the poet can and must:

> reges armare, in bella deducere, e navalibus classes emittere,
> celum, terras et equora describere, virginese sertis et floribus
> insignire, actus hominum pro qualitatibus designare, irritare tor-
> pentes, desides animare, temerarios retrahere, sontes vincire, et
> egregios meritis extollere laudibus, et huiusmodi plura; si quis
> autem ex his, quibus hic infunditur fervor, hec minus plene
> fecerit, iudicio meo laudabilis poeta non erit" (14. 7).

> [arm kings, marshal them for war, launch whole fleets from
> their docks, nay, counterfeit sky, land, sea, adorn young maid-
> ens with flowery garlands, portray human character in its vari-
> ous phases, awake the idle, stimulate the dull, restrain the rash,
> subdue the criminal, and distinguish excellent men with their
> proper meed of praise: these, and many other such, are the
> effects of poetry. Yet if any man who has received the gift of
> poetic fervor shall imperfectly fulfil its function here described,
> he is not, in my opinion, a laudable poet] (14. 7[7]).

It is just because poets are invested with this high mission that they love secluded and tranquil places favorable to meditation. Boccaccio, reversing the classical conception of solitude (felt as a condemnation or an anti-human refusal, from the myth of Bellerophon onwards), traces the figure of the poet, alone and meditative, not as a result of Petrarchan or romantic melancholy, but ascetically, for the good of mankind:

> . . . Ob id solitudines incolunt et coluere poetae, quia non in foro cupidinario, non in pretoriis, non in theatris, non in capitoliis aut plateis, publicisve locis versantibus, seu turbelis civicis inmixtis, vel mulierculis circumdatis sublimium rerum meditatio prestatur, absque qua fere assidua nec percipi possunt, nec perfici percepta poemata. . . .
>
> . . . Esto non adeo detestabile sit, ut hi arbitrari videntur, habitare silvas, cum in eis nil fictum, nil fucatum, nil menti noxium videatur; simplicia quidem omnia sunt nature opera. Ibi in celum erecte fagi et arbores cetere, opacitate sua recentes porrigentes umbras; ibi solum viridantibus herbis contectum atque mille colorum distinctum floribus, limpidi fontes et argentei rivuli, lepido cum murmure ex ubertate montium declinantes; ibi picte aves cantu frondesque lenis aure motu resonantes bestiole ludentes; ibi greges et armenta, ibi pastoria domus, aut gurgustiolum, nulla domestica re sollicitum, et omnia tranquillitate et silentio plena. . . .
>
> . . . Horrent atque recusant turpi atque deformi ypocrisi inertis vulgi mercari gratiam laudesque, et ab ignaris monstrari digito. Horrent fasces nedum exposcere, sed optare, aulas ambire regum, aut procerum quorumcunque assentatores fieri, auro pontificum infulas aucupari, ut ventri et inerti ocio latius indulgere queant, blandiri mulierculis, ut deposita subtrahant, pecunia quesituri, quod meritis quesisse non poterant. Horrent preterea et totis detestantur affectibus caturcenses ob pecuniam in celos evehere, et iuxta muneris quantitatem eis exhibere sedes. Quin imo, quos isti blasfemant, tenui contenti victu brevique somno, speculatione continua et exercitio laudabili componendo scribendoque sibi famosam gloriam et per secula duraturam exquirunt. O species hec hominum convitiis deturpanda, o detestanda solitudo talium! . . . Sed quid verbis insto? Haberem equidem

multa, que dicerem, ni spectabilis candor, ni virtus egregia, ni
laudabilis vita poetarum illustrium adversus tales se ipsam longe
validiori robore tueretur.

. . . Poets have sought and still seek their habitation in soli-
tudes because contemplation of things divine is utterly impossible
in places like the greedy and mercenary market, in courts,
theatres, offices, or public squares, amid crowds of jostling citizens and women of the town. Yet unless such contemplation is
practically uninterrupted, the poet can neither conceive his works
nor complete them. . . .

. . . It seems then that it is no such abomination as these
critics appear to think, to dwell in the woods where there is
nothing artificial nor counterfeit, nor noxious to the mind, for
all nature's works are simple.

There the beeches stretch themselves, with other trees, toward
heaven; there they spread a thick shade with their fresh green
foliage; there the earth is covered with grass and dotted with
flowers of a thousand colors; there, too, are clear fountains and
argent brooks that fall with a gentle murmur from the mountain's breast. There are gay song-birds, and the boughs stirred
to a soft sound by the wind, and playful little animals; and
there the flocks and herds, the shepherd's cottage or the little
hut untroubled with domestic cares; and all is filled with peace
and quiet. . . .

. . . They detest and abhor this purchase of cheap popularity
among idlers, of notoriety among the ignorant, by foul and
hideous hypocrisy. They abhor not merely to ask, but even to
desire the badges of office, or to haunt the halls of kings, to
flatter any man with a head higher than the rest, to be on the
track of pontifical robes, for pure idleness and their bellies'
sake to flatter poor women into a deposit of money from which
they graft, and get by foul means what they could never get on
their merits. They detest and abhor with all their hearts this
practice of sending souls of usurers to heaven for a price, and
assigning them seats in glory according to their contributions.

But the poets whom these fellows blaspheme are content with
plain living and little sleep, with constant speculation and the
laudable exercise of composition; thus they aspire to a glorious
fame that shall endure to the end of time. O strange sort of

men, so easily defiled with the hubbub of towns; O hateful solitude!

Enough! I could say more, were not the shining purity, the eminent virtue, the commendable lives of the great poets a stronger defence against such enemies than I can urge. (*Genealogia* 14. 11)[8]

Mostrano le ragioni delle cose, gli effetti delle virtù e de' vizi e che fuggire dobbiamo e che seguire, accio che pervenire possiamo, virtuosamente operando, a quel fine che è somma salute (*Trattatello* 22).

They reveal the reasons for things, the effects of the virtues and the vices, and what we must flee from and what follow, so that we may come, by acting virtuously, to that goal which is perfect health.

The image of the poet thus acquires a tone at once of the seer and of the hero. He has the voice of a teacher and is a model of life; he is a poet-bard and poet-hero.

This ideal picture in the *Genealogia* would not have been so precise and so evocative if it had been born only of literary and philosophical meditation. Instead it is clearly the projection of two incisive, direct and indirect experiences, experiences that caused the conception of poetry to evolve in Boccaccio's mind from a courtly and hedonistic accomplishment to a lofty moral and civil function. These are experiences arising from the assiduous study of, and an ever-increasing admiration for, Dante, "prima fax et prima lux" (first guiding light) of his life, and from intimate and uninterrupted conversations with Petrarch, "magister et praeceptor . . . splendidissimum tam morum spectaculum quam comendabilium doctrinarum iubar vividum" (master and mentor . . . as splendid an example of character as a living radiance of praiseworthy teaching). In fact, in the passages we have quoted, Dante and Petrarch are continually present as concrete examples of that ideal model, as the new heroes of poetry "anima mundi." And as such they are honored in the two biographies that Boccaccio dedicated to them, the first example of "lives" that are not about men of action, but about men of meditation and of poetry proposed as models, as the originators of a society, as the maximum expressions of a civilization—that is to say, as heroes. They constitute a significant diptych in which—only a few years apart—appear compared and complementary, as in a sublime tragic dialogue, the two greatest modern poets. (The complementary treatment of the poets is evident right from the very titles themselves, which are expressed in the same sequence of words: *De vita et moribus domini Francisci Petrarchi; De origine vita et moribus viri clarissimi, Dantis Aligerii*).

The eternal reasons for poetry are confirmed by the concrete examples of the two great masters, and the most characteristic traits in the ideal portrait of the poet traced out in the *Genealogia* correspond exactly to the concrete portraits of the two poets (love of solitude; contempt for popularity, appointments and wealth; temperance in food; frankness; dedication to the fostering of a virtuous life singly and socially). It would be easy to point to a series of parallel passages in Dante's life and the theoretical pages of the *Genealogia*. Or rather it would be possible —as I hope to do soon—to identify, by means of the evolution of the *Vita di Dante* (in three different versions between 1351 and 1372) a progressive stylization of the portrait of the poet as hero in a new civilization, the communal and popular one. In the first and more ample version Boccaccio has let himself go in his discussion of Dante as a man; it is anecdotal and fictionalized, almost gossipy. In the second, the 1361 version (repeated with some small variations in the third), he concentrates, instead, most of all on actually portraying the poet as bard and hero, characterized by the eternal reasons for poetry, and interrelates also texts from Cicero and from Petrarch. That highly evocative diptych, Dante-Petrarch, thus becomes more categorical, more exemplary and heroic. Perhaps also—as I hope my pupil and colleague Enzo Quaglio will show in the near future —the *Vita di Dante* grew more heroic because it was remodelled between 1351 and 1361 by two pairs of hands, by Boccaccio and by Petrarch himself, with the allusive use of texts by the latter. The figures of the two poets are fixed, because of this devoted rewriting, as those of the two greatest heroes in history in the thirteenth and fourteenth centuries (that history in which Boccaccio complained of the absence of great personalities who were not famous only for their iniquity and violence [*Ep.* 17; Intr.,

De casibus]). They enter, with complete right and all honors as men of thought and letters, among the great men of action in *De casibus virorum illustrium,* and they are in a superior position, in an exemplary sense, to the other figures (3.14; 8.1; 9.23,27; and see also: 4.1; 6.12; 8.18). Finally, Dante is presented and discussed as bard and hero—a really unique case— in a church, Santo Stefano di Badia, by Boccaccio himself in his last years, precisely with the insistent and amplified repetition of the great exemplary motifs already developed in the *Vita di Dante* and in the *Genealogia.*

In this way the model of the new hero, still completely unknown to Petrarch before his meetings with Boccaccio, was established. This new myth was already prevailing at the end of the fourteenth century in the clear and direct imitations by Filippo Villani and Domenico Bandini, and it was then developed in the series of biographies by Leonardo Bruni and Giannozzo Manetti (who, in their sequences of illustrious men, always placed those of meditation and poetry side by side with those of action; in fact Bruni reproaches Boccaccio for not having made Dante sufficiently serious). The new hero then triumphs in the great frescoes, by then decidedly humanistic and renaissant, by Biondo and Filelfo.

But when Boccaccio closed his eyes on 21 December 1375, he was already for his contemporaries almost hieratically composed in the model of the hero of poetry "ex Dei gremio originem ducens . . . ad omnes virtutis calcar" (leading an ancestry from the bosom of God . . . a spur to virtue for all). Boccaccio himself had alluded to his great work only with a very simple phrase, "studium fuit alma poesis" (life-giving poetry was his study), on the tablet that he had prepared for his earthy tomb in his favorite church of Santi Michele e Jacopo, of which he had been "rettore."

He had evidently wanted to consecrate, in this way, most of all the faith and the passion that had become increasingly the very reason for his life; he had wanted to insist, with that adjective *alma,* on the moral and civil function of the poet.

But almost as if in reply to the humble yearning for the fame that had smiled on Boccaccio while he was creating the new myth of the hero-poet ("nulla est tam humilis vita que dulcedine

glorie non tangatur" [no life is so humble as not to be touched
by the sweet savor of glory]), Coluccio Salutati wrote under
that candid epitaph:

> Inclyte cur vates, humili sermone locutus,
> de te pertransis? . . . Etas te nulla silebit.

> [Celebrated bard, why do you who have spoken in humble
> voice pass on? . . . No age will silence you.]

He calls him explicit *vates*, and then commemorates him in
his poem as *hero* of wisdom and of poetry. In those same days
Sacchetti exalted the noble intelligence of the artist so "divul-
gato e richiesto che infino in Francia e in Inghilterra l'hanno
ridotto alla loro lingua" (well-known and in demand that even
in France and in England they have translated him into their
language), and he complains "morte ci ha tolto ogni valore"
(death has deprived us of every value). He was echoing the
tones of the Homeric laments for the death of Hector, that
hero *per eccellenza*.

These are clear pronouncements by Salutati, the most authoritative classicist and moralist, but Florentine political leader
and administrator as well, and by Sacchetti, the most successful
narrator in the vernacular, but also a highly respected merchant. Thus Boccaccio is not only placed decisively beside Dante
and Petrarch to form a triptych, but he is himself stylized in
the new myth of the hero that, from *The Decameron* to the
Dantesque *Esposizioni*, he himself had created with such inspiration and generosity.

Notes

1. Joseph Campbell, *The Hero with a Thousand Faces* (New York: Meridian Books, 1956); Sidney Hook, *The Hero in History: A Study in Limitation and Possibility* (Boston: Beacon Press, 1955); Simone Weil,
"*L'Illiade* ou le poème de la force," *Cahiers du Sud*, no. 284 (1947).

2. Daniela Branca, "La morte di Tristano e la morte di Arcita," *Studi sul
Boccaccio* 4 (1967): 255–64.

3. Vittore Branca, "Un biadaiuolo lettore di Dante," *Rivista di Cultura
Classica e Medievale* 7 (1965): 200–215.

4. Vittore Branca, "Per la genesi dei 'Trionfi'," *La Rinascita* 4 (1941): 681–708; "L' 'amorosa visione': tradizione, significati, fortuna," *Annali Regia Scuola Normale Superiore di Pisa,* 2nd series, 11 (1942): 263–90.

5. Vittore Branca, *Boccaccio medievale* (Florence: Sansoni, 1970); *Boccaccio: The Man and His Works* (New York: New York University Press [in press]); *Giovanni Boccaccio: profilo biographico* (Milan: Mondadori, 1967).

6. Henri Hauvette, *Boccace* (Paris: Colin, 1914), p. 261.

7. Charles G. Osgood, trans. *Boccaccio on Poetry* (1930; reprint Indianapolis and New York: Bobbs-Merrill, 1956), pp. 39–40.

8. Osgood, pp. 55–58.

(Professor Branca's article was translated from the Italian by John Guthrie.)

Suggested Reading

GENERAL WORKS

Albany, Pierre. *Mythes et mythologie dans la littérature française*. Paris: Colin, 1969.
Bachelard, Gaston. *L'Air et les Songes*. Paris: Corti, 1943.
——. *La Terre et les rêveries de la volonté*. Paris: Corti, 1947.
Baudouin, Charles. *Le Triomphe du héros*. Paris: Plon, 1952.
Bénichou, Paul. *Morales du Grand siècle*. Paris: Gallimard, 1957.
Bowra, Cecil Maurice. *From Virgil to Milton*. London: Faber, 1963.
Brelich, Angelo. *Gli eroi greci: un problema storico-religioso*. Rome: Edizioni dell'Ateneo, 1958.
Campbell, Joseph. *The Hero with a Thousand Faces*. New York: Meridian Books, 1956.
Flitner, Wilhelm. *Europäische Gesittung*. Zürich: Artemis, 1961.
Gauthier, R. A. *La magnanimité*. Paris: Vrin, 1951.
Graves, Robert. *The Greek Myths*. London: Penguin Books, 1955.
Hook, Sidney. *The Hero in History: A Study in Limitation and Possibility*. Boston: Beacon Press, 1955.
Jung, Carl G. *Métamorphoses de l'âme et ses symboles*. Geneva: Georg, 1953.
Kerényi, Karoli. *Gli Dei e gli Eroi della Grecia*. Milan: Mondadori, 1963.
Maurer, François. *Dichtung und Sprache des Mittelalters*. Bern: Franck, 1963.
Raglan, Fitz Roy. *The Hero: A Study in Tradition, Myth and Drama*. New York: Vintage Books, 1956.
Rank, Otto. *Der Mythus von der Geburt des Helden*. Leipzig and Vienna: Deuticke, 1909.
Sellier, Philippe. *Le mythe du héros*. Paris: Bordas, 1970.
Steadman, John M. *Milton and the Renaissance Hero*. Oxford: Oxford University Press, Clarendon Press, 1969.
Taeger, Fritz. *Charisma: Studien zur Geschichte des antiken Herrscherkultes*. Stuttgart: W. Hohlhammer, 1957–1960.
Waith, Eugene M. *The Herculean Hero*. London: Chatto, 1965.

Weil, Simone. "*L'Iliade* ou le poème de la force." *Cahiers du Sud*, no. 284 (1947). (Also in her *La source grecque*. Paris: Gallimard, 1953.)

Weise, Georg. *L'ideale eroico del Rinascimento*. 2 vols. Naples: Edizioni Scientifiche Italiane, 1961–65.

Wittkower, Rudolf and Margot. *Born under Saturn*. London: Weidenfeld and Nicolson, 1963.

WORKS PRIMARILY ON BOCCACCIO

Battaglia, Salvatore. *Mitografia del personaggio*. Milan: Rizzoli, 1968.

Branca, Vittore. *Boccaccio medievale*. Florence: Sansoni, 1970.

——. *Boccaccio: The Man and His Works*. New York: New York University Press, 1975.

——. *Giovanni Boccaccio: profilo biografico*. Milan: Mondadori, 1967 (also in *Tutte le opere di Giovanni Boccaccio*. Vol. 1. Edited by Vittore Branca. Milan: Mondadori, 1967.)

Getto, Giovanni. *Vita di forme e forme di vita nel Decameron*. Turin: Petrini, 1966.

Hauvette, Henri. *Boccace*. Paris: Colin, 1914.

Neuschäfer, Hans-Jörg. *Boccaccio und der Beginn der Novelle*. Munich: Fink, 1969.

Scaglione, Aldo. *Nature and Love in the Late Middle Ages*. Los Angeles: University of California Press, 1963.

Šklovskij, Viktor. *Chudozestvennaja proza*. Moscow: Sovetskij Pisatel', 1961 (translated into Italian as *Lettura del Decameron*. Bologna: Mulino, 1969.)